# LEARN TO PLAY
# CHESS
# LIKE A BOSS

by Patrick Wolff

ALPHA

**Publisher:** Mike Sanders
**Development Editor:** Monica Stone
**Illustrator:** Laura Robbins
**Art Director:** William Thomas
**Cover Designer:** Lindsay Dobbs
**Book Designer/Compositor:** Ayanna Lacey
**Proofreader:** Lisa Starnes
**Indexer:** Celia McCoy

First American Edition, 2019
Published in the United States by DK Publishing
6081 E. 82nd Street, Indianapolis, Indiana 46250

001-313888-SEP2019

Published in the United States by Dorling Kindersley Limited.

International Standard Book Number: 978-1-4654-8381-2
Library of Congress Catalog Card Number: 2019936935

**Note:** This publication contains the opinions and ideas of its author(s). It is intended to
provide helpful and informative material on the subject matter covered. It is sold with
the understanding that the author(s) and publisher are not engaged in rendering
professional services in the book. If the reader requires personal assistance or advice, a
competent professional should be consulted. The author(s) and publisher specifically
disclaim any responsibility for any liability, loss, or risk, personal or otherwise, which is
incurred as a consequence, directly or indirectly, of the use and application of any of the
contents of this book.

**Trademarks:** All terms mentioned in this book that are known to be or are suspected of
being trademarks or service marks have been appropriately capitalized. Alpha Books,
DK, and Penguin Random House LLC cannot attest to the accuracy of this information.
Use of a term in this book should not be regarded as affecting the validity of any
trademark or service mark.

DK books are available at special discounts when purchased in bulk for sales
promotions, premiums, fund-raising, or educational use. For details, contact: DK
Publishing Special Markets, 1450 Broadway, Suite 801, New York, NY 10018 or
SpecialSales@dk.com.

Printed in the United States of America

Reprinted from *The Complete Idiot's Guide® to Chess, Third Edition*

**A WORLD OF IDEAS:**
SEE ALL THERE IS TO KNOW

**www.dk.com**

# Contents

# Introduction

You (or maybe someone you know) have never played chess, but it seems fascinating, and you'd like to learn the rules. Or maybe you know how to play, but you've never understood how to tell whether a move was good or bad. Or maybe you've even picked up a few pointers somewhere, but you'd really like to be able to play a decent game—and once you get better, you want to take your chess game to the next level by finding people to play (whether online or in person) and by learning how to develop a training regime so you can beat all those new people you will be playing! Plus, it would be really cool to understand the difference between how regular computers play chess and how computers using artificial intelligence (AI) play chess.

This is the book for you.

I played in national and international chess competitions for almost 20 years, both as a child prodigy and then as a full-time pro. During that time, I became one of the best chess players in the country and in the world, including being the US champion twice, in 1992 and 1995. So I have the expertise to explain it all to you.

But just as importantly, I also have years of experience teaching people at all levels how to play chess. I know lots of people think chess is for highbrows, but that's nonsense. Chess is an incredibly fun game. It offers a lifetime of excitement, beauty, and challenge to anyone who takes it up. Sure, chess exercises your brain: that's what makes it so great! But it's not just for intellectuals. Anyone can learn chess and learn to play it well, and just about everyone who does so loves it forever after. I bet you'll love chess, too.

I wrote the first edition of this book more than twenty years ago to provide people with a guide to learning and playing chess. Since then, I've been so gratified by all the wonderful feedback I received that I wanted to write this revised edition and take the best suggestions I received during that time to make this book even better. I hope you'll find it a fun and helpful introduction to the best game in the world.

## How to Use This Book

I've divided this book into four parts.

**Part 1, "Let's Play Chess,"** gets you started. Chapter 1 gives you some background, and it's mostly for fun, while Chapters 2 and 3 teach you the rules and how to read and write chess moves. If you've never played chess before, start here! Even if you have played chess, you might want to check these chapters out to make sure you've got everything straight. In particular, the rest of the book uses chess notation, so if you're not sure how to read and write chess moves, make sure you read Chapters 2 and 3! Chapter 4 teaches you how to checkmate a lone king with just a queen or a rook and a king. Not only is it good to know how to do this just for itself, but also it is an excellent way to learn other things, such as the power of the queen and the rook and how to make plans in chess.

**Part 2, "Tactics,"** teaches you the importance of capturing your opponent's pieces while holding onto your own, explains how to do so, and shows you some very important and typical ways to use your chess army to capture your opponent's forces. The last chapter in Part 2 shifts the focus from capturing the rest of your opponent's army to checkmating the king. (You do know that the aim of chess is to checkmate the king, right? If not, make sure you read Chapter 3 in Part 1!)

**Part 3, "Strategy,"** gets into some subtler stuff than Part 2. You learn how to strengthen your position, even when there's no move that will capture one of your opponent's pieces or menace your opponent's king. This part explains how to tell which moves are good or bad and why. By the time you've finished reading this part, you'll be able to choose the right strategies to set up the winning tactics. Your opponents won't know what hit them!

**Part 4, "Beyond the Basics,"** covers two topics: how to keep learning and how computers play chess. Chapter 15 explains how you can develop a training regime that will allow you to take your game far beyond this book; it also explains the range of digital chess resources out there and shows you how to find chess competition online, in clubs, and in tournaments. Additionally, Chapter 15 recommends some chess resources designed just for kids. Chapter 16 gives you the complete rundown on how computers play chess: from the first machines in the 1950s, to the IBM computer that first beat a world champion, to how AI (artificial intelligence) works. And check out the chess game at the end of Chapter 16 between two top computers—it's amazing!

## Diagrams

A diagram is a picture of a chess position. A lot of this book, especially Parts 1–3, require you to follow the progress of a chess game as each player makes moves. This presents a dilemma. Even experienced chess players find it difficult to do this without setting up the position on a chess set, and I'm sure you would, too. But that means you would have to have a chess set with you (or maybe an app on your phone) whenever you wanted to read this book. That would be a pain in the neck, which is certainly something I want to avoid.

The solution is diagrams, and lots of them. In the first half of the book, you'll find that every single position and almost every single move from each position gets a separate diagram. As the book progresses, I've assumed that you're becoming more comfortable with following one or two moves from a chess position, but you'll still see lots and lots of diagrams. My goal is to make it easy for you to read this book anywhere you want, not to force you to have a chess set with you to do so. I still recommend that you have a chess set handy (or use your phone!) for when you want to look at certain positions or moves carefully, but for the most part, you can read this book without a chess set if you want.

## Exercises

When you learn to play chess well, you're learning a skill. And as with any skill, you can't learn it without practice. Therefore, at the end of Chapters 2–14 I've included a number of exercises. I strongly recommend that you do each set of exercises after reading each chapter.

The exercises vary in difficulty. Some are relatively easy, and some are quite hard. Don't expect to be able to answer all of the exercises perfectly. I have constructed the exercises so that some of them reinforce what you've already learned, while some of them take you beyond what was covered in the chapter. Try your best to do the exercises and then compare your work with the answers in the back of the book. (You may want to try to do them just from looking at the accompanying diagram, or you may want to set the position up and move the pieces as you think. Either way you do the exercises is fine.) The exercises are not meant to be a test; their purpose is to help you learn the material better. Although the harder exercises will force you to work more, I think you'll find them especially instructive and rewarding.

## Special Note to the Reader

In later chapters of this book, I will be using positions from real games between grandmasters. Chess players have a standard way of referring to those games. For example, if Smith played White against Jones playing Black, in Walla Walla, Washington, in 1997, that game would be referred to by writing "Smith–Jones, Walla Walla, WA, 1997."

## Acknowledgments

Each successive edition of this book has driven home the lesson that writing a book is a collaborative effort. One person may be the author, but many people make the project possible, and (hopefully) a success. I owe many people thanks for their involvement with this book.

Thanks to Allen Kaufman, then–executive director of Chess-in-the-Schools, for suggesting that I would be a good person to write the first edition of this book. You got it all started!

Thanks to my terrific editor, Monica Stone, who provided many helpful suggestions and did copious fact-checking. (Whatever errors remain are my responsibility.) Thanks also to Elliott Winslow and Abel Talamantez, each of whom contributed some new material and reviewed parts of the manuscript.

Many thanks to the people who have helped me in the earlier editions. Christopher Chabris, my friend and colleague, helped me enormously in writing the first edition of this book through his editing, research, and writing contributions. Frisco Del Rosario reviewed the manuscript for the second edition and made many helpful suggestions along the way. Macon Shibut contributed new material to the third edition and did a great job reviewing the manuscript.

Most of all, thanks to my family: my wife, Diana Schneider, and our two wonderful children, Samuel and Athena. You bring me joy every day and I hope I do the same for you. I love you more than anything—even more than chess.

*Illustration credits:*

p. 5 Photograph by Jerome Bibuld, Courtesy of the Russell Collection.

p. 15 House of Staunton, Courtesy of the Russell Collection.

## Trademarks

All terms mentioned in this book that are known to be or are suspected of being trademarks or service marks have been appropriately capitalized. Alpha Books and Penguin Random House cannot attest to the accuracy of this information. Use of a term in this book should not be regarded as affecting the validity of any trademark or service mark.

# Part 1

# LET'S PLAY CHESS

If you've never played chess before, this part gets you started. First you get a little history, and find out what makes chess such a wonderful game. Next you learn the rules for playing chess, as well as reading and writing chess moves. Finally, I show you how to give checkmate with just the queen or the rook (with the help of your king).

Some people think it is hard to learn the rules and feel intimidated. I promise you that with a little patience, you'll find they're easy to learn. By the end of this part, you'll even start learning the skills you need to win!

# Chapter 1

# Why Play Chess?

Many people feel intimidated by chess. They often think that chess is just for intellectuals or that chess is too hard to learn unless you can do calculus in your head, and if you must be smart to play chess, how could it be much fun?

But chess is some of the most fun there is! Get the idea out of your head that you must be some kind of genius to learn how to play chess. Would millions of people in the United States alone play and *enjoy* chess if they had to be a genius to learn it? The truth is hundreds of millions of people around the world play chess, and more people are learning the game every day because chess is the most fascinating, most exciting, and most enjoyable game in the world!

Yet chess still has a reputation for being intimidating. Many people find chess intriguing, but they don't think that they could learn it. And you know, I totally understand why people think that. Look at any chess app on your phone or computer. See those weird-looking symbols, letters, and numbers that don't make any sense? Who wouldn't be intimidated? Or maybe you know an eight-year-old who plays chess, and you think to yourself, "I'm not going to be shown up by someone who's still in second grade!"

Well, if you think chess is kind of interesting, but also maybe a bit intimidating, this book is written for you. I teach you the rules, show you how to play, and even tell you how you can find an opponent to play with. And it's not going to hurt.

# Are We Having Fun Yet?

I remember how it feels not to understand the basics of chess. I'll take you through those basics slowly and explain everything step by step. Because I really understand the ins and outs of chess, I can teach you quite a lot without getting you confused. Before you even finish the book, I bet you'll beat that eight-year-old!

Most importantly, I want to make sure you enjoy learning chess as much as I know you'll enjoy playing it. After all, chess is a game. What's the point of playing a game if you don't enjoy it?

Part of the reason I'm so sure you'll enjoy chess is that I know from my own experiences how wonderful a game it is. After all …

+ Chess is easy to play anywhere. For just a few dollars, you can buy a set that fits in your pocket; or you can play against one of the many computer programs or apps on the market; or you can find an opponent online, and play a game literally 24 hours a day!

+ Chess is the fairest game I know. No dice spoil a good play by a bad roll; no umpire robs one side of a deserved victory. All that matters is how well you play.

+ No matter how big or small you are, no matter how old or young you are, you can learn to play as well as anyone.

+ The rules of chess are easy to learn. Trust me: after you read the next few chapters, you'll have the rules down cold.

+ Once you learn the rules, there's always more strategy to learn to improve your play—you can never be bored by chess. Every game has potential for the tension of battle, the beauty of new ideas, and the excitement of conquest!

People have been enjoying chess for more than 1,000 years, and chess has never been more popular than it is today. Let me tell you about the amazing history of chess and then I'll tell you how popular it is today.

# Once the Game of Kings

Chess is so old that nobody knows for sure when or where it began. People have played games with pieces on some kind of board for thousands of years. The earliest known game that is definitely linked to chess was played in India almost 1,400 years ago and was called *chaturanga*. Yet there is controversy about whether chaturanga is the oldest version of chess. Artifacts that seem to be chess pieces have been excavated in Italy, and some people claim the pieces should be dated at the second century C.E. Because it's so hard to draw definite conclusions from scanty evidence, we may never know the exact origins of chess.

What we do know is that chaturanga moved east before it came to the West. Buddhists who traveled to spread their religion brought the game with them to China, Korea, and Japan. In fact, both China and Japan have their own versions of chess (called Chinese chess and *shogi,* respectively). But very little else is known about the eastward movement of chaturanga.

We know much more about the journey of chaturanga through the West. It reached Persia, where it was called *chatrang.* When Persia was conquered by Arabs in the middle of the seventh century, the game was again renamed, this time to *shatranj.* And this is the game that was brought to western Europe in the eighth and ninth centuries by the early invaders of Spain and Sicily. The following two pictures show examples of ancient chess pieces.

*An ancient chess piece.*

*"Berserker" (rook) from the Isle of Lewis pieces believed to be from the twelfth century.*

By about the year 1000, shatranj was widely known throughout Europe and was popular among religious orders, in the courts of kings, and among some soldiers. Although shatranj is the ancestor of chess, it is not the same game! Shatranj was probably played on the same board, but some of the pieces are not ones we would recognize today, and some of the rules that govern the pieces were different.

Sometime in the late fifteenth century, the game radically changed. Beforehand, the queen existed, but its powers were limited; afterward, the queen's powers were enhanced. Additionally, the bishop replaced another piece, and some of the rules changed to make the game more exciting. Now, the lowly pawn moved two steps on its first move rather than just one, speeding up clashes, and it was required to promote another piece in its place when it reached the other side of the board, which *definitely* made for spectacular possibilities! (You will learn about these rules and more in Chapters 2 and 3.) And the game was renamed, again: *chess.*

Chess must have been a huge improvement over shatranj, because it spread like wildfire throughout Europe and replaced the old game completely. Suddenly, chess was played by more people: some masters even started writing and selling books on how to play chess well (see the following illustration). There was even a period of time during the seventeenth century in Italy when the leading chess players were sponsored by royal patrons! (Ah, that was the time to be a grandmaster!)

Unfortunately, the royal subsidies for chess died out, but the game was still very popular. During the eighteenth century, chess was played in popular coffeehouses throughout Europe. A few professionals could make a living by playing against the regular patrons of whichever coffeehouse they inhabited. Eventually, this gave rise to clubs devoted to chess, which sprang up in big European cities.

*An illustration from* Game and Playe of the Chesse, *the first printed book on chess in Europe.*

People weren't just playing chess in Europe! Over here in America, they began to play chess more and more. For example, both Thomas Jefferson and Benjamin Franklin played and wrote about chess. Whereas chess had once been the game of the aristocracy—why else would it have kings, queens, and knights?—by the start of the 1800s, it was becoming more popular with ordinary folks like us, both in Europe and in America.

Many have heard of the great twentieth-century American grandmaster Bobby Fischer, but did you know that the United States had a nineteenth-century version of Bobby Fischer? The first great American chess genius was Paul Morphy. He was born in New Orleans in 1837 and by the age of 20 was recognized as the strongest chess player in America. At that time, all the best chess players lived in Europe; so in 1858, Morphy voyaged overseas to challenge them. Amazingly, Morphy proceeded to crush the top European chess players by wide margins! When he returned to the United States in 1859, he was hailed a national hero for defeating the European champions at their own game. At the young age of 21, Morphy retired from chess and began a career as a lawyer. Sadly, his law career was unsuccessful, and his personal life was tragic: he suffered from mental illness and died shortly after turning 47. Still, Morphy helped popularize the game of chess in America as well as in Europe, and we still honor his brilliant achievements.

One of the people who did the most to popularize chess in the middle 1800s was Howard Staunton, one of England's greatest chess players. Staunton advocated standards for laws, notation, and timing moves. Until then, there were slightly different variants of chess played in different regions, and there was no standard system for recording the moves. Another problem was that a game would sometimes be abandoned because one player would take so long to move, the other would fall asleep! The solution for this was to impose a time limit on how long you could think about a move.

As chess continued gaining popularity throughout the nineteenth century, it was only a matter of time before chess tournaments were organized. In 1851, after standardizing the rules, Staunton organized the first international chess tournament, in which the best players from around the world came to London and competed. (The one missing player was Paul Morphy, who arrived in Europe afterward.) Staunton even designed an aesthetic and practical set of pieces that are still the standard, known as *Staunton pieces.*

*Paul Morphy*

From that point on, chess blossomed into the most popular game in the world. Tournaments were held everywhere, adopting the standard rules. Newspapers began printing columns devoted to chess. One by one, countries organized national federations to coordinate chess activities. Matches between the strongest players were held to determine the world champion. Eventually, a world federation to govern all the national federations and to run the world championship title evolved, and it exists to this day. The game that started as chaturanga, a lowly pawn among games, had grown to become chess: king of all games!

# Now the King of Games

Today, hundreds of millions of people play chess, making it the most popular game in the world. You can find players matching wits in parks, in schools, or simply across the kitchen table at home. Of course, there are also thousands of chess clubs. Formal tournaments allow for even more serious competition. (In Chapter 15, I'll tell you how to find clubs and tournaments that are near where you live.)

The explosive growth of technology and the internet that began in the late twentieth century opened vast, exciting new opportunities to enjoy the King of Games. Literally thousands of websites are devoted to chess. You can find hundreds of chess apps for your Android or Apple devices. There are online chess clubs where you can find opponents at every level of strength, from all around the globe, 24 hours a day. Although a big part of the fun of chess is in the opportunity it gives you for meeting interesting people, you don't even need a real living opponent. Most online chess-playing sites have computer programs set up to accept invitations at various playing strengths. And there are myriad chess engines available, both free and commercial. The latter always have graphic interface options, tutorial and training features, and other attractions.

Believe it or not, chess is a spectator sport, too! That might sound funny if you're conditioned to the fast-paced action of televised sports: "Two guys playing chess—isn't that a bit like watching grass grow?" In fact, chess has special qualities that make it one of the very best spectator sports. Chess spectators actually get to *play alongside* their superstars. When you follow a live game in progress, you evaluate positions, speculate about each player's plan, and weigh possible moves. In other words, you do exactly the same things as the actual players are doing!

Here again, technology has added to the ways chess enthusiasts enjoy their favorite pastime. In big international tournaments, games are played using special boards and sets with embedded electronic sensors that display the current positions onscreen for spectators to follow. At the same time, wireless headsets deliver expert commentary to chess tournament audiences. Major tournaments stream the games live to tens of thousands of spectators worldwide with running commentary—both expert and not so expert, because fans can post their own observations of the unfolding battle. Many online spectators of the highest-level games enjoy running the positions as they happen on their own chess programs, letting them play along and have the feeling that "*I* know what they should do!"

A brilliant novelty in tournament broadcasting was how the semifinals and finals of the 2018 PRO-Chess League were handled. The four final teams were flown to San Francisco, where they played their matches facing their opponents but with large monitors between them with their position on them. They wore noise-cancelling headsets; meanwhile, commentary was broadcast over the speakers at the venue so that the hundred or so live spectators could follow along, while seeing the games on huge wall-mounted monitors. And of course, the rest of the world was watching and listening on their computers.

# One Hundred Years of On-screen Chess

With so many people playing, it's no surprise that chess shows its face in popular culture. Most of these appearances are in a supporting role in advertising, in movies, or on TV. However, sometimes chess takes the center stage for itself.

The granddaddy of chess movies is the silent film *Chess Fever,* filmed during the Moscow International Tournament of 1925. The footage of the top players of the day, including World Champion José Capablanca, is excellent. It is, in fact, a romantic comedy in which chess saves the day.

In 1957, Swedish director Ingmar Bergman catapulted to world renown with *The Seventh Seal,* starring Max von Sydow as a fourteenth-century knight who talks Death into a chess game to decide his fate against the Black Plague.

A modern movie that puts chess front and center is the Oscar-nominated film *Searching for Bobby Fischer* (1993), based on the 1988 book of the same name. It tells the (mostly) true story of a real-life talented, young player Josh Waitzkin. Many pro chess players from the era are featured as extras, including Josh himself! Starring Ben Kingsley, Laurence Fishburne, and Joe Mantegna, it has plenty of Hollywood stars, as well.

In 2000, Vladimir Nabokov's novel *The Luzhin Defence* (1930) was made into a chess movie starring John Turturro. The story is not-so-loosely based on the life of Curt von Bardeleben (1861–1924), whom it is claimed Nabokov knew, and it chronicles the demise of a world-class player's sanity.

There is even a major Broadway musical titled, simply, *Chess.* Its creator, Tim Rice, has written such hit shows as *Evita* and *Jesus Christ Superstar* and the lyrics to Disney's *The Lion King* and *Aladdin.* The concept album *Chess* was released in 1984 and featured the hit song, "One Night in Bangkok." The plot loosely adapts personalities and events from the real 1972, 1978, and 1981 World Championship chess matches.

Lots of famous, heroic pop characters have been featured playing chess. For example, one of the pivotal scenes in the movie *Harry Potter and the Sorcerer's Stone* (2001) is a chess battle. Pursuing the forces of darkness, Harry, Ron, and Hermione must somehow traverse a chessboard battlefield where behemoth stone pieces are crushing captured rivals to rubble. The heroes themselves become pieces in this deadly game. At its climax, Ron sacrifices himself (well, he survives) so that Harry can deliver checkmate and proceed safely.

The opening scene in the 1963 James Bond classic *From Russia With Love* presents a glamorous fantasy vision of how top-level matches are staged. (Alas, I'm afraid that tuxedoed waiters and audiences all in evening clothes are more typical of James Bond's world than that of real chess!) The scene introduced a villain, Kronsteen, as a chess player—intimating the calculating nature of his evil genius, I suppose. Kronsteen receives a summons from SPECTRE (Special Executive for Crime, Terror, Revenge and Extortion) headquarters just as he is about to win a prestigious international tournament. Rather than obey immediately, he risks the wrath of his SPECTRE bosses by staying at the board until the victory is sealed. The filmmakers used a position based on an actual game from the 1960 USSR Championship.

In the original Star Trek television series, Mr. Spock played a futuristic three-dimensional version of chess. One episode turned on Spock's reasoning that someone must have tampered with the Enterprise's computer. Otherwise, by Spock's logic, it should not have been possible for him to win against a chess program that he himself had coded. This isn't really a valid logical deduction (sorry, Mr. Spock!), but in Chapter 16 you can learn all about how computers actually play chess.

Other television characters who have revealed themselves as occasional chess players include everyone from Thomas Magnum (Tom Selleck's character in *Magnum, P.I.*) to Alex Keaton (Michael J. Fox, in *Family Ties*); from stylish detectives Tubbs and Crockett (Philip Michael Thomas and Don Johnson, in *Miami Vice*) to Bart Simpson (*The Simpsons*).

Sometimes chess itself plays a starring role. One example is an episode of *The West Wing* that centered on chess games between President Bartlet (Martin Sheen) and two of his staffers (Rob Lowe and Richard Schiff). The course of the games mirrors a simultaneous diplomatic "chess match" that plays out between the president and China. In an episode of *CSI: Crime Scene Investigation* called "Killer Moves," CSI searches for a killer whose victims and locations are patterned after moves on the chess board. There was even a 2011 Canadian drama series called *Endgame* in which the main character is a fictional chess grandmaster named Arkady Balagan!

The stories of youngsters from difficult worlds who find transformation through chess have spawned quite a few movies. Here are three acclaimed films, all based on true stories:

+ *Knights of the South Bronx* (2005)  Ted Danson stars as a teacher in a rough New York school who helps some kids find their way via chess, while finding his own as well.

+ *The Dark Horse* (2014)  New Zealand actor Cliff Curtis plays Genesis Potini, a Maori speed-chess champion with often-crippling bipolar disorder and a brother in a violent gang. He has an improbable dream of converting a ramshackle chess club of throwaway children into a group of champions against all odds (first using a sort of magic to teach them the game) and saves his nephew from a violent life in the process.

+ *Queen of Katwe* (2016)  The story of Phiona Mutesi, who was nine years old when she followed her brother to a collapsing community center in perhaps the worst slum in the world. There, she falls in love with all the pieces, especially the queen. The story follows Phiona as she goes from hoping every day just to have food, to crossing the globe and playing in world championships and olympiads. The film stars Daniel Oyelowo (*Selma*) and Lupita Nyong'o (*Black Panther*) with the remaining cast entirely Ugandan, almost all having never acted before.

Finally, we shouldn't neglect to mention how chess is featured online. YouTube is home to quite a few regular broadcasters of entertaining, as well as instructional, videos. Quite a few grandmasters, many otherwise barely known, are stars there; even some amateurs have built up big followings. The king of chess YouTubers? One fairly average Croatian player named Antonio Radic, otherwise known by his screen name, *agadmator*. He has 407,000 subscribers. Not views. Subscribers.

More and more one can watch tournament games as they are happening, for example, on chess.com or Twitch.tv. These are often productions beyond just a commentator coming up with variations. (We'll talk about this further in Chapter 15, as we cover chess training.)

# Brave New World of Chess

One of the most remarkable technology stories of the last century was the defeat of then–World Chess Champion Garry Kasparov by IBM's computer Deep Blue in a six-game match in 1997. Literally millions of onlookers swamped the IBM server that was providing live coverage of the game, making this match perhaps the biggest online chess event in history. Kasparov's loss was much more than just a chess story—it made newspaper and TV headlines around the world! Pundits of all sorts weighed in about "what it all meant" for the relationship between computers and humans.

Fast-forward twenty years to the end of 2017, and the big chess-and-computers story was not man versus machine, but rather (old) machine versus (new) machine! The strongest chess playing computer in the world, a program called Stockfish, lost decisively to an artificial intelligence (AI) program called AlphaZero. Even though the Deep Blue–Kasparov match got more media attention, the AlphaZero victory over Stockfish was much more significant, in my opinion. In Chapter 16, I explain why and teach you all about how AI plays differently than traditional computers.

In the twenty-first century, we are becoming a society of people who depend upon and celebrate the products of our intellect more and more. What better game for us than chess? Computers on our tables or in our hands can provide more information and training for chess than could have been imagined just a few decades ago, while the internet has made it possible to find a new partner any time we want. There's never been a better time to start playing the world's greatest game. Let's get started!

# Chapter 2

# Drawing the Battle Lines

You are about to learn how to play the world's greatest game of war, strategy, and conquest. A chess game pits two armies, evenly matched, across a simple terrain. Only pure skill decides who is victorious and who is defeated. The aim of the game is simple: kill your opponent's king while protecting your own. But you will accomplish that goal only by using strategy and tactical foresight.

# Meet the Chessboard

The chessboard (yes, it's called a *chessboard*, not a checkerboard) has 64 squares arranged in eight vertical rows and eight horizontal rows. The squares alternate between one color and another, usually white and black. Sometimes other colors are used—such as tan and green or yellow and brown—but the squares are always referred to as *white* and *black*. (In other books, they are sometimes referred to as *light* and *dark*, but in this book, to keep it simple, we'll just use white and black.)

To begin a game, the board must be placed so that the right-corner square nearest each player is white. Throughout this book, we will reference pictures of the board (called *diagrams*) that look like Diagram 1. Notice that the bottom-right corner in this and every diagram is white!

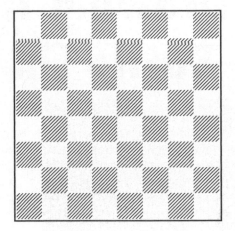

*Diagram 1: A typical example of the chessboard diagram.*

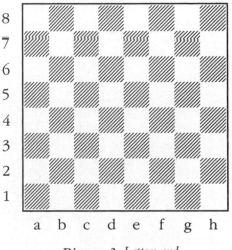

*Diagram 2: Letters and numbers of the files and ranks.*

# Name the Squares

Now that we've oriented the board, we can give each square a specific name. This is absolutely essential so that we can refer quickly and easily to where each piece is placed at any moment in a game. It will also allow us to say quickly and easily where each piece has moved, is moving, or can move.

The way we name the squares is simple and efficient. Look again at the chessboard in Diagram 2. A vertical column of squares is called a *file*, and the file at the very left is called the *a-file*. The file to its right is called the *b-file*, and so on to the rightmost file, which is called the *h-file* (because h is the eighth letter of the alphabet). Meanwhile, a horizontal row of squares is called a *rank*, and the rank at the bottom of Diagram 2 is numbered 1 and is called the *first rank*. The one just above it is numbered 2 and is called the *second rank*, and so on to the topmost rank, which is numbered 8 and is called the *eighth rank*.

Each square is named by putting the letter of its file next to the number of its rank. So, for example, the bottom-right corner square is called the *h1 square*, or simply *h1* for short. To help you remember the letters and numbers of the files and ranks, every chess diagram in this book will be lettered and numbered like Diagram 2.

In addition to files and ranks, chess players also refer to *diagonals*. A diagonal is a set of squares whose corners connect to make a straight line. For example, the squares b1 and a2 form one of the shortest diagonals on the chessboard; and the squares h1, g2, f3, e4, d5, c6, b7, and a8 form one of the longest diagonals on the chessboard.

# Meet the Pieces

A chess set is a collection of all the chess pieces you need to play a game of chess (see Diagram 3). A game of chess is played between two sides. One side is called *White*, and the other side is called *Black*. Just as in the case of the chessboard, other colors are sometimes used, but the two sides are always White and Black. Each side gets exactly the same number and kinds of pieces.

*Diagram 3: Here is a picture of the White side of a typical chess set; left to right, the pieces are king, queen, bishop, knight, rook, and pawn.*

You'll soon learn how each piece moves. But first, these are the basic rules:

✛ The aim of the game is to checkmate your opponent's king while keeping your own king safe. (*Checkmate* means the king is attacked and there is no way to prevent it from being captured on the next move. You will learn all about checkmate in Chapter 3.)

✛ White always makes the first move of the game.

✛ The players move alternately. That is, first White moves, then Black moves, then White moves, then Black moves, etc.

+ Only one move can be made at a time. The way to make a move is to take one of your pieces and put it onto another square. When you have done that, your turn is over, and it's your opponent's turn.

+ Only one piece can occupy a square at one time. If one of your own pieces occupies a square, you cannot move another one of your pieces there.

+ If one of your opponent's pieces occupies a square that you could move one of your pieces to, then you can move your piece to that square and take your opponent's piece off the board at the same time. This is called *capturing a piece*. After a piece is captured, it can't come back into the game. You don't have to move a piece to a square that is occupied by your opponent's piece, but if you do, capturing it is mandatory, not optional.

+ You must move when it is your turn, even when there are no good moves to be made.

Now let's learn how each of the chess pieces moves.

## The Pawn

The pawn is the grunt, the foot soldier in your army. In a game of kings, queens, and knights, the pawn is a lowly peasant, drafted to fight for his monarch. But don't let that fool you into thinking it is unimportant! The great eighteenth-century chess player André Philidor said, "The pawn is the soul of chess," and with good reason! The strategy of most chess games is largely determined by the placement of these humble fellows. Every grandmaster knows that the difference of one pawn is often the difference between victory and defeat.

Each side gets eight pawns. The pawn in this book is represented by Diagram 4. At the start of the game, White puts the pawns along the second rank, and Black puts the pawns along the seventh rank, as illustrated in Diagram 5. Remembering the names of the squares, we can say that White puts the pawns on a2, b2, c2, d2, e2, f2, g2, and h2 at the start of the game; while Black puts the pawns on a7, b7, c7, d7, e7, f7, g7, and h7 at the start of the game.

*Diagram 4: This is what a pawn looks like for reference in this book.*

Here's how the pawn moves:

+ Pawns never move sideways, backward, or diagonally backward.

+ Pawns always capture one square ahead diagonally to the left or right.

+ On its first move—and only on its first move—each pawn may move either one or two squares forward. After it has made its first move, it can only move one square forward in a turn.

+ The pawn is the only piece that captures differently than it moves!

+ If there is a piece (regardless of whether it is one of your pieces or one of your opponent's pieces) on the square in front of it, the pawn is blocked and cannot move forward. However, being blocked does not affect the pawn's ability to capture.

In Diagram 6, the pawn on h4 cannot move because it is blocked, but the pawn on f2 can move to either f3 or f4. Black's pawn on h5 cannot move because it is blocked, but the pawn on c5 can move to c4.

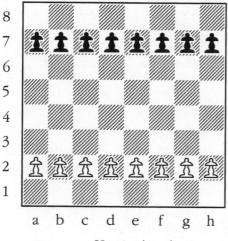

Diagram 5: Here is where the pawns start the game.

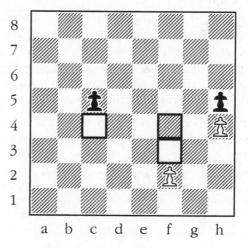

Diagram 6: Each pawn can move to any of the squares highlighted in front of it.

In Diagram 7, White's pawn on g4 can capture any Black piece on f5 or h5, and Black's pawn on g5 can capture any White piece on f4 or h4. Notice that either pawn may make a capture even though it is blocked by an opposing pawn.

The pawn is the least powerful of all the pieces, but is never to be taken for granted.

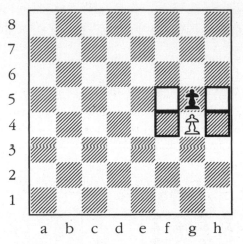

*Diagram 7: Each pawn can capture any enemy piece on either of the highlighted squares diagonally in front of it.*

# The Knight

The knight is usually depicted as a horse or a horse's head. As you'll see, there is good reason for this, because the knight literally moves as though it were leaping over the other pieces.

Each side gets two knights. The knight in this book is represented by Diagram 8. At the start of the game, White puts the knights on b1 and g1, and Black puts the knights on b8 and g8, as illustrated in Diagram 9.

*Diagram 8: This is what a knight looks like for reference in this book.*

Here's how the knight moves:

✛ The knight moves in the shape of an *L*: two squares up and one square to the left or the right, or two squares to either side and one square up or down, or two squares back and one square to the left or right.

✛ It does not matter whether there are any pieces in the way of the *L* path.

✛ If one of the opponent's pieces is at the end of the *L* path, the knight may land on that square and capture it. But if a piece of the same color as the knight is on a square at the end of the *L* path, the knight cannot move to that square.

In Diagram 10, the knight on d5 may move to e3, c3, b4, b6, *c*7, e7, f6, or f4. In Diagram 11, the knight on e5 may move to g6, g4, f3, d3, or c6, or it may capture the black pawn on c4 or d7. However, it may not move to f7. The knight is more powerful than the pawn and about as powerful as the bishop—which you're going to learn about next.

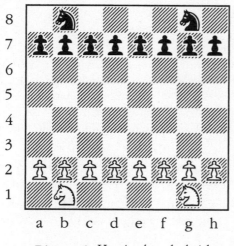

*Diagram 9: Here is where the knights start the game.*

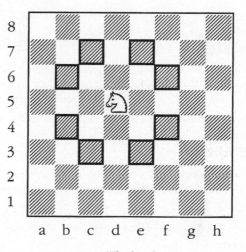

*Diagram 10: The knight can move to any of the highlighted squares.*

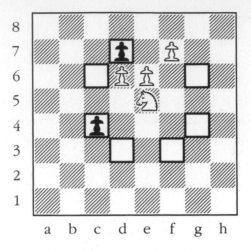

*Diagram 11: The knight can move to any of the highlighted squares.*

## The Bishop

Are you curious why a representative of the Catholic Church is fighting for the king? Apparently, when chess arrived in England, the shape of the piece was thought to resemble a bishop's miter. That seemed to fit somehow, and so it was christened *bishop* in English. Interestingly, the bishop is not thought of as a cleric in other languages. For example, in Italian it is *alfiere*, which means "standard-bearer"; in German it is *läufer,* which means "runner"; and in French it is *fou,* which means "fool," a reference to the court jester.

Each side gets two bishops. The bishop in this book is represented by Diagram 12. At the start of the game, White puts the bishops on c1 and f1, and Black puts the bishops on c8 and f8, as illustrated in Diagram 13.

*Diagram 12: This is what a bishop looks like for reference in this book.*

Here's how the bishop moves:

+ The bishop moves only along the diagonals.

+ It can move as far as it wants along any diagonal, forward, or backward, until it encounters an edge or a piece.

+ If there is a piece of the same color along a diagonal, the bishop cannot move to that square, nor can it move beyond that square.

+ If there is an opposing piece along a diagonal, the bishop can move to the square occupied by the enemy piece and capture it.

+ The bishop only moves on the squares of the same color as it starts on.

In Diagram 14, the bishop can move to a2, b3, c4, e6, f7, g8, h1, g2, f3, e4, c6, b7, or a8. In Diagram 15, the bishop can move to a2, b3, d5, e6, f7, g8, b5, d3, e2, or f1. (Notice that the bishop can't move to a6 where the white knight sits, but it can capture the black knight on f1.)

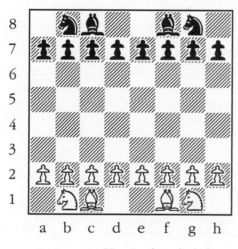

*Diagram 13: Here is where the bishops start the game.*

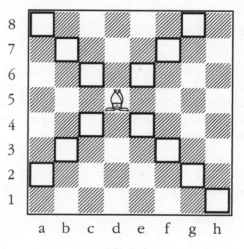

*Diagram 14: The bishop can move to any of the highlighted squares.*

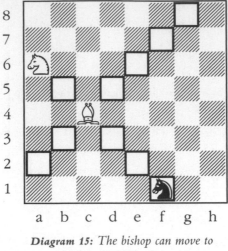

*Diagram 15: The bishop can move to*
*any of the highlighted squares.*

The bishop is about as powerful as the knight (and maybe just a smidgen more), but less powerful than the rook—which we'll talk about next.

## The Rook

Sometimes people call this piece a "castle," but that is not correct. The rook did not originally symbolize a castle's tower, but rather a warrior's chariot, as it was in the ancient Indian version of the game. As chess became popular in Europe, the piece evolved to look like something that was more familiar to Europeans in that time period.

*Diagram 16: This is what a rook looks*
*like for reference in this book.*

Each side gets two rooks. The rook in this book is represented by Diagram 16. At the start of the game, White puts the rooks on h1 and a1, while Black puts them on h8 and a8, as illustrated by Diagram 17.

Here's how the rook moves:

✛ The rook moves only along the files and the ranks.

✛ It can move as far as it wants along a file or a rank, forward or backward, left or right, until it encounters an edge or a piece.

✛ If there is a piece of the same color along a rank or a file, the rook cannot move to that square, nor can it move beyond it.

✛ If there is an opposing piece along a rank or file, the rook can move to the square occupied by the enemy piece and capture it.

In Diagram 18, the rook can move anywhere along the d-file or anywhere along the fourth rank. The rook in Diagram 19 can capture the pawn on d6, but it can't move to d7 or d8. The rook also can't move to g4 or h4.

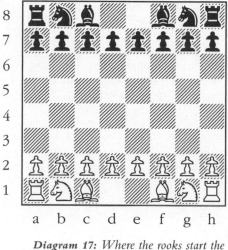

*Diagram 17: Where the rooks start the game.*

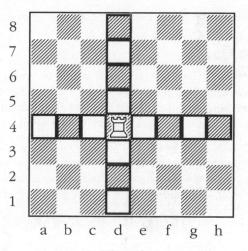

*Diagram 18: The rook can move to any of the highlighted squares.*

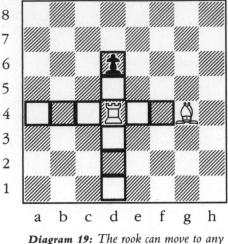

*Diagram 19: The rook can move to any of the highlighted squares.*

The rook is heavy-duty artillery, but even it pales before her royal highness: the queen.

## The Queen

Chess is a game of royalty, so it should be no surprise that the royal couple reigns supreme. The queen's supremacy is her power: she is the most powerful piece of all. Each side gets only one queen. The queen is represented in this book by Diagram 20. At the start of the game, White puts the queen on d1, and Black puts the queen on d8, as illustrated by Diagram 21.

Sometimes people get confused about whether the white queen starts on d1 or e1, and whether the black queen starts on d8 or e8. The trick is to remember that the queen always starts on the square that is the same color as she is: the white queen starts on the white square (d1), and the black queen starts on the black square (d8).

*Diagram 20: This is what a queen looks like for reference in this book.*

Here's how the queen moves:

+ The queen moves along the diagonals, the ranks, and the files. (In other words, it moves like both a rook and a bishop.)

+ It can move as far as it wants along a diagonal, rank, or file—backward or forward, left or right—until it encounters an edge or a piece.

+ If there is a piece of the same color along a diagonal, rank, or file, the queen cannot move to that square nor can it move beyond it.

+ If there is an opposing piece along a diagonal, rank, or file, the queen can move to the square occupied by the enemy piece and capture it.

According to the location of the queen in Diagram 22, it can move anywhere along the d-file or the fifth rank, as well as anywhere along the diagonals that the d5 square is on.

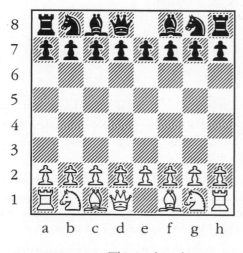

Diagram 21: This is where the queens start the game.

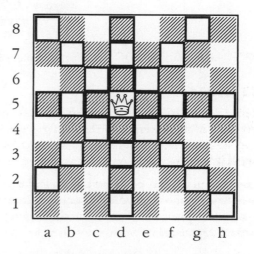

Diagram 22: The queen can move to any of the highlighted squares.

In Diagram 23, the queen on d5 can capture the bishop on d2, but it can't move to d1; it can also capture the pawn on b7, but it cannot move to a8; and the queen cannot move to g5 or h5.

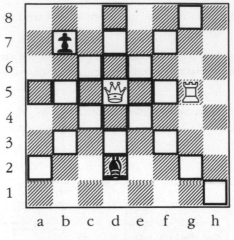

*Diagram 23: The queen can move to any of the highlighted squares.*

Bobby Fischer once wrote, "The queen is boss!" It moves like a rook and bishop put together, and it's even more powerful. But it's not the most important piece. That honor is reserved for the king.

## The King

Every version of chess going back to ancient times has the king, a male monarch whose capture is the object of the game. Each side gets only one king. The king is represented in this book by Diagram 24. At the start of the game, White puts the king on e1, and Black puts the king on e8, as illustrated by Diagram 25. Diagram 25 also shows how to set up the board at the beginning of a chess game.

(By the way, notice in Diagram 25 that the starting positions of each side's pieces are completely symmetrical, except for the king and the queen. Because of this, chess players often refer to the half of the board from the a-file to the d-file as the "queenside," and the other half from the e-file to the h-file as the "kingside.")

*Diagram 24: This is what a king looks like for reference in this book.*

Here is how the king moves:

✢ The king moves one square, and only one square, along a rank, file, or diagonal—forward or backward, left or right.

✢ If there is a piece of the same color on one of the squares next to the king, the king can't move to that square.

✢ If there is an opposing piece on one of the squares next to the king, the king can move to the square occupied by the enemy piece and capture it, but only so long as doing so would not put the king into check.

✢ When an opposing piece threatens to capture the king, we say the king is "in check." When your king is in check, you must get it out of check in the very next move.

✢ The king can never move onto a square that will put it into check.

In Diagram 26, the white king can move to c5, c4, c3, d3, e3, e4, e5, or d5.

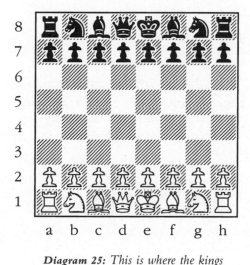

*Diagram 25:* This is where the kings start the game.

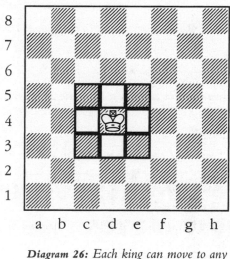

*Diagram 26:* Each king can move to any of the highlighted squares immediately next to it.

Remember that the king can never move into check. So in Diagram 27 the white king can move to c5 or e5, or it can capture the pawn on d5. The black king can move to a1, b1, c1, c2, b3, a3, or a2.

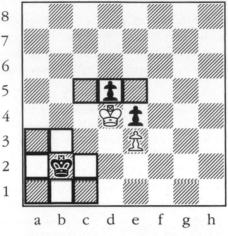

*Diagram 27: Each king can move to any of the highlighted squares immediately next to it.*

The object of the game is to put your opponent's king into checkmate, which means there is no way to prevent the king from being captured on the next move. A funny thing about chess is that checkmate ends the game, so the king is never actually captured! (The idea of killing the king probably violated ancient sensibilities.) You will learn all about checkmate in Chapter 3.

# The Two Rs: Reading and 'Riting Chess Moves

One of the most wonderful things about chess is that we can save every game ever played. All you have to do is write down the moves as you play them, and you can re-create the game whenever you want. Likewise, I can tell you to set up any particular chess position and then tell you what moves to play over. But before you can read or write these moves, you need to learn how.

People who do not already know how to read the notation for chess moves often freak out when they see it or hear it the first time. Once, I brought a chess book to read while waiting for an acquaintance who doesn't play chess. When he arrived, he saw my book and said, "Oh, I didn't know you read ancient Greek!" Chess notation really was Greek to him.

Actually, after you know the names of the squares and the pieces, it's very easy to learn and it completely makes sense. I think the best way to explain chess notation is to break it down as follows: how to read and write pawn moves with or without capture, and how to read and write all *other* moves with or without capture. So, let's take each step by step.

# Pawn Moves without Capture

The way to express where a pawn moves if it does not capture a piece is simply to name the square to which it moves. Consider Diagram 28, which is identical to Diagram 25, the starting position.

If I want to write that White's first move is to move her e-pawn from e2 to e4, I simply write "1.e4" (see Diagram 29). The "1" indicates that it is the first move of the game. (If it were, say, the forty-second move, it would be written as "42.e4".) The "." after the "1" is written to make it easier to read—it is not spoken. And of course, "e4" expresses what square the pawn moved to.

The exact same system is used for Black moves as well as White moves, with one very small difference. When a Black move is written by itself, it is written in the same way, except that instead of one period separating the move number from the name of the square, there are three. Suppose that White's first move is to move her pawn from e2 to e4, and Black responds by pushing his c-pawn one square forward. If Black's move is written alone, it is written as "1...c6" (see Diagram 30). If both moves are written together, they are written as "1.e4 c6", which means, "White's first move was to push her e-pawn two squares forward, and Black's first move was to push his c-pawn one square forward." (Notice that if two moves are written after a number, the first move is always White's move and the second move is always Black's move.)

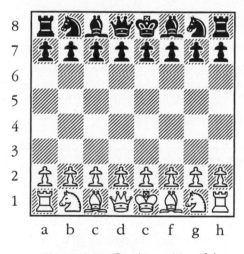

*Diagram 28: Starting position of the chessboard and pieces.*

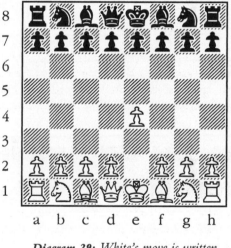

*Diagram 29: White's move is written "1.e4".*

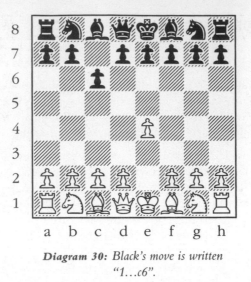

*Diagram 30: Black's move is written "1...c6".*

## Pawn Moves with Capture

When a pawn captures another piece, the way to express it is as follows:

1. Write the letter of the file the pawn is on.

2. Write an "x" which indicates a capture.

3. Write the name of the square the captured piece was on (which is now the name of the square to which the pawn has moved).

For example, suppose the first two moves (for both sides) of a game are 1.e4 c6 2.d4 d5, as shown in Diagram 31. Now suppose that for her third move White captures the pawn on d5 with her pawn on e4. The way to write this is "3.exd5", which is spoken as "three e takes d5". See Diagram 32 for an illustration of this move.

If Black responds by capturing the pawn with his pawn on c6, the move is written, "3...cxd5". If Black's move is written in conjunction with White's move, it is written "3.exd5 cxd5". See Diagram 33 for an illustration of this. Notice that once again the exact same system is used for Black moves as well as White moves, with the small difference that when a Black move is written alone, three periods separate it instead of only one.

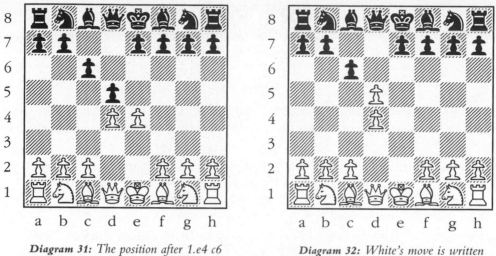

**Diagram 31:** *The position after 1.e4 c6 2.d4 d5.*

**Diagram 32:** *White's move is written "3.exd5".*

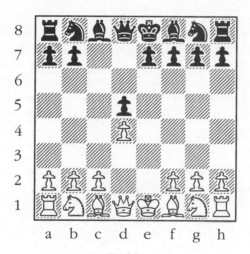

**Diagram 33:** *Black's move on its own is written "3…cxd5". White's and Black's moves together are written "3.exd5 cxd5".*

# All Other Moves without Capture

The way to express how a piece other than a pawn moves if it does not capture a piece is simply to name the piece and then name the square it moves to. Because it would be awkward to write the whole name for the piece on every move, the pieces are abbreviated as follows:

K=King          Q=Queen          B=Bishop          R=Rook          N=Knight

"N" is used for "knight" because "K" is already taken for the king. (When the moves are spoken aloud, you say the name of the piece, not the letter that is used as its abbreviation. The letters are used only when writing the moves.)

Suppose in the starting position you (playing White) want to move your knight on g1 to f3. (Remember you can do this because the knight can't be blocked the way other pieces can—it jumps over other pieces!) How do you write this? Easy: "1.Nf3" which is spoken "one knight f3" or just "knight f3" if nobody is interested in which number move it is.

If Black wants to respond by moving his knight from g8 to f6, the move is written "1...Nf6" if the move is written alone, and "1.Nf3 Nf6" if it is written next to White's move. See Diagrams 34 and 35 for an illustration of this.

Sometimes two pieces of the same color can move to the same square, and we need to make it clear which piece actually moved there. When this happens, we write the name of the file after the piece that moved, for example, "32.Nde6", to make clear that it was the knight on the d-file that moved to the e6 square on the thirty-second move. If naming the file doesn't work (for example, if there are knights on d4 and d8), we write the name of the rank after the piece that moved, "32.N4e6", to make clear that it was the knight on the fourth rank that moved to the e6 square on the thirty-second move. These moves are spoken as "thirty-two knight d e six" and "thirty-two knight four e six", respectively. Diagrams 36 and 37 illustrate this.

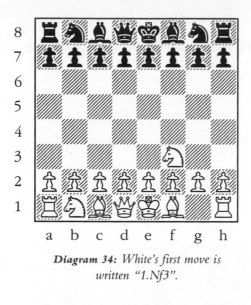

*Diagram 34:* White's first move is written "1.Nf3".

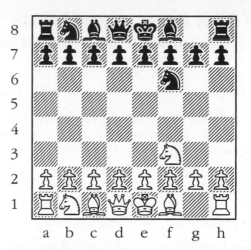

*Diagram 35:* Black's response is written "1...Nf6". White's and Black's moves together are written "1.Nf3 Nf6".

*Diagram 36:* If White's thirty-second move is to move the knight from d4 to e6, it's written "32.Nde6".

*Diagram 37:* If White's thirty-second move is to move the knight from d4 to e6, it's written "32.N4e6".

# All Other Moves with Capture

The way to express where a piece other than a pawn moves if it captures a piece is as follows:

1. Name the piece that moves.

2. Write an "x" which (just like with pawns) indicates a capture.

3. Name the square it moves to. (This should be sounding pretty familiar by now.)

Suppose the first three moves of a game are as follows: 1.e4 c5 2.Nf3 d6 3.d4 cxd4. (See Diagram 38.) If White's fourth move is to capture the pawn on d4 with her knight, the move is written "4.Nxd4". (See Diagram 39.) The "x" is read as "takes" or "captures", so the move, "4.Nxd4" is announced "four knight takes d four" or just "knight takes d four" if nobody cares what number move it was.

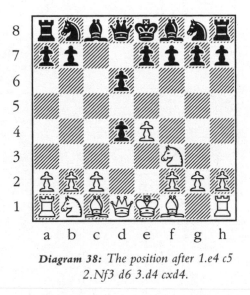

*Diagram 38: The position after 1.e4 c5 2.Nf3 d6 3.d4 cxd4.*

Once again, it's possible for two pieces of the same color to be able to capture the same piece (thereby moving to the same square). The system for making clear which piece did the capturing is the same as for moves without capture: the file of the piece is distinguished, and if that doesn't work, the rank is distinguished. For example, suppose that on the twenty-sixth move Black has rooks on a8 and f8, and wants to capture a piece on d8 with the rook. We would write, "26...Raxd8" to make clear that it was the rook on the a-file that made the move. Sometimes, distinguishing the file doesn't work. If, for example, Black wants to capture a piece on a7 and has rooks on a6 and a8, we would write, "26...R8xa7" to make clear that it was the rook on a8 that captured the piece on a7. Diagrams 40 and 41 illustrate this.

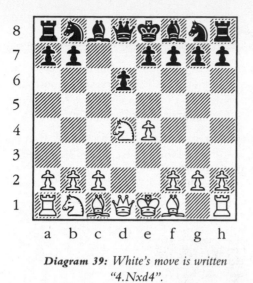

**Diagram 39:** *White's move is written "4.Nxd4".*

**Diagram 40:** *If Black's twenty-sixth move is to capture the queen with Black's rook on a8, it's written "26...Raxd8".*

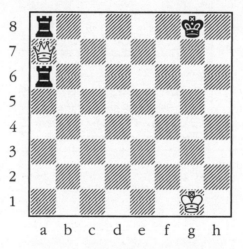

**Diagram 41:** *If Black's twenty-sixth move is to capture the queen with the rook on a8, it's written "26...R8xa7".*

# Exercises: Take a Deep Breath

You've learned a lot already! You've learned the names of the squares, how to set up the board and the pieces, most of the rules of play, how the pieces move, and how to read and write chess notation. In fact, you're just about ready to start playing chess. You only have to learn a few more rules, which are covered in Chapter 3.

Before you start that chapter, you may want to do these exercises to test your mastery of what you've learned here. If you have any trouble, don't get flustered; simply look at the answers found in Appendix B and refer back to the relevant section in the chapter.

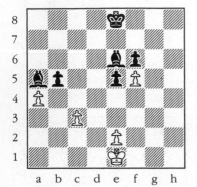

**Exercise 1:** List all the squares to which White can move each pawn. Write each move each pawn can make in correct chess notation.

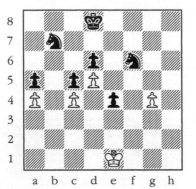

**Exercise 2:** Can Black move either of his knights? If so, say where each one can go. Write each move either knight can make in correct chess notation.

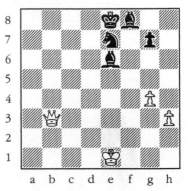

**Exercise 3:** List all the squares to which Black can move either bishop. Write each move either bishop can make in correct chess notation.

**Exercise 4:** *List all the squares to which White can move the rook. Write each move it can make in correct chess notation.*

**Exercise 5:** *List all the squares to which Black can move the queen. Write each move it can make in correct chess notation.*

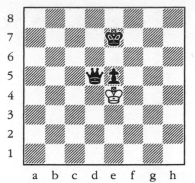

**Exercise 6:** *List all the squares to which White can move the king. Can it capture the queen on d5? Can it capture the pawn on e5? Write each move it can make in correct chess notation.*

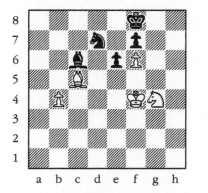

**Exercise 7:** *Whose turn is it? List all the legal moves in the position. Write each move in correct chess notation.*

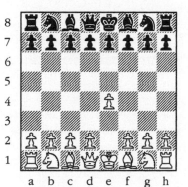

**Exercise 8:** *List all of Black's legal moves in the position. Write each move in correct chess notation.*

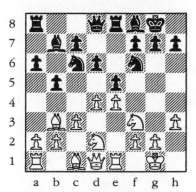

**Exercise 9:** *It is White's move. List all the legal moves White can make with each pawn. Then list all the legal moves White can make with either bishop. Write each move in correct chess notation.*

**Exercise 10:** *It is Black's move. List all the legal moves Black can make with either knight. Then list all the legal moves Black can make with either rook. Write each move in correct chess notation.*

**Exercise 11:** *What moves can Black play? Write each move in correct chess notation. What do you think is Black's best move?*

**Exercise 12:** *It is White's move. List all of White's legal moves and then write each one in correct chess notation. What do you think is White's best move?*

# Chapter 3

# Rules of Engagement

You're almost ready to start playing chess. After you finish this chapter, you'll know all the rules. You only have two things more to learn. First, you'll learn the three special moves that aren't like all the others. Second, you'll learn all the ways a game of chess can be won, lost, or declared a tie. Then, you'll be ready to play a game with anyone!

# Three Special Moves

In Chapter 2, you learned how each piece moves. But there are three special moves that need a little more explanation. More specifically, the pawn has two special moves, and the king has one special move. What makes these moves special is they are only possible under certain circumstances. After you learn these three special moves, you'll know everything there is to know about how the pieces move.

You might find each special move a little confusing at first, especially the last special move—the one the king can do. That's normal. Almost everyone finds these three moves a little strange when they first learn them. That's why I've devoted half of this chapter to explaining them. If you read through the explanations carefully, and take the time to do the exercises, you'll soon find these moves come naturally. As you get more experience playing chess, you'll come to appreciate each of these three special moves: each one greatly enriches the game!

## Pawn Capturing a Pawn en Passant

The pawn has two special moves. The first one is a special way for it to capture another pawn by capturing *en passant*, which is French for "in passing." The idea is that a pawn gets one (and only one) chance to capture an enemy pawn that uses its first move (where it moves two squares instead of just one) to pass by it.

Consider Diagrams 1, 2, and 3. As I'm sure you remember from Chapter 2, pawns normally move only one square at a time, but when a pawn is on its starting square, it has the option of moving either one or two squares forward. In Diagram 1, if the white pawn were to move only one square forward, it would be on the d3 square, where the black pawn could capture it. But what if it moves two squares forward? Then it lands on the d4 square, where the black pawn normally can't capture it. The white pawn has passed right by the black pawn.

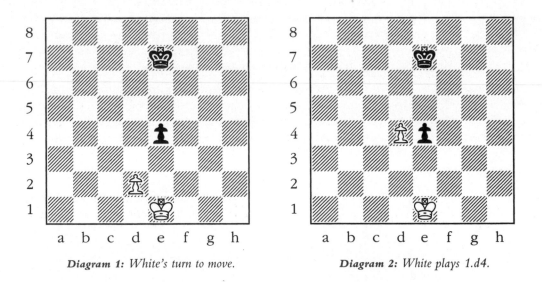

*Diagram 1: White's turn to move.*    *Diagram 2: White plays 1.d4.*

---

*Diagram 3: Black plays 1...exd3,
capturing the white pawn en passant.*

But here is where the pawn's first special move applies. When a pawn moves two squares forward and by doing so lands on the square immediately to the left or right of an opposing pawn, then on the very next move, *and only on the very next move*, that pawn may be captured by the opposing pawn *as if it had only moved one square forward.*

The easiest way to remember this rule is to understand its point. The idea is to not let a pawn sneak by an opposing pawn without giving the opposing pawn one chance to capture it. In Diagrams 1 and 2, by moving two squares forward the white pawn was able to skip over the d3 square, which the black pawn controls, and get to safety on d4. In doing so, it "passed by" the opposing pawn's control of the square in front of it. The en passant rule gives the opposing pawn one chance to capture the pawn as if it had moved only one square. But the opposing pawn only gets one chance! If it doesn't capture the pawn on the very next move, the en passant capture is no longer possible.

Notice from the caption to Diagram 3 that an en passant capture is written just like a normal pawn capture, as though the captured pawn had moved only one square instead of two. In some books, you may see "e.p." written after such a capture to indicate that it's an en passant capture, but strictly speaking that isn't necessary, and we won't write *e.p.* after an en passant capture in this book.

## Promoting the Pawn

The pawn's second special move is truly amazing. Many chess games are won or lost because of this special move. I like to imagine that this special move is an answer to a complaint I would make if I were a pawn.

What's the complaint? Well, remember that unlike all the other pieces, the pawn can't move backward. This means that as the pawn marches forward, it's on a one-way trip. Consider the plight of the pawn in Diagram 4.

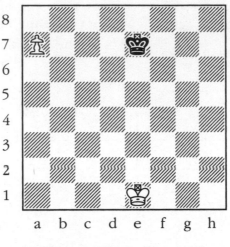

**Diagram 4:** *White's pawn nears the opposite end of the board.*

This pawn has almost managed to arrive at the opposite end of the board. Suppose he advances one more square. Is that it for the poor little guy? Does he have to sit uselessly on the edge of the board for the rest of the game?

In fact, the pawn has an exciting future ahead of it! When the pawn reaches the edge of the board, it is "promoted." That pawn can be transformed into any piece (of the same color) that you want, except the king. Actually, it *must* be transformed. Once the pawn reaches the edge of the board, promoting it is mandatory, not optional. But nobody ever complains, because it's such an advantage to be able to turn what would be a useless pawn into a knight, a bishop, a rook, or especially the most powerful piece of all: a queen. The transformation happens in the same turn as moving the pawn to the edge of the board, and the turn ends once the pawn has been replaced by the piece you choose.

The only two limitations to pawn promotion are that you can only promote to a piece of the same color, and you can never promote to a king. You can promote as many of your pawns as you can get to the edge. Even if none of your pieces of a certain kind has been captured, you may still promote the pawn into another one of that piece. For example, even if you still have your queen, you may promote your pawn to a queen; even if you still have both your knights, you may promote your pawn to a knight, and so on.

Writing the move for a pawn promotion is easy. You simply write the pawn's move in the normal way, and then put "=" followed by the abbreviation for whatever piece to which the pawn was promoted. If the pawn is promoted to a queen, for example, you write the pawn's move in the normal way, plus "=Q" after it.

Consider Diagram 5, where it's White's turn and she has two pawns that she can push to the eighth rank and promote. If the pawn on f7 moves forward one square and becomes a knight (see Diagram 6), the move is written "1.f8=N". If the pawn on a7 moves forward one square to become a queen (see Diagram 7), the move is written "1.a8=Q".

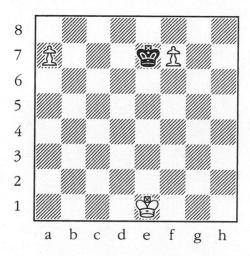

*Diagram 5: It's White's turn to move. White can promote either the pawn on f7 or the pawn on a7.*

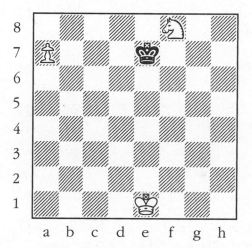

*Diagram 6: Pawn being promoted to knight, written "1.f8=N".*

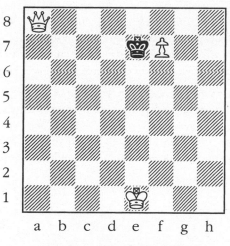

*Diagram 7: Pawn being promoted to queen, written "1.a8=Q".*

# King's Special Privilege

There's only one more move for you to learn: the king's special move. On its very first move, so long as certain conditions are met, the king has the privilege of *castling*. When the king "castles," it moves either two squares to the right or two squares to the left and then the rook that the king has moved closer to jumps over the king to land on the square immediately on the other side of the king.

Sound confusing? Don't worry: everybody finds this move hard to understand at first. I will list the rules for castling, but first let me show you what castling looks like. Look at Diagram 8.

Let's suppose it's White's turn to move, and she decides to castle. In fact, White can castle to either the kingside or the queenside, so let's consider each case in turn.

If White castles kingside, she moves her king two squares to the right, to g1, and then moves the rook on h1 to f1. This is all done in one turn. Notice that the *only* time you can ever move two of your pieces in a single turn is when you castle. Diagram 9 shows White castling in this way.

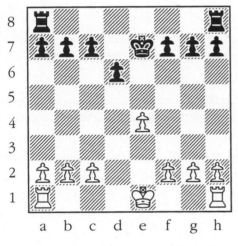

*Diagram 8: White can castle kingside or queenside.*

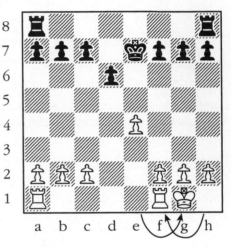

*Diagram 9: White castling kingside.*

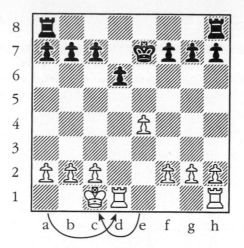

*Diagram 10: White castling queenside.*

If White castles queenside, she moves her king two squares to the left, to c1, and then moves the rook on a1 to d1. Once again, this is all done in one turn. Diagram 10 shows White castling in this way.

Here are the rules for how to castle:

✦ The move of castling takes place in one turn, and it involves moving two pieces. First, the king moves two squares to the right or to the left and then the rook it has moved closer to moves to the square immediately on the other side of the king.

✦ There must be no pieces, either yours or your opponent's, on any square between the king and the rook being used for castling. (You may not capture a piece while castling!)

✦ Castling must be the first move of the king. After the king has moved, it may not castle for the rest of the game. (Because castling is a move of the king, this means that each player may castle only once per game, if at all.)

✦ The rook used to castle must not have moved yet, too. But the fact that one rook has moved doesn't disqualify you from using the other rook to castle.

✦ The king can't use castling to get out of check. This does not mean that being in check disqualifies the king from castling later in the game. If the check is removed in some way other than by moving the king, it may still castle on another move (as long as the other requirements are met). But when the king is actively in check, it may not castle to escape check.

✦ The king can't castle into check. (Naturally, because the king can never move into check anyway.)

+ If one of your opponent's pieces controls the square the king must "jump over" to castle, castling is prohibited. That means if White wants to castle kingside, but the f1 square is controlled by an enemy piece, White can't castle kingside while that square is controlled. And if White wants to castle queenside, but the d1 square is controlled by an enemy piece, White can't castle queenside while that square is controlled. Similarly, Black can't castle kingside while the f8 square is controlled by an enemy piece, nor can he castle queenside while the d8 square is controlled by an enemy piece. But once there is no longer any enemy piece that controls the crucial square next to the king, the prohibition is lifted.

+ There is a special way to write the move of castling. Kingside castling is written as "O-O", and queenside castling is written as "O-O-O". For example, if White's twelfth move is to castle kingside, it is written "12.O-O", and if Black's ninth move is to castle queenside, it's written "9...O-O-O".

Let me show you another illustration of castling for both sides, plus how it's written, in the next three diagrams.

In Diagram 11, it's White's turn to play move eight. White can't castle kingside, because the bishop on f1 is in the way. White decides to castle queenside. This is written "8.O-O-O".

In Diagram 12 Black can't castle queenside, because the queen on d8 and the bishop on c8 are in the way. Black decides to castle kingside (see Diagram 13). This is written "8...O-O".

Don't worry if you find castling confusing. Everybody does at first. You'll get the hang of it. Take a careful look at the rules of castling and the exercises at the end of the chapter to test your understanding of this rule.

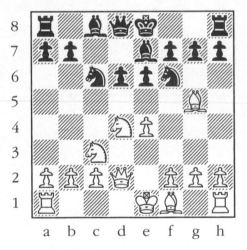

*Diagram 11: The bishop on f1 prevents White from castling kingside. White can castle queenside.*

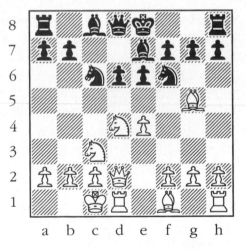

*Diagram 12: White has played 8.O-O-O, and now it's Black's turn. Black can't castle queenside because of the queen on d8 and the bishop on c8, but Black can castle kingside.*

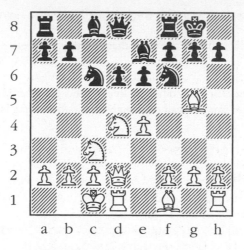

*Diagram 13: Black has played 8...O-O.*

# Win, Lose, or Draw

When you play a game of chess, it can end in one of three ways: you can win, you can lose, or you can draw. (A draw is a tie.) In chess competitions, a win is worth one point to the winner, a loss is worth zero points to the loser, and a draw is worth half a point to each player.

Let's first learn how a game is won or lost and then we'll learn how a game can be a draw.

## Checkmate—the Aim of the Game!

Remember from Chapter 2 that the aim of the game is to put your opponent's king in a position where it can't escape being captured on the next move. When the king is in check (threatened with capture) and there is no move that can *prevent* it from being captured in the very next move, then we say the king is "checkmated." Checkmate ends the game. When you checkmate your opponent, you win; when your opponent checkmates you, you lose. It's that simple.

Sometimes, someone who's just starting to play chess will try to answer checkmate with a check. Nice try, but no dice. Checkmate is immediate and final. In fact, it doesn't even matter if you could checkmate your opponent in the very next move! Checkmate is checkmate, and it ends the game. Period.

It takes a little time to be able to recognize checkmate when it happens. Just remember that it's checkmate when all of the following are true:

✦ The king is in check.

✦ The king can't move to a square where it's not in check.

✦ The piece giving check can't be captured.

✦ There is no piece to put in the way between the king and the piece giving check.

Here are two important points about reading and writing chess moves regarding check and checkmate:

+ If a move puts the opponent's king into check, a "+" is put after the move. For example, if Black's fortieth move is the rook to f3, and this move puts White into check, the move is written "40... Rf3+".

+ If a move puts the opponent's king into checkmate, a "#" is put after the move. For example, if you see the move "28.Be6#" then you know that White's twenty-eighth move put Black into checkmate.

## An Example of Checkmate

It's White's turn to move (see Diagram 14), and she decides to move her rook from d1 to d7 where it will attack two of Black's pawns, on b7 and f7 (see Diagram 15). But White's aggression is misplaced here, because she has left her own king very vulnerable. Black takes advantage of White's mistake by playing 1...Re1# (see Diagram 16). There is no move White can play to remove the king from check in the next move, so she is in checkmate, and Black wins the game.

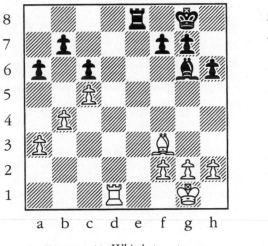

Diagram 14: White's turn to move.

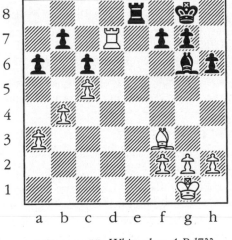

Diagram 15: White plays 1.Rd7??

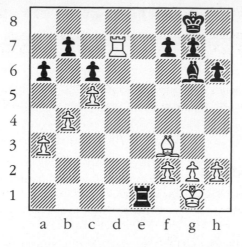

*Diagram 16: Black plays 1...Re1#.*

## What's Up with the Punctuation?!?

Did you notice that in Diagram 15 there are two question marks after the 1.Rd7 move? Chess players use question marks and exclamation marks to express an opinion about a chess move. A "!" means that a move is good (with "!!" meaning really, really good) while a "?" or "??" means that a move is bad or really bad. White's decision to move the rook to d7 was really bad because it let Black give checkmate on the very next move. You will see a lot more "!" and "?" symbols later in the book.

## Throw in the Towel

There is one other way to win. A player may give up at any time during a game, just like a boxer may throw in the towel at any time during a fight. Giving up is called *resigning*. If you're just starting to play chess, my advice is never to resign. Play every game to the end! As you get better, however, you'll start to recognize when your position has deteriorated to the point that—even though you may not be able to see exactly how it will happen—you will inevitably be checkmated. If your game has reached such a dreadful state, it may make sense to resign rather than to continue a hopeless struggle. By far the most common way for a grandmaster to lose a chess game is to resign before the inevitable checkmate.

# Sometimes Nobody Wins

A game of chess doesn't always have a winner and a loser. When no one wins and no one loses, both players draw. In fact, games between grandmasters end in draws more often than one side wins or loses. There are four ways that a game can end in a draw; let's go through them one at a time.

## Insufficient Material to Deliver Checkmate

Sometimes so many pieces have been captured on both sides that it's simply no longer possible to put the enemy king into checkmate. If checkmate is no longer legally possible, the game is a draw. This is pretty rare, however, because it has to be absolutely impossible for checkmate to happen.

In Chapter 4 you will learn how to force checkmate with just a lone queen or a lone rook against a king. So if one side has at least a rook or a queen, checkmate is still possible. And if one side has a pawn, remember that it could always promote to a rook or a queen. Furthermore, two knights, a knight and a bishop, or two bishops can all give checkmate against a lone king.

The bottom line? Insufficient material is usually just king versus king or when one side only has a knight or a bishop; so don't worry too much about it. Just keep in mind that if it is impossible for either player to checkmate the other, the game is drawn.

There are also some positions where even though there are more pieces on the board, it turns out to be impossible to construct a checkmate, usually because of the way the pawns block each other and also block the other pieces. Don't worry about this: it's extremely rare! But if you like playing with puzzles, you might try to figure out what such a position could be.

## Friendly Agreement

Just as either side can at any time resign the game, both players can at any time simply agree to a draw. Sometimes it can be polite to agree to a draw. If it's absolutely clear that neither side has any realistic chance to win, the gracious thing to do is to offer a draw. Or if you are playing a friendly game and your opponent suddenly has to leave—and you don't think you have an obviously better position—again, the gracious thing to do is to agree to a draw.

When grandmasters play against one another, it's common for them to agree to a draw even in fairly complicated positions. Sometimes this is because the position only seems complicated, and both players realize the game really should be a draw. Sometimes grandmasters agree to a draw because each player is afraid of losing! Because you are just starting to learn chess, I strongly urge you to play out every position to the end. Losing a game here or there is not nearly so bad as losing a chance to learn more and improve your game.

Maybe these first two ways for a game to end in a draw seem a little obvious or boring to you. But pay attention! The next two ways are not so obvious at all.

## Perpetual Check

Remember that whenever your king is in check, you must remove it from check on the very next move. And remember, too, that the king is in checkmate when it is in check and there is no way to remove the check on the very next move. But suppose your king is in check, and you remove it from check, and then it's in check again, and then you remove it from check, and then it's in check again, and so on.

When one side continually checks the other side, it's called *perpetual check*. If one side announces that he'll give perpetual check, and there's no way to escape from it, the game is drawn.

It's important to remember that perpetual check is different from simply giving a lot of checks. Perpetual check occurs only when one side can put the other side in check forever. That's why, if one player announces she will give perpetual check, the game is drawn. What would be the point of continuing the game?

So often in chess, a picture is worth a thousand words. See the following diagrams for some examples of positions that are and are not cases of perpetual check.

In Diagram 17, Black is in check. Can White give perpetual check? The answer is no, it isn't perpetual check because after 1...Kc7 (Diagram 18), White has only one more check with the rook (2.Rc8+ or 2.Rd7+), whereupon Black will capture the rook. Then there certainly won't be any more checks!

In Diagram 19, Black is in check. Can White give perpetual check? Black has no move other than 1...Ka7 (see Diagram 20). When White plays 2.Rd7+ (see Diagram 21), Black must move the king to either b8 or a8. White will play 3.Rd8+, then 4.Rd7+, then 5.Rd8+, and so on. If White demonstrates this and announces that she will give perpetual check, she can claim a draw.

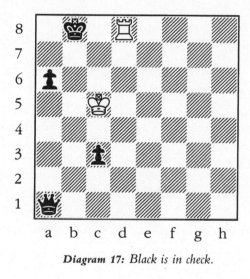

Diagram 17: Black is in check.

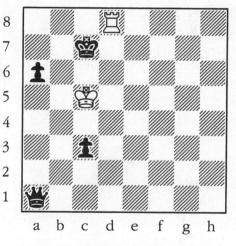

Diagram 18: Black plays 1...Kc7, and now it's clear that White can't give perpetual check.

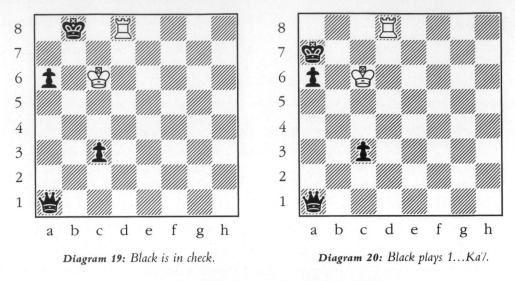

Diagram 19: *Black is in check.*

Diagram 20: *Black plays 1...Ka7.*

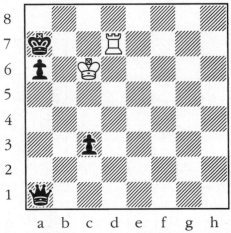

Diagram 21: *White plays 2.Rd7+ and can give perpetual check by playing Rd8+ and Rd7+ forever.*

# Stalemate

Suppose there is literally no move you can make. This means that it's your turn to move, but there is simply no square to which you can move any piece. (This isn't common, but it happens more often than you might think.) What do you think happens in this case?

Many people who are just learning the rules assume that if one side can't make any legal move, that side loses the game. But in fact, what happens is the game is a draw. Often when I explain this rule to people, they think it doesn't make sense. After all, if someone can't make a single move, doesn't that mean the person is helpless? And if the person is helpless, why should the game be a draw?

I understand that thought. But on the other hand, remember that the object of the game is to capture the enemy king. The whole point of stalemate is that it is "stale" because you haven't attacked the king. And you can't win without attacking the king. See the following diagrams for some examples.

✛ In Diagram 22, it's White's turn to move. (Chess players express this as "White to move" as seen in the caption.) This position is not stalemate because White has one legal move: 1.g4.

✛ In Diagram 23, it's White's turn to move. This position is stalemate, because White has no legal moves at all, so the game is a draw.

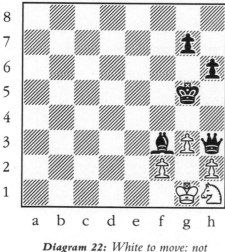

*Diagram 22: White to move: not stalemate.*

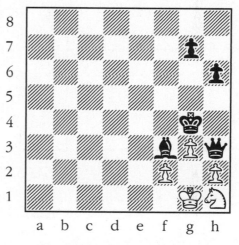

*Diagram 23: White to move: stalemate.*

+ In Diagram 24, it's Black's turn to move. This position is stalemate because Black has no legal moves at all, so the game is a draw.

+ In Diagram 25, it's Black's turn to move. This position is not stalemate because Black has two legal moves: 1…h6 and 1…h5.

Diagram 24: *Black to move: stalemate.*

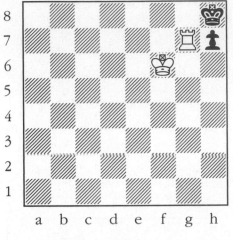

Diagram 25: *Black to move: not stalemate.*

# Exercises: You're Almost Ready to Play!

Don't worry if you're still a little unsure about a few of the rules. It may take a little time before you've got them down cold. Use the exercises to train your knowledge and understanding. If you have trouble with any of the exercises, reread the appropriate section and study the illustrative diagrams.

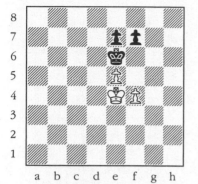

**Exercise 1:** *If Black plays 1... f5+, can White respond with 2.exf6 or not?*

**Exercise 2:** *It's White's turn. If White wants to promote the pawn on c7 to a queen, what is the only move to do this? Write the move down.*

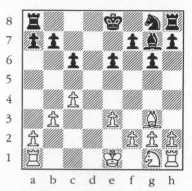

**Exercise 3:** *White to move and wants to castle queenside. Write that move down. If White castles queenside, can Black respond by immediately castling queenside himself?*

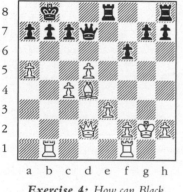

**Exercise 4:** *How can Black give White perpetual check?*

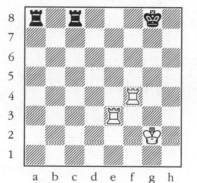

**Exercise 5:** *White to move. How can White checkmate Black in two moves?*

**Exercise 6:** *Black to move. Is it stalemate?*

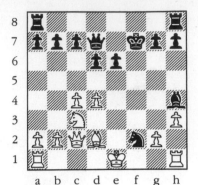

**Exercise 7:** Can White castle kingside or queenside? If castling on either side (or both sides) is legal, write down the move in correct chess notation.

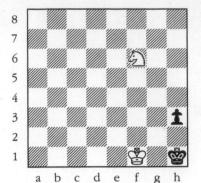

**Exercise 8:** White to move. Should this position be declared a draw? Can White force a win with best play?

**Exercise 9:** Black to move. This position is very similar to Exercise 8. Black has two legal moves; one of them loses, the other draws. Which is the right move, and why?

**Exercise 10:** White to move (Kasparov–Kramnik, Holland, 2001). If White plays 1.g4, can Black capture en passant?

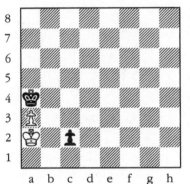

**Exercise 11:** It is Black's turn. Black can and should promote his pawn. What should he promote it to? Why?

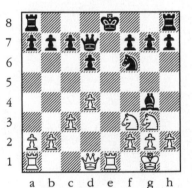

**Exercise 12:** It is Black's turn. (How could you know even if I didn't tell you?) Can he castle kingside? Can he castle queenside?

# Chapter 4

# How to Win with Just One Piece

In this chapter, I teach you how to force a lone king into checkmate with a queen and how to force a lone king into checkmate with a rook. What's the point of learning how to do this? Well to begin with, it's a useful skill to have in its own right. After you study this chapter, you can be confident about winning a position where you have only a queen or only a rook remaining.

But there are two other important reasons to learn this skill. First, there's no better way to get a feel for the power of the queen or the rook than by learning how to use it to force checkmate against the lone king.

Second, learning how to force a lone king into checkmate is an excellent way to learn how to plan. Chess is a war between two evenly matched armies. Such a war can be won only if you lead more effectively than your opponent. To lead your army effectively you must lead it in accordance with a plan that fits the needs of your position at any moment. In subsequent chapters, you'll learn how to recognize what those needs are and how to achieve them. But even before you begin learning the strategies and tactics your plan should include, you should get a sense for how to form a plan in the first place. This chapter will help you do that.

It may be useful to read this chapter with a chess set by your side, so you can play out all the moves. But don't worry if you don't have a set—I have included diagrams so you can follow all the moves just by reading the book.

As I explain how to force checkmate with the queen or with the rook, there is not enough space to examine every single defensive possibility. Focus on the key ideas. After you think you understand it, you might want to play these positions with a friend or a computer, so you can practice giving checkmate against all possible king moves.

# Checkmate with Queen and King Versus King

Consider the position shown in Diagram 1. Suppose you're playing White. Obviously, you have the advantage because your opponent has only his king, and you have a king and a queen! In fact, you should win this position. How should you play?

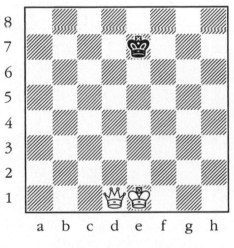

*Diagram 1: What is White's plan to win this position?*

## Make a Plan

Let's not make any moves right away. Let's think about this first. What should your plan be? Well, it's hard to imagine aiming for anything except checkmate. After all, Black doesn't have anything else on the board except his king, so there isn't anything in Black's position to attack except his king. If there was ever a time to go for checkmate, this is it!

"But wait a minute," you might ask, "isn't checkmate always the goal? What's different about saying I should go for checkmate now?"

That's a good question, and it brings up a mistake that many beginning players make. While it's always the *ultimate* goal to checkmate your opponent's king, it's not always correct to have that as your *immediate* goal. You should always choose your moves with some kind of plan to improve your position. Often, the right way to improve your position (or attack your opponent's position) will not directly involve checkmate. In fact, if you try to attack your opponent's king before you're ready to do so, you may overextend yourself and make your own position worse! This will become clearer to you as you learn more about chess strategy.

At any rate, since Black literally has nothing left on the board but the king, it's clear that in this position checkmate is the thing to aim for. That's the goal. What plan should you make to achieve it?

Here are two very important hints:

✛ The queen can't checkmate a lone king on an open board by herself—the queen needs the help of the king.

✛ The queen and king can't checkmate the opposing king unless it's on the edge or the corner of the board.

If it's not clear to you why either point is true, try to construct a checkmate with just a queen and king against a lone king in a way that contradicts the two points above, and you'll see why it can't be done.

Now then, what plan can you make to give checkmate? Taking your cue from the two hints above, it should be clear that you must use your own king, and you must drive the enemy king to the edge or the corner. And in fact, the winning plan is to do just that. Here's how to do it.

*Diagram 2:* White to move.

## Constrict the King

In case you've forgotten the position we're starting from, Diagram 2 gives the same position as Diagram 1. Step one is to constrict the king's movements as much as possible. This will make it easier to drive the king to the edge of or corner of the board. To accomplish this end, the best first move is 1.Qd5 (see Diagram 3). Why is this such a good move? Look how much the black king is constricted by the queen in Diagram 4. The queen blocks the king from crossing either the d-file or the fifth rank. This first move enormously helps the plan to drive the king to the edge (or the corner) of the board.

When they first try to give checkmate with a queen and a king, many beginning chess players instinctively give check and then give check again, and again, and again, and again. But how would that help drive the king to the edge of the board? It doesn't. In fact, the best way to force checkmate doesn't involve giving check before it's time to give checkmate, not even once!

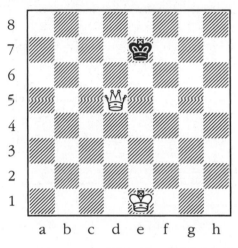

*Diagram 3: White plays 1.Qd5! to constrict the king's movement as much as possible.*

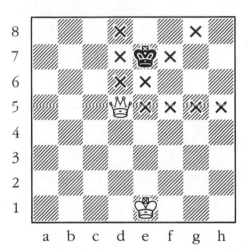

*Diagram 4: The Xs show all the squares Black's king can't move to.*

## Bring Your King Up to Help

Let's go back to the position after 1.Qd5. How will Black respond? Black realizes that the king is in greatest danger on the edge of the board, so he should try to keep the king away from the edge. Keeping this in mind, let's suppose he plays 1...Kf6 (see Diagram 5). Is there any queen move you can make that will constrict the king even further? You might think 2.Qe4, but I think this move gives up just about as much as it gains: if you play 2.Qe4, you take the e-file away from the king, but you give up the fifth rank. For the moment, there is no better square for the queen than d5. Since the queen is so well placed, let's bring the king up to help the queen by playing 2.Kf2 (see Diagram 6). This is a very good move because it helps accomplish the other thing we need to achieve to give checkmate: it brings the king closer to the queen.

Suppose Black responds by moving his king back to where it was before and plays 2...Ke7, as in Diagram 7.

Now what should White do? Actually, White has two very good moves. If you are thinking "Keep bringing the king up to help the queen by playing 3.Ke3, 3.Kf3, or 3.Kg3," give yourself a pat on the back because those are all very good moves. However, I'm going to show you a different way to proceed. Before bringing the king up, we're going to use the queen to drive Black's king into the corner.

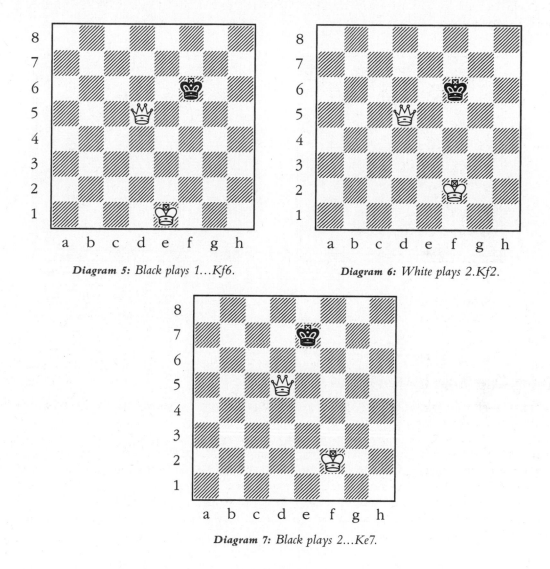

**Diagram 5:** *Black plays 1...Kf6.*          **Diagram 6:** *White plays 2.Kf2.*

**Diagram 7:** *Black plays 2...Ke7.*

# Drive the King to the Corner

Diagram 7 shows the white queen at d5. The plan is to drive the king back to the corner using just the queen. The black king will then be helpless, so you can bring your own king up for the final kill. My suggestion is for White to drive the king farther back by playing 3.Qc6 (see Diagram 8).

By the way, do you notice how the queen is always played a knight's move away from the king? Doing this enables the queen to take the maximum number of squares away from the king. In fact, the next several moves are all going to put the queen a knight's move away from the king. Suppose Black plays 3...Kf7; now you should play 4.Qd6, as in Diagram 9.

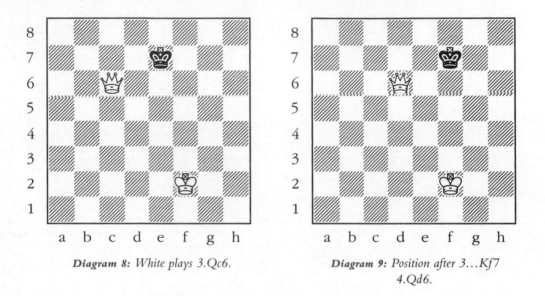

*Diagram 8: White plays 3.Qc6.*

*Diagram 9: Position after 3...Kf7 4.Qd6.*

The next several moves are all going to follow the same pattern; therefore, if Black plays 4...Ke8, then White plays 5.Qc7, as shown in Diagram 10.

Now keep pushing the king into the corner: 5...Kf8 6.Qd7 Kg8 7.Qe7 Kh8, as Diagram 11 shows.

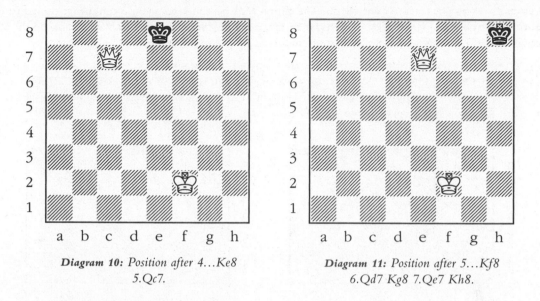

*Diagram 10: Position after 4...Ke8 5.Qc7.*

*Diagram 11: Position after 5...Kf8 6.Qd7 Kg8 7.Qe7 Kh8.*

## Beware of Giving Stalemate!

What should you play now? Look at Diagram 12. If your first instinct was to play 8.Qf7??, then slap yourself on the wrist. *You've just put Black in stalemate!* (You remember stalemate, right? If not, refresh your memory by reviewing it in Chapter 3.)

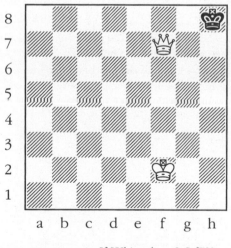

*Diagram 12: If White plays 8.Qf7??, then Black is in stalemate, and the game is a draw.*

# Go for the Kill

Let's go back to Diagram 11, with the queen still on e7. There's no way you can improve the position of the queen because the black king is as far back as possible. Now it's time for White to bring the king up for the kill, so let's play 8.Kg3, as shown in Diagram 13.

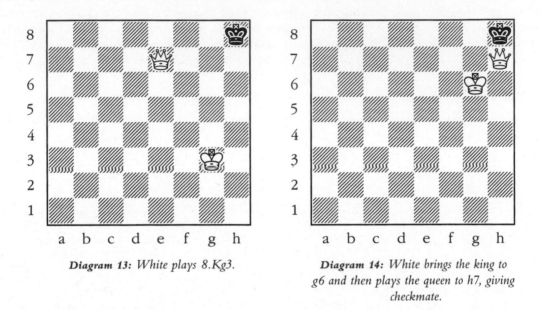

Diagram 13: *White plays 8.Kg3.*

Diagram 14: *White brings the king to g6 and then plays the queen to h7, giving checkmate.*

Black has nothing to do but to move his king back and forth. While he's doing that, you bring your king up and, when you're ready, give checkmate. The game might finish: 8...Kg8 9.Kg4 Kh8 10.Kg5 Kg8 11.Kg6 Kh8 12.Qh7#. The final checkmate is shown in Diagram 14. It took only 12 moves and a good plan to force checkmate!

Is it clear to you how White forced checkmate? If not, go back over this section. Don't worry too much about particular moves, and focus on understanding what the main ideas are and how White realizes them: driving the king into the corner, avoiding stalemate, and bringing up the king to deliver checkmate. See how much more effective it is to follow a logical plan than to merely give check after check with the queen!

# Checkmate with Rook and King Versus King

In many ways, the procedure for giving checkmate with the rook is similar to doing it with the queen. Once again, you must drive the king back to the edge or a corner; and once again, you must use your own king to help. But because the rook is a weaker piece than the queen, you need to use your king more actively in this procedure. In particular, you need to use your king in the process of driving the opposing king to the edge of the board, because the rook (unlike the queen) can't do it alone.

## Constrict the King

Consider the position in Diagram 15. How can you best constrict the king with the rook? The best move is 1.Ra6! which prevents the king from crossing the sixth rank, as in Diagram 16.

Why is this the best move? Well, the goal is to force the king to the edge of the board; after this move, the king can't go beyond the seventh rank. That's a lot of progress for one move!

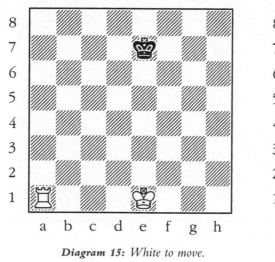

*Diagram 15: White to move.*

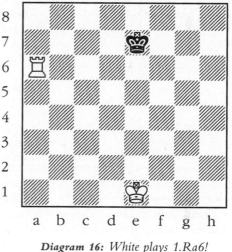

*Diagram 16: White plays 1.Ra6!*

# Bring Your King Up to Help

White has just moved 1.Ra6, and it's Black's move. How will Black respond? If Black moves the king backward and plays 1...Kf8, then White can play 2.Ra7 and restrict the black king's movement even more. So let's suppose Black plays 1...Kd7. Since there is no way the rook can do anything more to restrict the king, it's time for White to bring up her king by playing 2.Kd2. Look at Diagram 17 to see the position after these moves.

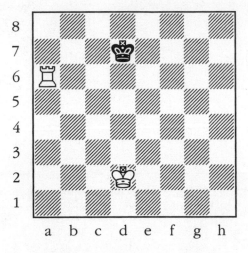

*Diagram 17: Black plays 1...Kd7, and White responds with 2.Kd2.*

Black moves the king over to attack the rook by playing 2...Kc7 3.Kc3 Kb7, reaching Diagram 18. Notice that the black king is now attacking the white rook. This illustrates how the rook is weaker than the queen. The king can never move next to the queen, but it can move diagonally next to the rook, so the plan of always staying a knight's move away from the king isn't going to work. The rook needs the king's help!

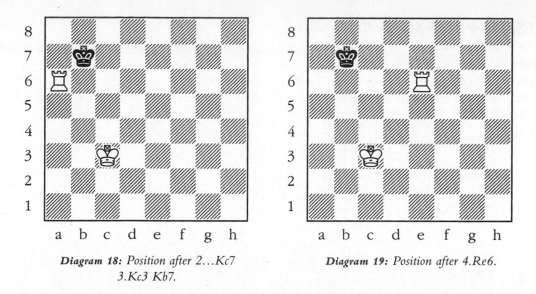

Diagram 18: Position after 2...Kc7 3.Kc3 Kb7.

Diagram 19: Position after 4.Re6.

There's no reason for concern, however, just because the black king is attacking the rook. You can simply move the rook to another square along the sixth rank where the king isn't attacking it, for example, 4.Re6 (see Diagram 19). This will keep the black king constricted and give you time to bring up the white king to participate in the hunt.

Black may try to move the king over to attack the rook again by playing 4...Kc7, as in Diagram 20.

White brings up the king to join the fight: 5.Kc4 Kd7 6.Kd5! (see Diagram 21). Now the rook on e6 is protected by the white king. Black's plan was to attack the rook and try to free his king, but here the active white king foils Black's plan by coming to the aid of the rook. The black king can't capture the rook because it's protected by the white king.

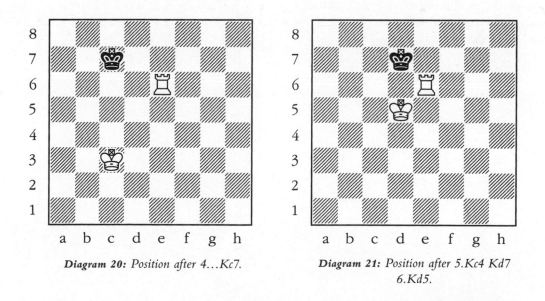

Diagram 20: Position after 4...Kc7.

Diagram 21: Position after 5.Kc4 Kd7 6.Kd5.

# Drive the King Back

Notice how much the black king is constricted in Diagram 21. Not only is it blocked from crossing the sixth rank, it's also blocked from crossing the e-file. The next step in White's plan is to continue taking more squares away from the black king, driving it back to the edge or the corner. This is just like what we did with the queen; the big difference is that the rook needs to work with the king to carry out this plan.

Let's continue playing the game out. The black king runs, and the white rook chases: 6...Kc7 7.Rd6 Kb7 8.Rc6 (see Diagram 22). Now the black king is confined to a tiny box of four squares: b7, b8, a7, and a8!

On the next move, as shown in Diagram 23, Black plays 8...Kb8. How should White progress from here? Once again, White needs to use the king. Because Black's king is confined to the squares b8, b7, a8, and a7, it makes sense for White to bring the king over so it is closer to those squares.

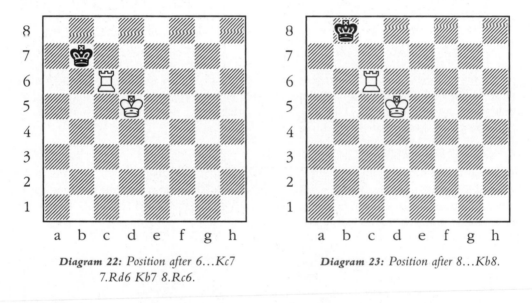

*Diagram 22: Position after 6...Kc7 7.Rd6 Kb7 8.Rc6.*

*Diagram 23: Position after 8...Kb8.*

In Diagram 24, White brings the king closer to the action: 9.Kc5 Kb7 10.Kb5. The black king is confined to the same four squares, but now the white king is nearby, ready to help the rook drive the black king even further back.

Suppose Black plays 10...Ka7 (as shown in Diagram 25)? Now we can see how useful it is to have the king nearby. White responds by playing 11.Rb6, as shown in Diagram 26, and the black king is really driven into the corner! But whenever the king starts getting close to running out of moves, you must be careful not to give stalemate.

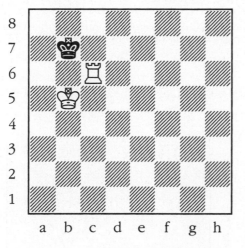

*Diagram 24: Position after 9.Kc5 Kb7 10.Kb5.*

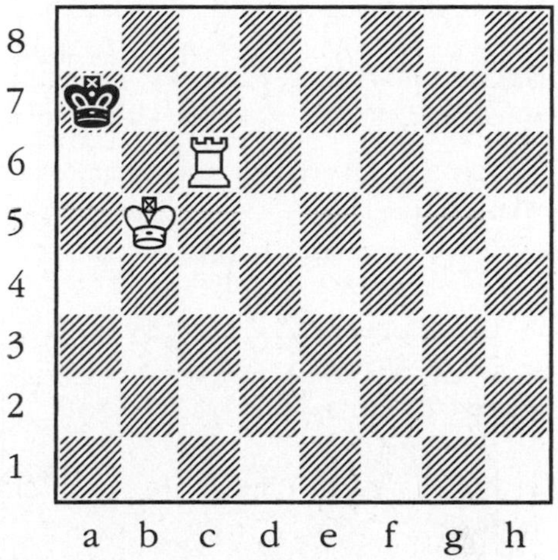

*Diagram 25: Position after 10...Ka7.*

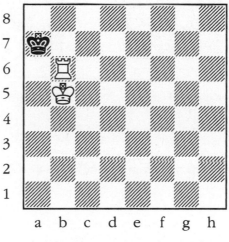

*Diagram 26: Position after 11.Rb6.*

## Beware of Giving Stalemate!

Consider Diagram 27, which shows the position after Black plays 11...Ka8. White can't improve the location of her rook, so it's time to move the king. Should the white king move to a6 or c6?

If you thought White should play 12.Ka6?? (see Diagram 28), give yourself another slap on the wrist! That move puts Black into stalemate and the game would be a draw. Just as with the queen, you must always be careful not to take away all the squares from the king while you are hunting it down with the rook.

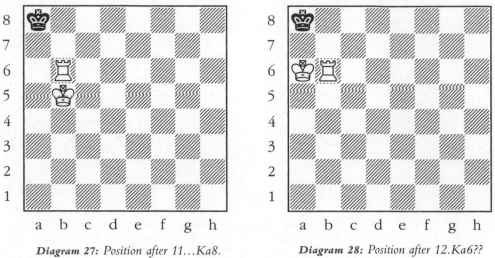

*Diagram 27: Position after 11...Ka8.*      *Diagram 28: Position after 12.Ka6?? and stalemate.*

# Go for the Kill

The right way for White to play is 12.Kc6, as shown in Diagram 29. This move brings the king closer without giving checkmate. Now play continues: 12...Ka7  13.Kc7 Ka8. Do you see in Diagram 30 how White can give checkmate now?

White can give checkmate with 14.Ra6# (see Diagram 31).

Did you notice that you never gave check before checkmate? There was never any reason to give check, so it was never part of our plan.

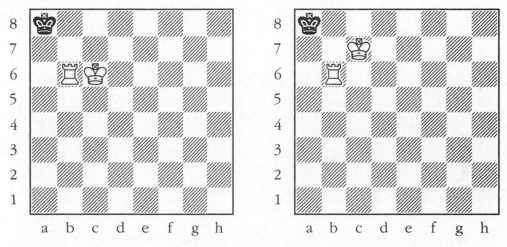

*Diagram 29: Position after 12.Kc6.*

*Diagram 30: Position after 12...Ka7 13.Kc7 Ka8.*

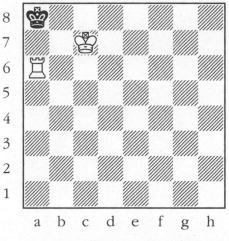

*Diagram 31: Position after 14.Ra6#.*

# Could You Do It Again?

Do you feel comfortable about giving checkmate with a queen or a rook against a king? If you have a friend who's also learning how to play chess, you may want to practice together. Take turns forcing checkmate with the rook or the queen against each other. If you're learning on your own, go over the chapter carefully. Imagine how you would have played if at various points Black had moved the king to a different square than we considered here.

Finally, use this chapter to think about the importance of playing moves according to a plan. The plan doesn't have to be as detailed and thorough as the plan we use in this chapter. Most chess positions are too complicated for anyone—even a grandmaster—to make a plan that goes much beyond a few moves. The important thing is to make your moves in accordance with an idea—a goal you want to achieve that meets the needs of the position.

# Exercises: A Plan to Win

Use these exercises to test your mastery of checkmate.

**Exercise 1:** *How can White force checkmate in two moves? Is 1.Qe6 a good move or a bad move?*

**Exercise 2:** *How can White force checkmate in two moves?*

**Exercise 3:** *Name all the squares on which Black could put a queen to give checkmate.*

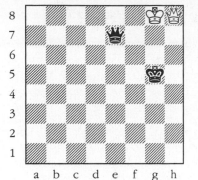

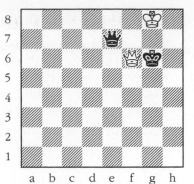

**Exercise 4:** *Although White has only a lowly pawn, she still has a winning plan. What is the plan, and how can it be achieved?*

**Exercise 5:** *Black to move. What is the best move? Can Black win?*

**Exercise 6:** *How should Black capture the queen?*

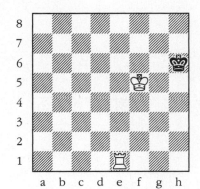

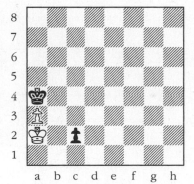

**Exercise 7:** *White to move. How can White force checkmate in two moves?*

**Exercise 8:** *Black to move. This is the same position as Exercise 11 in Chapter 3. Suggest a reasonable series of moves leading to Black checkmating White.*

# Part 2

# TACTICS

Now that you're ready to play chess, it's time to learn how to play better! This part and the next one teach you how to play chess *well*. Chess thinking is divided into two areas: tactics and strategy. This part teaches you tactics, and Part 3 teaches you strategy.

A tactic is a move or a sequence of moves designed to achieve a goal. The most common goals are to capture your opponent's pieces and to give checkmate. I teach you the tactics you need to make sure you capture more of your opponent's pieces than he or she captures of yours. I also show you some tactics to apply directly to the attack against the king, and you get to see some examples of successful attacks against the king. Let's get ready to rumble!

# Chapter 5

# It's a Material World

In Chapter 4, you saw how to win with an extra rook or queen at the end of the game. In fact, if you did Exercise 4 in Chapter 4, you saw that even having just one extra pawn at the end of a game can be enough to win. As you will see in the following chapters, having more pieces or pawns than your opponent is useful throughout the game in many other ways.

In the starting position of a chess game, neither side can capture any of the opponent's pieces or pawns. But that changes very quickly! So the first things you need to learn are how to watch out for threats to your side and how to take advantage of any opportunity to capture your opponent's forces, as well.

In this chapter, you'll learn the relative value of each piece and how to decide whether a move is advantageous or not by making basic calculations when capturing a piece or when allowing your opponent to capture one of your pieces. The next two chapters (6 and 7) will then show you lots of advanced strategies for capturing your opponent's pieces.

# The Concept of Material

Chess is a game of war. In chess, as in war, the bigger army will win if all other things are equal. It's just common sense: if you have more forces to attack with than your opponent has to defend with, your attack has a better chance to overwhelm the defense; and if you have more forces to defend with than your opponent has to attack with, your defense has a better chance to turn away the attack.

When you have more forces with which to attack and to defend with than your opponent does, you have more power, which chess players call *material*. A *material advantage,* as chess players call it, is an advantage in power. When you have a material advantage over your opponent, you have a more powerful army than your opponent.

## Sometimes Fewer Pieces = More Material

Let's develop this "chess as war" analogy a little more. Most people probably agree that the United States has the most powerful military in the world. So even if the United States went to war with a country that had a bigger population, the United States would probably win. (Let's leave weapons of mass destruction out of this little thought exercise!) But wait a minute, if the other country has more people than the United States, then it could potentially field a bigger army. So why wouldn't the other country win?

Without getting bogged down in military science, one thing at least is clear: a bigger population might translate into more soldiers, but the number of soldiers is not the only thing that matters. It also matters what weapons (and other equipment) are used and how well the soldiers are trained. Even if one army has more soldiers, and maybe even more weapons, an opposing army with better soldiers and better weapons might be more *powerful*.

Now imagine that the pawn is a foot soldier and the rook is a tank, and you can see how this applies to chess.

Sometimes a material advantage means having more pieces than your opponent. But other times, a material advantage means that the pieces you have are worth more.

## The Relative Value of Pieces

So just how powerful is each piece relative to every other piece? There is a standard scale that answers this question. This is a very useful scale to know, and you should commit it to memory. Do keep in mind that it's only an approximation, but it's a heck of a good approximation! The relative values of the pieces are as follows:

| | |
|---|---|
| Pawn | 1 point |
| Knight | 3 points |
| Bishop | 3 points (plus a teensy bit more) |
| Rook | 5 points |
| Queen | 9 points |

There are two words chess players use to talk about capturing one piece for another: *trade* and *exchange*. To trade a piece for another is to capture one of your opponent's pieces in return for allowing one of your pieces to be captured. To trade bishops, for example, is to capture your opponent's bishop and allow your bishop to be captured in return. But a trade doesn't have to be one piece for its counterpart; you can trade a knight for a bishop or trade two rooks for a queen, for example.

The word *exchange* is used similarly; you can exchange knights or exchange two pawns and a bishop for a rook. But the word *exchange* has a very specific meaning: it indicates that a player has one rook more than his or her opponent, and the opponent has only an extra knight or bishop to compensate. For example, if you have an exchange for a pawn, it means you have a rook more than your opponent, while your opponent has either an extra knight or bishop and also an extra pawn. In this example, you have the "advantage of the exchange," while your opponent has an extra pawn in return for a disadvantage.

Notice that the bishop and the knight are worth about the same, even though they are very different pieces. One of the eternal questions in chess is whether you trade a bishop for a knight in any given case. Each thrives in different kinds of positions. The bishop can zoom across the board, so it likes positions where the pawns do not get in the way of its diagonals. The knight likes to find a secure square it can sit on that's in the middle of the action; its leaping ability means the knight is not hampered by the presence of other pieces.

In general, you should favor the bishop in positions where it can find long diagonals and where it can move around a lot. In contrast, you should generally favor the knight in positions with lots of pawns, especially when you can find a secure square for the knight to sit on and influence the action. In the long run, pawns tend to get exchanged, so it's not a bad bet that the bishop will become more powerful toward the end of the game. That is why I have said that the bishop is a teensy bit more powerful than the knight. But whether the bishop or the knight is really the better piece in any particular position is usually more important than the long-term tendency for the bishop to become stronger as pawns are traded and come off the board.

You will learn more about the relative value of the knight and the bishop in Chapter 10. For now, consider them of about equal worth.

## What about the King?

Notice that the king isn't on the scale. Why not? Well, the loss of the king means the loss of the game, so you aren't about to give up your king for another piece! In that sense, the king has an infinite value.

But it still makes sense to ask how powerful it is. After all, just because you dare not lose the king doesn't mean that you can't use it to attack and defend. The scale tries to give a relative weight to the power of each piece. Even though we can't exchange the king for another piece, wouldn't it be nice to know how powerful it is in relation to the other pieces?

Here's the answer: it's worth about three points, which is to say it's about as powerful as the knight or the bishop. Just be careful when you use the king, though, because its *importance* goes far beyond its power!

## How Do You Use This Scale?

Generally, you want to trade up when you can. If you can grab a pawn, do so. If you can give two pawns to get a bishop, that's a good trade. If you can get a rook for three pawns, that's an even better trade. And so on.

This is only a rough scale. It is not a perfect indication of the relative value of each piece. There are particular piece combinations that work well together, and there are particular piece combinations that don't work so well together. There are also certain situations where the value of some pieces increases while the value of others decreases. You will learn some of these situations in later chapters, and experience will teach you additional situations. (See Chapter 15 for how to learn more once you finish this book.) Although it is only a rough scale, it works very well. Grandmasters use it regularly and so should you.

## A Piece by Any Other Name

Sometimes the word *piece* includes pawns, and sometimes it doesn't. Because the relative value scale of pieces is so useful, chess players often use it to distinguish between three different kinds of pieces:

+ **pawn**   So low on the value scale that it does not deserve to be called a piece; it just goes by its name most of the time.

+ **minor pieces**   The bishop and the knight because they are less powerful and have less value.

+ **major pieces**   The rook and the queen because they are so powerful and have the most value.

Look at how the word *piece* is used in context. This may be confusing at first, but you will get the hang of it over time.

# How to Win Material and Avoid Losing Material

It's simple: Capture your opponent's pieces, and don't let your own pieces get captured. If you capture one of your opponent's pieces and one of yours can be captured, make sure the piece you take is worth more than the one your opponent takes.

I can imagine what you're thinking, "Okay, it sounds simple, but how do I make sure that I capture pieces when I can and that I don't let my own pieces be captured? And if there is a trade of pieces, how can I make sure that I trade up?"

## "How Do You Get to Carnegie Hall?"

The answer: practice, practice, practice. Hey, you didn't think you were going to be able to get better without practice, did you? But don't despair! I will explain how you should practice, and I will give you a lot of exercises to practice with. Are you ready to go to work? Let's start with Diagram 1.

It's White's turn to move. Study this position, and before you continue reading, list (or just think to yourself) every single capture White can make. Next, try to decide which capture (if any) White should make. (In chess, we refer to these move choices as "1," although the board reflects a game further along.)

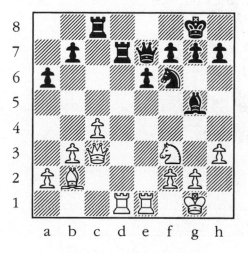

*Diagram 1: White to move.*

There are four captures White can make:

+ White can capture the pawn on e6 with the rook on e1 (1.Rxe6).

+ White can capture the knight on f6 with the queen on c3 (1.Qxf6).

+ White can capture the rook on d7 with the rook on d1 (1.Rxd7).

+ White can capture the bishop on g5 with the knight on f3 (1.Nxg5).

Which capture (if any) should White make? Using our relative value scale of pieces, we can see that there are two captures White should definitely *not* make, one capture that is neutral, and one capture

White should definitely make. See Diagrams 2 and 3 for an illustration of the first capture White shouldn't make.

(By the way, remember that "?" and "??" are used to denote a bad and very bad move, relatively, while "!" and "!!" are used to denote a good and very good move, relatively.)

White should not play 1.Rxe6?? because Black will then recapture the rook with either the queen on e7 or the pawn on f7, and White will lose a rook for a pawn—a very bad trade. (By the way, Black has another way to win a rook other than by capturing the one on e6 with either the pawn or the queen. Do you see what it is?) Next see Diagrams 4 and 5 for an illustration of the second capture White shouldn't make.

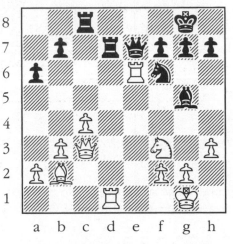

*Diagram 2: White plays 1.Rxe6??*

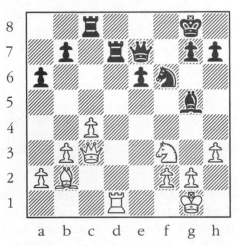

*Diagram 3: Black responds 1…fxe6 and wins a rook for a pawn.*

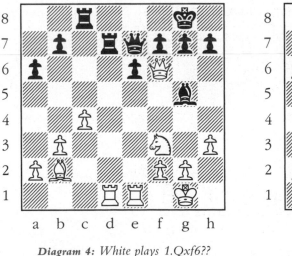

*Diagram 4: White plays 1.Qxf6??*

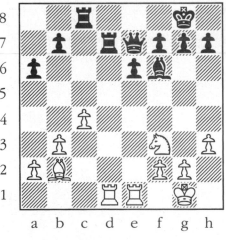

*Diagram 5: Black responds 1…Bxf6 and wins a queen for a knight.*

White also should not play 1.Qxf6??, because Black will then recapture the queen with either the pawn on g7 or the bishop on g5, and White will lose a queen for a knight—another *very* bad trade. Now see Diagrams 6 and 7 for an illustration of the third capture, the one that is basically neutral.

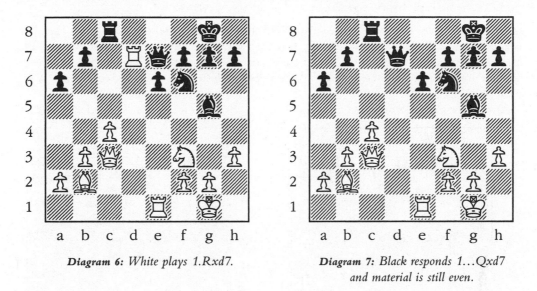

*Diagram 6: White plays 1.Rxd7.*          *Diagram 7: Black responds 1…Qxd7 and material is still even.*

It is neither good nor bad for White to play 1.Rxd7 because Black will recapture the rook with the queen, and White will simply have made an even trade: rook for rook. Now look at Diagram 8 for the fourth possible White capture, the one White should play.

The capture of the bishop with 1.Nxg5! is excellent because there is no way Black can recapture the knight that takes this bishop. White gains a whole bishop for nothing!

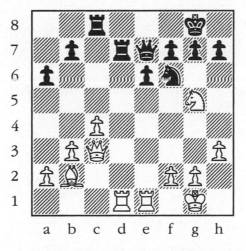

*Diagram 8: White plays 1.Nxg5!*

Here's another position for you to study (see Diagram 9). It's White's turn to move. Once again, either make a list or tell yourself mentally all the captures White can make and then decide which one (if any) White should choose.

There are three captures White can make:

✛ White can capture the pawn on b5 with the knight on c3 (1.Nxb5).

✛ White can capture the pawn on d5 with the rook on d2 (1.Rxd5).

✛ White can capture the pawn on d5 with the knight on c3 (1.Nxd5).

Try to decide for each capture whether White should play it or not and then read what I think about it. See Diagrams 10 and 11 for an illustration of the first capture White can make.

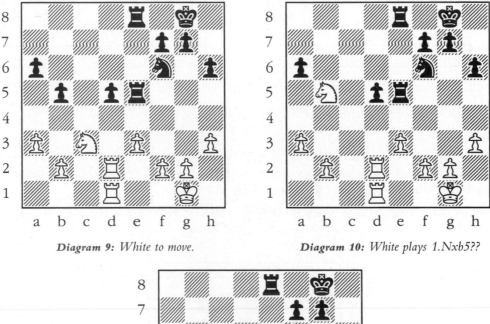

*Diagram 9: White to move.*      *Diagram 10: White plays 1.Nxb5??*

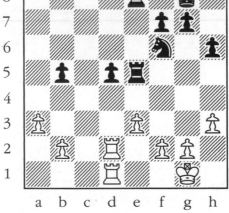

*Diagram 11: Black responds 1...axb5 to capture the knight.*

If White plays 1.Nxb5??, Black will respond 1...axb5 and gain a knight for a pawn. White should not do this! Now for an illustration of the second capture White can make, see Diagrams 12, 13, and 14.

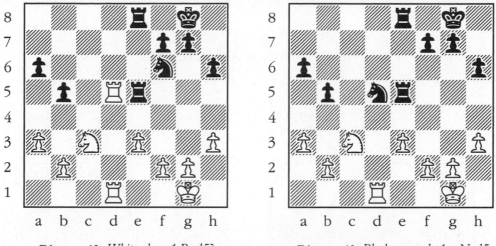

Diagram 12: White plays 1.Rxd5?

Diagram 13: Black responds 1...Nxd5 to take the rook.

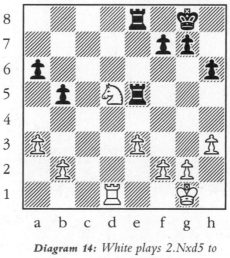

Diagram 14: White plays 2.Nxd5 to take the knight.

If White plays 1.Rxd5?, Black will respond 1...Nxd5 (see Diagram 13) and gain a rook for a pawn. But we can't stop here, because White can make another capture: she can take the knight on d5 with 2.Nxd5 (see Diagram 14). But at this point, Black has taken a rook, and White has only taken a knight and a pawn in return. (Do you see why Black will not want to take White's knight on d5 now?) This sequence of moves has given Black a material advantage, so 1.Rxd5? is a mistake.

The best move is the third possible capture: 1.Nxd5! (see Diagram 15). Now suppose that Black responds with 1…Nxd5 (see Diagram 16). Then White can play 2.Rxd5 (see Diagram 17), and if Black plays 2…Rxd5 (see Diagram 18), White responds with 3.Rxd5. White begins by capturing a pawn and then every capture and recapture is just an even trade, which still leaves White with a material advantage of one pawn.

How can you be sure that a series of captures will come out in your favor? One thing you must do is count the number of pieces (or pawns) attacking and defending whatever you want to capture. If you attack it one more time than it is defended, the last piece standing will be one of yours.

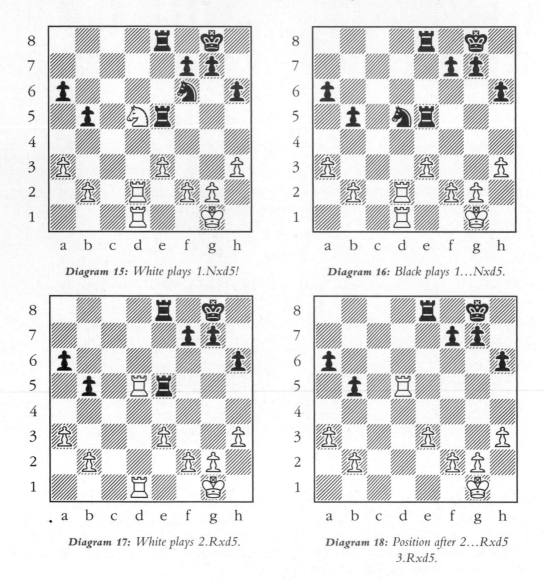

*Diagram 15: White plays 1.Nxd5!*

*Diagram 16: Black plays 1…Nxd5.*

*Diagram 17: White plays 2.Rxd5.*

*Diagram 18: Position after 2…Rxd5 3.Rxd5.*

But that doesn't mean you should automatically capture something if you attack it one more time than your opponent defends it! You must also make sure that you do not lose a more valuable piece for a less valuable piece. (Think about Diagrams 12 and 13. White got a knight and a pawn, but it cost her a rook. Even though she had the last piece standing, she came out behind.)

The only way to make sure things work out for you is to calculate the consequences of each capture. Here is a good rule of thumb: start a series of captures with your least valuable piece (or a pawn), and keep recapturing with the least valuable piece available. That way, you keep your most valuable piece for the end of the capture-and-recapture sequence.

## "Do I Really Need All of This Practice?"

There have been a lot of diagrams for you to study in the last few pages. It may feel somewhat overwhelming. Don't worry if you feel you can't work through it all at once. Take your time and read at the pace that feels most comfortable for you. However, I strongly recommend that you think about all the positions. (In fact, in some positions other captures are possible that I didn't explain. You should try to figure out the consequences of those captures for yourself!) You will find a lot of exercises at the end of the chapter, and I recommend that you do these as well.

Why do I recommend all this work? The answer is simple: learning how to capture your opponent's pieces and how not to let your own pieces be captured, teaches you certain skills. It's not hard to get the idea that it's good to have more material than your opponent and bad to have less material than your opponent. The harder part is actually recognizing when you can win material and when you're in danger of losing material. There is no other way to develop these skills than by practicing.

What skills do you need to develop in order to win material and avoid losing material? There are just three:

+ You need to develop the ability to see in any position which pieces (and pawns) are attacking other pieces (and pawns) and which are being attacked.

+ You need to be able to calculate what the result of a capture will be.

+ You need to be able to assess whether the result of a capture will give you a material advantage or not. (Always remember the relative value scale of pieces!)

The way to develop these abilities is to train yourself by looking at many different positions and seeing which pieces attack other pieces, what will happen in each case if you capture a piece, and whether the resulting position will give you a material advantage. The exercises at the end of this chapter are there for you to do just this kind of training.

# How to Defend One of Your Pieces

In the next two chapters, you learn many useful patterns for winning material. But before we close this chapter, let's address one more thing: how do you defend against a threat to one of your pieces? After all, we've been looking at all the ways to capture material. But what about when you are the one who is being threatened with capture? What should you do?

There are five ways to meet a threat to one of your pieces:

+ Move the piece that is being attacked.

+ Defend the piece that is being attacked.

+ Block the attack on the piece.

+ Capture the piece that is attacking you.

+ Attack something else in your opponent's position.

Let's illustrate each one of these ways to meet a threat to one of your pieces with an example.

## Move the Piece That Is Being Attacked

Look at Diagram 19. Suppose you are Black, and you see that your queen on b6 is being attacked by the bishop on e3. It's your move. What do you do? Well, the simplest thing to do is to move it away to where it's no longer being attacked, right? Diagram 20 shows the position after Black has done just that. It is White's turn again, and the black queen can't be captured because it has moved away.

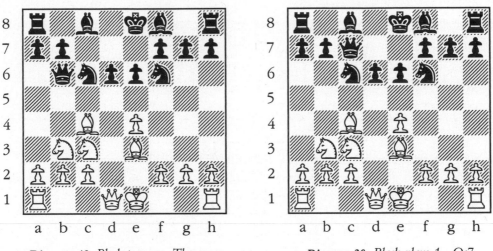

*Diagram 19: Black to move. The queen is attacked by the white bishop on e3.*

*Diagram 20: Black plays 1...Qc7.*

## Defend the Piece That Is Being Attacked

This works well so long as the piece of yours that is being attacked is not more valuable than whichever one of your opponent's pieces is attacking it. But if your piece is more valuable, this is not a good way to meet the threat.

Suppose you are White in Diagrams 21 and 22. In Diagram 21, Black is attacking the rook on c1 with his queen on f4. White defends that rook with her other rook, as shown in Diagram 22. Now it would be a mistake for Black to capture the rook on c1, because White would recapture the queen with the rook on d1 and White would win a queen for a rook—a very good trade for White!

But in Diagram 23, Black is attacking the rook on c1 with his bishop on f4. Now it would be a bad idea for White to defend this rook, because if Black takes the rook with his bishop, then even if White recaptures the bishop, Black has won the exchange (a rook for a bishop), which is a good trade for Black and a bad trade for White.

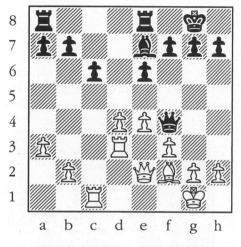

*Diagram 21: White to move. The rook on c1 is attacked by the queen on f4.*

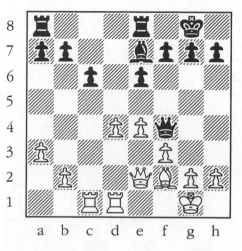

*Diagram 22: White plays 1.Rdd1.*

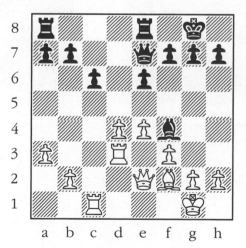

*Diagram 23: White to move: the rook on c1 is attacked by the bishop on f4.*

## Block the Attack on the Piece

You must keep two things in mind if you want to do this. First, if a knight attacks a piece, there is no way to block it. (Remember, knights jump over pieces!) Second, the piece that blocks the attack must be defended, and it must be of lower or equal value to the piece that is attacking. Diagrams 24 and 25 illustrate this second point. In the first diagram, White attacks the queen on c7 with the bishop on g3. In the second diagram, Black defends the attack by moving the bishop to d6. White can capture the bishop, but then Black will recapture the bishop with the queen, and the result will simply be an even trade.

## Capture the Piece That Is Attacking You

Again, whether this is a good idea depends on whether the piece you are thinking about capturing is protected and what the relative value of the piece is. Look again at Diagram 24. It would be a very bad idea for the black queen to capture the bishop on g3, because White would recapture with either the h-pawn or the f-pawn, and Black would lose a queen for a bishop.

But Black has another piece that can capture the bishop.

Certainly, it is a bad idea for Black to take the bishop with his queen, but what about taking it with the knight on h5? In Diagram 26, Black captures the bishop with the knight. White will recapture the knight with one of the pawns, and the result will be an even trade of knight for bishop.

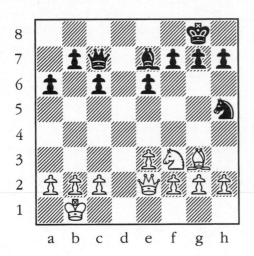

*Diagram 24: Black to move. The black queen is attacked by the bishop on g3.*

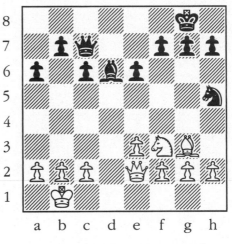

*Diagram 25: Black plays 1...Bd6.*

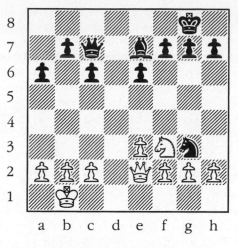

***Diagram 26:*** *Black plays 1...Nxg3.*

## Attack Something Else in Your Opponent's Position

The final way to meet an attack on one of your pieces is just to ignore it altogether and do something else. In that case, just make sure that whatever you do is important enough to be to your advantage if you both carry out your threats! Also, be sure that your threat can't be parried in such a way that you leave yourself vulnerable to the original threat.

Consider Diagram 27. Black attacks the knight on c3 with his rook on c8. White decides to parry this threat by attacking the queen on f8 with her bishop. In Diagram 28, White has attacked the queen. Now it would be a very bad idea for Black to capture the knight, because White would capture the queen, and even after Black recaptured the bishop with his king, White would have won a queen for a knight and a bishop—an excellent trade (see Diagram 29).

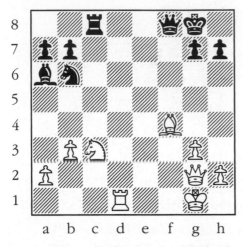

*Diagram 27: White to move. The knight on c3 is attacked by the rook on c8.*

*Diagram 28: White plays 1.Bd6.*

*Diagram 29: Position after 1…Rxc3?? 2.Bxf8.*

Just a small change in the position can make all the difference! Consider Diagram 30. Once again, the knight on c3 is attacked, and once again White decides to meet the threat by attacking the queen on f8 with her bishop on d6. Diagram 31 shows the position after White does this. But this time the white queen is on a slightly different square—f2 instead of g2—so now Black can capture the queen with his own queen and with check! White has to meet the check, so she recaptures the queen. Then the threat to Black's queen is gone, and Black can capture the knight on c3 with his rook. See Diagrams 32 and 33.

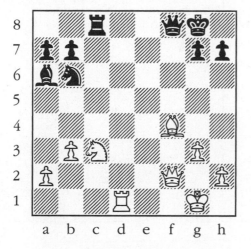

*Diagram 30: White to move. The knight on c3 is attacked by the rook on c8.*

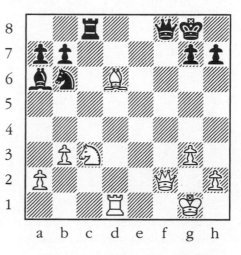

*Diagram 31: White plays 1.Bd6??*

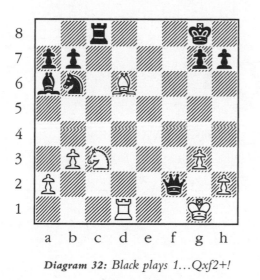

*Diagram 32: Black plays 1...Qxf2+!*

*Diagram 33: Position after 2.Kxf2 Rxc3.*

# Exercises: Practice, Practice, Practice!

It is *so* important to develop the skills of winning material (and not losing material) that the next two chapters are devoted entirely to teaching you the most common tricks for winning (and losing) material. Before you start the next chapter, I recommend that you do these exercises. Yes, I know there are a lot of them, but they are there for your benefit! Don't worry if you have some trouble with them. You can always turn back to the relevant section of the chapter if you are unclear about something. By trying to solve the exercises, and studying the answers if they give you trouble, you will develop the skills you need to win at chess. And believe me, chess is always more fun when you win!

**Exercise 1:** *It's White's turn. List all the pieces and pawns the knight on d4 attacks. Should White capture any of them?*

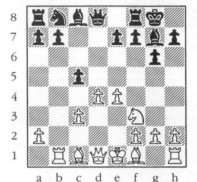

**Exercise 2:** *It's White's turn. Does either 1.Rxb7 or 1.dxc5 win a pawn?*

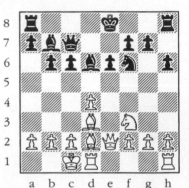

**Exercise 3:** *It's White's turn. What two pawns does White attack? Should White capture either of them?*

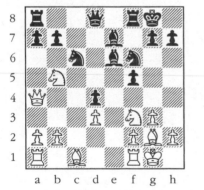

**Exercise 4:** *It's White's turn. Does either 1.Nfxd4 or 1.Nbxd4 win a pawn? Does 1.Qxd4 win a pawn?*

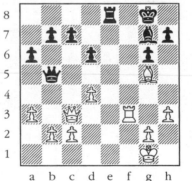

**Exercise 5:** *It's Black's turn. What is Black's best move?*

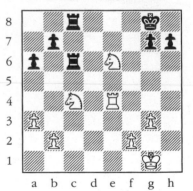

**Exercise 6:** *It's Black's turn. Which knight should Black capture?*

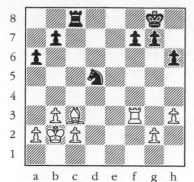

***Exercise 7:*** *It's Black's turn. Can Black win material by capturing the bishop on c3 with either the rook or the knight?*

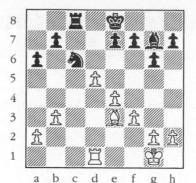

***Exercise 8:*** *It's White's turn. Will White have a material advantage after the sequence 1.dxc6 Rxc6, and if not is 1.dxc6 still the best move?*

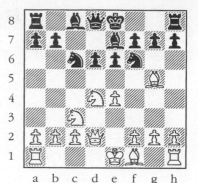

***Exercise 9:*** *It's White's turn. List all of the captures White can make. Do any of them give White a material advantage?*

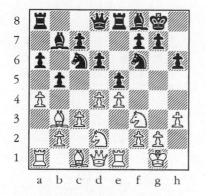

***Exercise 10:*** *It's White's turn. List all of the captures White can make. Do any of them give White a material advantage?*

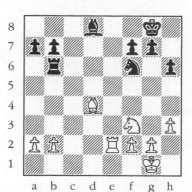

***Exercise 11:*** *It's White's turn, and White attacks both the knight on f6 and the rook on b6. Should White capture either of them?*

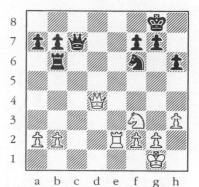

***Exercise 12:*** *It's White's turn. Should White capture any of Black's pieces?*

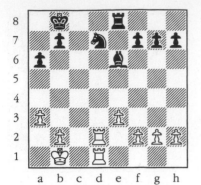

**Exercise 13:** *It's White's turn. Should White capture the knight on d7?*

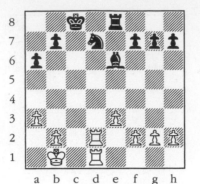

**Exercise 14:** *It's White's turn. Should White capture the knight on d7?*

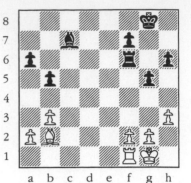

**Exercise 15:** *It's Black's turn, and the rook on f6 is attacked by the bishop on b2. Does Black have any other way to defend against this threat than by moving the rook?*

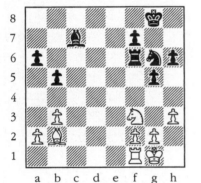

**Exercise 16:** *It's Black's turn, and once again the rook on f6 is attacked by the bishop on b2. Does Black have any other way to defend against this threat than by moving the rook?*

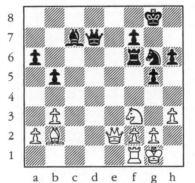

**Exercise 17:** *Once again it's Black's turn, and once again the rook on f6 is attacked. Now does he have any other way to meet the threat of its capture than to move it?*

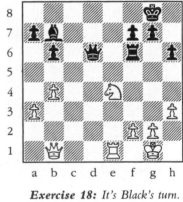

**Exercise 18:** *It's Black's turn. What is Black's best move?*

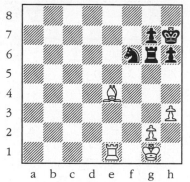

**Exercise 19:** *It's Black's turn. What is Black's best move?*

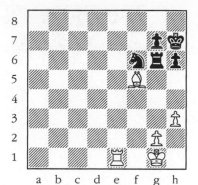

**Exercise 20:** *It's Black's turn. Can Black prevent White from capturing the rook next turn?*

**Exercise 21:** *It's Black's turn. How can Black prevent White from capturing the rook next turn?*

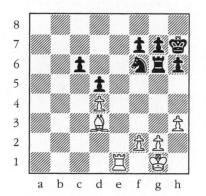

**Exercise 22:** *What happens if Black tries to save the rook the same way as in Exercise 21?*

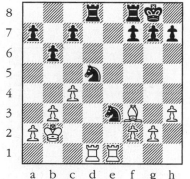

**Exercise 23:** *It's White's turn. Which knight should White capture, and why?*

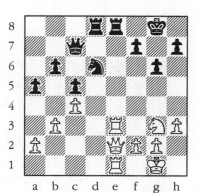

**Exercise 24:** *It's White's turn. Can White win material by capturing the rook on e8?*

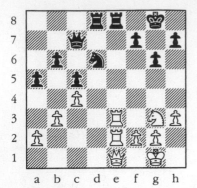

**Exercise 25:** *It's White's turn. Can White win material by capturing the rook on e8?*

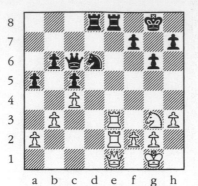

**Exercise 26:** *It's White's turn. Can White win material by capturing the rook on e8?*

**Exercise 27:** *Black to move. White has just played the knight from c3 to d5. Black's queen is now attacked, as well as the bishop on e7. How can Black defend both pieces at once? What is the best move?*

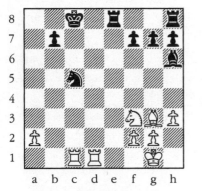

**Exercise 28:** *Black to move. What should Black play? Who will be ahead in material?*

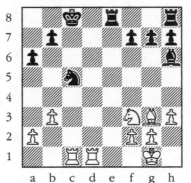

**Exercise 29:** *Black to move. What should Black play? Who will be ahead in material?*

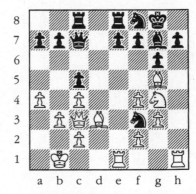

**Exercise 30:** *This one is very hard! Black has just played the knight to f3 from d4. How can White save the queen (attacked by the bishop on g7) and rook (attacked by the rook on f3) at the same time? What is White's best move?*

# Chapter 6

# Tricks of the Tactical Trade

A tactic is a sequence of moves, generally a few moves long, played with a specific goal in mind. Often the goal is either to give checkmate or to win material. One of the neat things about chess is that there are common patterns that recur with tactics. Once you learn these patterns, you'll find it much easier to spot tactical threats and opportunities.

In this chapter and the next, I'll show you some of the most important tactical patterns (which chess players just call *tactics*) for winning material. Are you ready? Let's dive in!

# The Fork

When one piece attacks two pieces at the same time, it's called a *fork*. I'll show you examples of forks by each different piece. Let's start with the pawn.

## Pawn Forks

Consider Diagram 1. It's White's turn to move. Black is threatening to capture the pawn on e4, so White could defend it with 1.Bd3 or exchange pawns with 1.exd5 exd5. But White has a much better move: 1.e5! (see Diagram 2). White attacks both Black's bishop on d6 and Black's knight on f6. There is no way Black can defend both of them. Black must lose either the bishop or the knight for a pawn.

The paradox of pawn forks is that pawn forks are dangerous precisely because pawns are worth so much less than the other pieces. It's useless to protect a piece against a pawn because if you lose even a knight or a bishop for a pawn, you've lost a lot of material.

In fact, it's often worth giving up a pawn to set up a pawn fork. Take a look at Diagram 3.

It's White's turn. Notice that Black's pawn on e5 is attacked twice (by White's pawn on d4 and White's knight on d3) and defended twice (by Black's knight on d7 and Black's bishop on d6). But if White could get one of her own pawns to e5 and if that pawn were protected, Black's knight on f6 and bishop on d6 would be forked. Do you see a way to do that?

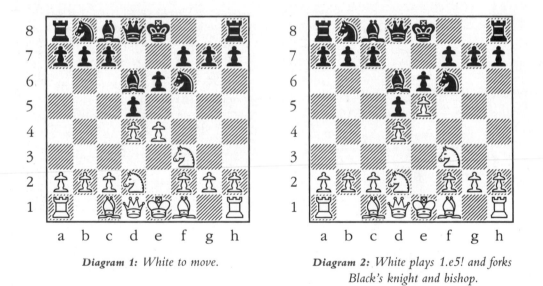

*Diagram 1: White to move.*

*Diagram 2: White plays 1.e5! and forks Black's knight and bishop.*

White cleverly plays 1.f4! (see Diagram 4), which attacks the pawn on e5. Because it's attacked by two pawns, it's useless to defend it with a piece, and there is no way to defend it with a pawn. Unless Black wants to lose a whole pawn for nothing, Black had better capture one of White's pawns. So in Diagram 5 Black plays 1...exd4.

But now White can carry out the plan of establishing the pawn fork by playing 2.e5 (see Diagram 6). White has lost a pawn but is attacking two pieces and will win one of them for a pawn. So White comes out ahead a piece for two pawns.

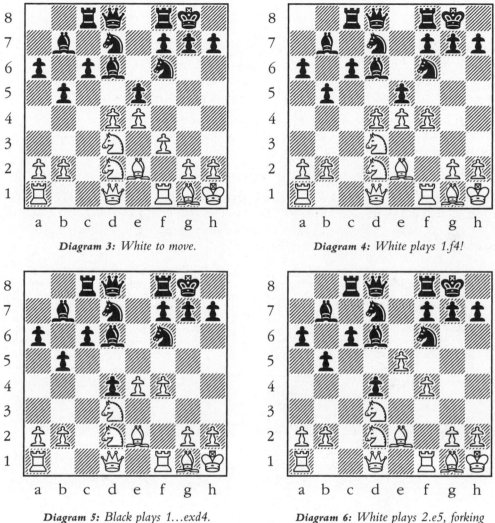

*Diagram 3: White to move.*

*Diagram 4: White plays 1.f4!*

*Diagram 5: Black plays 1...exd4.*

*Diagram 6: White plays 2.e5, forking Black's knight and bishop.*

# Knight Forks

Knights strike terror into the hearts of the rooks and the queen because they're so tricky. Two pieces that seem to be far apart and out of range of anything suddenly can find themselves forked by a knight. Watch out for these guys!

Consider Diagram 7, in which it's White's turn. What danger could there possibly be to Black in this position? All the danger in the world after 1.Ne4, as you can see in Diagram 8. Both Black's queen and rook are attacked by the knight. There is no way to remove the threat to both pieces in his next turn, so Black must lose material. By the way, Black should make the best of a bad deal by moving the queen to a square where it can recapture the knight once it captures the rook on c5. For example, 1...Qe7 is a good move.

Part of the danger of knights is that because they don't move like any other piece, when they fork two (or more) pieces, they often do not have to be defended. (Compare to the pawn fork in Diagram 2, for example.) Diagram 9 shows the deadliest knight fork of all: the family fork, so called because the knight forks both the king and queen. Black is in check, so he must move the king, and White will win a whole queen!

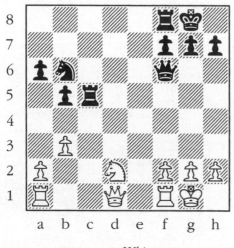

*Diagram 7: White to move.*

*Diagram 8: White plays 1.Ne4! and forks the rook and the queen.*

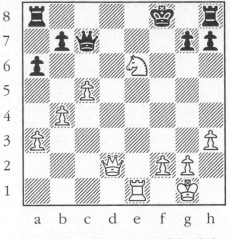

*Diagram 9: White's knight forks Black's
king and queen.*

This brings us to an important point: Why would you want to promote a pawn to anything other than a queen? The most common reason is when promoting to a knight sets up a family fork. Promote to a queen, and you just gain a queen. Promote to a knight while forking the king and queen, and you gain a knight, plus you capture a queen. Diagrams 10 and 11 demonstrate this.

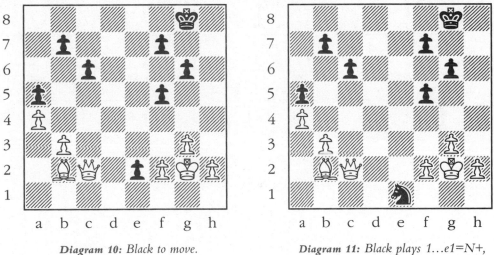

*Diagram 10: Black to move.*

*Diagram 11: Black plays 1...e1=N+,
forking the king and queen.*

## Bishop Forks

The other pieces may not be quite as dangerous forkers as the pawn and the knight, but they are not to be trifled with! Consider Diagram 12. It's White's move, but Black has a material advantage of a knight, a rook, and a pawn. How much damage could White possibly do?

Lots! White starts with 1.Bxc6+ (see Diagram 13), which not only captures a knight but also forks Black's rook on d5 and king on e8. Black responds with 1...Ke7. Maybe Black figures that even after losing the knight and the rook, he will still have a material advantage of a pawn.

But after 2.Bxd5, White is again forking two pieces: the knight on g8 and the rook on b3 (see Diagram 14). Black must lose one or the other, which will leave White with the large advantage of a bishop for a pawn. Notice how Black's pawns on b6 and g7 are getting in his way. If Black didn't have the pawn on b6, he could play 2...Rb8 to move the rook out of the attack and also protect the knight. If Black didn't have the pawn on g7, he could play 2...Rg3, which would move the rook out of the attack and also protect the knight at the same time. But the pawn on b6 stops 2...Rb8, and the pawn on g7 blocks the g-file, so that 2...Rg3 doesn't protect the knight. What a bishop!

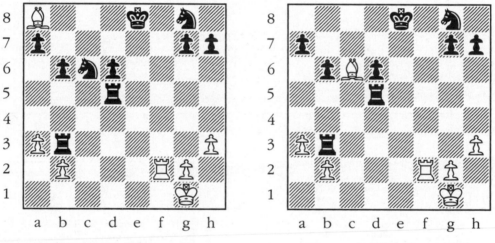

*Diagram 12: White to move.*　　　　*Diagram 13: White plays 1.Bxc6+.*

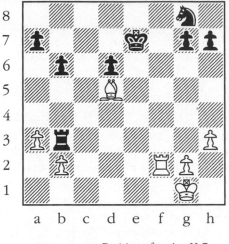

*Diagram 14: Position after 1...Ke7 2.Bxd5.*

## Rook Forks

Whenever you see two pieces along the same file or the same rank, and a rook nearby, watch out! There may be a fork just waiting to happen.

Consider Diagram 15. Material is just about equal. In a game between two grandmasters, a draw would be the most likely result. However, in this case Black isn't satisfied with a draw, and Black plays 1...Ne2?? (see Diagram 16) to attack the rook.

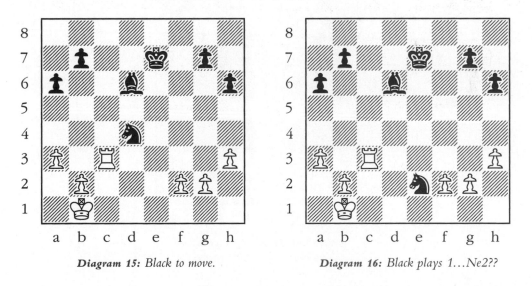

*Diagram 15: Black to move.*

*Diagram 16: Black plays 1...Ne2??*

This is a horrible blunder! Notice how Black has put the knight onto the same file as the king. White snatches the opportunity to fork the two pieces by playing 2.Re3+. Black must get out of check and then White captures the knight (see Diagram 17) in the next move, leaving Black with a lost position.

Diagrams 18 and 19 give another example of a rook fork. Here Black even has a material advantage, but it will not last. White plays 1.Rd7! and attacks both the knight on e7 and the bishop on b7. One or the other must go: the fork gives White a winning material advantage.

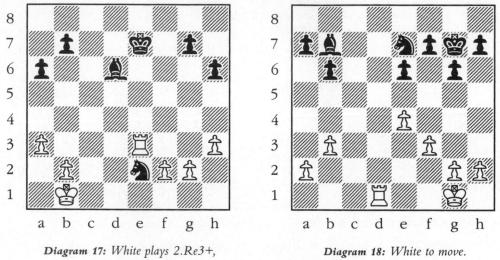

**Diagram 17:** White plays 2.Re3+, forking king and knight.

**Diagram 18:** White to move.

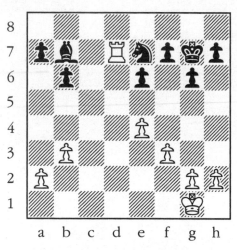

**Diagram 19:** White plays 1.Rd7, forking knight and bishop.

# Queen Forks

You can never be too careful with the queen. When thinking about your opponent's queen, always check twice to make sure that there is not a fork hiding somewhere. And when thinking about your own queen, look to see whether an opportunity for a queen fork might be present. Because the queen combines the power of the rook and the bishop, it can attack two or more pieces from almost any square on the board.

Diagrams 20 through 22 show one example of how the queen's ability to combine the rook's move and the bishop's move makes it such a dangerous piece. Black decides to play 1...Ng5??, but this is a grave error. White spots the flaw and plays 2.Qd8+! forking the king and the knight. Black must defend against the check, for example by playing 2...Kh7 and then White wins a knight for free by 3.Qxg5.

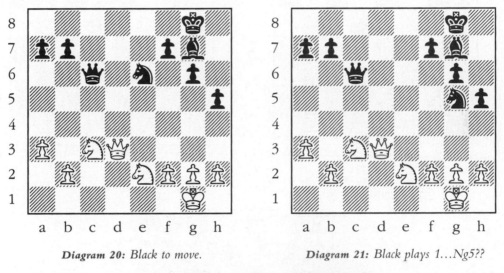

*Diagram 20: Black to move.*

*Diagram 21: Black plays 1...Ng5??*

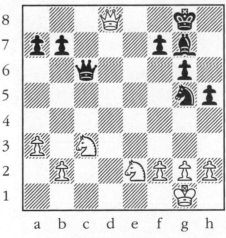

*Diagram 22: White plays 2.Qd8+,*
*forking king and knight.*

Diagrams 23 through 25 show another example. In Diagram 23, Black wants to move the bishop. A good move would be 1...Be6, which puts the bishop on the sensitive diagonal in front of the king on g8. But Black plays 1...Bb7?? (see Diagram 24), a terrible mistake. White pounces on the error by playing 2.Qb3+! (see Diagram 25), forking the bishop and the king. Black must defend against the check, which will leave the bishop defenseless to the queen. (Notice that blocking the check with the bishop by playing 2...Bd5 fails to save the bishop because White can safely capture the bishop on that square with the pawn, knight, or queen.)

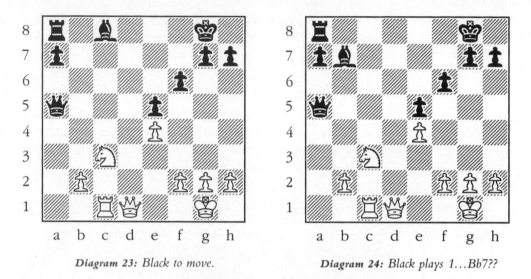

Diagram 23: *Black to move.*          Diagram 24: *Black plays 1...Bb7??*

Diagram 25: *White plays 2.Qb3+,*
*forking king and bishop.*

Have you noticed in the last two examples how an attack against the king was part of the fork? The king does not like to be exposed along a rank, file, or diagonal! Among the many dangers of being so exposed is that there might be a fork lurking. And since the king must be protected at all costs, the other piece being attacked is often helpless. So if you notice that your opponent's king is exposed along an open rank, file, or diagonal, look for a way to take advantage of it. And if your own king is so exposed, try to get it out of harm's way.

## King Forks

Because the king is so vulnerable, it's unusual for the king to be used aggressively before many pieces have been exchanged, so it is not common for the king to fork pieces or pawns. But it can happen just the same!

Consider Diagram 26. Black notices that his rook is attacked by the knight on g4, so he should move the rook away from the attack. Where should it go?

A good move would be 1...Re7, but Black tries to be too aggressive. Black spots a check and wants to play aggressively, so why not do it? Black plays 1...Rg3+? (see Diagram 27), but after 2.Kf2! Black's rook and knight are forked by White's king (see Diagram 28). The best Black can do is to play 2...Rxg4, but after 3.Rxg4, Black has lost the exchange (rook for knight).

*Diagram 26: Black to move.*

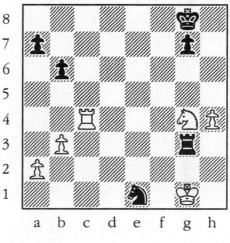

*Diagram 27: Black plays 1...Rg3+?*

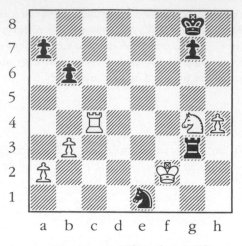

*Diagram 28: White plays 2.Kf2,*
*forking Black's rook and knight.*

King forks typically occur when there are very few pieces left and it's safer for the king to be used aggressively. In Diagram 29, there are very few pieces left, and Black's king has managed to make it all the way behind White's pawns. Now Black reaps the benefits by playing 1...Kb2! (in Diagram 30), which attacks three pawns at the same time. Now that's a fork fit for a king! (See Chapter 14 for more about how the king can be used aggressively when there are only a few pieces left on the board.)

By the way, there's a saying in chess: "Patzer sees a check; patzer gives a check." (A *patzer* is a weak player.) It's good to play aggressively, but don't play a check just because you can: think about it like any other move.

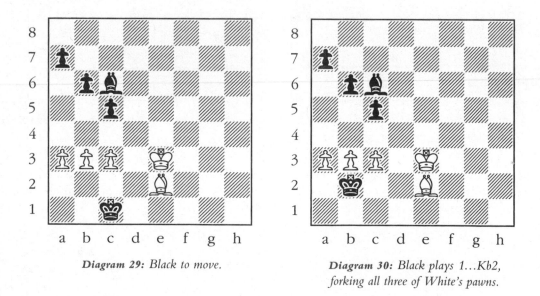

*Diagram 29: Black to move.*

*Diagram 30: Black plays 1...Kb2,*
*forking all three of White's pawns.*

Before we move on to other tactics, keep in mind that the fork is not an automatic winner. Sometimes one piece can move out of the attack and defend the other piece at the same time, for example. The fork is just a pattern, like all the other tactics we review. Sometimes it works, and sometimes it doesn't. Knowing the pattern directs your attention to analyze the move, but you still have to figure it out. (Hey, you didn't think this game was going to be easy, did you?)

# The Pin

When you attack a piece, and that piece cannot move without exposing another piece behind it to capture, you are pinning the first piece to the piece behind it. Only long-range pieces—the bishop, the rook, and the queen—can pin one piece to another. The ability to pin one piece to another is part of what makes those long-range pieces so dangerous!

I'll show you some common ways for bishops, rooks, and queens to pin pieces. But keep this in mind: there's a difference between pinning a piece to any ordinary piece and pinning a piece to the king. When a piece is pinned to the king, the pinned piece can never move off the line of attack (because that would be exposing the king to check). Therefore, pinning a piece to the king is especially effective. In contrast, if a piece is pinned to an ordinary piece, you should always remember that it's legal (though often undesirable) to move it even though it's pinned.

What should you do if your opponent is pinning one of your pieces and you want to remove the pin? There are four ways to break a pin:

+ Capture the piece that is doing the pinning.

+ Attack the piece that is doing the pinning, and force it to move away.

+ Block the pin: either put something between the pinning piece and the piece that is pinned, or put something between the pinned piece and the piece it's pinned to.

+ Get out of the way. If all else fails, you can move the piece behind the pinned piece out of the line of fire.

## Bishop Pins

The position in Diagram 31 is the same position as Exercise 20 in Chapter 5. The bishop on f5 pins the rook on g6 to the king. Black cannot move the rook from attack because that would expose the king to check. So White will win the rook for the bishop.

When a piece is pinned to your opponent's king, sometimes it's better to bring another piece over to reinforce the attack before capturing it. That way, you can win the pinned piece without allowing your opponent to recapture the piece that captured it. Alternatively, you can capture the pinned piece with a piece of lower value than the one you are pinning it with.

The next few diagrams illustrate what I mean. It's Black's move in Diagram 32. Black can only hope that White would be so foolish as to capture the rook right away with the bishop—then Black would recapture the bishop, and material would be equal. But Black realizes the real danger is that White might play 1.Ne5!, attacking the rook again so that White can win it for nothing. It's Black's move, and he plays 1...Nd5 (Diagram 33). Black's idea is that if White plays 2.Ne5, Black can play 2...Ne7, defending the rook and even attacking the bishop, gaining time to remove the king from the pin while still protecting the rook by playing 3...h5 and 4...Kh6.

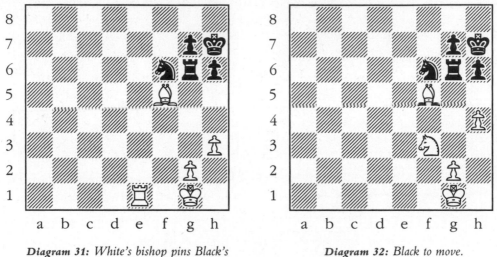

**Diagram 31:** *White's bishop pins Black's rook to the king.*

**Diagram 32:** *Black to move.*

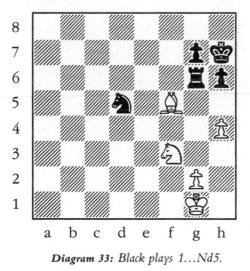

**Diagram 33:** *Black plays 1...Nd5.*

It's a good plan, but it fails because White plays 2.h5! in Diagram 34, attacking the rook with a pawn. There is nothing for Black to do. If Black plays 2...Ne7 (see Diagram 35), then White plays 3.hxg6+, and if Black is so foolish as to recapture the pawn with 3...Nxg6? (see Diagram 36), then White will play 4.Ne5, winning the knight as well. What a pin!

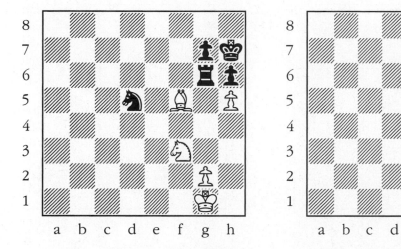

*Diagram 34: White plays 2.h5!, attacking the pinned rook with the pawn.*

*Diagram 35: Position after 2...Ne7 3.hxg6+.*

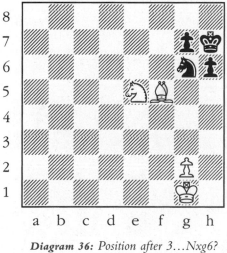

*Diagram 36: Position after 3...Nxg6? 4.Ne5.*

Diagrams 37 and 38 show something else to watch out for. Suppose you pin your opponent's rook to the queen with your bishop. Make sure that the rook can't move away and give check at the same time, especially if your bishop isn't protected! This is really a version of "two attacks at once," which I will explain to you later in the chapter.

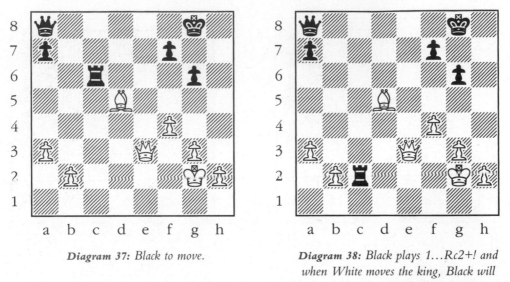

*Diagram 37: Black to move.*

*Diagram 38: Black plays 1...Rc2+! and when White moves the king, Black will play 2...Qxd5.*

Finally, here are some typical pins: bishop pinning knight to king (see Diagram 39) or queen (see Diagram 40). Notice that there is no reason for the side with the pinned knight to panic yet. Although there is a pin, there is no threat to win the pinned piece. Even so, the bishop is often well used in such a pin; not only is the bishop being used actively, it's also reducing the effectiveness of the knight.

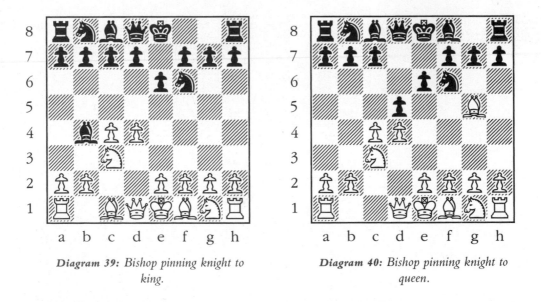

*Diagram 39: Bishop pinning knight to king.*

*Diagram 40: Bishop pinning knight to queen.*

# Rook Pins

Diagrams 41 through 43 show some examples of rook pins. Notice in Diagram 43 that if the rook is going to pin the queen, it had better be protected! (The same holds true for a bishop pinning the queen, of course.)

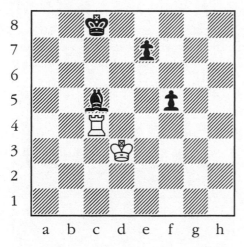

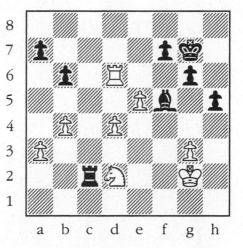

*Diagram 41: White's rook pins Black's bishop to the king.*

*Diagram 42: Black's rook pins White's knight to the king.*

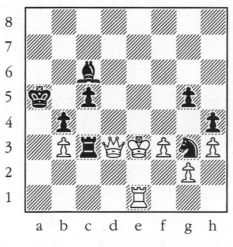

*Diagram 43: Black's rook pins White's queen to the king.*

One of the most common uses of the rook pin is to pin a piece to the uncastled king along the open e-file, if one side has castled early and the other side has not. Diagrams 44 and 45 show what I mean. In Diagram 44, because White has castled and Black has not, Black's knight and king are precariously placed on the same file. In Diagram 45, Black pays the price. White attacks the knight, which cannot move because it is pinned. Even if Black defends the knight, it can't be saved because in the next move White will attack the knight with a pawn, and the knight will have to stand his post while he is slaughtered by the pawn.

Don't let this happen to you! I can't stress strongly enough how important it is to castle early. Castling gets your king to safety and makes it much easier to use the rooks effectively. As you get better at chess, you will gradually learn all the exceptions to this rule. But for now, follow the rule and make sure you castle before it's too late!

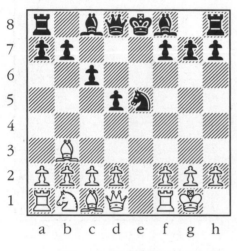

*Diagram 44: White to move.*

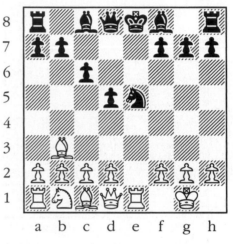

*Diagram 45: White plays 1.Re1! and pins the knight to the king.*

# Queen Pins

The queen moves like the rook and the bishop, so it can pin like the rook and the bishop: along ranks, files, and diagonals. Diagrams 46 shows an example.

Keep in mind that because the queen is so powerful, if your opponent is able to protect the piece that is pinned, you won't want to capture it with the queen. But that doesn't stop you from attacking the piece with something else, perhaps even a lowly pawn. The queen holds the piece down, and the other piece or pawn goes in for the kill. Diagram 47 shows an example of this.

I have been concentrating on showing you how to use pins to win material. But keep this in mind: pins are also effective ways to immobilize your opponent's pieces. Even if there's no immediate way to win the piece being pinned, just by pinning it you have severely limited its ability to move.

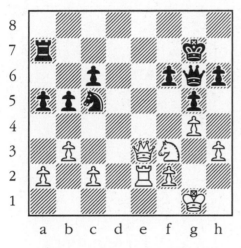

*Diagram 46: White pins the knight to the rook, and Black must lose a piece.*

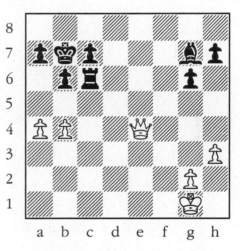

*Diagram 47: White pins the rook to the king and threatens to play 1.b5.*

# The Skewer

The skewer is a variation on the pin. In a skewer, you attack a piece, force it to move, and then win the piece behind it. Usually the piece you force to move away is more valuable than the piece behind it.

Diagrams 48 through 51 show some examples of skewers. Keep in mind that king skewers (skewers where you give check because you want to capture the piece behind the king when it moves) are the most dangerous skewers of all.

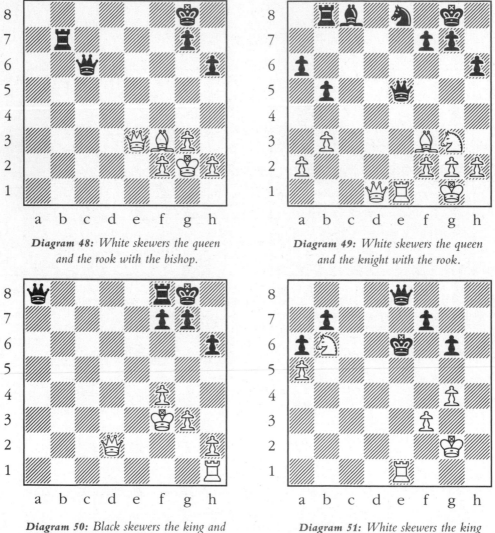

Diagram 48: *White skewers the queen and the rook with the bishop.*

Diagram 49: *White skewers the queen and the knight with the rook.*

Diagram 50: *Black skewers the king and the rook with the queen.*

Diagram 51: *White skewers the king and the queen with the rook.*

# Two Attacks at Once

When you give two attacks at once, one move creates two attacks by two different pieces at the same time. Notice how this is different than the fork, where one piece attacks two pieces at the same time.

Does that sound impossible? The idea is simple, really. One piece moves and attacks something, and after it is out of the way, another piece behind it is "discovered" attacking something else. (This is why the "two attacks at once" tactic is sometimes called a *discovered attack*.) Let's take a look at two examples of this.

In Diagram 52, Black notices that the bishop would attack the queen if the knight were not in the way on c6. This gives Black an idea. Is there some useful square where the knight can move to and, therefore, use the fact that the bishop will be attacking the queen?

In Diagram 53, we see the answer. Black plays 1...Nb4!, an extremely strong move. Because the bishop on b7 now attacks the queen, White must meet this threat. But the knight on b4 also attacks the rook. White cannot meet both threats at the same time and so must lose material.

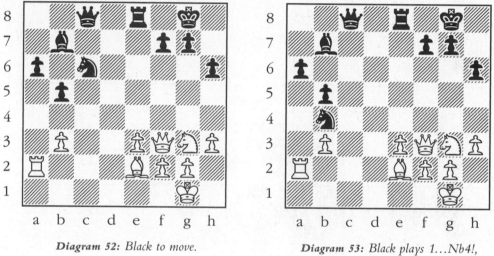

*Diagram 52: Black to move.*

*Diagram 53: Black plays 1...Nb4!, attacking the rook with the knight and the queen with the bishop.*

When I was a kid, someone gave me a great piece of advice: "When you see a good move, don't play it right away; sit on your hands and make sure there isn't an even better move." Our second example shows this piece of advice in action. The discovered attack is such a strong tactic that there may be more than one good move, so you want to look for the strongest possible discovered attack.

Take a look at Diagram 54. One possible discovered attack is to capture the pawn on a6. The bishop can't be captured (see Diagram 55) because of the threat to the queen. But this only wins a pawn. Is there a stronger move? Yes, there is! White can play 1.Bg4! (see Diagram 56) which attacks the rook on c8. Black must move the queen, and White will win the rook for the bishop.

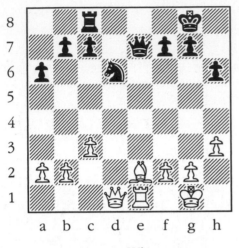

Diagram 54: *White to move.*

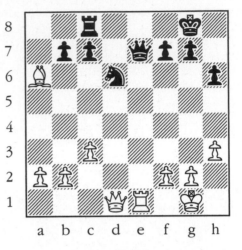

Diagram 55: *White plays 1.Bxa6 and wins a pawn, but White had a stronger move.*

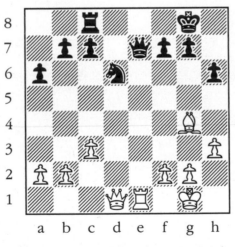

Diagram 56: *White plays 1.Bg4! and wins the rook for the bishop.*

# Discovered Check

The most potent way to give two attacks at once is the discovered check. When you give discovered check, you move one piece, and thereby uncover a check by another piece to the king. (The king suddenly "discovers" that it is in check!) I cannot emphasize strongly enough how powerful this tactic is. Every grandmaster has deep respect for the discovered check—so much respect that if there is a discovered check it is usually the first move the grandmaster considers.

Diagrams 57 through 60 show how powerful discovered check can be. Diagrams 58 and 60 show a discovered check that wins the queen, because there is no way to remove the king from check and prevent the queen from being captured. (In particular, notice in Diagram 60 that 1...Qc7 can be answered by 2.Nxc7.)

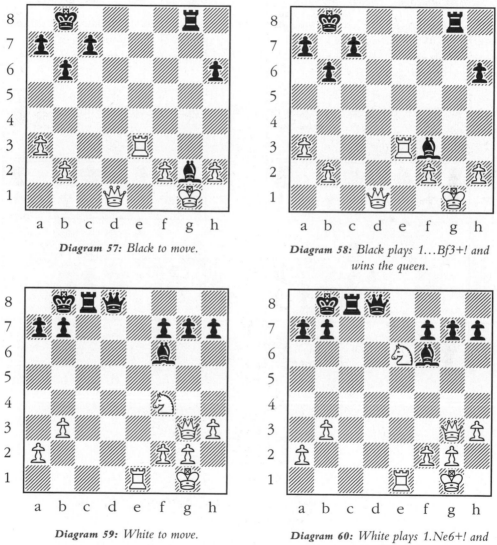

Diagram 57: Black to move.

Diagram 58: Black plays 1...Bf3+! and wins the queen.

Diagram 59: White to move.

Diagram 60: White plays 1.Ne6+! and wins the queen.

# Double Check

A double check is an interesting twist on discovered check. The double check is a discovered check in which the piece moving away decides to attack the king! The king finds itself being checked by two pieces at once, and so there is no other way to meet the check than to move.

Basically, the double check is not a tactic to win material, but a tactic to attack the king. Still, because it's a variant of the discovered check, I thought I would introduce you to it now—especially since it gives me a chance to end the chapter by showing you a beautiful combination of moves that forces checkmate using double check!

Diagrams 61 through 66 show an example of double check leading to checkmate. At the moment, in Diagram 61, Black has an extra knight. Probably he expected White to just win back the piece by using the pin on the e-file and playing 1.Re1. Instead, White plays a move that begins a forced sequence leading to checkmate!

In Diagram 62, White plays 1.Qd8+!!, catching Black off guard. What is White up to? Well, it doesn't matter—there is only one legal move anyway—so Black captures the queen with 1...Kxd8 (see Diagram 63).

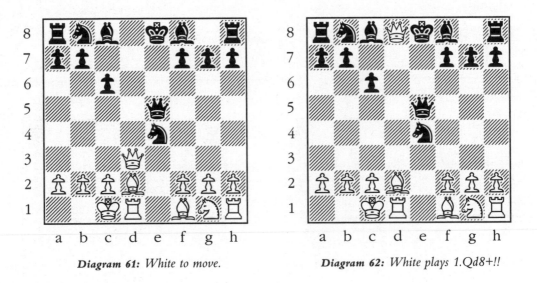

*Diagram 61: White to move.*          *Diagram 62: White plays 1.Qd8+!!*

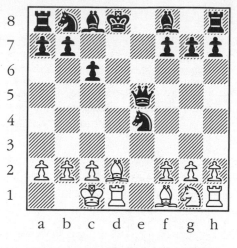

*Diagram 63: Black plays 1...Kxd8.*

But now White's clever plan is revealed with 2.Bg5+!! (see Diagram 64), putting Black in double check. Because Black is in check from two pieces at once, the king must move. The king has only two moves, to c7 or to e8. But no matter which way the king goes, White will give checkmate.

I urge you to figure out for yourself how White would give checkmate if Black moved the king to c7. (Here's a hint: White gives checkmate with her bishop.) Black decides to play 2...Ke8 (see Diagram 65).

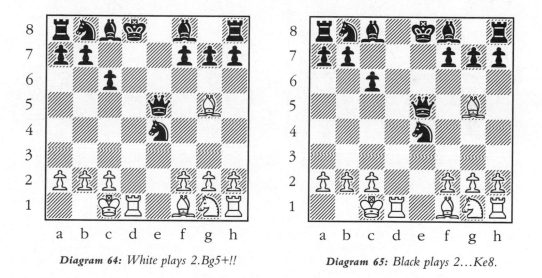

*Diagram 64: White plays 2.Bg5+!!*   *Diagram 65: Black plays 2...Ke8.*

Now White has only one check, but it's the check that ends the game: 3.Rd8# (see Diagram 66). What a finish!

*Diagram 66:* White plays 3.Rd8#.

# Exercises: Forks, Pins, and Skewers

Practice recognizing these tactics by working through the following exercises. Forks, pins, skewers, and two attacks at once are effective tactics for winning material.

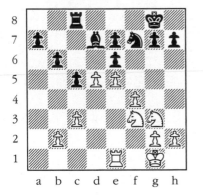

*Exercise 1:* White to move. How can White win a pawn by threatening a pawn fork between Black's knight and bishop?

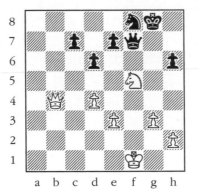

*Exercise 2:* White to move. Should Black be worried about 1.Nxh6+, or should White be worried because the knight is being attacked?

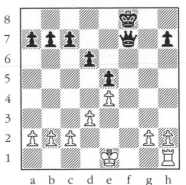

*Exercise 3:* White to move. What is White's best move?

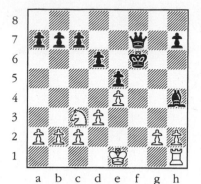

*Exercise 4:* White to move. Can White win Black's queen? What is White's best move?

*Exercise 5:* Black to move. Who should win this position?

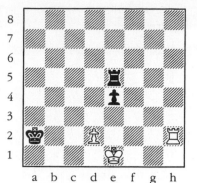

*Exercise 6:* White to move. What is White's best move?

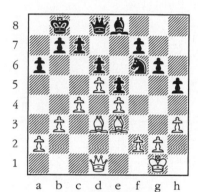

*Exercise 7:* White to move. White plays 1.Bg5 in this position. What is White's threat? Can Black defend?

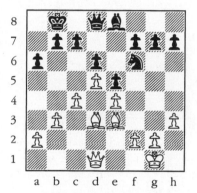

*Exercise 8:* White to move. White plays 1.Bg5 in this position. Does Black have the same problem as in Exercise 7?

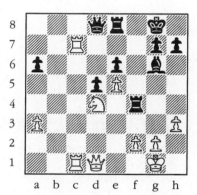

*Exercise 9:* White to move (Wolff–Sagalchik, North Bay, 1996). I played 28.Nxe6, forking the queen and the rook on f4. What was my idea if Black played 28…Rxe6?

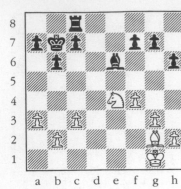

*Exercise 10: White to move. What is White's best move?*

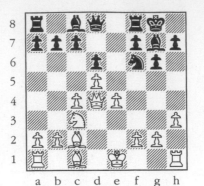

*Exercise 11: Black to move. What is Black's best move? (Hint: the solution involves combining two different tactics.)*

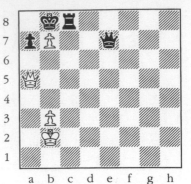

*Exercise 12: White to move. This is a tough one! White thinks about playing 1.bxc8=Q+ Kxc8, giving both sides equal material and the position should be a draw. But White also sees the possibility to do better. How?*

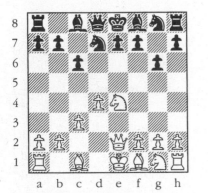

*Exercise 13: White's last move was 1.Qe2. What is the threat? Should Black play 1...Ngf6 or not?*

*Exercise 14: Black played an amazing move in this position, 1...Qg1+. What on Earth was the idea after White captures the queen with the king?*

*Exercise 15: White to move (Volchok–Kreslavsky, USSR, 1970). It looks like Black will win back the bishop because of the pin against the rook. But White found a terrific way to turn the tables and win.*

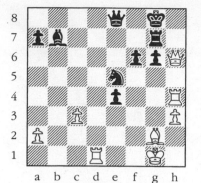

**Exercise 16:** *White to move (Szabo–Bronstein, Zurich, 1953). Material is roughly even in this complicated position, but White found a way to cut through the complications and get a winning material advantage. How? (Hint: 1.Qh8+ is not the right first move, but it is the right idea.)*

**Exercise 17:** *White to move. White wins by finding the right way to give discovered check with the rook.*

**Exercise 18:** *White to move (Sznapik–Bernard, Poznan, 1971). White could capture Black's f-pawns, but then Black defends with 1...Ra7. Instead, White found a beautiful way to win. How?*

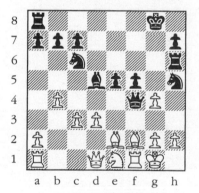

**Exercise 19:** *Black to move (Kosalopov–Nezhmetdinov, Kazan, 1936). Black found an incredible way to win with 1...Qxh2+!! 2.Kxh2. What should Black play now?*

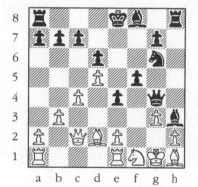

**Exercise 20:** *White to move (Yermolinsky–Abroskin, Leningrad, 1972). How did White win Black's queen?*

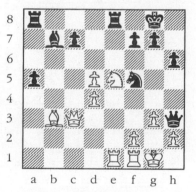

**Exercise 21:** *Black to move (Morozevich–Adams, Holland, 2001). How did Black force White to resign in one move?*

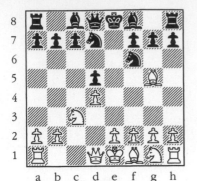

**Exercise 22:** *White to move. Can White safely capture the pawn on d5 with the knight? Why or why not?*

**Exercise 23:** *Black to move. Does the forking pawn move 1...e5 win a piece? This is tricky! (Hint: the fork is not the only tactical trick at play here.)*

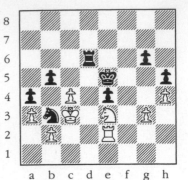

**Exercise 24:** *Black to move. Why does 1...Rd3+! win material no matter which way the king runs? (Hint: the winning fork is straightforward after 2.Kc2, but after 2.Kb4, Black has to figure out how to set up a winning fork. Try starting with the same move that wins after 1.Kc2.)*

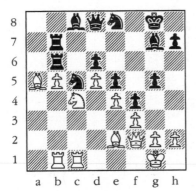

**Exercise 25:** *White to move. How can White use the pin of the rook on b6 to maximum advantage? Here's a hint: don't give Black time to fortify the defense of the knight on c5.*

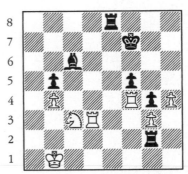

**Exercise 26:** *Black to move. Black plays the very strong move 1...Re1+. Can you work out how Black uses pins to gain a decisive material advantage?*

# Chapter 7

# Dirtier Tricks

In Chapter 6, you learned the most basic tactics you can use to win material. Now I will show you some tactics that are more sophisticated. You will probably see the tactics in Chapter 6 more often than the ones in this chapter, but the ones here are pretty common, too. You'll have plenty of chances to use them against your opponents!

# Getting an Enemy Piece out of the Way

Many times, if you could only force your opponent to move one of his pieces to another square, you could take advantage of some weakness in his position. Forcing your opponent to move a piece to a different square is called *deflecting* that piece. Deflection comes in many different forms, but it falls roughly into two categories.

## Attacking the Defender

In Diagram 1, does White have any way to win material? Well, the only piece that is attacking any of Black's pieces is the knight on e5, which attacks Black's bishop on d7 and his pawn on f7. But if White captures either one, Black can recapture the knight. Taking the pawn on f7 by playing 1.Nxf7?? would be a bad idea because after 1…Kxf7, Black wins material, capturing a knight and only losing a pawn. Taking the bishop on d7 by playing 1.Nxd7+ is not so bad, but after 1…Nxd7, White has only exchanged a knight for a bishop, which is basically an even trade.

Okay, so there is nothing for White to capture right away that will give her a material advantage. But is there any way for White to deflect one of the black pieces crucial for the defense? Suppose Black's knight could be driven away from the f6 square, so it wouldn't defend the bishop any more. Then White could capture the bishop for free! Do you see how to do it?

White plays 1.g5 in Diagram 2, attacking Black's knight with a pawn. Black is really in trouble now. Since Black's knight is attacked by a measly pawn, there is no way to defend it. In vain, Black looks for some way to attack White, but there is nothing to do. Black is caught between a rock and a hard place: either White captures a whole knight for only a pawn, or—even worse—Black moves the knight, so the bishop is no longer defended, allowing White to win a whole bishop for free!

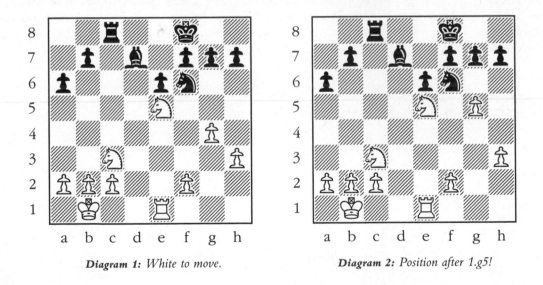

*Diagram 1: White to move.*          *Diagram 2: Position after 1.g5!*

Let's look at another example in Diagram 3. It's Black's turn to move. Is there any way for Black to use deflection to his advantage? Well, what does Black attack? Black attacks the pawn on h3 with the bishop, but that doesn't look very promising because that pawn is defended by the pawn on g2, and how would you deflect that pawn? But Black attacks something else that looks much more promising: the bishop on e2. Black's queen attacks it, and it is only defended by White's queen. If there were only some way to drive the queen away, Black could take the bishop.

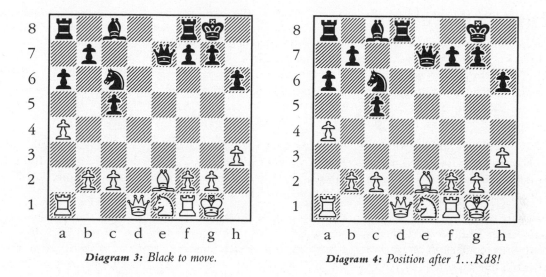

Diagram 3: Black to move.     Diagram 4: Position after 1...Rd8!

Sure enough, Black can play 1...Rd8! (see Diagram 4) to attack White's queen. What can White do? She can't take the rook because it's defended by Black's queen. Is there any square to which White can move the queen where it still defends the bishop? No, the queen can only move to c1 or b1, and neither of those lets it defend the bishop. The only chance is to block the attack, so White plays 2.Bd3 in Diagram 5. (White could also block the attack by playing 2.Nd3, but this move would lose material in the same way that 2.Bd3 does.)

White has defended the queen from attack and moved the bishop off the sensitive e2 square. It looks like White is safe. But Black has seen farther! The right move uses one of the ideas from last chapter to win material. Do you see how?

Black plays 2…c4! in Diagram 6, to attack the bishop. Black realizes that White's bishop is pinned to the queen, so White must either lose the bishop or let the queen be captured. (Notice that if White had played 2.Nd3, then 2…c4 would have won the knight because of the pin in a similar way.)

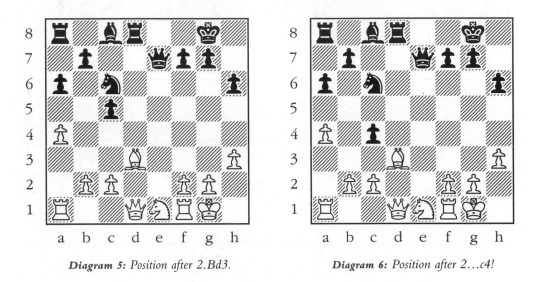

Diagram 5: Position after 2.Bd3.          Diagram 6: Position after 2…c4!

Do you see how Black combined two different tactical ideas in this last example? Black started with deflection and then followed up with a pin. It's often a good idea to look for ways to combine tactics!

# Overloading the Defender

Everyone knows how hard it can be to do two things at once. Well, the same is true for chess pieces. When one piece must defend two things at the same time, sometimes the piece is unable to do both.

In Diagram 7, Black has two possible captures: 1...Rxc2 and 1...Qxe3+. White defends both pieces with the queen, which means the queen is doing double duty. Black takes advantage of this by playing 1...Rxc2! in Diagram 8.

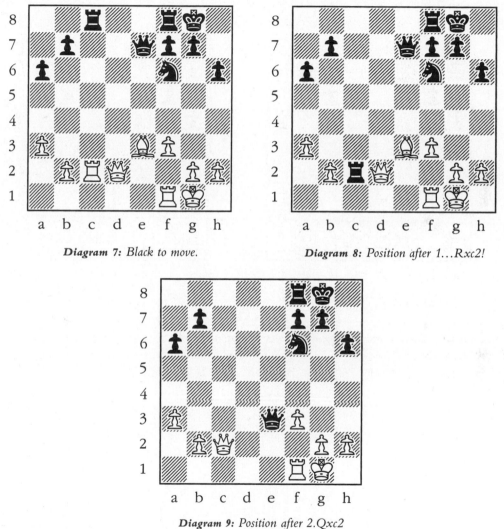

Diagram 7: Black to move.

Diagram 8: Position after 1...Rxc2!

Diagram 9: Position after 2.Qxc2
Qxe3+.

When White recaptures with 2.Qxc2, the queen leaves the defense of the bishop, and Black wins a whole piece for nothing with 2...Qxe3+ (see Diagram 9).

Sometimes when a defender in your opponent's army is overloaded, it's worth using a stronger piece to take a piece of lesser value, even though your piece will be recaptured. This can work to your advantage because the defender is deflected from the defense of another piece that you can capture, and the two pieces together are worth more than the one piece you lost. Diagrams 10-12 show an example of this.

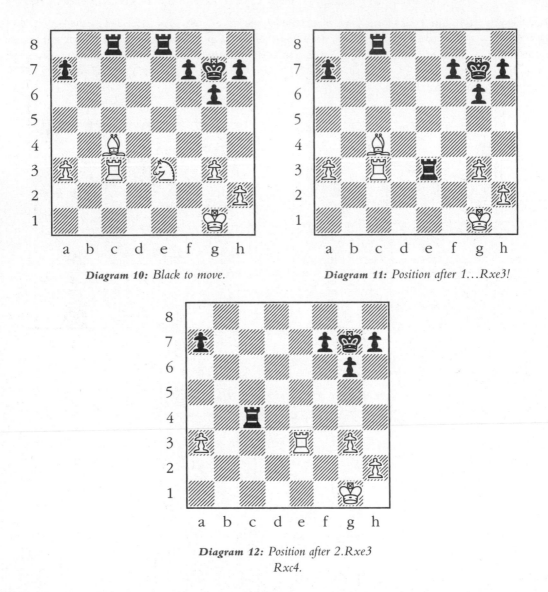

Diagram 10: Black to move.

Diagram 11: Position after 1...Rxe3!

Diagram 12: Position after 2.Rxe3 Rxc4.

In Diagram 10, White counts the material, and assumes things stand about equal: a knight and a bishop add up to six points (maybe even a little more) and are at least as good as a rook and a pawn. White sees that Black's rooks are attacking the knight and bishop, but it seems that everything is defended well enough by the rook—the knight is even defending the bishop to boot! What could go wrong?

Black plays 1...Rxe3! in Diagram 11, and suddenly the roof caves in. White has no choice but to recapture the rook with 2.Rxe3, after which Black plays 2...Rxc4 (see Diagram 12). Black has won two pieces for a rook and now has an extra pawn, as well as all the chances to win.

Keep in mind that a defensive piece can be overloaded in ways other than just having to defend another piece from capture. For example, sometimes it might have to defend against check or checkmate.

In Diagram 13, White attacks only one piece: the knight on e7, which is defended by the bishop on f8. But White is alerted to the possibility of decoying the bishop away from defending the knight because Black's king is exposed to check along the diagonal, and the only defense to the check is to block it with that same bishop on f8. White plays 1.Bf6+! (see Diagram 14), and after 1...Bg7 plays 2.Bxe7 (see Diagram 15), winning the knight for nothing.

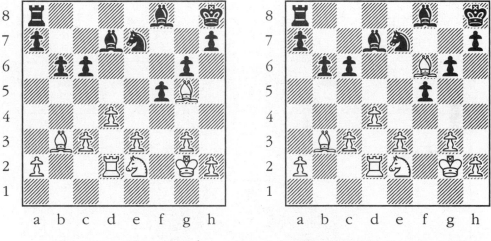

Diagram 13: White to move.          Diagram 14: Position after 1.Bf6+!

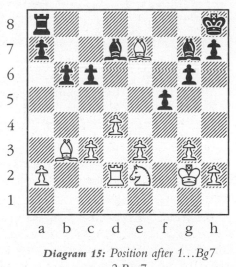

Diagram 15: Position after 1...Bg7
2.Bxe7.

# When You Are Your Own Worst Enemy

Sometimes one of your pieces is on a square which another one of your pieces would just love to reach. When that happens, you should look for the most advantageous way possible to get the piece out of the way. Sometimes the best way to get the piece out of the way is to sacrifice it. When you sacrifice a piece to get it out of the way, it's called a *clearance sacrifice*.

Let's see how this works by taking two examples from former World Chess champions. The first example is a position from the game Tal–Parma, played in Bled, 1961 (see Diagram 16). Bruno Parma was a very strong grandmaster in his day, but he was no match for the Latvian genius Mikhail Tal, known as "the Wizard from Riga" because of his brilliant and inventive play. Tal sees that he has a rook for a bishop and a pawn, giving him a material advantage. But he also sees that if his knight were on e6 instead of his queen, he would be forking Parma's Black king and queen. What's the best way to get the queen out of the way? For a genius like Tal, it couldn't have taken more than a millisecond to find 29.Qxf5! (see Diagram 17).

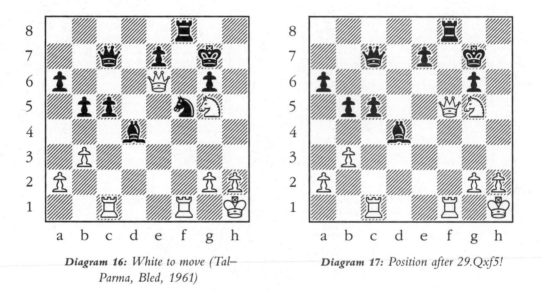

*Diagram 16: White to move (Tal–Parma, Bled, 1961)*

*Diagram 17: Position after 29.Qxf5!*

Tal captures the knight with his queen, because even though Black can recapture the queen, White will then follow up with 30.Ne6+ and win Black's queen in return, pocketing the knight as profit. Parma resigned, yet another victim to Tal's magic.

Just a year before Tal played that game, he had taken the World Championship title from Mikhail Botvinnik, a man 25 years his senior. Yet Botvinnik would retake the title from Tal later in 1961. Let's look at a game Botvinnik played before he reached his full strength. Even though he was not yet world champion, he was good enough to teach us a thing or two!

Botvinnik played White against Georgiy Stepanov in this game in 1931 (see Diagram 18). Perhaps Stepanov hadn't suspected anything yet, but we can assume that Botvinnik already noticed that his opponent's queen was in a precarious position. How did Botvinnik take advantage of this circumstance? Are any of his own pieces in the way?

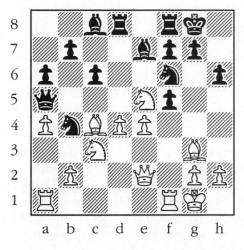

Diagram 18: White to move (Botvinnik–
Stepanov, Leningrad, 1930)

Diagram 19: Position after 19.Bxf7+!!

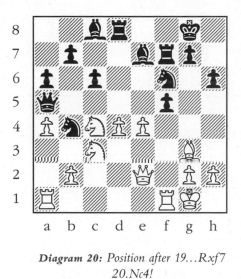

Diagram 20: Position after 19…Rxf7
20.Nc4!

Botvinnik played 19.Bxf7+!!, which at first blush seems crazy. What could the idea of this move possibly be? After all, Black has the square f7 securely defended, so it looks like White is simply trading a bishop and knight for a rook and pawn. But the real point was revealed after Black recaptured the bishop, 19…Rxf7. (Because Stepanov was in check, he had no better move than to take the bishop.)

It turns out that f7 was not White's real target at all. Now Botvinnik played 20.Nc4!, attacking the black queen. What Botvinnik noticed and his opponent missed is that the queen has no safe square to run to. If you can't believe it, try to find a safe square for the queen. But don't forget that because the knight has moved from e5, the bishop on g3 controls the c7 square! The young Botvinnik exploited his material advantage and eventually won the game.

# Wishing Can Help You Make It So

It often takes a flash of inspiration to find a clearance sacrifice because it's hard to see the possibility of putting one of your pieces on a square that another one of your pieces already occupies. You can help that flash of inspiration to come by asking yourself this question: "What move do I wish I could play?"

Sometimes you may find that the only thing preventing you from making your wish come true is one of your own pieces. And if that's the case, maybe you can do something about it.

Look at Diagram 21 and suppose you are Black in this position. Things look pretty dismal. White has an extra pawn, and Black doesn't have any obvious threats. Maybe you even start daydreaming. "I was so stupid to lose that pawn. Not only am I behind in material, but also my pieces don't look that great. My knight is the only piece beyond the first rank, and the only one doing any good for me! Well, maybe my queen is doing a little good because it's attacking the rook on c6. Come to think of it, White's rook and queen are lined up in a typical knight fork position. If only I could play 1…Nb4. I wish I could play 1…Nb4, but my pawn on b4 stops me."

Even though White has an extra pawn, Black has a killer move here, and daydreaming has taken Black halfway to finding it. If your pawn offends you, push it: 1…b3! is deadly (see Diagram 22). Actually, this move begins a sequence that combine three tactics: a fork, a clearance sacrifice, and a deflection. Because White's bishop and queen are forked, the pawn can't be ignored. Because Black's queen attacks White's rook on c6, 2.Qxb3 simply loses the rook to 2…Qxc6 (see Diagram 23). So White plays 2.Bxb3, but then Black forks the queen and rook with 2…Nb4 (see Diagram 24).

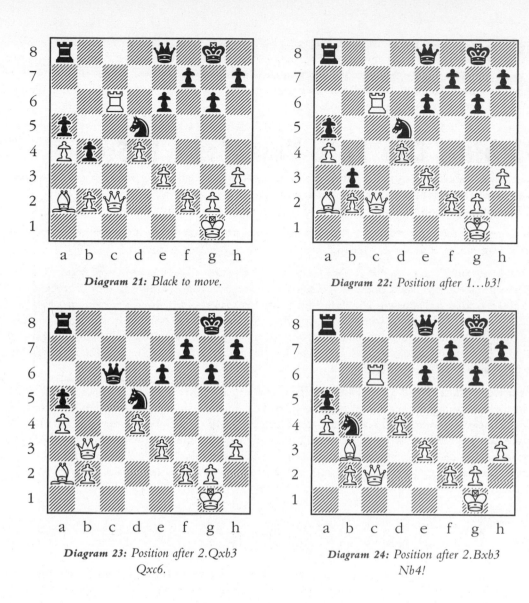

**Diagram 21:** *Black to move.*

**Diagram 22:** *Position after 1...b3!*

**Diagram 23:** *Position after 2.Qxb3 Qxc6.*

**Diagram 24:** *Position after 2.Bxb3 Nb4!*

# Superman's Not the Only One with X-Ray Vision!

I used to love reading comic books—okay, I still love reading them—and Superman was one of my favorite heroes. In fact, I first started reading comic books around the same time I first started learning how to play chess! Maybe that's why I have a special fondness for this next tactic, the x-ray. The name comes from the idea that sometimes a piece can "see through" an enemy piece.

Sometimes if an enemy piece captures one of your pieces, another of your pieces suddenly has its scope increased so that it can now capture the enemy piece on the same square. This is the idea of the x-ray tactic.

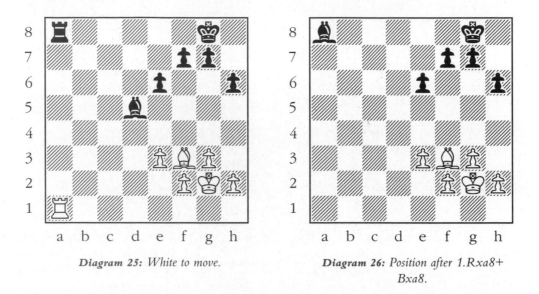

Diagram 25: White to move.     Diagram 26: Position after 1.Rxa8+ Bxa8.

Let me illustrate what I mean with a simple example in Diagram 25. It might look as though Black's bishop on d5 adequately protects the rook on a8, so if White plays 1.Rxa8+, Black can just recapture the rook with 1...Bxa8, and the result is an even trade. But look at the position after 1.Rxa8+ Bxa8 (see Diagram 26), and it becomes easier to see that White will play 2.Bxa8 and win a bishop for free! The white bishop on f3 can "see" the a8 square through the black bishop on d5 because if the black bishop ever captures anything on that square, the white bishop on f3 suddenly has a clear path to a8. That is the nature of the x-ray tactic.

The idea behind the x-ray is pretty simple, but being able to spot these tactics can be hard and takes practice. What makes it hard is that somehow it just doesn't seem natural that a piece that is "blocked off" from a square (like the white bishop was blocked off from the a8 square in Diagram 25) can have any control over it. The key to the x-ray is if the piece that is blocking another piece from controlling a square is used to capture something on that square, it suddenly no longer blocks access to that square.

Whew, that last sentence was a mouthful, wasn't it? Maybe I'd better just show you what I mean. The next position is taken from a game played by the most famous chess player of all time: Bobby Fischer. Fischer played this game in the 1963–64 US Championship, which was just one of the eight US Championships Fischer won! (Even more incredible is that he only played eight times!) Fischer's brilliant career culminated in his becoming world champion in 1972 by crushing the champion from the Soviet Union, Boris Spassky.

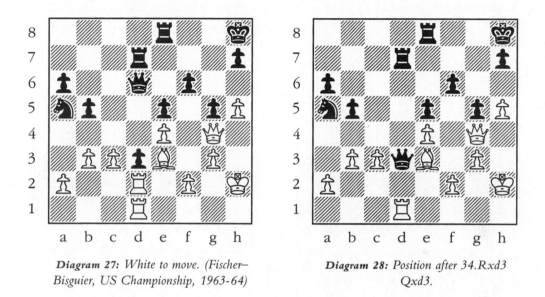

*Diagram 27: White to move. (Fischer–Bisguier, US Championship, 1963-64)*

*Diagram 28: Position after 34.Rxd3 Qxd3.*

In this game, Fischer is playing another American grandmaster Arthur Bisguier (see Diagram 27). Bisguier has calculated that the pawn on d3 is adequately protected. He figured that if White captures the pawn, he will maintain material equality as follows: 34.Rxd3 Qxd3 35.Rxd3 Rxd3. White will have traded two rooks for a queen and one pawn, which amounts to about an even trade.

Sure enough, Fischer took the pawn, and Bisguier recaptured the rook (see Diagram 28). Now Bisguier expects Fischer to capture the queen on the next move, after which Bisguier will recapture the rook. This is only an even trade for Fischer, but what else could Fischer have been thinking?

*Diagram 29: Position after 35.Qxd7!*

Fischer's idea was to use the x-ray tactic to his advantage! Instead of taking the queen on d3, he captures the rook on d7 (see Diagram 29). The method to his madness is that the queen is now protected by the rook on d1. If Black plays 35...Qxd7, White just plays 36.Rxd7. After the dust settles from all the captures, White emerges with an extra pawn.

# The "In-Between" Move

Huh? What's this? In between what?

No, this doesn't mean in between the squares, or in between the lines, or in between the king and the queen. *In between* refers to a move that comes in between two moves that you expect your opponent to have to play consecutively. (Sometimes this is called a *zwischenzug,* which is German for "in-between move.") Suppose you capture one of your opponent's pieces which is protected. You naturally expect your opponent to recapture. But you must always be careful not to overlook the possibility that your opponent may have a move that can be played "in between," perhaps a threat to another one of your pieces or a check. And that little in-between move may make a world of difference.

Take the position in Diagram 30, for example. Black has every reason to be happy. With a material advantage of a rook for a bishop, Black is looking to win. Black decides to exchange a pair of rooks, figuring that after 1...Rxh4?? White has nothing better than to recapture with 2.Qxh4. Black notices that White could also give check with 2.Qd8+ (see Diagram 31), but there doesn't seem to be any point to it because Black can just move the king with 2...Kh7.

But Black has failed to consider the power of this in-between move! Black just assumed that White would have nothing better than to recapture the rook. Had Black thought more carefully about the consequences of allowing the check, he might have realized that the queen on d8 is forking the king and the rook, so White is not giving up on recapturing the rook. And once Black moves the king to h7, White will capture the rook on h4 with check (see Diagram 31).

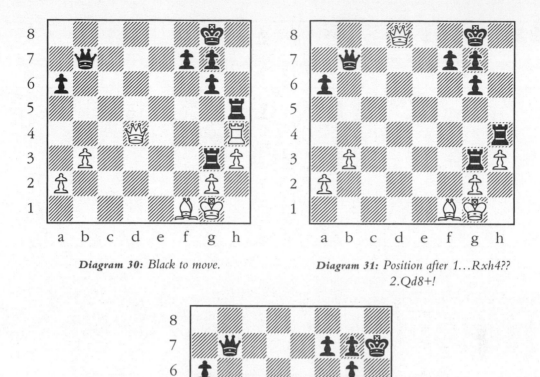

*Diagram 30: Black to move.*

*Diagram 31: Position after 1...Rxh4??*
*2.Qd8+!*

*Diagram 32: Position after 2...Kh7*
*3.Qxh4+.*

But it's not just check; it's another fork of the king and the rook! Black is obliged to move the king back to g8 and then White will capture the rook on g3, winning a rook for nothing and gaining a decisive material advantage. Carelessly thinking that White had nothing better than to recapture, Black went from a winning position to a losing position!

Powerful in-between moves are often checks. So at some point in your calculations, you should proceed extra carefully when you see that your opponent can give a check. And always take a thoughtful look at a check that you can give before playing some obvious move: it might just turn the whole game upside down!

# Exercises

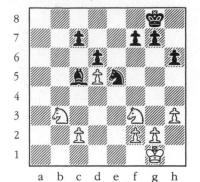

**Exercise 1:** *White to move. White wants to take advantage of the fact that the pawn on d6 defends two pieces at the same time. How can White win material?*

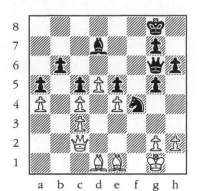

**Exercise 2:** *Black to move (Spassky–Fischer, World Championship match, 1972). Bobby Fischer knew how to take advantage of deflection in this game. Can you find the winning move?*

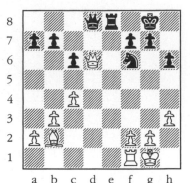

**Exercise 3:** *White to move. Would it be a good idea for White to play 1.Rd1 to protect the queen? If not, then why?*

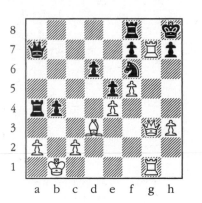

**Exercise 4:** *White to move. Would White prefer another piece on g7 besides the rook? How should White arrange for it to happen?*

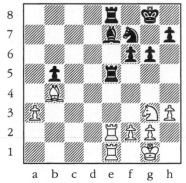

**Exercise 5:** *White to move. Does 1.Bxe7 win material by using the x-ray attack? Does it matter which rook Black selects to recapture the bishop?*

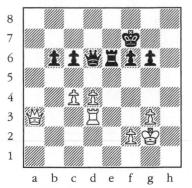

**Exercise 6:** *White to move. White can win a pawn with 1.Qa7+, but she has an even better move. The two keys here are deflection and the in-between move!*

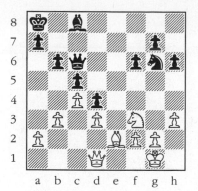

**Exercise 7:** *White to move. How can White win material?*

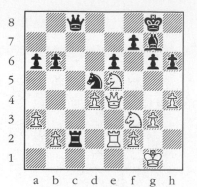

**Exercise 8:** *Black to move (Illescas–Wolff, Biel, 1993). Miguel Illescas is a tough grandmaster, but I was able to win a pawn by using a variation of deflection and a clearance sacrifice to set up a fork. Can you see what I played? (This is a tricky one!)*

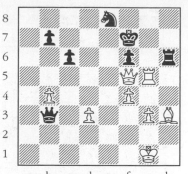

**Exercise 9:** *Black to move (Shirazi–Wolff, US Championship, 1992). I wanted to capture White's rook, but my pawn was pinned to my king. How did I manage to deflect the queen away so I could pocket some extra material?*

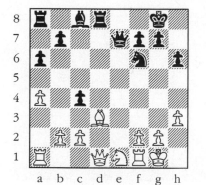

**Exercise 10:** *White to move. This position is identical to Diagram 3 of this chapter, except that the knight is on f6 instead of c6. That small difference allows White to save the bishop. How?*

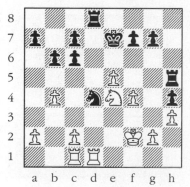

**Exercise 11:** *White to move (Kasparov–Kramnik, Holland, 2001). Kasparov rejected 1.g4 because he did not want to allow 1...hxg3+ 2.Nxg3 Rxh3. But he missed a crushing move at this point in his calculations. What is it? (Hint: White has the same move no matter which square Black moves the rook to along the h-file after 2.Nxg3.)*

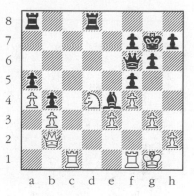

**Exercise 12:** *White to move and win.*

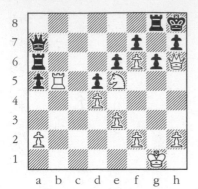

**Exercise 13:** White to move
(Gauzel–Ginting, Novi Sad,
1990). It looks like Black has
everything defended, but White
was able to overload and deflect
the defending pieces to win.
How?

**Exercise 14:** Black to move
(Ehlvest–Yermolinsky, Las
Vegas, 1994). White—Ehlvest,
a top grandmaster—has just
played 1.Qd5. Yermolinsky,
another top grandmaster,
captured the queen and lost the
game. What strong in-between
move did both grandmasters
miss?

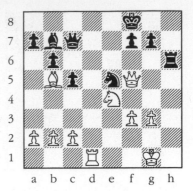

**Exercise 15:** White to move
(King–Benjamin, USA, 1962).
How did White win a piece by
exploiting the overloaded black
queen?

**Exercise 16:** White to move. If
1.Qg3 or 1.Qg4, then 1...Qh6
defends. Nor does 1.Qxc1 Rxc1
2.Rg7 Be8 make headway.
How can White force either
checkmate or a decisive win of
material?

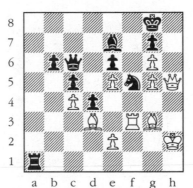

**Exercise 17:** Black to move. It
looks like White has a crushing
attack. But Black can not only
defend, but win! How? (Hint:
Black needs to nudge the white
king to the right square.)

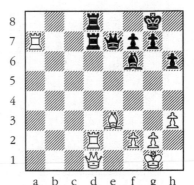

**Exercise 18:** Black to move.
Can Black win material by
capturing either rook? Why or
why not?

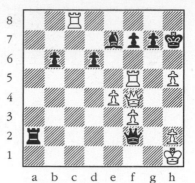

**Exercise 19:** *White to move (Maroczy–Vidmar, Ljubljana, 1922). White is attacking, but Black has an extra pawn and seems to be defending. White found an incredible winning move. What is it? (Hint: White combines deflection with getting Black to block the defense of a key square.)*

**Exercise 20:** *White to move. White wants to play g3-g4 checkmate, but Black's queen pins the g-pawn. How can White deflect the queen and win?*

**Exercise 21:** *White to move (Carlsen–Karjakin, World Chess Championship 2016). World Chess Champion Magnus Carlsen dramatically defended his title by finding a brilliant move to force checkmate. What did he play?*

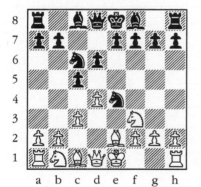

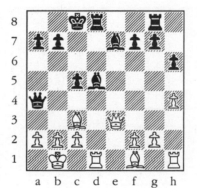

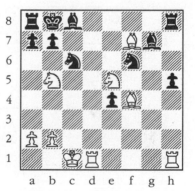

**Exercise 22:** *White to move. How can White win a piece?*

**Exercise 23:** *White to move (Li Chao–Bu Xiangzhi, Chinese Championship, 2009). White, a very strong grandmaster, played 18.Qxe7?? because he couldn't see what was wrong with taking the bishop on e7. How did Black force checkmate?*

**Exercise 24:** *Black to move. White has just played 1.Bf4. What is the threat? Does 1... Bh6 defend?*

*Exercise 25:* Black to move (Gulbrandsen–O'Kelly, Stockholm, 1937). How can Black win material?

*Exercise 26:* Black to move (Carlsen–Anand, World Championship, 2014). At this pivotal moment, Anand missed a chance to win material! Can you do better? What is the right move for Black?

# Chapter 8

# Hunting Down the King

In Chapters 5 through 7, I stressed the importance of having a material advantage, and I showed you some useful tactics for gaining a material advantage. In this chapter, I expand on these two concepts a little more.

First, I explain another way to think about having a material advantage and how to use it to attack the king. Then I show you some special tactics that are useful when attacking the king, as well as some ways to use the tactics you've already learned!

# When a Material Advantage Is Relative

Let's start by thinking a little more about having a material advantage. What good is having more material? Remember in Chapter 5, I said the point of having more material is that when you have more material, your attack overwhelms your opponent's defense, and your defense turns your opponent's attack.

Now this is certainly true, in the long run, for attacks in general. But in the short run, the success of a particular attack doesn't depend on overall material but on how much material the players have in the *relevant* part of the board.

Think of it this way: If you have more material overall, then as long as nothing is happening right away, you have an overall advantage in force. But if something is happening somewhere, the person with more material where that "something" is taking place will have the advantage in force as far as that something is concerned.

When does it matter to have an advantage in force in a relevant part of the chessboard? Well, nothing is more important than the safety of the king, so it can *really* matter when the king is under attack! Take a look at Diagram 1 to see what I mean.

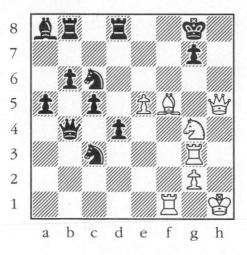

*Diagram 1: White has a winning attack against Black's king.*

Black has a huge material advantage. If Black's king were safe, Black could expect to use that advantage in material to win the game in the long run. But there isn't going to be a long run because White is about to slaughter Black's king!

Even though White has much less material than Black, all of it (except for the one pawn on g2 and the king) is right near the Black king and ready to go for the kill. Notice, also, that Black has only one measly pawn in front of the king to beat back White's attack. One pawn is no match for a queen, two rooks, a knight, and a bishop! Black's pieces are too far away to defend the king, and they are not in position to attack White's king. Even though Black has much more material overall, White's massive advantage in material near Black's king is what is going to decide the game.

If it isn't clear to you that Black is about to lose, then you might want to play around with this position on your own to convince yourself that White's attack is overwhelming. Here's a hint to get you going: if it's White's turn, 1.Be6# is checkmate, so you had better assume it's Black's turn to move!

This was a pretty exaggerated example just to make the point. Now we'll look at some more realistic situations where the side with more material near the opponent's king can launch a successful attack.

# The Emperor Has No Clothes!

One way that having more material near the opponent's king can make a difference is if the opponent's king has very few pieces or pawns around it for defense. When this happens, we say that the king is "exposed." Don't let your king walk around naked in the middle of the chess game! (I'm talking metaphorically here.) As a general rule of thumb, when your king is castled, it's a good idea to have at least two connected pawns in front of the king and at least one minor piece (knight or bishop) near the king for defense.

Diagrams 2 through 9 show you an example of this rule in action. At first glance, it might look like Black's king is not in danger. But take another look: White's knight on e5, rook on g3, and bishop on c2 all control squares that are very close to the king. And Black has only two pawns in front of the king to shield it. Furthermore, Black's queen and knights are very far away from the king, so they may not be useful for defense. Is there some way White can bring more material near the black king to attack it?

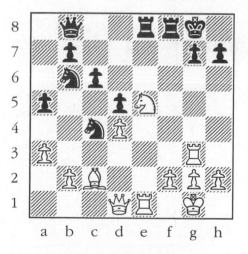

*Diagram 2: White to move.*

Yes, there is! In Diagram 3, White plays 1.Qh5! to attack the pawn on h7. Suddenly, White's material advantage near the king is huge, with the queen on h5, a rook on g3, a bishop on c2, and a knight on e5 all aimed at Black's king. In fact, Black has no adequate defense and is lost. I'll show you two plausible tries for Black to defend himself and how White defeats both. You may want to try to find other defenses for Black and how White defeats those as well.

The first try is for Black to play 1…h6 (see Diagram 4). Black removes the pawn from attack on h7 and puts it on a square where it is protected by the pawn on g7. Except it isn't really protected, because the g7 pawn is pinned to the black king by the rook on g3! White can simply play 2.Qxh6 in Diagram 5, capturing the pawn, renewing the threat of check ("checkmate") mate on h7, and creating a new threat on g7. Black can't meet all these threats. (If this is not clear to you, set the position up on a board and try to find the best moves for both sides.)

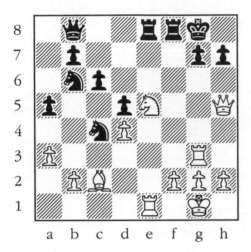

Diagram 3: White plays 1.Qh5!, which threatens 2.Qxh7#.

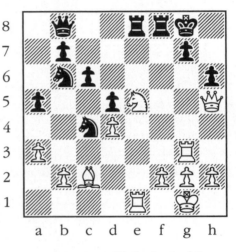

Diagram 4: Black tries 1…h6.

Diagram 5: White plays 2.Qxh6.

The second try is for Black to play 1...g6 (see Diagram 6). This blocks the attack to the h7 pawn. Black figures if White captures the pawn on g6, then Black recaptures the piece with the h7 pawn, and Black will gain a material advantage. But who cares about material if you can give checkmate? White plays 2.Bxg6! in Diagram 7, renewing the threat to the h7 pawn and creating new threats of discovered check. Alternatively, 2.Rxg6+ would also force checkmate quickly, after either 2...hxg6 3.Qxg6+ Kh8 4.Qh7# or 2...Kh8 3.Rg8+ followed by 4.Qxh7#. Black has nothing better than 2...hxg6, when 3.Rxg6# is checkmate (see Diagram 8).

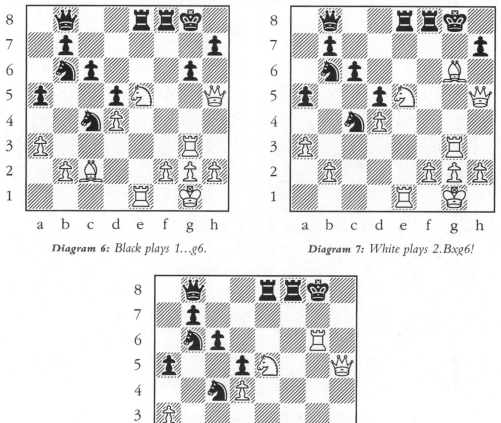

**Diagram 6:** *Black plays 1...g6.*     **Diagram 7:** *White plays 2.Bxg6!*

**Diagram 8:** *Position after 2...hxg6*
*3.Rxg6#.*

Black's troubles were caused by having too few pieces close enough to the king to help with its defense. (And in this case, the pieces near the king—the rooks on f8 and e8—weren't much help.) If we make two small changes, things become much better for Black. Let's suppose that the knight on b6 is now on f6 and the queen on b8 is now on c7, as shown in Diagram 9. Suddenly, Black has two more pieces near the king for defense. The queen on c7 protects the sensitive pawn on g7 and can travel along the second rank to protect the king. The knight on f6 protects the sensitive pawn on h7 and also prevents the white queen from coming to h5. Now Black's king is much safer and White has no prospects for a sudden attack.

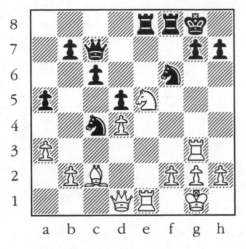

*Diagram 9: Black's king is safe.*

# Exposing Your Opponent's King

Because your opponent may not be so obliging as to leave the king so open to attack, you often have to work at making your opponent's king more exposed. Now I'll show you an example from a game between grandmasters where one player saw an opportunity to expose the opponent's king and used that chance to go for the kill.

Let me warn you: in this example, we will be looking at a lot more moves than we have been doing in previous examples. I'll make it as easy to follow as possible, but if you haven't been using a chess set, you may want to get one to follow this example. If you don't have one—don't worry—just follow along as best you can. The most important thing is that you understand the main ideas.

## Anand–Kasparov, 1995

This example is etched in my memory because it comes from the 1995 World Chess Championship match in New York City, where I was one of Viswanathan Anand's coaches in his bid to challenge the world champion, Garry Kasparov. Anand unfortunately lost that match, and this game is one reason why. (But I'm happy to report that this setback did not stop Anand from later earning the World Chess Championship crown, first from 2000-2002 and then again from 2007-2013.)

Kasparov, playing Black in Diagram 10, is temporarily behind one pawn. He can recapture the pawn by playing 20...Qxe6 or 20...fxe6, which would restore the material balance. But Kasparov plays a much stronger move with 20...c4! as shown in Diagram 11.

The idea behind this move is to prevent White from castling either on the kingside or the queenside. White can't castle kingside because now the black queen controls the g1 square. White could castle queenside, but it would be a bad idea because after 21.O-O-O, Black would play 21...cxb3 22.axb3 Qxb3 for a winning position.

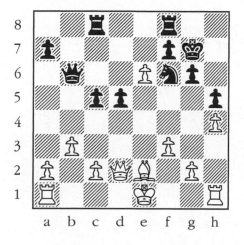

*Diagram 10: Black to play (Anand–Kasparov, World Championship, 1995).*

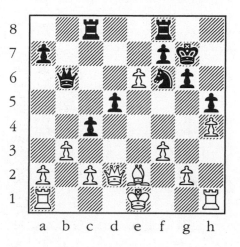

*Diagram 11: Black plays 20...c4!*

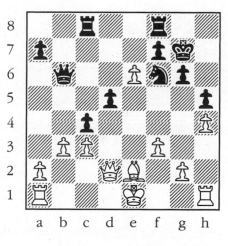

*Diagram 12: White plays 21.c3.*

Anand was afraid of allowing Black's pawn to c3, but he didn't want to play 21.bxc4 dxc4 because he judged this would dangerously expose his queenside to Black's queen. Anand played 21.c3 as shown in Diagram 12. Now Kasparov could have captured either of White's pawns on b3 or e6, but doing so would have slowed down his attack against the king. Instead, Kasparov brought more material to bear against White's increasingly, precariously positioned king by playing 21…Rce8! (see Diagram 13).

(By the way, do you notice that Black's king is castled while White's king is not? Kasparov's attack is made possible because Anand left his king uncastled in the center of the board for too long. Keep your king safe by castling early! And if your opponent delays castling for too long, look for a good way to attack!)

Now Anand did not want to play 22.exf7, because after 22…Rxf7, the rook on f8 would join the attack. Not only would the f-file suddenly be open, but also the rook would be ready to play 23…Rfe7, threatening to capture the bishop on e2, which is pinned to White's king. Anand felt that he needed to have some material to compensate for Black's growing attack, so he played 22.bxc4 as shown in Diagram 14. Kasparov responded by bringing his rook into the action by playing 22…Rxe6 (see Diagram 15).

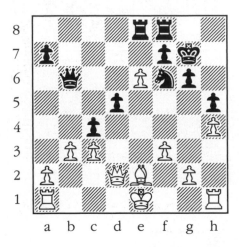

*Diagram 13: Black plays 21…Rce8!*

*Diagram 14: White plays 22.bxc4!*

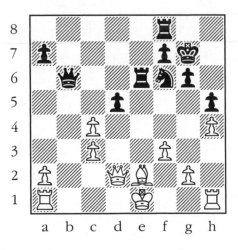

*Diagram 15: Black plays 22…Rxe6.*

After 22...Rxe6, Black was threatening to play 23...Rfe8, which would win material by attacking the pinned bishop. Anand moved his king out of the pin by playing 23.Kf1 (see Diagram 16). This move did meet the threat, but it had the drawback of giving up the right to castle, which practically ensured that White's king would not soon find safety. Black played 23...Rfe8! anyway (see Diagram 17). Even though this move doesn't win the bishop, it is still a very good move. It brings another piece closer to White's king, forcing White to defend against a specific threat (to capture the bishop on e2) and stopping White from improving his position in any other way. White defended against the threat by playing 24.Bd3, as shown in Diagram 18.

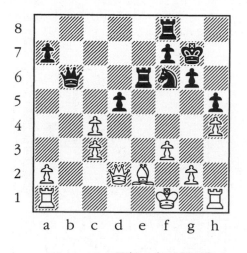

*Diagram 16: White plays 23.Kf1.*

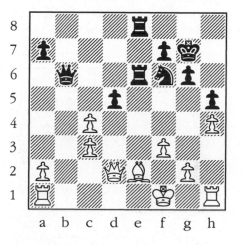

*Diagram 17: Black plays 23...Rfe8.*

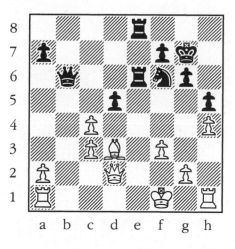

*Diagram 18: White plays 24.Bd3.*

Kasparov now spots a magnificent way to expose White's king even more and goes in for the kill. He begins with what is basically a deflection tactic: 24...dxc4 (see Diagram 19). White recaptures the pawn with 25.Bxc4 as shown in Diagram 20. Then Kasparov shows why he wanted to deflect the bishop from the defense of the e4 square with his next move: 25...Ne4!! (see Diagram 21).

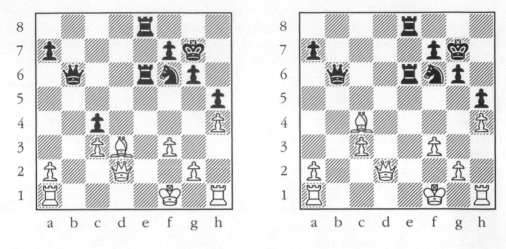

Diagram 19: *Black plays 24...dxc4.*     Diagram 20: *White plays 25.Bxc4.*

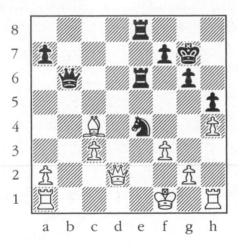

Diagram 21: *Black plays 25...Ne4!!*

Black ignores the threat to the rook and instead moves the knight to a square where it can be captured! Yet the move is so strong that Anand resigned. I hated to watch Anand lose, but I have to take my hat off to Kasparov for playing a beautiful game. He gave us all a valuable lesson in how to conduct an attack against the king.

Some amateurs emulate grandmasters too closely by resigning at the first sign of trouble. This is a big mistake. It made sense for Anand to resign the position in Diagram 21 because for him and Kasparov, the key moves were easy to calculate. But it would not be obvious to you, to your opponent, or to almost anyone else in the world! Chess players like to say, "Nobody ever saved a lost position by resigning." So don't give up the ship unless it's really, truly hopeless.

## Variations

Now let's dive into the position that Anand chose to resign so we can understand why Kasparov's attack was overwhelming. I urge you to use a chess set (or a computer) to play over the following variations of Diagram 21, so you can follow all the ideas. As you do so, notice how effectively Black is using all the pieces in the attack, while White's two rooks stand on the sidelines doing nothing.

Black has just played 25…Ne4 and threatens to capture the queen on d2 with check. Let's closely examine each one of White's plausible moves:

> **Variation 1:** 26.fxe4 Rf6+ 27.Ke1 (27.Ke2 Rf2+ 28.Kd1 Rxd2+ 29.Kxd2 Rxe4 not only gives Black a material advantage, but with White's king so exposed to attack, Black would win quickly) 27…Rxe4+ 28.Kd1 (28.Be2 Qf2+ 29.Kd1 Rxe2! 30.Qxe2 Rd6+ gives Black a huge material advantage) 28…Rxc4 is hopeless for White: Black threatens both 29…Rd6 and 29…Rf2, and White will not survive in the face of Black's attack.

> **Variation 2:** 26.Qd4+ Qxd4 27.cxd4 Nd2+ forks the king and bishop, giving Black a winning material advantage. This demonstrates two very important ideas about attacking the king. First, a plausible defense for White is to exchange queens, in order to remove Black's most powerful attacking piece. Second, Black's attack is made all the more effective by combining the attack against the king with threats against other pieces. (Note the use of the fork!) Black is willing to break off the attack against the king if there is a way to gain a large material advantage safely.

> **Variation 3:** 26.Qf4 Qf2#.

> **Variation 4:** 26.Qc2 Ng3#.

> **Variation 5:** 26.Qe1 defends both f2 and g3, so it is a better try than variations #3 and #4 26…Rd6! and White is helpless. Black threatens 27…Nd2+. If White plays 27.Rd1 to protect the d2 square, then 27…Rxd1 28.Qxd1 Ng3# is the end. If White plays 27.fxe4, then 27…Rf6+ 28.Ke2 Rxe4+ wins material and keeps the attack going.

# Useful Tactics for Attacking the King

Good for you if you had the patience to read through the analysis of that game (including the variations at the end)! I know it's hard work, but it will really pay off. Now, I'm going to show you a couple of useful tactics to keep in mind for attacking the king.

A successful attack does not always require having more material near the king. Having more material near the king is useful, but it doesn't guarantee a successful attack and it's not always necessary for an attack to succeed. Sometimes an attack succeeds not because you have more pieces near the king but simply because the pieces you do have near the king work really well together. The remaining pages of this chapter show two common patterns for how pieces can coordinate when attacking the king and then the exercises at the end of the chapter demonstrate some more.

# Nowhere to Run!

When the king is castled, it often has three pawns right in front of it, blocking all the squares on the rank above it. That's generally useful, as the pawns provide shelter for the king. However, having the pawns all in a row in front of the king when the king is on the back rank can also be a problem. If a rook or the queen should come along and give check, and there is no way to capture it or block the check, the king will be checkmated! That is called the *weak back rank,* and it is an incredibly common theme. You've already seen this theme in this book; for example, the very first checkmate I showed you (Chapter 3, Diagram 21) was a checkmate on the weak back rank. But the idea is so important, I'll show you another example.

In Diagram 22, White has moved her h-pawn from h2 to h3, thereby giving the king a square to which it can move on the second rank. But because this square is attacked by the black bishop on c7, White's king still suffers from a weak back rank, which Black can exploit with 1...Ra1+. White can block the check with the rook or the knight, but these pieces will be captured and then the check will be checkmate.

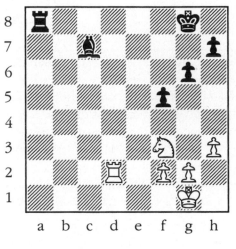

*Diagram 22: Black to move.*

# Death by Suffocation

You would think that the king would be safe if it surrounded itself with lots of pieces, right? Well, that certainly blocks any check from most pieces, but not the knight! You can't block a knight's check. And if you've taken away all the squares the king can move to, that one check might be mate. When that happens, it's called the *smothered mate.*

A quick look at Diagram 23 gives the impression that Black is in no danger of smothered mate here. But in fact, White can force checkmate in just a few moves by combining no fewer than four tactical ideas: deflection, weak back rank, double check, and smothered mate. Can you see how?

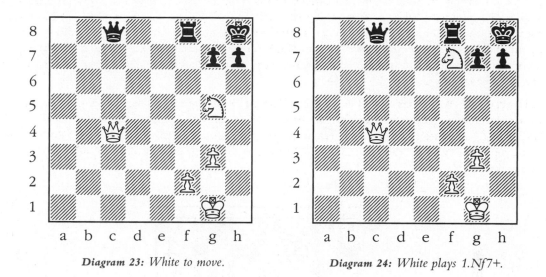

Diagram 23: White to move.     Diagram 24: White plays 1.Nf7+.

Since we are looking for a way for White to force checkmate, it's good to look at a check. And indeed, the right first move is 1.Nf7+, as shown in Diagram 24. Now Black can't capture the knight because that would leave the queen on c8 unprotected, and White would play 2.Qxc8+, with mate to follow on the back rank. (Here is where deflection and the weak back rank play their roles.)

Since the knight can't be captured, Black must play 1...Kg8 (see Diagram 25). Now what? Again, we should look for a check, but no ordinary discovered check will work because the queen on c4 is attacked by the queen on c8. So we have to use double check and play 2.Nh6+ in Diagram 26, after which Black has only one possible response: 2...Kh8 (see Diagram 27).

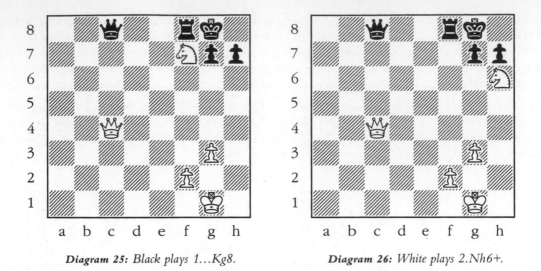

**Diagram 25:** *Black plays 1...Kg8.*

**Diagram 26:** *White plays 2.Nh6+.*

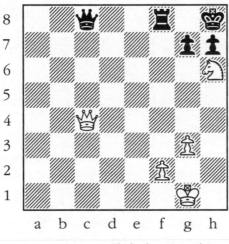

**Diagram 27:** *Black plays 2...Kh8.*

It may look like White now has nothing better than to force perpetual check by playing 3.Nf7+ Kg8 4.Nh6+ Kh8 5.Nf7+, and so on. After all, White is behind in material, and how could Black be vulnerable to attack? But think about this: when White plays Nf7+, the only square to which Black's king can go is g8. Can White force Black to occupy this square with the rook? If so, then when White plays Nf7+ Black's king will be smothered by its own pieces, and it will be checkmate.

And yes, there is a way to do it: the queen sacrifice 3.Qg8+!! (see Diagram 28). Black's only move is to capture the queen with 3…Rxg8, as shown in Diagram 29 and then 4.Nf7# is checkmate (see Diagram 30). Notice that not only did 3.Qg8+!! force Black to occupy the g8 square with his rook, it also deflected the rook away from the defense of the f7 square.

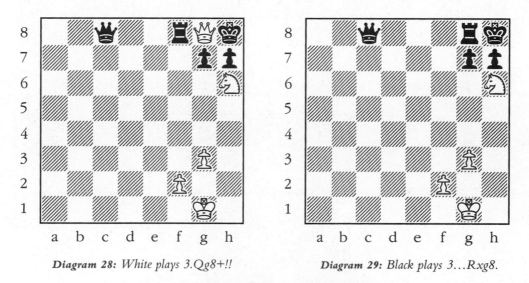

Diagram 28: *White plays 3.Qg8+!!*     Diagram 29: *Black plays 3…Rxg8.*

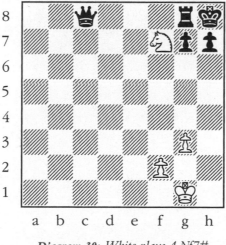

Diagram 30: *White plays 4.Nf7#.*

# Exercises: The Infinite Variety of Checkmates

Weak back rank and smothered mate are two of the most important tactics to keep in mind when looking for checkmate. But there are literally thousands of other checkmate tactics. In the following exercises, I challenge you to find ways to give checkmate that may not fit into some of the tactics you've already seen. It's up to you to learn these tactics and keep them in mind for future use. (I'll give you a hint if the exercise uses a new tactic.)

Always be on the lookout for new tactics to use, both to win material and to checkmate the king, and *always* look for ways to combine tactics!

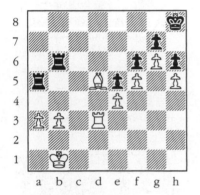

**Exercise 1:** *White to move (Wolff–Rao, Philadelphia, 1992). Black has a weak back rank. What is the best way for White to take advantage of it? (Hint: White uses a tactic called interference, using one piece to physically block another piece from moving to a certain square.)*

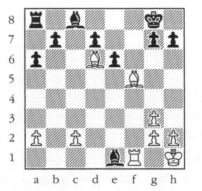

**Exercise 2:** *White to move (Wolff–Dimitrijevic, Boston, 1994). Again, Black has a weak back rank! How can White force checkmate in two moves using that back rank?*

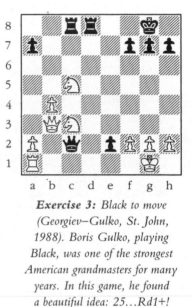

**Exercise 3:** *Black to move (Georgiev–Gulko, St. John, 1988). Boris Gulko, playing Black, was one of the strongest American grandmasters for many years. In this game, he found a beautiful idea: 25...Rd1+! Show how Black wins after either 26.Nxd1 or 26.Rxd1. (Hint: after 26.Rxd1, find a deflection.)*

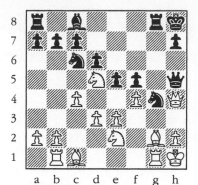

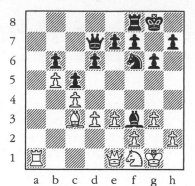

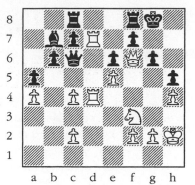

**Exercise 4:** *White to move. Why can't White capture the queen? If White plays 1.Qe1, then 1...Qxh2# is checkmate. Suppose White plays 1.Qg3 instead to protect h2. How does Black force checkmate using a deflection?*

**Exercise 5:** *Black to move wins, but White to move can defend. If it's Black's turn to move, how does Black force checkmate in two moves? (Hint: bring the most powerful piece into the attack.) If it's White's move, how should White defend against the threat?*

**Exercise 6:** *White to move (Short–Timman, Amsterdam, 1991). Here's an amazing position from a game between two former world championship contenders which uses the same idea as the last exercise, with a twist. White played 32.Kg3, and after 32...Rce8 he played 33.Kf4. What was White's idea? Can Black defend?*

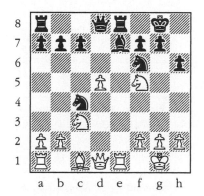

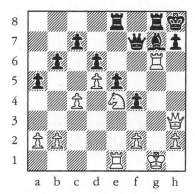

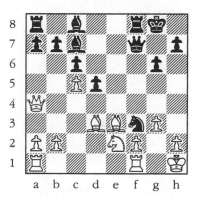

**Exercise 7:** *White to move (Wolff–Formanek, Chicago, 1994). How can White expose the black king to launch a devastating attack? (Here are two hints: one, don't overlook the white bishop on c1; and two, consider that after 14.Qd3 Nd6, if 15.Qg3 were check, then Black's king would be in great danger.)*

**Exercise 8:** *White to move. It looks like White will have to retreat the rook, giving Black time to defend. But White has a deadly blow. What is it? (Hint: White uses deflection to deliver smothered checkmate.)*

**Exercise 9:** *Black to move. How can Black combine an attack against a white piece to reposition himself for a deadly blow against White's king?*

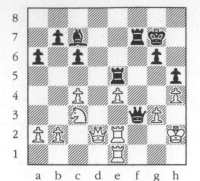

***Exercise 10:*** *Black to move (Rohde–Yermolinsky, Philadelphia, 1992). Two strong American grandmasters are battling in this position. Black missed a brilliant sacrifice to rip open White's king and then give checkmate. Can you find it? (Hint: think about how to draw the White king out and maximize the power of the bishop on c7.)*

***Exercise 11:*** *White to move. Does White have a stronger move than retreating the knight to e4 or f3?*

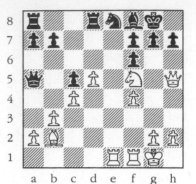

***Exercise 12:*** *White to move (Khalifman–Seirawan, Holland, 1991). White, a top grandmaster, started a brilliant winning combination with 1.Nh6+!! gxh6. How should White continue the attack against the king?*

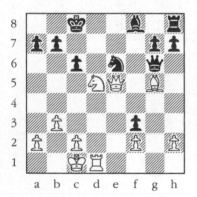

***Exercise 13:*** *White to move. How can White deliver checkmate on d8? (Hint: White needs to get the knight out of the way and make sure the king will not have access to the c7 square when the knight has moved out of the way.)*

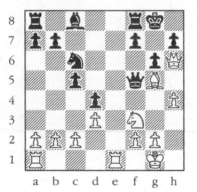

***Exercise 14:*** *White to move. How can White exploit the back rank to force checkmate?*

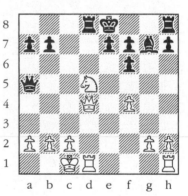

***Exercise 15:*** *White to move (Girsch–Man, Canada, 1963). Once again, White can exploit the weak back rank, this time with a deflection sacrifice.*

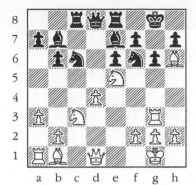

**Exercise 16:** *White to move (Keene–Miles, Hastings 1975/76). How should White continue the attack against Black's king?*

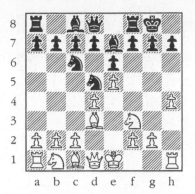

**Exercise 17:** *White to move. Believe it or not, this position is taken from a chess book dating back to the year 1620! The winning idea here is a familiar pattern that comes up over and over again. How can White launch a winning attack against the black king?*

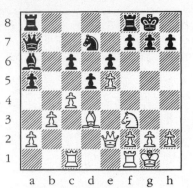

**Exercise 18:** *White to move (Winslow–Manvelyan, San Francisco, 2016). Do you see the same pattern in this position as in Exercise 17? Work out how the game should go after White plays 17.Bxh7+.*

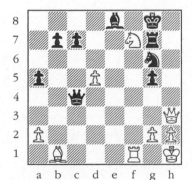

**Exercise 19:** *White to move. (Matlakov–Nabaty, Batumi, 2018). It looks like White is going to win by setting up a discovered check, but actually the win uses a different pattern. What is White's best move?*

**Exercise 20:** *Black to move (Alekseev–Mamedov, Batumi, 2018). White is forking Black's knight and bishop, and the b-pawn is one square away from making a queen. Can Black crash through White's defenses to force checkmate?*

# Part 3

# STRATEGY

If there's no move to capture one of your opponent's pieces, and you can't see how to attack the king, how can you know what move to play? Which positions are good for you, and which are bad? How can you tell? The answers to these questions come from knowing chess strategy, and that's the subject of this part.

The traditional way to teach chess strategy—and who am I to break with tradition?—is to divide the course of a chess game into three phases: the beginning phase (called the *opening*), the middle phase (called the *middlegame*), and the final phase (called the *endgame*). Similar strategies apply to each phase, but there are some differences in how the strategies should be applied in each phase. By the time you finish this part, you'll know what to do and when to do it!

# Chapter 9

# In the Beginning

So far, we've looked at lots of different kinds of chess positions that might arise in a game. But we haven't looked at the one chess position that always arises in every game: the starting position. "All these tactics are fine and dandy," you might think to yourself, "but what the heck should I do when I actually start the game?" That's the subject of this chapter. You will learn what your goal should be in the first 8 to 12 moves, as well as the crucial principles to keep in mind as you work toward that goal.

# The Beginning, Middle, and End of a Chess Game

Chess can be divided into three distinct phases. The first phase is called the *opening* and is the first 8 to 12 moves of the game. The second phase, the one that comes after the opening, is called the *middlegame*. The third phase is called the *endgame*, which is when there are relatively few pieces left for each side. This chapter focuses on the opening.

So why do special considerations apply to the opening? At the beginning of a chess game, all the pieces and pawns are crammed into two ranks for each side, and there are four ranks of unoccupied squares. It would be foolish to rush out and attack your opponent before you brought out your pieces and pawns to good squares. After all, would a general mount an attack on the enemy before the army was ready to fight? If you're going to be a good general to your chess army, you have to know how to bring out your pieces and where they belong. That's what the opening is all about. Once you have your army fairly well mobilized, the middlegame begins. And although the number of moves it takes to reach that stage varies from game to game, 8 to 12 moves is a good rough estimate.

# "The Opening" or "an Opening"?

"The opening" refers to the general phase of the game where you're moving your pieces into position to start maneuvering for advantage. But we can also talk about "an opening," which is a specific sequence of moves that one plans in advance to start the game with. There are literally thousands of such sequences of moves. The more advanced one becomes at chess, the more time one spends studying specific opening moves. In a game between grandmasters, sometimes the whole game can be won or lost because of a new idea—even just one new move—that one grandmaster plays against another in an opening sequence.

If you want to progress beyond this book, you need to learn more about these specific openings. In Chapter 15, you can  learn more about exploring the world of chess openings. But you must learn to walk before you can run. Before you learn any specific openings, you must learn the basic principles for playing the opening. Those principles are the subject of this chapter.

# When Does the Beginning End?

When do you know the opening has ended? The simple answer is that you know it's over when you've achieved the goals of the opening. You have two goals during the opening: first, to get most of your pieces and some of your pawns off their starting squares and onto better squares; and second, to get your king to safety. There are five basic principles (discussed in the following sections) to keep in mind for the opening while you achieve those goals.

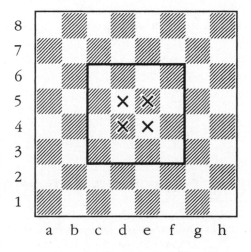

*Diagram 1: The square in bold outlines the center of the board; the Xs show the four most important center squares.*

## Principle #1: The Center Is Where the Action Is

Okay, so you want to bring your pawns and pieces into play. That makes sense, but where should you put them? The answer is simple: you want to put them on squares where they control the center of the board. Diagram 1 shows the center.

Why control the center? Basically, there are two reasons. First, when you control the center, you can move your pieces from one area of the board to any other area in the most efficient way possible, since the easiest way to move from side to side is to go through the middle. Second, controlling the center gives you more control over the sides of the board. So it comes down to flexibility and raw power, both of which are increased by controlling the center.

Keep in mind that occupying the center is not always the same thing as controlling it, because a piece or pawn does not control the square it's sitting on. That doesn't mean that you shouldn't put pieces or pawns in the center! It just means that when you do, you have to make sure that those pieces or pawns are adequately supported by other pieces or pawns.

# Principle #2: Center Pawns First

Which pawns and pieces should you bring out to control the center? Different considerations apply to pawns and pieces, so we'll discuss each separately. Principle #2 covers the pawns.

For the pawns, the rule of thumb is to use the e-pawn and the d-pawn first, plus sometimes the c-pawn. The reasons to push the e-pawn and the d-pawn are that they are the center pawns and have a bigger influence on the battle for the center, and pushing them lets the bishops and the queen get into the game. The reasons to push the c-pawn are that it can have some effect on the center (although less than the center pawns), and pushing it also opens a diagonal for the queen to use. (Even if the queen does not use it right away, it may be useful later in the game.)

Deciding whether to push the f-pawn is tricky; there are times when it can be a good idea, but there are also times when it's bad to do so because pushing this pawn exposes the king. An experienced player will often know when it's good to push this pawn and when it's bad, but even an experienced player can come to regret pushing the f-pawn too early in the opening. For example, take another look at the Anand-Kasparov game in Chapter 8. Because Anand's pawn was on f3, Kasparov's queen on b6 was able to prevent him from castling, which enabled Black's attack against the white king. This is a perfect example of the problems that can result from pushing the f-pawn too soon.

What about the other four pawns? There are times when you want to push them; in particular, later in the chapter I mention the *fianchetto*, which can be quite good and requires you to push either your g-pawn or your b-pawn. But in general, the pawns on either side of the board shouldn't be pushed until you have finished the opening, unless you have a good reason.

Here's a last thought about pawns and the center: Pawns that can have more influence on the center are worth just a little bit more than other pawns. That means the d-pawn and e-pawn are just a little better than the c-pawn and f-pawn, and more than just a little bit better than the other four pawns. So don't exchange a center pawn for a noncenter pawn without a good reason!

# Principle #3: Minor Pieces before Major Pieces

When you move a piece for the first time, chess players say that you *develop* it. (But for some reason, chess players don't talk about "developing" the pawns—and the king should be "protected," not "developed.") The rule of thumb for developing pieces is to develop the less powerful pieces first and the more powerful pieces later. Develop the knights and the bishops first (some people emphasize that you should develop the knights before the bishops), the rooks second, and the queen last.

Some beginning players think they should bring the queen out right away. I understand the thought: since the queen is so powerful, why not use it right away to attack? But often, this is wrong. You're not going to be able to attack anything before you get the rest of your army into action, so you'll just waste time. And even worse, the queen will be exposed to attack by your opponent's pieces. Your opponent will gain time to develop more pieces by simultaneously developing a piece and attacking the queen and force you to use more time by moving the queen to safety.

Of course, any rule has its exceptions, and there are openings grandmasters play where the queen plays a role early in the opening. But these cases are rare, and they have been carefully thought through in advance. You will learn the exceptions to the rules as you learn more about chess. For now, keep the queen home in the opening!

## Principle #4: Time Is of the Essence

I said that one reason you should not bring the queen out too early in the opening is that your opponent will "gain time" to develop pieces by attacking your queen. The concept of time is important in chess, especially during the opening.

Think of it this way. Suppose you and I are playing a game. In my first few moves, I move each center pawn once, each knight once, and each bishop once, and then I castle; while in your first few moves, you move the same one center pawn twice and take two moves to develop each piece. Obviously, I'm going to have more pieces and pawns playing a role in the game earlier on, and that's going to give me an advantage in any early skirmishes we might have. You've wasted time in the opening.

Of course, there will be times when you really do want to move the same piece twice or even more times in the opening. (For example, you may need to move a piece that is being attacked.) But as much as possible, you should develop each piece to a good square and then turn your attention to developing the other pieces.

## Principle #5: Castle Early!

Castling is a wonderful move. It does two things: it hustles the king out of the center of the board to one of the wings, where it will be out of the way of the other pieces; and it makes it easier to develop the rooks.

Maybe it's not obvious why castling helps develop the rooks. If you are following my advice, you'll be pushing the e-pawn and/or the d-pawn, maybe the c-pawn, and possibly the f-pawn in the opening. If the rooks are going to get into the game, they're going to need open files, i.e. the files where pawns have been pushed forward or exchanged (the e-pawn, the d-pawn, the c-pawn and maybe the f-pawn). So you need to get the rooks to those files, and castling helps do that.

You might wonder which side you should castle on. The answer is always going to depend on the particulars of the position, but a key consideration is to castle wherever the king will be safer. Remember from last chapter that the castled king should have at least two, and preferably three, pawns in front of it to keep it safe. So make sure you haven't moved too many of the pawns on whichever side you castle the king!

# Two Openings to Illustrate the Five Principles

This section shows examples from actual openings that grandmasters might play, illustrating good play in the opening according to the principles you've just learned.

# Queen's Gambit Declined

The first opening we look at is called the *Queen's Gambit Declined*. White begins Diagram 2 by playing 1.d4, to which Black responds 1...d5 (see Diagram 3). With the first move, White stakes out territory in the center and opens up the diagonal for the queen's bishop. Black does the same.

White's next move is 2.c4 (see Diagram 4). The purpose of this move is to fight for the central square d5. White uses the c-pawn to intensify the struggle for the central squares, but the move also places the pawn on a square where Black can capture it. This is why the opening is a gambit: White offers Black a pawn as part of the opening strategy. (A gambit in chess is a sacrifice, usually of one or two pawns, that has become a known opening idea.)

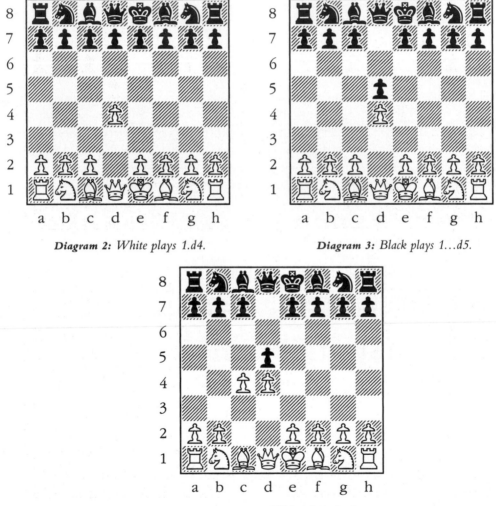

**Diagram 2:** *White plays 1.d4.*   **Diagram 3:** *Black plays 1...d5.*

**Diagram 4:** *White plays 2.c4.*

Black decides not to capture the pawn and plays 2...e6 (see Diagram 5). (It is also possible for Black to capture the pawn: then the opening is called the *Queen's Gambit Accepted*.) Notice that Black's second move not only helps develop the king's bishop, it also enables Black to recapture on d5 with a pawn if White should play cxd5. This is important, as it means that Black can maintain the very strong pawn on d5.

The next several moves by each player are developing moves aimed at controlling the center. In Diagram 6, White plays 3.Nc3, and Black plays 3...Nf6; in Diagram 7, White plays 4.Bg5, and Black plays 4...Be7. (If Black were to play 3...dxc4 or 4...dxc4, White would respond strongly with 4.e4 or 5.e4; Black would not be able to keep the pawn and would lose control of the center to boot.) Notice that White's fourth move pins Black's knight to the queen, while Black's fourth move breaks the pin by putting the bishop between the knight and queen.

In Diagram 8, White plays 5.e3, and Black plays 5...O-O. Having developed the queenside minor pieces, White begins to focus on developing the kingside minor pieces. Black, on the other hand, hurries to castle kingside.

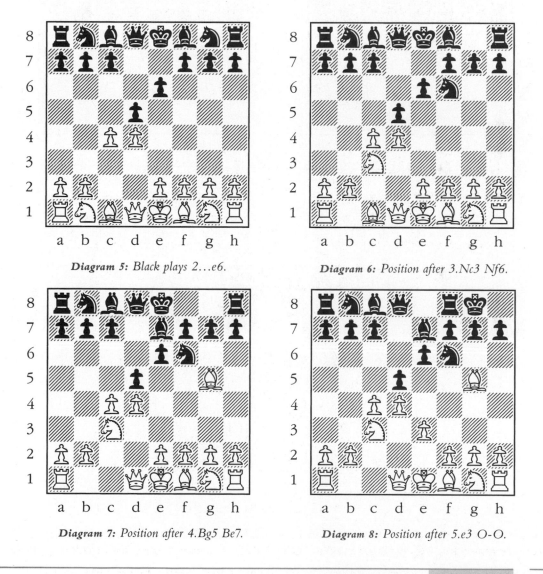

Diagram 5: Black plays 2...e6.

Diagram 6: Position after 3.Nc3 Nf6.

Diagram 7: Position after 4.Bg5 Be7.

Diagram 8: Position after 5.e3 O-O.

White's next move is 6.Nf3, developing the knight to an excellent square. Black responds with 6...Nbd7 (see Diagram 9). This move puts the knight into the fight for the center, but the black knight is not as aggressively placed here as White's queen's knight on c3. Black decides to develop the knight to this less active square rather than to c6 because Black wants to use the c-pawn in the fight for the center, either by pushing it to c5 to attack White's pawn on d4 or by pushing it to c6 to support the pawn on d5.

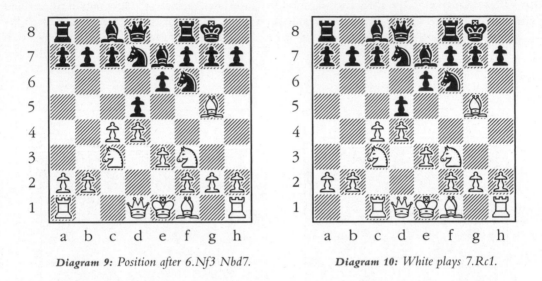

**Diagram 9:** *Position after 6.Nf3 Nbd7.*            **Diagram 10:** *White plays 7.Rc1.*

In Diagram 10, White plays 7.Rc1. Perhaps this move seems surprising; it might seem that White would do better to play 7.Be2 or 7.Bd3, in order to develop the bishop and castle before developing the rook. The explanation is that White wants to make the best possible use of time by anticipating Black's likely next move. White realizes that one plan for Black is to capture the pawn on c4 and then to play ...c5 himself.

For example, if 7.Bd3, then Black would play 7...dxc4 8.Bxc4 c5; although Black has exchanged a center pawn for a noncenter pawn, it is all right because Black will soon exchange a noncenter pawn back for a center pawn again. White anticipates this idea by developing the rook first; now if Black plays 7...dxc4 then after 8.Bxc4, White will have gained the Rc1 move over the previous sequence. Black decides not to allow White to gain time in that way and chooses instead to support the center by playing 7...c6 (see Diagram 11).

Now White plays 8.Bd3 (see Diagram 12), developing the last minor piece. How should we evaluate this position? White's control of the central squares is somewhat stronger than Black's, but Black has still secured a good stake in the center. White has not yet castled, but soon will. Because White's pieces control the center a little better than Black's and because White's pawns are slightly farther advanced than Black's, it's fair to say that White has a small advantage. But this advantage is not much; and if Black plays well, a satisfactory position can be secured. (In fact, in Chapter 12, I show you Black's best way to continue.)

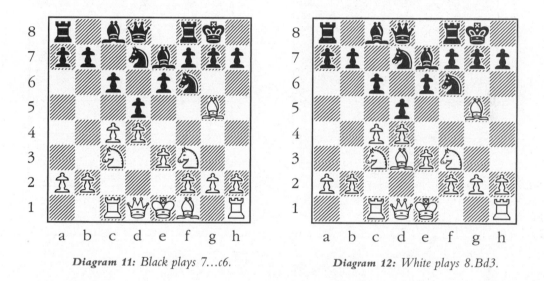

*Diagram 11: Black plays 7...c6.*    *Diagram 12: White plays 8.Bd3.*

## Sicilian Defense

The second opening we will look at is called the *Sicilian Defense*. White plays 1.e4, a move that fights for the center in a similar way to 1.d4, but in contrast to the last example, Black does not mimic

White's first move and plays 1...c5 instead (see Diagram 13). Black decides to grab territory on the side of the board that White's first move slightly neglected. On the plus side, Black may stand better on the queenside than White because of this bold strike; on the minus side, Black's first move does not help develop pieces, and the pawn on c5 controls less of the center than the pawn on e4. This provocative opening often leads to very exciting games!

In Diagram 14, White's next move is 2.Nf3, while Black plays 2...d6. White's move develops the knight toward the center, while Black's move prepares to develop the queen's bishop and controls the e5 square.

White's third move is quite bold: 3.d4 (see Diagram 15). On the plus side, this move fights for control of the d4 square and enables White to develop the queen's bishop. On the minus side, it allows Black to exchange a noncenter pawn for a center pawn. Such dynamic imbalances are typical for the Sicilian Defense.

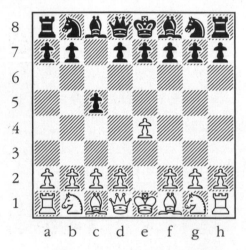

*Diagram 13: Position after 1.e4 c5.*

*Diagram 14: Position after 2.Nf3 d6.*

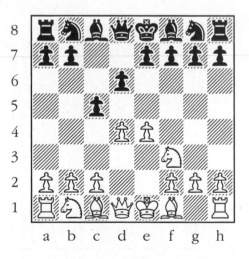

*Diagram 15: White plays 3.d4.*

Black takes White up on the offer to exchange pawns (see Diagram 16), and White recaptures with the knight. (White doesn't recapture by playing 4.Qxd4, because then the queen would be exposed to attack by 4...Nc6.)

In Diagram 17, Black develops the knight to an excellent square while attacking the e4 pawn by playing 4...Nf6, and White defends the pawn by developing the knight with 5.Nc3. Now Black wants to develop the king's bishop and then castle. What's the best way to do this?

Black plays 5...g6 (see Diagram 18), with the intention of putting the bishop on g7 next move. This is not the only solution to the problem, but it is a good one. The move 5...g6 defines a particular variation of the Sicilian Defense, called the *Dragon Variation*. (Openings often have many variations with separate names. This is especially true of the Sicilian Defense, which has literally dozens of separately named variations!)

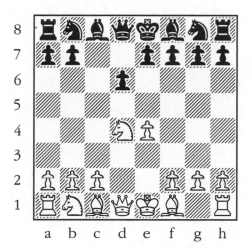

Diagram 16: Position after 3...cxd4 4.Nxd4.

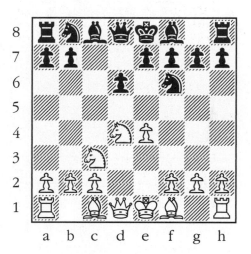

Diagram 17: Position after 4...Nf6 5.Nc3.

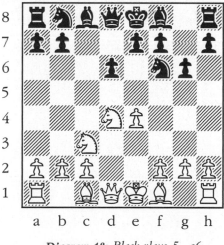

Diagram 18: Black plays 5...g6.

## A Brief Digression: Fianchettoing the Bishop

Moving either the g-pawn or the b-pawn up one square and then putting the bishop onto the square the pawn used to be on is called *fianchettoing the bishop*. (*Fianchetto* is Italian for "little flank.") You should be careful about adopting this strategy for two reasons:

+ The pawn move does little to fight for control of the center squares, so it loses time in the opening.

+ Once you advance the pawn, it no longer guards the squares it once did. This is especially important if the king castles to that side of the board, since the king might be more exposed now that the pawn has advanced.

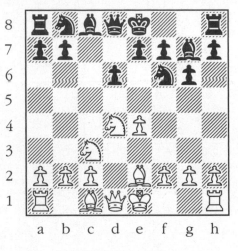

*Diagram 19: Position after 6.Be2 Bg7.*

Nevertheless, the fianchetto is often a good way to develop the bishop. In the position in Diagram 19, it is especially effective because White's d-pawn has been exchanged and no longer stands on d4, so the bishop's diagonal will be relatively unobstructed by White's pawns. Black's bishop often has a powerful influence from its post on the g7 square in the Dragon Variation of the Sicilian Defense.

## Back to the Sicilian Defense

Both sides continue their development. White plays 6.Be2 and Black plays 6...Bg7 (see Diagram 19). White castles and then Black castles (see Diagram 20). On the eighth move, White decides to develop the queen's bishop to e3, where it fights for control of the d4 square, and Black develops the queen's knight to c6, where it also fights for control of d4 (see Diagram 21).

White's ninth move, in Diagram 22, may not make sense unless you understand Black's intention. Black would like to advance the d-pawn to d5. This would exchange White's last center pawn, weakening White's control of the center, and leaving Black with only one center pawn. Therefore, White decides to retreat the knight to b3 with 9.Nb3. Although this takes a piece away from the center, it also increases the scope of White's queen; in particular, it increases its control of the d5 square. Besides, White was nervous about the possibility of the knight on d4 coming under heavy pressure because of the knight on c6 and the bishop on g7. Although the fianchettoed bishop is currently blocked by the knight on f6, it always has the potential to strike if the knight uncovers it!

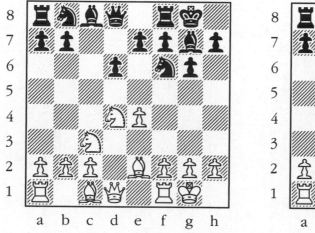

*Diagram 20: Position after 7.O-O O-O.*

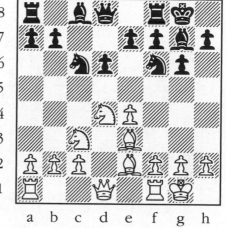

*Diagram 21: Position after 8.Be3 Nc6.*

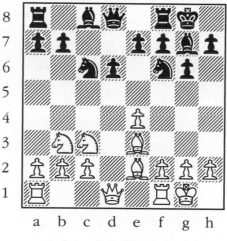

*Diagram 22: White plays 9.Nb3.*

Black develops the last minor piece by playing 9...Be6 (see Diagram 23). This move reinforces Black's control of the d5 square and prepares the possibility of playing 10...d5.

White responds by playing 10.f4 in Diagram 24. Although this move goes against the caution of thinking carefully before pushing the f-pawn in the opening, in this position it is justified. Remember that the reason not to play the move is that it exposes the king. But in this position, White's king is already castled, and the diagonal which this pawn move exposes is shielded by the bishop on e3. Plus, moving the pawn to f4 has an important point: now if Black plays 10...d5, White does not have to allow Black to exchange this pawn, but instead can respond by playing 11.e5, as the e5 square is protected by the f-pawn. Finally, White is also poised to cause trouble for Black's bishop on e6 by pushing the pawn to f5 at some point.

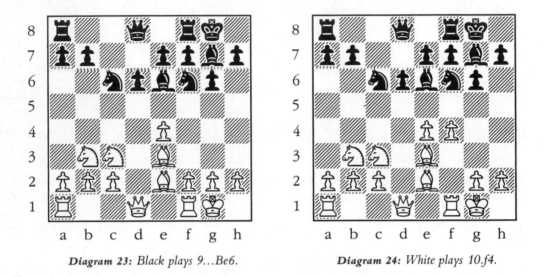

*Diagram 23: Black plays 9...Be6.*     *Diagram 24: White plays 10.f4.*

Now let's take stock of the result of the opening for both sides. White's pawns are more aggressively posted, but Black's position has no weaknesses. Both sides have developed all the minor pieces to active squares, and each side's king is safely castled. Chances are about equal, and a tough fight lies ahead in the middlegame.

# Exercises

Use the following exercises to develop your understanding of the principles discussed in this chapter. Above all, remember that your goals in the opening are to develop your pieces to good squares as quickly as possible, control the center, and get your king to safety!

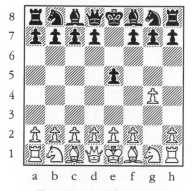

**Exercise 1:** *White to move. White has played 1.g4, to which Black responded 1...e5. Who has played better in the opening so far, and why? White is thinking about playing 2.f3. Why would this move be a terrible mistake?*

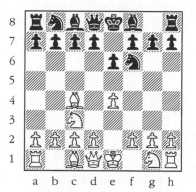

**Exercise 2:** *Black to move. Black is thinking about playing 1...d5. Would this be a good move or a bad move? Why?*

**Exercise 3:** *White to move. This position was reached after 1.d4 Nf6 2.c4 d5 3.cxd5 Qxd5. Black's first move is excellent, but his second and third moves are not; explain why, and suggest a good move for White to play next.*

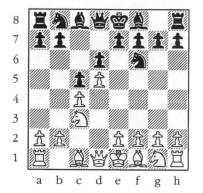

**Exercise 4:** *Black to move. Do you think this is a good position for Black to fianchetto the king's bishop? Why or why not?*

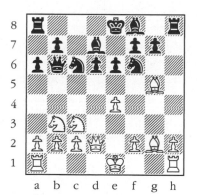

**Exercise 5:** *White to move. It's been a pretty wild opening so far; now White wants to castle. Should White castle kingside or queenside? Why?*

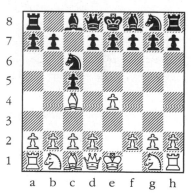

**Exercise 6:** *White to move. This position was reached by 1.e4 c5 2.Bc4 Nc6. Is 3.Qh5 a good move or a bad move? Why?*

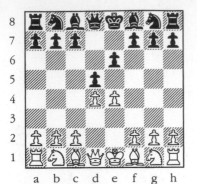

**Exercise 7:** *White to move. This position was reached by 1.e4 e6 2.d4 d5; this opening is called the French Defense. List all the moves that you would consider for White here. Why do you list those moves? What are the best moves to consider? Is 3.f3 a good move or a bad move? Why?*

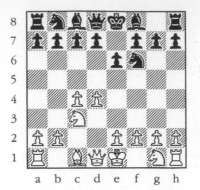

**Exercise 8:** *Black to move. This position was reached after 1.d4 Nf6 2.c4 e6 3.Nc3. Black is considering three moves: 3… Bb4, 3…Be7, and 3…d5. One of these moves is a bad move, the other two are good moves. Which is the bad move and why?*

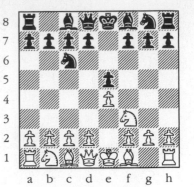

**Exercise 9:** *White to move. This position was reached by 1.e4 e5 2.Nf3 Nc6. Here White usually plays 3.Bb5 or 3.Bc4. Why do people not play 3.Bd3 or 3.Be2? Explain why these two moves are not as good as the normal moves.*

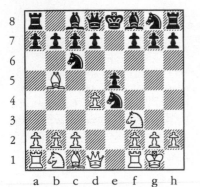

**Exercise 10:** *Black to move. This position was reached after 1.e4 e5 2.Nf3 Nc6 3.Bb5 Nf6 4.O-O Nxe4 5.d4. The normal move is 5…Nd6, which after 6.Bxc6 dxc6 7.dxe5 Nf5 8.Qxd8+ Kxd8, leads to a complicated endgame. Why do you think 5…exd4 is not normally played? Analyze this position and decide how White should continue.*

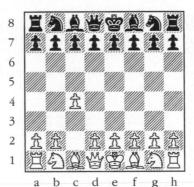

**Exercise 11:** *Black to move. White has just played 1.c4; this opening is called the English Opening. Consider the relative merits of playing 1…e5 versus 1…c5 in response. What other moves might Black consider? Would 1…d5 be a good move?*

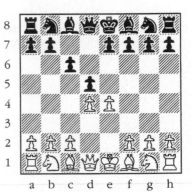

**Exercise 12:** *White to move. This position was reached by 1.e4 c6 2.d4 d5; this opening is called the Caro-Kann Defense. (You may want to compare this position to Exercise 7.) List all the moves that you would consider for White here. Why do you list those moves? What are the best moves to consider? Is 3.f3 a good move or a bad move? Why?*

# Chapter 10

# Making the Most of Your Pieces

The middlegame is where most of the action is, so we spend the next four chapters on it. In this chapter, you learn how to use your pieces more effectively. Later in the chapter, we consider each piece separately: knight, bishop, rook, and queen. (We talk about the pawns in Chapter 11; and as for the king, you should be keeping him in a safe place until the endgame!) But first, let's talk about two very important concepts that apply to all the pieces.

# Mobility: Give Me Room!

A piece tends to be more powerful if it controls more squares. And when it controls more squares, we say it's more mobile. Of course, controlling more squares isn't the only thing that's important; obviously it matters *which* squares your pieces control. We'll come to that in a moment. For now, just appreciate the importance of making sure your pieces control more squares, rather than fewer squares.

By the way, controlling the center is a really great way to increase the mobility of your pieces. So make sure you control the center of the board!

# Attack Your Opponent's Weaknesses

Your pieces will be more effective if they attack the weakest spots in your opponent's position. A weak spot can be the king, a pawn or group of pawns, a piece, or even a particular square.

A lot of the challenge in chess is identifying the weak spots in your opponent's position. Later in this chapter, we will go through lots of specific examples of well-placed and poorly placed pieces, so you can learn common patterns of what are weak spots and strong spots in a position.

Now let's look at each piece and see how to increase its mobility and use it to attack your opponent's weak spots.

# The Knight

The disadvantage of the knight is that it is not a long-range piece like the bishop, rook, or queen. It must be relatively close to the action in order to have any effect, and it takes a knight a lot longer to get somewhere than it takes a bishop, rook, or queen. But the knight also has the big advantage that it can hop over other pieces. Once you get the knight close to the action, it doesn't matter whether the squares next to it are occupied or not—it still has the same power.

What does this mean? Well, the knight wants to find a strong square somewhere in the middle of the board or close to some weak spot in the opponent's position and then the knight wants to sit there. The knight doesn't care about getting a "clear view" of anything, because it always has the same view no matter what. But the knight also doesn't have to move around too much, because it is so much slower than the other pieces.

In Diagrams 1 and 2, both players follow this advice. Each side has played well so far. (Notice how well each side controls the center!) Now White sees a way to increase the power of the knight on f3 and plays 1.Ne5! This is an excellent move; the knight now occupies a powerful post in the center from which it won't be easily dislodged. Notice in particular that Black cannot easily attack the knight with a pawn.

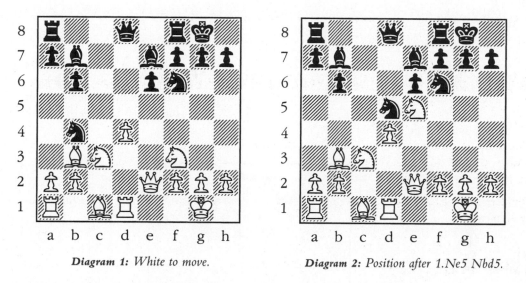

*Diagram 1: White to move.*  *Diagram 2: Position after 1.Ne5 Nbd5.*

But Black also has the opportunity to increase the power of one of the knights, and so plays 1...Nbd5!, also an excellent move. Each side has found a good square for the knight, where it is relatively secure, and where it controls many important squares.

Note that Black could have moved either knight to d5, but correctly moved the one farther from the center in order to maximize control of the center. There is an old saying in chess: "A knight on the rim is dim." This means that a knight on the edge of the board is usually not well placed, because it controls fewer squares on the edge than in the center.

Pawns and knights can often work very well together. A knight may be able to occupy a square deep in the heart of your opponent's territory if it is supported by a pawn. Diagram 3 shows an example of this. In the diagrammed position, I had just managed to maneuver the knight to d6, where it stands very well thanks to the pawn on e5. Notice how the knight attacks Black's pawns on f7 and b7. Even though these pawns are protected, the fact that they are attacked still causes Black serious problems, because Black is forced to divert pieces to defend these pawns. Notice the bishop on e8 in particular; it's forced to languish on the edge of the board because it has to protect the pawn on f7. And of course, Black's king is none too happy about having an enemy knight so close to it! In fact, it took me fewer than 10 more moves to win the game from this position, largely thanks to my powerful knight on d6.

Chess players often use the terms *active* and *passive* to describe chess pieces. A piece that attacks another pawn or piece, particularly when it controls many squares, is active, while a piece that lacks mobility and/or is tied down to defending other pieces or pawns is passive. In Diagram 3, the knight on d6 is active, while the bishop on e8 is passive. In general, you want your pieces to be active and your opponent's pieces to be passive!

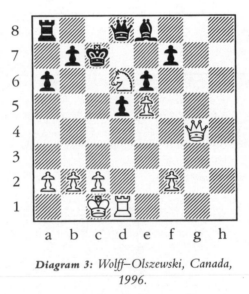

*Diagram 3: Wolff–Olszewski, Canada, 1996.*

A knight often stands very well when it attacks two connected pawns at once, as long as one of the pawns is not itself defended by another pawn. This is illustrated in Diagram 4. If Black's h-pawn were on h7 instead of h6, Black could play 1…g6 to dislodge the knight on f5, and the game would be about equal. But because the pawn is on h6, the knight cannot be chased away so easily, since if Black plays 1…g6?, then White wins a pawn with 2.Nxh6+. Therefore, White has the advantage, because the knight on f5 is very powerful: it both controls important central squares and also puts pressure on Black's king position (see Diagram 4). In fact, if it is White to move, White can immediately exploit the strong position of the knight by playing 1.Qg3!, which threatens checkmate on g7, and to which Black has no adequate response. For example, if 1…Nh5 then 2.Qg4! attacks the knight, when 2…g6 loses the pawn to 3.Nxh6+, and 2…Qg6?? is even worse because of 3.Ne7+. The best defense after 1.Qg3! is 1…g6, but after 2.Nxh6+, White wins a pawn. If Black's h-pawn were on h7, Black could respond to 1.Qg3 with 1…g6 without losing the h-pawn.

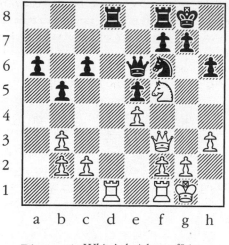

*Diagram 4: White's knight on f5 is very powerful.*

It is important to be able to tell when a knight that *looks* well placed is not. Look at Diagram 5. Is Black's knight actively placed on c6? At first it would appear so, because it attacks squares in the center and is hardly in any danger of being dislodged from its post. But in fact, it is passively placed because White's pawns on c3 and d4 "control" the knight. That is, they attack many of the same squares the knight attacks, and this lessens the knight's effectiveness considerably. White's knight, although it sits on the first rank at the moment, has a much brighter future because it can maneuver quickly to a very strong square.

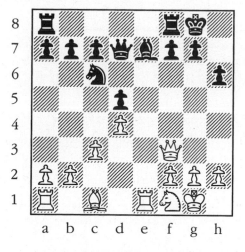

*Diagram 5: White to move.*

In Diagram 6, White has played 1.Ne3! Rfd8—Black must move one or the other rook to d8 to protect the d-pawn—2.Nf5, and suddenly the white knight occupies a terrific square. In fact, working with the bishop on c1, the queen on f3, and the rook on e1, this knight leads an attack against Black's king.

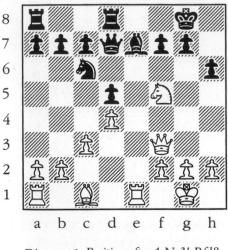

*Diagram 6: Position after 1.Ne3! Rfd8 2.Nf5.*

# The Bishop

In many ways the bishop is the knight's opposite. Whereas the knight moves slowly, the bishop zooms across the board. So the bishop doesn't care so much about getting right up next to the action because it can influence things from far away. But unlike the knight, who hops over pieces, the bishop can be blocked. So the bishop cares very much about its diagonals being clear of pieces or pawns.

In Diagram 7, even though White's bishop is far away from the action on g2, it is extremely active because it controls a long, unobstructed diagonal, along which it attacks Black's pawn on c6. (Notice how badly Black's knight on g6 is placed, because it is forced to defend the pawn on e5 and because it is controlled by the white pawn on g3. Also notice that White's queen, attacking the e5 pawn, is more active than Black's queen, which is stuck defending the e5 pawn.) Black's bishop, on the other hand, is very passive, as it is forced to defend the pawn on c6. Although each bishop has moved only one square from its starting position, White's fianchettoed bishop is much more active.

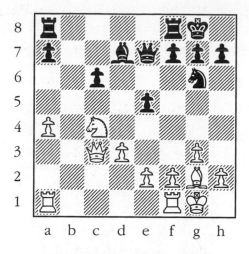

*Diagram 7: White's bishop is more active than Black's bishop.*

A bishop is called *bad* or *good* based on whether its mobility is blocked by having lots of its own pawns on the same color square as the bishop uses (bad) or not (good). As the name suggests, you should avoid the bad bishop and aim for the good bishop. Diagram 8 shows the contrast; Black's bishop is blocked by its own pawns (especially on e6 and c6, but also on b7, d5 and f7), so it is bad. White's bishop, on the other hand, coordinates very well with the pawns (especially on c3, d4 and e5), so it is good. You should not put too many pawns on the same color square as your bishop, as this will tend to make your bishop bad.

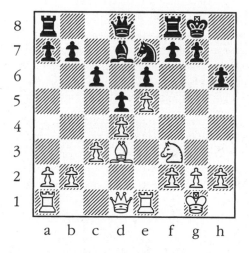

*Diagram 8: White's bishop is good; Black's bishop is bad.*

But having your pawns are on the same color as your bishop doesn't *always* mean your bishop is bad. In Diagram 9, Black's bishop is no longer constrained by its pawns; even though Black's pawns are on the same color squares as the bishop moves on, the bishop is active. You should always be careful about putting pawns on the same color squares as your bishop moves on, but if you do, usually it's better to get the bishop "outside" the pawns so it can be active.

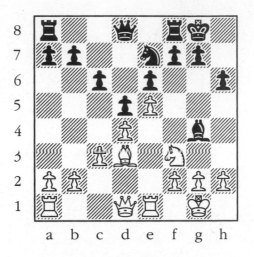

*Diagram 9: Black's bishop is not bad because it's actively placed outside the pawns.*

## Which Is Better: Bishop or Knight?

Many positions are equally suited for the bishop or the knight, but some positions definitely favor one or the other.

Diagram 10 shows an example of a position that clearly favors the knight. The player of the white pieces is Emanuel Lasker, who was world champion for almost 30 years! Lasker knew that Black's bishop, so badly hemmed in by its own pawns, is a weak piece in this position. But Lasker also understood that his own knight was not the strongest piece at the moment, either, because Black's pawns are controlling many of the squares the knight controls. And Lasker also knew that the knight is happiest when it finds a secure square from which it can control lots of central squares. Lasker saw a way to improve the position of his knight.

Lasker played 1.Na4! (see Diagram 11). This violates the rule about not putting the knight on the edge of the board, but it's okay here, because the knight isn't going to stay there long; it's going to c5.

Black's queen is attacked, so it retreats to e7, to which Lasker responds 2.Qd4! (see Diagram 12). This move controls the c5 square, enabling White to play Nc5 next move. The knight will stand very well on this square, and it will be totally secure; the queen protects the knight, and the knight can be further supported by moving the b-pawn to b4 if necessary.

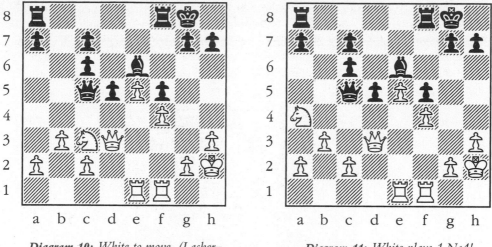

**Diagram 10:** *White to move. (Lasker–Cohn, St. Petersburg, 1909)*

**Diagram 11:** *White plays 1.Na4!*

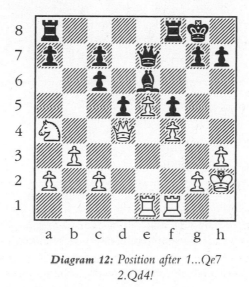

**Diagram 12:** *Position after 1...Qe7 2.Qd4!*

Notice how Black's bishop, restricted to the white squares, is incapable of fighting for control of the black squares. In positions where the knight is stronger than the bishop, it is common for the knight to sit securely on a square of the opposite color of the enemy bishop. Notice also that the center is "closed," meaning there are lots of pawns in the middle of the board blocking the files, ranks, and (most importantly for the bishop) the diagonals. (By contrast, positions where the files, ranks and diagonals are not blocked by pawns are called *open*.) Closed positions often favor the knight over the bishop.

When the center is clear of pawns and the knight lacks any strong squares to settle on, the bishop tends to be the stronger piece. Diagram 13 shows an example of this. Black's bishop has a magnificent diagonal, at the end of which lies a white pawn and the white king: perfect targets. Clearly, the relevant area is the kingside, but White's knight is practically a spectator to any kingside activity. In particular, notice how the black pawns on b6 and c5 control the white knight. Black has a large advantage in this position.

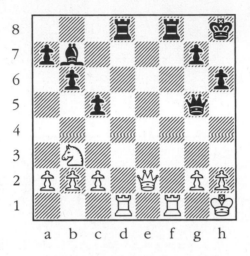

*Diagram 13: Black's bishop is much stronger than White's knight.*

## The Two Bishops

Often, the bishop's power is felt most strongly in the middlegame when it joins forces with its companion bishop. It is frequently an advantage to be the only player with both bishops. Some people go so far as to say that having both bishops is worth an extra half-point of material! (Recall the chart in Chapter 5.) You should remember that everything depends on position; when the position is sufficiently closed, having two bishops may not be an advantage. Still, closed positions often open up over time, so one must never underestimate the potential—or danger—of two bishops.

Diagram 14 shows a typical situation where the two bishops confer an advantage. White may be able to attack Black on either the kingside or the queenside. Black's minor pieces are passive; the knight is on a stable square, but it does not attack any important points in White's position—and it is hard to see how it could do so soon. Black's bishop is good for the defense of the king, but it also attacks nothing in White's position. White's position is preferable, thanks largely to having the two bishops.

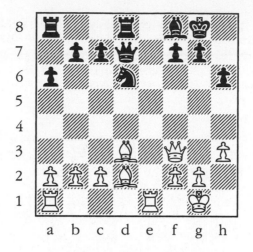

*Diagram 14:* White has the better
position thanks to the two bishops.

But a small change in the position can change the assessment. Suppose that Black's bishop was on e6, rather than f8, as in Diagram 15. In this case, the bishop and the knight coordinate much better together, so Black's position has improved. For example, if it is Black's move, Black might play either 1…Bc4 or 1…Bf5. By exchanging White's strong bishop on d3, Black's knight would become more active, since it was the bishop on d3 that restricted the activity of Black's knight.

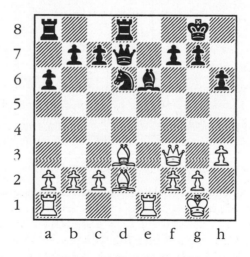

*Diagram 15:* Here the two bishops
are not so large an advantage, because
Black's knight and bishop work well
together.

If an opposing knight is off to the side of the board, the two bishops may be worth a pawn or more. Diagram 16 shows a position where Black has a large advantage, even though White has an extra pawn. Black's bishop on e4 totally dominates the board, preventing the white knight in particular from maneuvering to a position that is closer to the center. (In fact, this position is taken from a game I once played as White, except in that game Black did not have a pawn on g7, so actually, I had two extra pawns. But even with two extra pawns, I could only draw because Black's two bishops were so powerful!)

The two bishops do not always confer an advantage, however. Particularly when one or both bishops is blocked by pawns, the position may favor knights. In Diagram 17, White's bishops are clearly not playing a very active role at the moment. If it were Black's turn to move, Black could play 12…c5! to keep White's black-squared bishop blocked up for the foreseeable future. Since it was White's turn, White stopped this move by playing 12.c5, but even so, Black gained the advantage after 12…dxc5 and won by attacking White's king. Because White's "extra" dark-squared bishop was never able to become active, having two bishops was not an advantage.

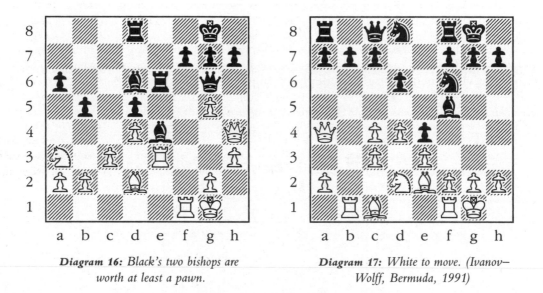

*Diagram 16: Black's two bishops are worth at least a pawn.*

*Diagram 17: White to move. (Ivanov–Wolff, Bermuda, 1991)*

Notice that White has two pawns on the same file in Diagram 17; it's quite common for one side to exchange a bishop for a knight to create this pawn formation, called *doubled pawns*. (You'll learn more about doubled pawns and other pawn formations in Chapter 11.)

Here are some general rules to follow for playing positions where one side has the two bishops.

If you have the two bishops …

+ Don't let the center become blocked with pawns.

+ Create open diagonals, especially for the "extra" bishop you have that your opponent lacks; sometimes it's worth a pawn to do it.

✛ Keep the enemy knights away from wherever you are attacking, and keep them from settling on secure squares in the center.

If you are playing against the two bishops …

✛ Block the center with pawns.

✛ Put most of your pawns on the opposite color of your bishop. This both strengthens your bishop and blunts the power of the enemy bishop, for which you have no counterpart.

✛ Find a strong square for the knight, or at least keep it close to wherever the bishops might attack.

## Opposite-Colored Bishops

You'll see in Chapter 14, that even if one side has the advantage of one or two pawns and the players have opposite-colored bishops, the game may be drawn. (When each side has only one bishop, and each bishop travels on different colored squares, we say that the players have "opposite-colored bishops.") In the endgame, opposite-colored bishops often favor the defender, because it's easier to block passed pawns from advancing. But exactly the reverse is true in the middlegame. In the middlegame, opposite-colored bishops favor the attacker. The reason is that when you use your bishop to attack, your opponent can't use his or her bishop to defend any of the threats your bishop creates, because they all occur on the wrong-colored squares.

Diagram 18 demonstrates an example of the opposite-colored bishops helping the attacker. White threatens 1.Bxf7+, because if Black uses the rook on f8 to capture the bishop, the rook on d8 will be lost. Black can defend only by moving the rook away from d8, but then White still maintains the attack against f7 and also gains the d-file for the rook to boot. White's advantage is so large here that it is probably enough to win. Notice how Black's knight and bishop simply fail to attack anything in White's position, whereas White has fastened on the pawn on f7 with deadly effect.

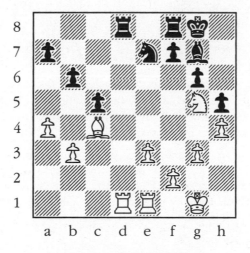

**Diagram 18:** Black to move.

# The Rook

Here are three things to keep in mind about the rook:

+ Rooks crave open files.

+ If you can penetrate with your rook into one of the first three ranks of your opponent's position, it will often be very strong for you.

+ Rooks work very well in pairs; if there is something to attack along a file or a rank, think about putting both rooks there. (Putting two rooks on the same file or rank is called *doubling the rooks*.)

We can continue the analysis from Diagram 18 to show the first two principles. Diagram 19 shows the position after Black plays 1...Rxd1 and White recaptures with 2.Rxd1. (Black could also try to defend by moving the rook to another square, e.g. by playing 1...Rde8, but then White would intensify the attack with 2.Rd7.) Now White's rook is clearly much more active than its counterpart on f8, which is forced to defend the pawn on f7. In addition, White threatens to play 3.Rd7, which will attack the knight on e7 and the pawn on a7 as well as put pressure on the pawn on f7. How can Black defend?

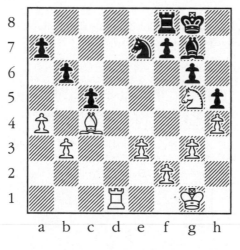

*Diagram 19: Position after 1...Rxd1 2.Rxd1.*

Actually, I don't think Black has any adequate defense. Diagrams 20, 21, and 22 show one possible sequence of moves to illustrate some of the themes of this position. Black tries to defend the knight with the bishop by playing 2...Bf6, and White attacks the bishop with 3.Ne4 (see Diagram 20). Black defends the bishop with the king by playing 3...Kg7, and White attacks the a-pawn with 4.Rd7 (see Diagram 21). If Black defends the pawn by playing 4...a5, then White forks the bishop on f6 and the pawn on b6 along the sixth rank by playing 5.Rd6 (see Diagram 22). White will win the pawn on b6 and the attack will only continue to intensify. (Alternatively, if Black defended the pawn by playing 4...Nc8, then 5.Ba6 is very strong and if 4...Nc6?? then 5.Rd6 wins material by forking the knight and bishop.)

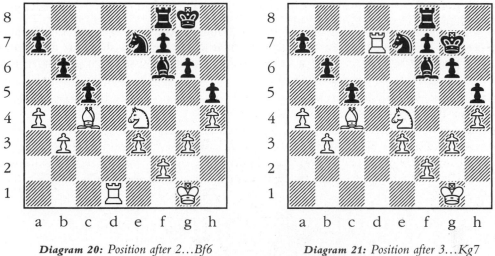

Diagram 20: Position after 2...Bf6 3.Ne4.

Diagram 21: Position after 3...Kg7 4.Rd7.

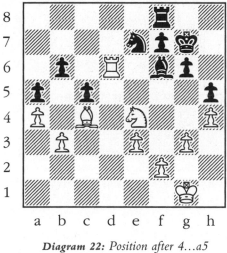

Diagram 22: Position after 4...a5 5.Rd6.

Did you notice in Diagrams 18 through 22 how powerful it was to push the rook down to the next-to-last rank? This is a common idea. And it can be even more effective if you can put both rooks on the next-to-last rank! Rooks that are doubled on the next-to-last rank are sometimes called *greedy pigs*, because they "eat" (capture) everything in their path!

Here is one last (and very important) trick to learn about making your rooks effective. Moving a rook to an already open file is not the only way to activate the rook along a file; you can also open the file by either pushing the pawn in front of the rook or making a capture with the pawn in front of the rook. You'll read more about this in Chapter 11, but here's one example to show you what I mean. This is another position from the Dragon Variation of the Sicilian Defense (which you learned about in Chapter 9). It is White's turn to move in Diagram 23. What is the best way for White to get the rook on h1 into the action?

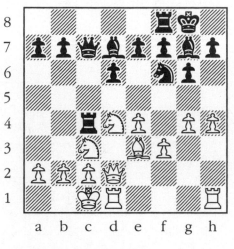

**Diagram 23:** *White to move.*

White plays 1.h5! as shown in Diagram 24, with the intention of playing hxg6 soon. This will open the h-file and facilitate an attack against the black king. (In fact, this tactic of pushing the h-pawn in order to open the h-file is one of the most dangerous ways of attacking a king that has castled into a fianchettoed bishop's position.) The open h-file will help White's attack enormously, and so it is a very effective plan. (Notice that if Black plays 1...gxh5, White still opens the h-file with 2.g5! Ne8 3.Qh2! followed by 4.Qxh5.) But Black may have one small compensation: if Black recaptures the pawn on g6 by playing ...fxg6, the f-file will open up to activate Black's rook on f8.

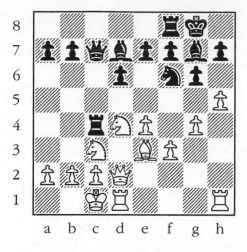

*Diagram 24: White plays 1.h5.*

# The Queen

Because the queen is so valuable, you have to be a little careful about how you use it. Just as in the opening, if you put the queen in the center of the board during the middlegame, it may find itself harassed by enemy pawns, minor pieces, or rooks.

The queen's power makes it difficult to define general principles for its use. Because it is so powerful, it can serve almost any purpose. The best way to use the queen is to put it on a flexible square, where it is out of harm's way, but also capable of quickly moving to wherever it may be useful. It is often a great advantage if the queen can safely occupy a central square. If you can establish it in the center without it coming under fire, it will greatly increase your control of the rest of the board because it can attack squares in all directions.

One important thing to keep in mind is that because the queen is so powerful, it's often worth a lot to try to trap it. If you send the queen into the middle of your opponent's position, be careful that you don't allow your opponent to surround it; and if your opponent sends his or her queen into your position, look for a way to cut off its escape (and then its head)!

Diagrams 25 through 30 show one example of how dangerous it can be to do a solitary raid with the queen. (The position comes from the opening, but the same principles apply here as in the middlegame.) Diagram 25 shows a position from another variation of the Sicilian Defense called the *Najdorf Variation*, in which it is Black's turn to play his seventh move. (The position arises after 1.e4 c5 2.Nf3 d6 3.d4 cxd4 4.Nxd4 Nf6 5.Nc3 a6 6.Bg5 e6 7.f4.) Black has several moves here; one of the most aggressive is to play 7...Qb6, as shown in Diagram 26.

Black clearly intends to capture the b-pawn. This is called the *Poisoned Pawn Variation* because of the danger to the queen of capturing this pawn. I should point out that this opening is in fact quite good for Black. Two former world champions made it a crucial part of their opening repertoires: Bobby Fischer and Garry Kasparov. But please bear in mind that they only played this highly risky and aggressive move because they convinced themselves after many, many hours of analysis that it is good for Black. Without preparation, you should not play so recklessly with the queen in the opening!

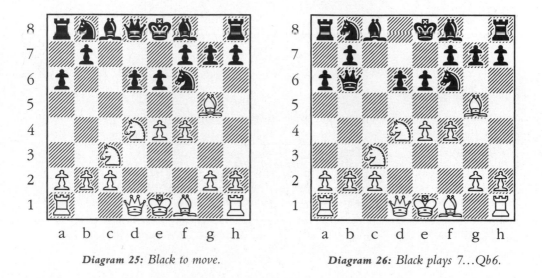

*Diagram 25: Black to move.*    *Diagram 26: Black plays 7...Qb6.*

The most common response for White is to gambit the pawn with 8.Qd2 Qxb2, as shown in Diagram 27. Then one plan for White is to protect the rook on a1 and simultaneously shut the queen in by playing 9.Nb3, as shown in Diagram 28.

Black has several moves here, the best perhaps being 9...Qa3. But above all, Black must look for White's threats and anticipate the danger to the queen. When your queen only has one square to run to in case it is attacked, an alarm should go off in your mind that says: *"Warning! Queen in danger of being trapped!"*

Let's suppose Black does not see White's idea (do you see it?), and plays the simple developing move 9...Be7 (see Diagram 29). As a general principle, this move is impeccable; Black wants to develop the bishop and castle quickly. But the general principle in this case is much less important than the problem of making sure the queen has a way back to safety.

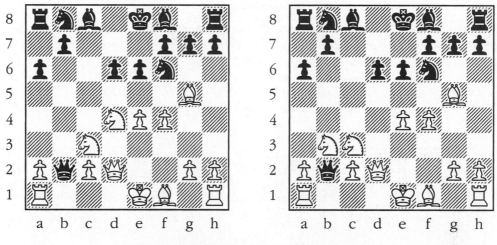

*Diagram 27:* Position after 8.Qd2 Qxb2.      *Diagram 28:* White plays 9.Nb3.

*Diagram 29:* Black plays 9...Be7.

Black pays the price in Diagram 30, when White plays 10.a3! Too late, Black realizes that White threatens to win the queen with either 11.Ra2 or 11.Nd1, and it will cost Black at least a piece to save the queen.

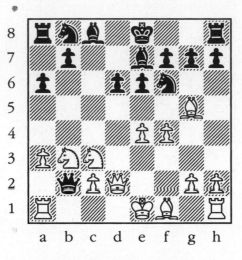

**Diagram 30:** *White plays 10.a3.*

# Exercises

---

You may find the upcoming exercises more difficult than the ones in previous chapters. Try your best to solve them and then study the answers. My goal in giving you harder exercises is to teach you more than I could explain in the chapter.

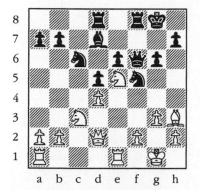

**Exercise 1:** *White to move (Wolff–Wen, Canada, 1996). Which minor pieces should White exchange in the next two moves? How would you then evaluate the position?*

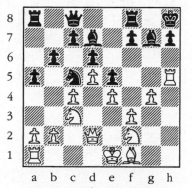

**Exercise 2:** *White to move (Nimzovich–Tartakower, Germany, 1929). The two players in this game were both among the finest of their day. White now played 17.Nh1. Why did White play this move?*

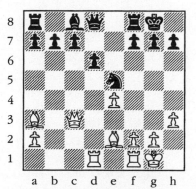

**Exercise 3:** *Black to move (Morphy–Amateur, New Orleans, 1858). Morphy played this game blindfolded, while playing five other blindfold games. His opponent had to decide between 15...f6 or 15...f5. One is correct; the other (which was played) is a terrible mistake. Which is the better move, and why?*

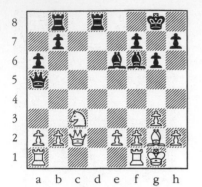

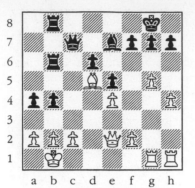

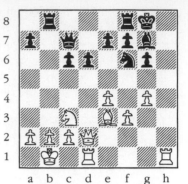

**Exercise 4:** *Black to move (Dzindzichashvili–Ehlvest, New York, 1990). Do the two bishops give Black enough compensation for his pawn deficit? What move would you play for Black, and what is the idea behind it?*

**Exercise 5:** *White to move. Can White use the opposite-colored bishops to advantage? Suggest a way for White to play. (Hint: try to identify Black's weakest point and then figure out a good way to attack it.)*

**Exercise 6:** *White to move. How can White use the open h-file to attack Black's king? (Hint: find a way to exchange the piece that is best defending Black's king from attack along the file, and then combine the power of the queen and the rook.)*

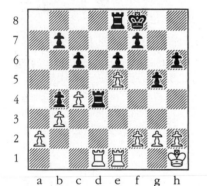

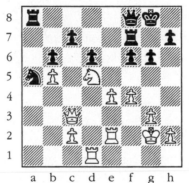

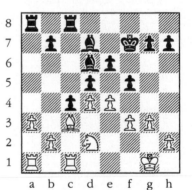

**Exercise 7:** *Black to move. How should Black use the open d-file to advantage? Find Black's best move, and suggest how the game might continue.*

**Exercise 8:** *White to move. Explain why White stands better in this position. Suggest a way that White could press the advantage by exposing the black king to attack. (The details are difficult here, so don't worry too much about them. I want you to find the best idea and try to analyze the resulting position the best you can.)*

**Exercise 9:** *White to move (Janowski–Capablanca, New York, 1916). This is a famous game. Janowski played 1.e5 and lost a long endgame. Grandmaster Alex Yermolinsky suggests 1.exf5 exf5 2.f4 as an improvement. What is the idea behind Yermolinsky's suggestion? (Hint: White wants to activate a piece.)*

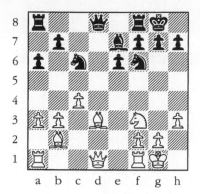

**Exercise 10:** *Black to move. Who has the advantage in this position, and why? Suggest a plan for Black.*

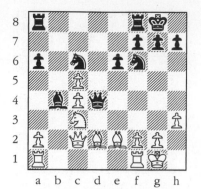

**Exercise 11:** *Black to move (Oll–Anand, Biel, 1992). Who has the advantage in this position, and why? Suggest a plan for Black.*

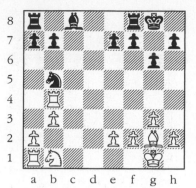

**Exercise 12:** *Black to move (Villamayor–Gallagher, Calcutta, 2001). Black's knight is attacked, but Black found a much stronger move than defending or moving the knight. What did he play?*

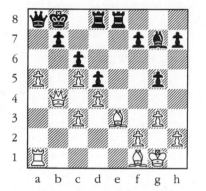

**Exercise 13:** *Black to move (Anand–Hubner, Germany, 1992). Black has the advantage of the exchange, but Black's queen is passive, and Black's king is exposed. Does White have enough compensation for the material? Why or why not?*

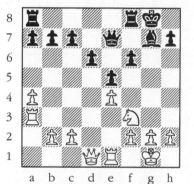

**Exercise 14:** *White to move. How can White exploit Black's bad bishop? Suggest a plan for White that moves the knight to a stronger square.*

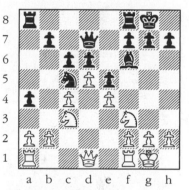

**Exercise 15:** *Black to move. Black's bishop is passive, and it is a bad bishop because it is trapped behind the e5 and d6 pawns. Can you suggest a way for Black to make this bishop more active?*

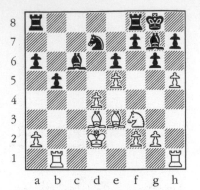

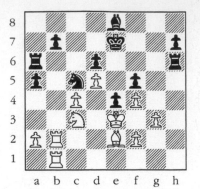

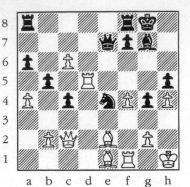

**Exercise 16:** *White to move (AlphaZero–Stockfish 8, London, 2018). This was a game between the two strongest chess computers in the world. (You can learn more about these computers in Chapter 16.) White played 19.h6 here. What is the idea of this move? Analyze this position for yourself, then turn to Appendix B to see how AlphaZero exploited Black's passive bishop.*

**Exercise 17:** *White to move (Carlsen–Vlassov, St. Petersburg, 2018). World Champion Magnus Carlsen played a surprising sacrifice here: 28.Rxb7+ Nxb7 29.Rxb7+. What do you think was the idea? Analyze how the game could continue.*

**Exercise 18:** *Black to move (Aronian–Anand, Mexico City, 2007). White is attacking the b5 and h5 pawns. White probably expected Black to defend the h5 pawn with tempo (in a single turn) by playing the knight to f6. Instead, Black played 26...Qe6! What was Black's idea after White captured the pawn on h5?*

# Chapter 11

# Pawn Shop

In Chapter 10, we looked at the pieces. Now it's time to look specifically at the pawns. Even though the pawn is the least powerful part of your chess army, in some ways it is the most significant. Many times, the way the pawns are arranged determines your best plan, and many times your best plan is to change the way the pawns are arranged! We'll soon get into the specifics of what you should do with different pawn structures. (A *pawn structure* is how chess players refer to the way the pawns are arranged.) First, let's understand what makes the pawns so important.

# "The Pawns Are the Soul of Chess"

There are three reasons why the pawns are especially important:

+ Because there are so many pawns and because they are worth so much less than the pieces, the position of the pawns limits and determines how the pieces can move. Since a piece normally cannot allow itself to be captured by a pawn, the squares that the pawns control are off limits to the pieces. That means it's important to use your pawns to control the right squares.

+ Because they move forward but capture diagonally, pawns often block each other. When this happens, they become a kind of fixed feature of the position, and the pieces have to move around the pawns. Not only do the pawns limit and determine how the pieces can move by what squares they control, they also do so by what squares they're on.

+ Because pawns only move forward and never move backward, each pawn move is a commitment. Put a piece on a bad square and you can still reposition it later. Put a pawn on a bad square and you may be stuck with it for the whole game! So you have to be extra careful to handle your pawns well.

Keep these three things in mind as you read the rest of this chapter!

# Chain Gangs

André Philidor, a Frenchman and the strongest chess player of the eighteenth century, famously wrote the above quote, "The pawn is the soul of chess." One of Philidor's contemporaries was the great philosopher Jean-Jacques Rousseau, who wrote that people are born free, yet are found everywhere in chains. The opposite is true of pawns. Pawns are born in a chain stretching from one side of the board to the other, but as they advance, they become separated. When they do so, they often form little groups. Let's take a look at some of the common ways pawns form groups.

## Side by Side Is Strongest

Generally speaking, pawns are best placed when they are two, or sometimes three, abreast. When they are in this formation, all the squares they control are lined up on the same rank, which maximizes their effectiveness. When two pawns are side by side they are known as a *pawn duo*; an example is shown in Diagram 1. This is a standard position from an opening called the *Pirc Defense*. Black does not stand too badly; Black has developed about as well as White and has good enough squares on which to develop the rest of the minor pieces. But most grandmasters agree that White has a small advantage in this position, thanks mainly to the powerful pawn duo on e4 and d4, which control the center squares c5, d5, e5 and f5 very well. In fact, this pawn duo is so powerful that it is essential for Black to challenge it by advancing one of the pawns to the fifth rank after proper preparations: the d-pawn to d5 (rarely), the c-pawn to c5 (sometimes), or the e-pawn to e5 (commonly).

Another advantage of the pawn duo is that since each pawn controls the square in front of its neighbor, each pawn supports the other's possible advance. This gives the pawns maximum dynamic potential. Diagram 2 shows a position we've already seen in Chapter 9, Diagram 24. White has just played 10.f4, which supports both f5 and e5. For example, if Black plays 10…d5, the support of the f-pawn makes 11.e5 strong. And if Black does nothing to stop it, on the next turn White might advance the f-pawn to f5 and chase Black's white-squared bishop away from the center. The move 10.f4 has increased the dynamic potential of White's position, thanks to the creation of the pawn duo on e4 and f4.

When a pawn duo has few or no pawns opposing it, the duo can be terribly strong because each pawn supports the other's potential advance. Look for an example of this feature in the exercises at the end of this chapter.

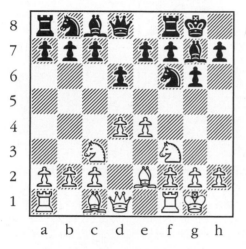

*Diagram 1: White's pawn duo on e4 and d4 is strong.*

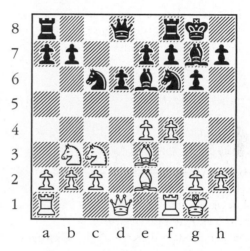

*Diagram 2: White's pawn duo on e4 and f4 generates dynamic potential in the center.*

## Forward Pawns and Backward Pawns

Often, one pawn in a pawn duo will march forward, at which point the pawns no longer harmoniously control all the squares of both colors in front of them. Instead, the forward pawn controls two squares of one color, and the backward pawn controls two squares of the same color—including the square on which the forward pawn sits. This pawn formation has the potential to be either strong or weak, depending upon the situation.

An example is shown in Diagram 3, from my game against the Armenian grandmaster Smbat Lputian. White's forward pawn controls two squares deep in Black's position: d6 and f6. The f6 square is close to Black's king, and that—plus the fact that White controls many more squares on the kingside— indicates that White's correct strategy is to attack on the kingside. Black's forward pawn on d5 controls the squares e4 and c4. Black's pieces are unable to take advantage of this pawn's control of e4, but they are well placed to control squares on the queenside. One strategy that suggests itself to Black is to attack on the queenside. Another strategy is for Black to attack White's strong pawn on e5 (and at the same time fight for control of the f6 square) by advancing the f-pawn to f6. In fact, my opponent combined both ideas, gained the upper hand, and won the game.

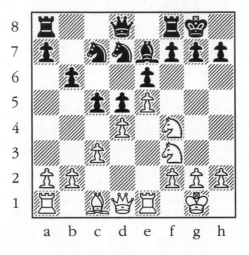

*Diagram 3: (Wolff–Lputian, Holland, 1993).*

Let's take a closer look at the pawn structure in Diagram 3. The e6 pawn is defended by the f7 pawn, and the f7 pawn is defended by the king. So Black's pawns are all well defended. White's pawn on d4 is defended by the pawn on c3, which is in turn defended by the pawn on b2 At first, it may seem like White's pawns are just as well defended as Black's. But Black could play …cxd4, and if White recaptures with the pawn, this will leave the d4 pawn undefended by another pawn. In the middlegame, with all the pieces left on the board, this pawn is usually not in any danger. But now let's imagine a scenario like that in Diagram 4.

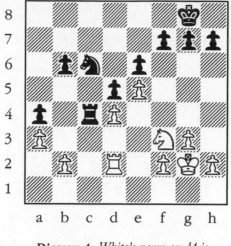

*Diagram 4: White's pawn on d4 is weak.*

Now the d4 pawn is under heavy fire from Black's pieces; White's rook and knight are passive because they are forced to defend the pawn, whereas Black's pieces are active, so only Black has any chance to win this position. One of the dangers for the less advanced pawn in a pawn chain is that it can become weak if it loses support from its fellow pawns.

While White's pawn structure in Diagram 3 has the potential to be more vulnerable than Black's, it confers other advantages to White: specifically, White has more space for the pieces to operate in, and Black's king may be more vulnerable due to the influence of the e5 pawn.

Chess author Jeremy Silman has suggested a useful rule of thumb for how to form plans based on pawn structure. He suggests that you should always consider the possibility of attacking on the side of the chess board where your pawn chain is "pointing." For example, in Diagram 3, White's pawn chain from b2 to e5 points to the kingside, so White should think about attacking there. And since Black's pawn chain from f7 to d5 points to the queenside, Black should think about attacking on that side of the board.

When judging the worth of different pawn chains, a crucial consideration is how easily one can advance the less advanced pawn to create a pawn duo again (see Diagram 5). Even though it's Black's move in Diagram 5, Black stands poorly because White is poised to advance the e-pawn, whereas Black's c-pawn and d-pawn are blocked by White's pieces. When White advances the e-pawn, Black's pieces will be pushed back to the first few ranks. Not only will White's pawns on e5 and d5 be extremely strong, but their strongly supported forward position will strengthen White's pieces behind them. (Notice that if it were White's move, 1.e5 would win material immediately because Black's knight would have nowhere to go.)

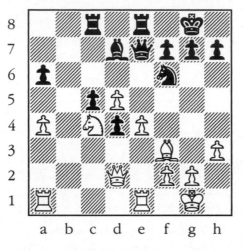

*Diagram 5: Black to move.*

Chess players sometimes use the phrase "backward pawn" to describe the specific case where (1) the less advanced pawn in a pawn duo can't be defended by another pawn, (2) the square in front of the less advanced pawn is not occupied by an opposing pawn, and (3) the less advanced pawn can't advance forward safely. An example of this is shown in Diagram 6. Notice how much of a liability the backward d6 pawn is; it can't be defended by another pawn, so it must be defended by pieces, which makes those pieces passive. Furthermore, Black has almost no hope of safely advancing the pawn to d5 to exchange it for White's e4 pawn, so it will remain a liability for a long time. Finally, because Black's e-pawn has advanced to e5, the square in front of the backward pawn (d5) lacks pawn protection and is therefore weak. White's knight could be very well placed at some point on this square, and it will always be difficult for Black to chase it away.

Can you see why chess players would call the pawn on d6 in Diagram 6 backward? It's a permanent weakness that will need protecting, and it can't do anything to control the square in front of it.

The conclusion you might draw from this example is that it is always bad to have a backward pawn. But things are not so simple. Compare Diagram 6 to Diagram 7. (Diagram 7 is a well-known position from the Najdorf Variation of the Sicilian Defense.) Black's position here is much better than in Diagram 6, for several reasons:

✛ Black's d-pawn is well defended by the bishop on e7, and although defending the d-pawn makes the bishop passive, it's not too serious because the bishop is usefully placed on e7 to defend the kingside.

✛ Black's minor pieces have enough influence over the d5 square to prevent White from permanently occupying it with a piece. (See Chapter 13 for more explanation about this factor.)

✛ Black's pawn on e5 helps to control White's knight on b3, which is a passive piece.

✛ Black's queen and rook are actively placed along the c-file.

For these reasons, the position in Diagram 7 offers approximately equal chances for both sides, in spite of Black's backward d6 pawn.

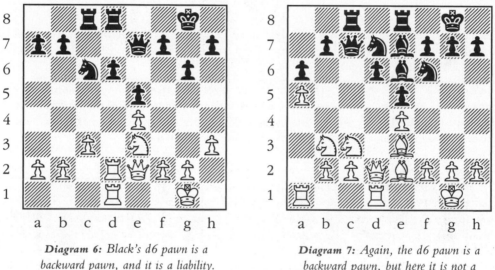

*Diagram 6: Black's d6 pawn is a backward pawn, and it is a liability.*

*Diagram 7: Again, the d6 pawn is a backward pawn, but here it is not a liability.*

The square in front of the backward pawn is almost always important. If the square is not occupied by an opposing pawn, then it is usually in each player's interest to control that square. The side with the backward pawn often wants to advance the pawn, while the side playing against the backward pawn generally wants to stop that from happening.

The bottom line: when one pawn advances and leaves the other behind, there are pluses and minuses. Unlike the pawn duo (side by side), it is not always a strong formation. Whom it favors, and why, depends on the particulars of the position.

# When One Pawn Holds Two

Notice in Diagrams 6 and 7 that White's e-pawn blocks Black's e-pawn from advancing, and it also stops Black's d-pawn from advancing because it controls the square in front of it. In general, it is good for you to have one pawn serve double duty like this, because it allows you to use your other pawns to greater effect.

In Diagrams 6 and 7, the advantage of the e-pawn "holding" two pawns is not so great, because White can't really use the other pawns to strong effect. (This is especially true in Diagram 7; because White's c-pawn is blocked by the knight on c3, it plays little part in the center. But notice that in Diagram 7, White's a-pawn also holds two pawns: this serves White well, as it gives White better control of the queenside.)

Diagrams 8 and 9 show a situation where "one pawn holding two" gives one side a large advantage. Consider Diagram 8. White's best plan is to push the e-pawn. Not only will this give White strong control of the center, it will also establish one pawn duo (e4 and f4), and create the potential to establish another, even stronger duo (d5 and e5). Another advantage of pushing the e-pawn is that it would enable White to push the f-pawn, which would threaten to expose Black's king and allow White to bring the bishop to f4. The bishop on f4 together with the strong knight on c4 could then attack Black's weak d-pawn.

White has the advantage, and 1.e4 is not a bad move. But pushing the e-pawn right away ignores Black's plan, which is to push the b-pawn to b5 and establish a pawn duo (c5 and b5), kicking White's knight away from its strong post.

The best move is 1.a5! as shown in Diagram 9. This move stops Black from establishing the pawn duo (because 1...b5? now loses a pawn to 2.axb6 en passant), and secures the knight's square at c4. Now that White's a-pawn holds Black's a-pawn and b-pawn, White practically has an extra pawn, which White will use to great effect on the next move by advancing the e-pawn to e4.

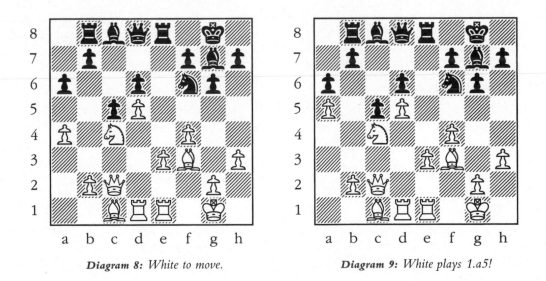

*Diagram 8: White to move.*   *Diagram 9: White plays 1.a5!*

## Some Pawns Are Islands

Each group of pawns separated by a file that has no pawns of the same color is called a *pawn island*. Generally, you want all your pawns working side by side, so only having one group of pawns is ideal. Don't take this to an extreme, but a useful principle is to have as few pawn islands as possible.

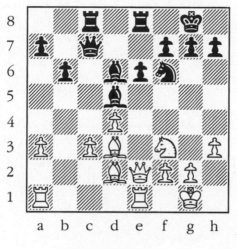

*Diagram 10: Black to move.*

Diagram 10 gives an example of the danger of having too many pawn islands. Black's pawn structure is free of any weaknesses, but White's pawns on a3 and c3 are weak. (If White had a pawn on b2 instead of a3, there would be nothing wrong with White's position.) However, White controls more squares on the kingside, so Black must be careful not to allow White to attack him there. Black's best move is 1…Bc4!, which does three things:  First, forces the exchange of a piece that could potentially attack Black's king. Second, it makes sure that the c-pawn cannot advance to c4 to establish a pawn duo. And third, it clears the d5 square for the knight, where it can attack the c3 pawn.

## The Isolated Pawn

When there are no pawns of the same color on either of the files next to it, we say that the pawn is "isolated." (It may be useful to think of an isolated pawn as a more extreme case of a backward pawn.)

The isolated pawn has the potential to be a serious weakness for two reasons. First, it must be defended by pieces, which may not be possible (and even if the pawn can be defended, the pieces defending it may be tied down and rendered passive.) Second, the side with the isolated pawn can't control the squares in front of it with pawns, so the opponent can use those squares more easily.

Diagrams 11 and 12 each present an example of the dangers of an isolated pawn. In Diagram 11, the isolated pawn is weak and cannot be defended. In Diagram 12, the squares in front of the isolated pawn cannot be controlled by any pawns, so the opponent's knight has settled on a powerful square where it will be difficult to dislodge.

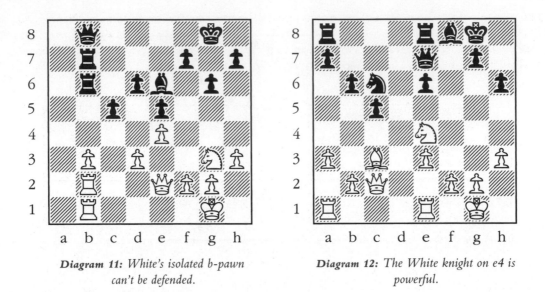

**Diagram 11:** *White's isolated b-pawn can't be defended.*

**Diagram 12:** *The White knight on e4 is powerful.*

However, the isolated pawn isn't always a bad thing. Diagrams 1 and 2 of Chapter 10 show a position where one side has the isolated pawn and the position offers roughly equal chances to both players. Exercise 7 of Chapter 8 shows a position where the isolated pawn confers an advantage because it yields such good control of the center. Here are a few important rules of thumb to keep in mind for playing with and against an isolated pawn, especially when it is a center pawn:

+ The isolated pawn usually wants to advance, both to gain space and to be exchanged for another pawn. Therefore, it's crucial for both players to control the square directly in front of the isolated pawn.

+ The side with the isolated pawn wants to keep as many pieces as possible on the board, because with more pieces, the extra space and central control can be used to generate an attack somewhere.

+ The side playing against the isolated pawn wants to exchange pieces because this will lessen any possible attack, whereupon the weakness of the isolated pawn will become more important.

# Double the Pleasure

Sometimes when a pawn makes a capture, you can get two pawns on the same file. Such pawns are called *doubled pawns*. Sometimes doubled pawns are a weakness, sometimes they're not so bad, and in other cases they can even be advantageous.

The worst doubled pawns are isolated pawns on an open file, like Black's c-pawns in Diagram 13. These miserable creatures are easy targets for White. They are easy to attack along the open file, and they are hard to defend because there's no way to protect one of them with a pawn. Avoid these doubled pawns unless you have a very good reason.

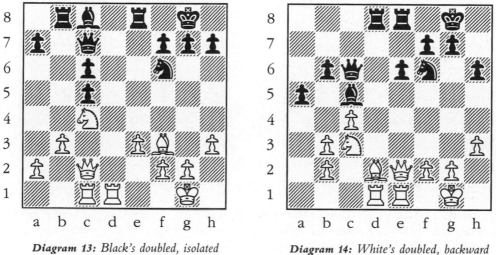

Diagram 13: Black's doubled, isolated        Diagram 14: White's doubled, backward
c-pawns are very weak.                          b-pawns are not good.

It's also bad to have doubled pawns that are fixed as backward pawns, such as White's b-pawns held by Black's a-pawn in Diagram 14. The problem with doubled, backward pawns is that the second backward pawn (in Diagram 14 the b2-pawn) usually contributes very little. It doesn't protect any adjacent pawn as the b3-pawn does, and it can't advance because it's got a pawn in front of it. The only time when the extra doubled pawn does anything useful is when the squares it controls happen to be important for some reason, but that's usually a lucky accident.

When doubled pawns create more pawn islands, they're often a liability, as in Diagram 15. In this case, the extra pawn island caused by the doubled f-pawns is significant because it weakens the squares around Black's king. Kevin Spraggett, a Canadian grandmaster who was Black in this game, has compensated by placing the bishops in front of the king. But this has the drawbacks of making the black-squared bishop passive and allowing White to gain the two bishops (by capturing the white-squared bishop) at any time. In this case, the knight on h4 is well placed, even though it is on the edge of the board, because it menaces the bishop *and* the king. I was at the tournament where this game was played, and I watched Michael Adams, a then-young British grandmaster playing White, win very nicely.

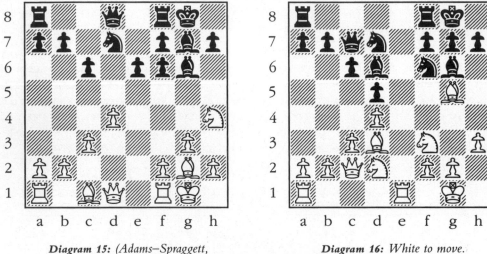

Diagram 15: (Adams–Spraggett, Hastings, 1989).

Diagram 16: White to move.

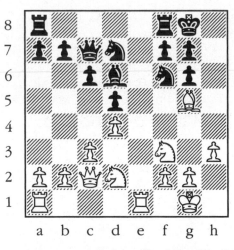

Diagram 17: Position after 1.Bxg6 hxg6.

So when are doubled pawns not bad? They're often okay when they're not isolated, they're not backward, and they don't make extra pawn islands. Diagrams 16 and 17 show an example of this. In Diagram 16, White sees an opportunity to double Black's pawns, as shown in Diagram 17 with 1.Bxg6 hxg6. But the pawn recapture doesn't create any more pawn islands or any new backward pawns, so it doesn't do much damage to Black's pawn structure.

There is a slight cost to the doubled pawns: the g5 square is weakened because Black has lost the possibility of controlling it by pushing the h-pawn to h6. On the other hand, Black has gained control of the f5 square, which compensates for that slight weakening. Here the doubled pawns are acceptable.

Notice that in Diagram 17 Black recaptured with the h-pawn and not with the f-pawn. This illustrates an important rule of thumb: when you have a choice of making a capture with one of two pawns, you should generally capture toward the center. While there are plenty of exceptions to this rule, depending on the specific features of the position, it is still a useful rule of thumb to remember.

There are two typical cases where doubled pawns are good: when doubling your pawns increases your control of the center, and when doubling your pawns opens a file or diagonal (usually a file) that you can use to your advantage. Diagrams 18 and 19 show an example of each. In Diagram 18, White's doubled pawns are otherwise healthy (not isolated, not backward, and not creating extra pawn islands), and the pawn on b4 helps White control the important square c5. (Notice that this formation of doubled pawns is extremely sturdy: the b4 pawn is protected by the c3 pawn, which in turn is protected by the b2 pawn, making it very hard for Black to attack.) These doubled pawns are good for White.

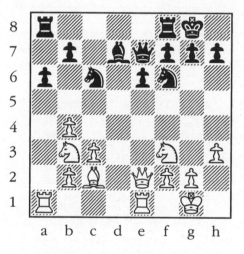

*Diagram 18: The doubled pawns are good for White.*

In Diagram 19, Black's position is littered with doubled pawns, but here they serve Black well because Black has used both the open files the doubled pawns have yielded (the d-file and the g-file) to attack White's position. In particular, the open g-file is contributing to White's king coming under heavy fire, and even if it's White's turn to move, I doubt White can survive. (Black threatens 1…Nf4, after which a catastrophe will occur on d3, g2, and h3.) Notice here that the doubled pawns are all controlling important squares: d4, e5, and e6. In this case, the doubled pawns are good for Black because the piece activity they generate far outweighs the structural weakness they constitute.

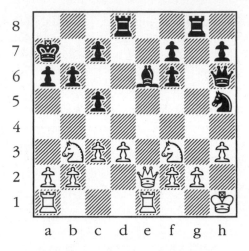

*Diagram 19: The doubled pawns open important files (the d-file and the g-file) for Black.*

However, while doubled pawns are sometimes acceptable or even strong, it is very rare for tripled pawns (three pawns on the same file) to be okay. Tripled pawns are almost comically weak and should be avoided unless you have a very, very good reason otherwise!

# Pawns: What Are They Good For?

Unlike the song about war, the answer for pawns is not "absolutely nothing!" There are lots of ways to use pawns, and I can't possibly show you all of them. In the remainder of this chapter we will review some of their most important uses. Pay close attention in your games and the games you study to look for other ways to use pawns effectively.

## Open Sesame!

Pawns are very useful for prying open a file or a diagonal. I've shown you one common way this is done in Diagrams 23 and 24 in Chapter 10, but there are many other ways to open either a file or a diagonal.

Diagrams 20 through 22 show White opening both a file and a diagonal with the same pawn move. If White's h-pawn were moved back one square, and Black's h-pawn were moved up one square (so that White's h-pawn were on h4 and Black's h-pawn were on h5), then Black's king would be much safer. White would have to sacrifice material in order to open any files or diagonals to the king. But with the pawns where they are, 1.g4! is very strong. Since Black's f-pawn is attacked several times, Black must play 1...fxg4 2.Qxg4, when White has a powerful attack with all the pieces aimed against the king.

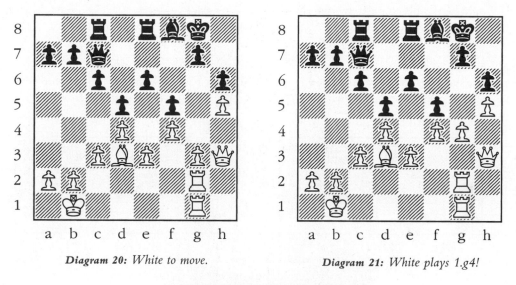

*Diagram 20: White to move.*       *Diagram 21: White plays 1.g4!*

*Diagram 22: Position after 1...fxg4*
*2.Qxg4.*

# Reconstructive Surgery

Another important way to use your pawns is to advance one pawn to exchange it for one of your opponent's pawns. That way you can change the pawn structure to get rid of some weakness in your position. This is different from the last case because the reason for exchanging pawns in that case was to open a file or a diagonal, whereas here the idea is more focused on changing the pawn structure itself.

In Diagram 23, White has backward doubled pawns. If Black could play 1...b5!, then White's bishop on b3 would be cut off completely from the center and kingside, reducing the bishop to complete passivity. If Black could play 1...b5, White would practically have to play without the use of the white-squared bishop.

Clearly, White must not allow this to happen, and the way to stop it is to play 1.c4! (see Diagram 24) to exchange one of the backward doubled pawns for Black's d-pawn. With the weak pawn ready to be exchanged and her bishop back in action, White's chances will be no worse than Black's.

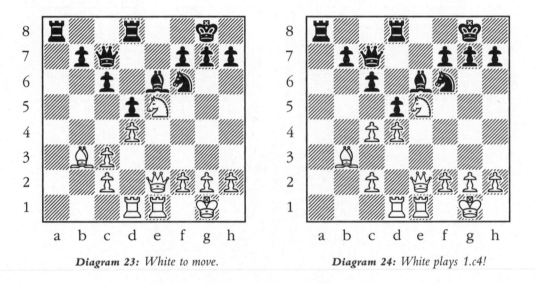

*Diagram 23: White to move.*      *Diagram 24: White plays 1.c4!*

In Diagram 25, Black has the advantage both because White's doubled, isolated pawns on c3 and c4 are weak and because the bishop on e2 is bad. Black has several good moves, and maybe 1...Qc7 is the best, since 2.Bxa7?? would lose the bishop after 2...b6! 3.Qa4 Ra8.

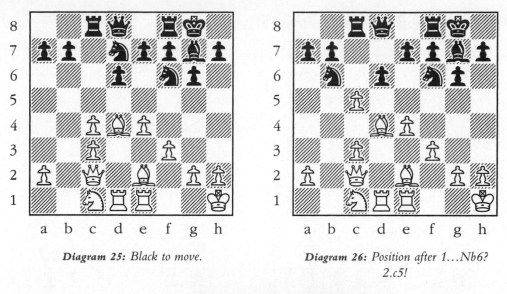

Diagram 25: Black to move.

Diagram 26: Position after 1...Nb6?
2.c5!

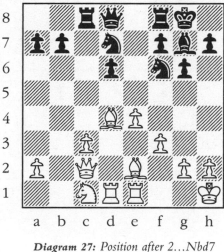

Diagram 27: Position after 2...Nbd7
3.cxd6 exd6

Black is too eager to attack the weak c4 pawn and pays a price: After 1...Nb6? White plays 2.c5! (see Diagram 26). Black cannot capture the pawn because White wins material with a discovered attack (2...dxc5?? 3.Bxf6!), so Black retreats the knight back to d7. (It doesn't help to put the knight on the awful a8 square with 2...Na8, because after 3.cxd6, if Black tries to prevent the pawn structure from being weakened with 3...Qxd6??, then White forks Black's queen and knight with 4.e5.)

After 2...Nbd7, White plays 3.cxd6 exd6, reaching the position in Diagram 27. Now each side has the same number of pawn islands. White's two bishops and better control of the center give her the advantage.

# Damaging Your Opponent's Pawn Structure

The example in Diagrams 25 through 27 illustrates the very important principle that when you attack a weak pawn, you must make sure it can't move forward with strong effect. By advancing the pawn, not only did White get rid of a weak pawn, White also damaged Black's pawn structure.

This brings up another important idea, which is that sometimes the opportunity will arise to use one of your pawns as an offensive weapon to damage your opponent's pawns, e.g. by making one of them isolated or by splitting them into more pawn islands. When you can do this without cost to your own pawn structure, it is often a good idea.

Diagrams 28 and 29 show an example of this. In Diagram 28, neither side has any pawn weaknesses. However, White has the opportunity to create pawn weaknesses in Black's position with 1.b5!, as shown in Diagram 29.

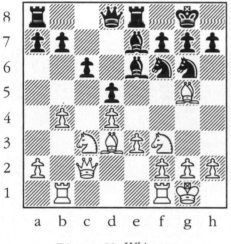
*Diagram 28: White to move.*

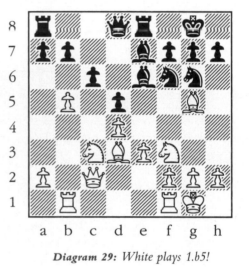
*Diagram 29: White plays 1.b5!*

No matter how Black responds to this pawn move, Black's pawn structure will be weakened:

+ If Black plays 1...cxb5, then after 2.Bxb5, Black will have three pawn islands (including an isolated pawn on d5). White will have only two pawn islands, and although the pawn on a2 is technically isolated, it is so difficult for Black to attack that it hardly counts as a weakness.

+ If Black plays 1...c5, then after 2.dxc5 Bxc5, Black's d-pawn will be isolated and on an open file as well, which makes it even weaker.

+ If Black ignores White's b-pawn, then after 2.bxc6 bxc6, Black will again have three pawn islands to White's two, and the c-pawn will be a backward pawn on an open file.

Diagrams 30 and 31 show another typical way a pawn structure can be damaged. While the previous example showed White attacking the "middle link" of Black's pawn chain, here White plays 1.a6! to attack the base of Black's pawn chain. By attacking the b7 pawn, White undermines the c-pawn's protection. In fact, Black cannot avoid some loss of material after this move. You might want to analyze this position for yourself to see why.

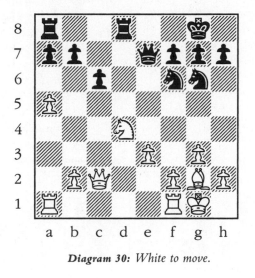

**Diagram 30:** *White to move.*

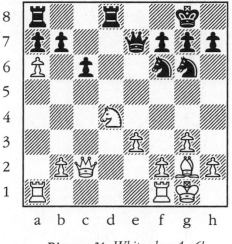

**Diagram 31:** *White plays 1.a6!*

# Exercises

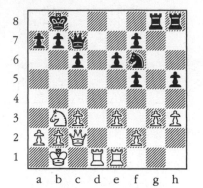

**Exercise 1:** White or Black to move. If it's Black's turn, what should Black play to get rid of an isolated pawn and damage White's pawn structure? If it's White's turn, what should White play to prevent Black's idea?

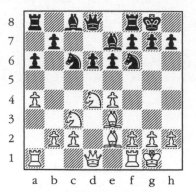

**Exercise 2:** White to move (Anand–Kasparov, World Championship, 1995). What pawn move should White play and why?

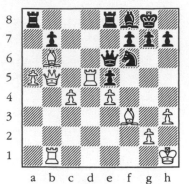

**Exercise 3:** Explain what compensation White has for the material after 27…Nxd5 28.exd5, and suggest what White's plan for the next several moves will be. (Note: This is an extremely difficult position. Kasparov himself misjudged it! Try your best to understand this position and then study the explanation in the answers to the exercises.)

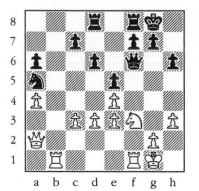

**Exercise 4:** Black to move (Kasparov–Anand, World Championship, 1995). Is White worse off for accepting doubled pawns? Explain why or why not.

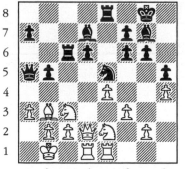

**Exercise 5:** White to move (Anand–Kasparov, World Championship, 1995). Is Black worse off for accepting doubled pawns? Explain why or why not.

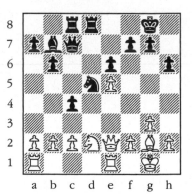

**Exercise 6:** Black to move. How can Black do great damage to White's pawn structure?

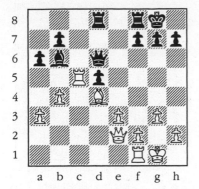

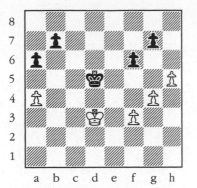

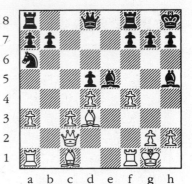

**Exercise 7:** *White to move (Gligoric–Euwe, Zurich, 1953). Black is hoping to give White an isolated pawn after the rook on c5 retreats, for example, 21.Rc3 Bxd4 22.exd4. But does White have to move the rook on c5? Suggest a move for White that protects d4 so White can eventually move the rook and avoid the isolated pawn. Evaluate the position after that move.*

**Exercise 8:** *White to move. Even though you may not yet have read Chapter 14, I bet you can solve this position using your knowledge of pawn structures! Each side wants to promote a pawn; if White can stop Black from promoting a pawn on the queenside, then White can win by promoting a pawn on the kingside. What is White's best move?*

**Exercise 9:** *White to move (Kasparov–Shirov, Holland, 2001). Black has just captured a knight on e5. Which way should White recapture? Why?*

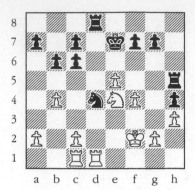

**Exercise 10:** *White to move (Kasparov–Kramnik, Holland, 2001). If you remember Exercise 11 in Chapter 7, you know that Kasparov rejected 1.g4 because he did not see the key tactic preventing Black from playing 1…hxg3+. Suppose you saw that you could play 1.g4 without allowing 1…hxg3+. Why is it to White's advantage to play this move?*

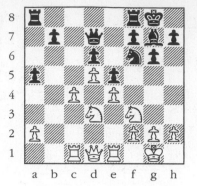

**Exercise 11:** *White or Black to move. If it is White's move, what move should White play, and why? If it is Black's move, what move should Black play, and why?*

**Exercise 12:** *Black to move. What pawn move should Black play? Why?*

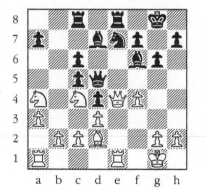

**Exercise 13:** *White to move (Kveinys–Yermolinsky, Vilnius, 1979). In this position, White played 1.b4. Is this a good move or a bad move? Justify your answer.*

**Exercise 14:** *White to move. White wants to attack on the kingside. What is the best move to start with, and why?*

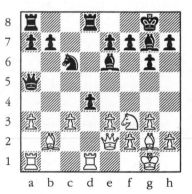

**Exercise 15:** *White to move (Arnett–Yermolinsky, New York, 1998). Black has just captured a pawn on d4. How should White recapture? Why?*

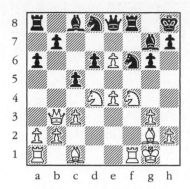

**Exercise 16:** White to move. Black has just played 1...c5, so that after White retreats the knight, Black can capture the pawn on e6. But White has a better move which secures the very strong pawn on e6. What should White play?

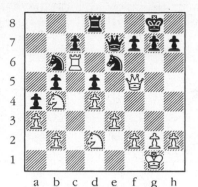

**Exercise 17:** White to move (Botvinnik–Keres, Moscow, 1948). How can White weaken Black's pawn structure even further to gain a large advantage?

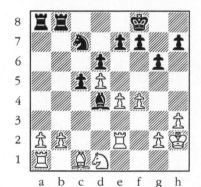

**Exercise 18:** Black to move (Camara–Benko, Sao Paulo, 1973). Black has a strong move to undermine White's pawn on d5. What is it? Find Black's best move and analyze the consequences.

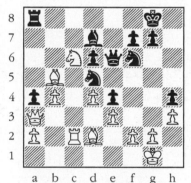

**Exercise 19:** Black to move (Stockfish 8–AlphaZero, London, 2018). White has an extra pawn, but at the cost of moving all of the pieces away from the king. Suggest a plan for Black that uses a kingside pawn push to attack White's king, and analyze how the game could continue.

# Chapter 12

# Space: The Final Frontier

In Chapter 10 we talked about pieces, and in Chapter 11 we talked about pawns. In the next two chapters, we talk about the squares. (You've got to agree this will take care of the whole chess set!) More specifically, we talk about two very important ideas: how many squares you control and which squares you control. As you read through this chapter and Chapter 13, think about the ideas you've learned in the previous three chapters. You'll find that what you've learned about the opening, the pieces, and the pawns has a lot to do with how many squares you control and which squares you control.

# The Advantage of Space

The amount of space you control is the total number of squares you control with your pieces and pawns. Generally speaking, the more space you control, the better it is for you. When you control more space, your pieces are more powerful because they have more squares on which to go. Although who has more space is determined by the squares controlled by both pieces and pawns, as you go through the examples in this chapter you should notice that the pawn structure often determines who has more space. (Recall Chapter 11.) Since the pawns largely determine the mobility of the pieces, the player whose pawns are farther advanced will have more room to maneuver and more space.

## Grabbing Space

One way to take more space is to occupy the center with your pawns. In some cases, it can be worth taking time away from developing your pieces to stake some ground in the center with pawns. Let's see how Bobby Fischer did this in a game he played on the way to winning the 1972 World Championship title.

Diagram 1 shows the position of Petrosian–Fischer in the sixth game of the final qualifying match for the World Championship. It would seem at first that White has a good position. White has developed two pieces, and they both control squares in the center. Black has yet to develop a piece, although we must admit that both pawn moves fight for the center. Because Black hasn't developed a single piece, we might expect the next move to do so now, e.g. with 3…Nc6 or 3…Nf6, and that's probably what Petrosian expected, too. Instead, Fischer played an extraordinary move: 3…f6! (see Diagram 2). Fischer is broke all our opening rules! How can we explain this?

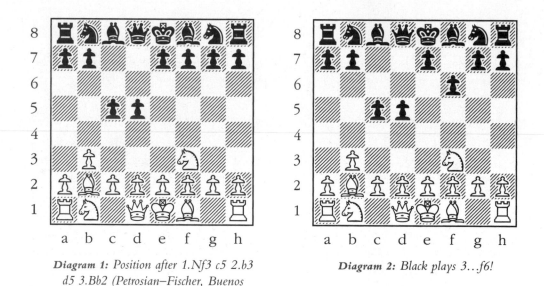

*Diagram 1: Position after 1.Nf3 c5 2.b3 d5 3.Bb2 (Petrosian–Fischer, Buenos Aires, 1971).*

*Diagram 2: Black plays 3…f6!*

Fischer realized that although pushing the f-pawn often puts the king in jeopardy, here his king is safe. Furthermore, the pawn move had an important idea behind it: Black wants to put a pawn on e5. Then with pawns on c5, d5, and e5, Black will control a lot more space in the center than White. Once Black establishes that wall of pawns in the center, White will have a hard time taking space in the center and then developing pieces to active squares. Black, meanwhile, will easily be able to develop pieces to active squares using all the space that the wall of pawns establishes.

Now we understand Fischer's strategy. By establishing this strong pawn bulwark in the center early on, he is able to control the lion's share of the board and to develop the pieces much more actively than White. (Notice in particular how establishing a pawn on e5, protected by a pawn on f6, drastically reduces the power of White's knight on e5 and bishop on b2.)

Let's see how Fischer's strategy worked out for him. Petrosian (playing White) decided to fight for the center with his pawns after all. But White didn't want to play 4.d4 because after 4...cxd4 followed by 5...e5, Black would keep a tight grip in the center, and White would have exchanged a more valuable center pawn for a less valuable noncenter pawn. So Black played 4.c4, and after 4...d4 5.d3 e5, reached the position in Diagram 3. Do you see how Black has established a powerful pawn wedge in the center? Notice that although White has developed two minor pieces, the bishop on b2 and the knight on f3, both of those pieces have their mobility severely restricted by Black's pawns.

Both sides then continued developing their pieces with 6.e3 Ne7 7.Be2 Nec6, reaching the position in Diagram 4. Although it looks strange for Fischer (Black) to develop his king's knight in two moves to a square he could have developed his queen's knight to in one move, the maneuver makes sense because Fischer has decided that most of his play will be on the queenside. Therefore, he wants to have both knights on that side of the board. If White exchanges pawns on d4, Black will recapture with the c-pawn (toward the center!) and then maneuver the queen's knight to the c5 square, where it will attack the two squares in front of the d4 and e5 pawns.

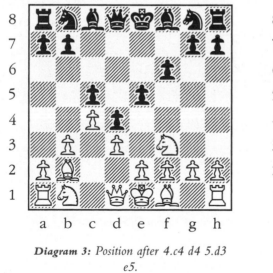

*Diagram 3: Position after 4.c4 d4 5.d3 e5.*

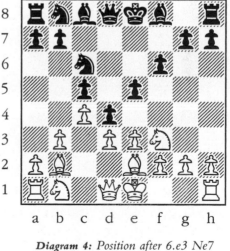

*Diagram 4: Position after 6.e3 Ne7 7.Be2 Nec6.*

More development and then castling ensued, reaching the position in Diagram 5 after 8.Nbd2 Be7 9.O-O O-O. Notice that even though White has developed more pieces, Black's pieces have much more mobility: White controls only four squares in Black's territory, whereas Black controls seven in White's territory. (Plus, Black controls the d4 square four times.) Even though White has developed more quickly, it is Black who has more active pieces. That is the benefit of a space advantage!

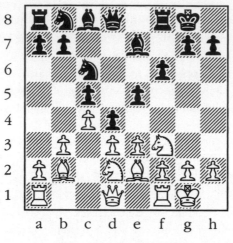

**Diagram 5:** *Position after 8.Nbd2 Be7*
*9.O-O O-O.*

# What to Do with More Space

Wherever you have more space, your pieces have more mobility than your opponent's, so an attack in the part of the board where you have more space has a better chance of overcoming your opponent's defense.

Let's zoom forward in this instructive game to see how Fischer used his space advantage. Diagram 6 shows the position after Black's twenty-third move. Fischer's plan is to push his c-pawn forward. After exchanging Black's b-pawn and c-pawn for White's b-pawn and d-pawn, Black will have a strong, protected passed pawn on d4, while White will have a weak, isolated a-pawn.

Diagram 7 shows how the game continued. Petrosian decided to force Fischer's hand immediately, rather than wait for Fischer to break through at his pleasure. He played 24.a4 and after 24...bxa4 25.bxa4 c4, reached the position in Diagram 7. Petrosian put up a tough defense, but eventually Fischer won the weak a-pawn and then the game.

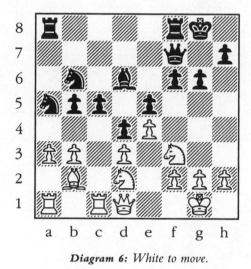

*Diagram 6: White to move.*

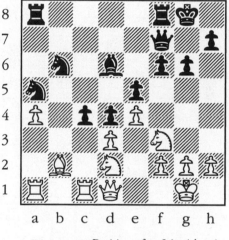

*Diagram 7: Position after 24.a4 bxa4 25.bxa4 c4.*

Attacking on the side of the board where you have more space is one good idea. Another good thing to do when you have space is to take some more space! Diagrams 8 through 10 show an example of this idea, which comes from a game by the late grandmaster and former New York Times chess columnist Robert Byrne. In Diagram 8, White clearly has more space than Black, but because White's c-pawns are doubled and Black's knight and bishop are stationed on the queenside, it's hard to see any way for White to attack on the queenside. What to do? White saw a good opportunity to take even more space by playing 16.f4 (see Diagram 9).

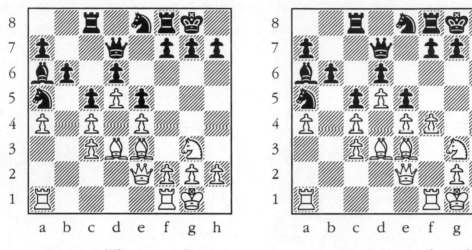

**Diagram 8:** *White to move (Byrne–Kotov, USA–USSR Team Match, 1954).*

**Diagram 9:** *Position after 16.f4.*

**Diagram 10:** *Position after 16...f6 17.f5.*

Black realized capturing the pawn with 16...exf4 would be a bad idea after 17.Rxf4 because the elimination of the e5 pawn would cause Black to lose ground in the center and open the f-file. The future potential for White to open the diagonal of the d3 bishop by playing e4–e5 would increase the dynamic power of White's pieces. This would be especially dangerous for Black since White's pieces would be concentrated near Black's king on g8! Black wisely kept the position tightly closed by playing 16...f6. But that gave White the opportunity to take even *more* space by playing 17.f5. Compare Diagram 10 to Diagram 8, and you will see how much more space White has taken. Now that White has gained space on the kingside, White is well positioned to use that space to attack Black there. Although the game was eventually drawn, White had the better position throughout, thanks to the very good idea of playing f2–f4–f5.

## But Don't Forget the Center!

Games like Petrosian–Fischer can give a misleading impression that by flinging your pawns forward, you'll squeeze your opponent to death. Actually, it's much trickier than that. The danger of pushing your pawns forward too quickly is that your opponent may be able to smash the center open with a well-timed set of pawn moves. At that point, your opponent's pieces may become more active and your aggressive pawn moves may expose weaknesses in your position.

You may remember Diagram 11; it's the same position as Diagram 11 from Chapter 9. When discussing this position in Chapter 9, I said that a good move for White is 8.Bd3, developing a piece. But after reading the first part of this chapter, you might prefer not to develop the bishop and instead gain space on the queenside with 8.c5? (see Diagram 12).

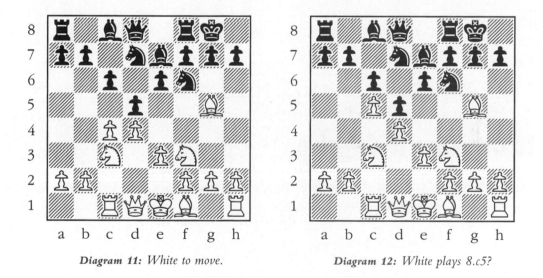

*Diagram 11: White to move.*          *Diagram 12: White plays 8.c5?*

This is a bad idea. In addition to neglecting development, the move has two other problems. It relieves the pressure on Black's vital d5 pawn, and White's c-pawn is not sufficiently supported. Black strikes back in the center by playing 8...e5! (see Diagram 13). Black would love to push this pawn to e4 because then suddenly Black would be the one with more space in the center. White thought this move had been prevented because the pawn on d4 and the knight on f3 each control the e5 square, while Black only controls the e5 square with the knight on d7. But a deeper look shows that once the d4 pawn captures on e5, the pawn that has just moved to c5 will become vulnerable.

Diagram 14 shows the result. After 9.dxe5 Ne4 10.Bxe7 Qxe7 Black will soon win back the pawn, and White is now on the defense. White must find a way to protect two weak pawns, complete development, and get the king to safety; whereas Black's king is safe, and the remaining pieces will develop easily.

*Diagram 13: Black plays 8...e5!*

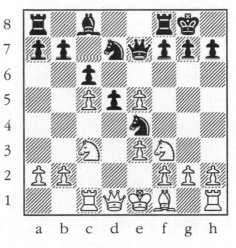

*Diagram 14: Position after 9.dxe5 Ne4 10.Bxe7 Qxe7.*

# Relieving a Cramp

We'd all like to have more space, but there are only so many squares on the chessboard, and someone's going to control more of them. Sometimes that's okay: having less space doesn't necessarily mean that you can't attack your opponent, and having more space doesn't necessarily mean that you can. But sometimes having less space is a real problem and you need to address it.

Here are three good strategies to adopt if you have less space:

+ Exchange pieces

+ Take some space of your own

+ Challenge your opponent's space advantage

# Exchange Pieces

If you've got less space to maneuver your pieces in, it stands to reason that you'd like to exchange some pieces so the pieces you're left with aren't tripping over their own toes. (Plus, your opponent will have fewer pieces to take advantage of the extra space.) Trading pieces is the first strategy you can adopt when your position is cramped.

Diagram 15 shows the opening position we saw in Chapter 9, Diagram 12. Black unquestionably has less space, which translates into difficulty developing the queen's bishop. But Black can solve that problem by exchanging some pieces.

Black starts by playing 8...dxc4 9.Bxc4 Nd5 in Diagram 16. By trading pawns, Black gives the knight a post on d5. If Black didn't have a specific strategy in mind, this would be risky because White's extra center pawn stakes out more space now. But Black has a concrete plan to remedy this.

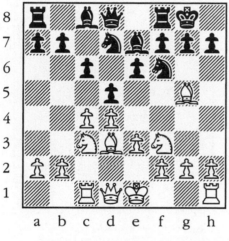

*Diagram 15: Position after 8.Bd3.*

*Diagram 16: Position after 8...dxc4 9.Bxc4 Nd5.*

White's bishop on g5 is attacked, so White exchanges bishops with 10.Bxe7 Qxe7 and then wisely decides to play 11.O-O, whisking the king out of the center (see Diagram 17).

Black continues the strategy of exchanging pieces in Diagram 18 with 11...Nxc3 12.Rxc3. At first it may look like Black hasn't accomplished anything. White still has more space, and Black seems to have surrendered control of the center to boot. But Black has benefited by trading pieces because the queen now joins the knight in supporting the important pawn push 12...e5! (see Diagram 19). With this move, Black fights back in the center and gains a more equal share of space. Plus, Black's white-squared bishop finally has its diagonal cleared of the e6 pawn so it can be developed as soon as the knight moves. Black has become much closer to obtaining equal chances after the pawn push 12...e5, but Black couldn't have accomplished it without trading the pawns and pieces that gave Black more room to operate.

Diagram 17: Position after 10.Bxe7 Qxe7 11.O-O.

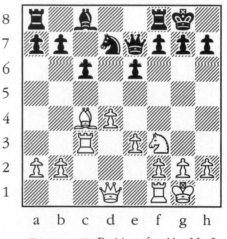

Diagram 18: Position after 11...Nxc3 Rxc3.

Diagram 19: Black plays 12...e5.

# Take Some Space of Your Own

If you have less space, go out and claim some territory! This strategy is fairly straightforward, and we can see it in action in an opening called the *King's Indian Defense*.

Diagram 20 shows a standard position from this opening. (It arises after 1.d4 Nf6 2.c4 g6 3.Nc3 Bg7 4.e4 d6 5.Nf3 O-O 6.Be2.) There is no doubt that White has more space. How should Black play?

Black begins by striking in the center with 6...e5 (see Diagram 21). Black isn't going to let White's pawn "duo"—a pawn trio!—in the center remain unchallenged. In Diagram 22, White castles (7.O-O), because taking twice on e5 does not win a pawn. (If 7.dxe5 dxe5 8.Nxe5, then 8...Nxe4! wins the pawn back. Can you see why?) Black develops the knight to c6 to put more pressure on White's d4 pawn with 7...Nc6. This prompts White to advance the pawn with 8.d5. The pawn now attacks the knight, so Black retreats it with 8...Ne7.

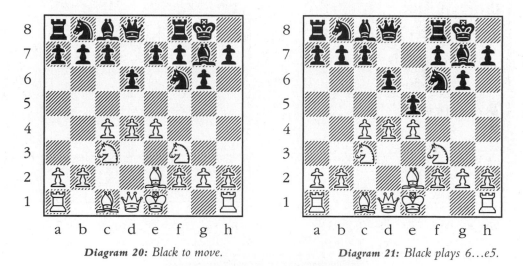

*Diagram 20: Black to move.*

*Diagram 21: Black plays 6...e5.*

*Diagram 22: Position after 7.O-O Nc6*
*8.d5 Ne7.*

White's next move looks strange at first: 9.Ne1 in Diagram 23. This is by no means the only reasonable move in this position, but it's a good one. White's idea is to gain more space on the queenside. The best way to do that is to push the c-pawn to c5. To support this advance, White's plan is to maneuver the knight to d3 and the bishop to e3, and 9.Ne1 is the first move in that plan. (Note that the reason both sides can afford to engage in some maneuvering at the expense of development in this position is that the pawn structure in the center is completely closed.)

Black's next move, 9...Nd7 (see Diagram 24), has both a defensive and an offensive idea behind it. The defensive idea is to lend support to the c5 square. If White wants to gain space on the queenside by pushing the c-pawn to c5, then Black wants to stop it! The offensive idea is to strike in the center and to gain space on the kingside by pushing the f-pawn to f5. Notice that after pushing the e-pawn to e5, the pawn supports staking out more territory on the kingside, a benefit Black is quick to capitalize on.

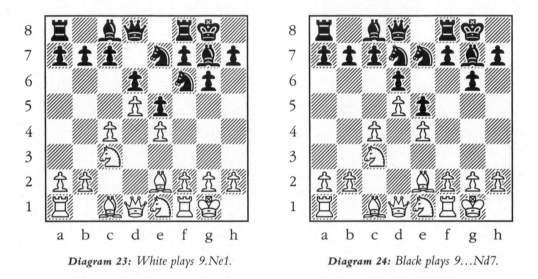

*Diagram 23: White plays 9.Ne1.*     *Diagram 24: Black plays 9...Nd7.*

Both sides proceed with their plans. White plays 10.Be3 to lend more support to the eventual c4-c5 push, and Black strikes in the center and kingside with 10...f5 (see Diagram 25). White's next move 11.f3, has two ideas: The first idea is to support the e-pawn with another pawn. Now if Black captures on e4, White can recapture with a pawn so Black won't have eliminated one of White's center pawns (and Black's knight on e7 won't be able to hop safely to the f5 square and fight for the center). The second idea is to allow the bishop to retreat to the f2 square if Black advances the pawn to f4. From f2 the bishop will still control the vital c5 square.

Sure enough, after White plays 11.f3, Black plays 11...f4 (see Diagram 26), taking more territory on the kingside. Finally, Diagram 27 shows the position after White retreats the bishop with 12.Bf2 and then Black takes even more space on the kingside with 12...g5. Compare Diagram 27 to Diagram 20 and 22, and notice the difference in space. White still has more space in the center and the queenside, but now Black has definitely grabbed space on the kingside to support active operations there. And because both kings live on that side of the board, you can bet the game will be exciting!

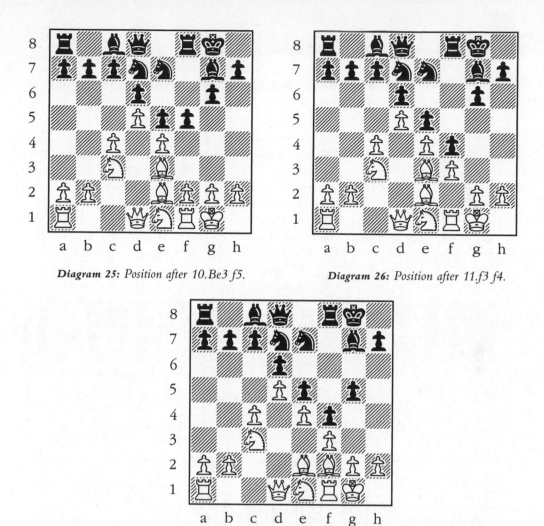

*Diagram 25: Position after 10.Be3 f5.*

*Diagram 26: Position after 11.f3 f4.*

*Diagram 27: Position after 12.Bf2 g5.*

Look at Diagrams 20 through 27 and notice that even after gaining space on the kingside, Black still has less space overall than White. That's because White's farthest advanced pawn (d5) is a center pawn, whereas Black's farthest advanced pawn (f4) is not. One more reason that center pawns are a little more valuable than other pawns is that you gain maximum space by advancing a center pawn.

## Challenge Your Opponent's Space Advantage

The third strategy for addressing a disadvantage in space is to fight for the territory your opponent has claimed. One common way to do this is to exchange one of your opponent's far-advanced pawns for one of yours that is close to home. This removes the enemy pawn's influence over squares in your own territory and opens more lines for your pieces to use.

Diagrams 28 through 32 illustrate an example of this strategy. Diagram 28 shows a position from an opening called the *French Defense*. (The position arises after 1.e4 e6 2.d4 d5 3.Nd2 Nf6 4.e5 Nfd7 5.c3 c5. Black's first move, 1...e6, defines this opening as the French Defense.) It's White's turn and there are two logical strategies. The first is to play 6.f4, as shown in Diagram 29. By supporting the e5 pawn with a second pawn, White ensures that Black can't force White to exchange it for Black's f-pawn. Since the e5 pawn is twice protected by pawns, if Black captures it with the f-pawn, then after White recaptures with the f-pawn, White will still have a pawn on e5. (The situation is similar to Diagrams 20 through 27: if Black plays the pawn to c6 and captures on d5, White can recapture with the c-pawn and still keep a pawn on d5.)

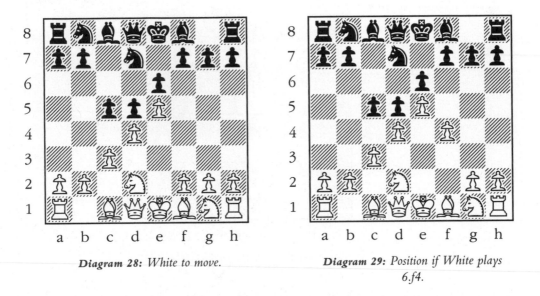

*Diagram 28: White to move.*

*Diagram 29: Position if White plays 6.f4.*

But 6.f4 has drawbacks as well. The move does nothing to contribute to White's development, and the pawn push makes the queen's bishop bad. Although 6.f4 is a perfectly respectable move, many grandmasters prefer to play 6.Bd3, as shown in Diagram 30. One common way for both sides to play from here is 6...Nc6 7.Ne2 cxd4 8.cxd4, and Black almost always plays 8...f6 next, as shown in Diagram 31.

The move 8...f6 is a perfect illustration of the strategy of challenging the opponent's space advantage. White's best move is to capture the pawn with 9.exf6 and then after 9...Nxf6, Black controls as much space as White, as you can see in Diagram 32. It should be said that Black has paid a price for equalizing space. Black has two new problems in Diagram 32 that didn't exist before: Black's pawn structure is weaker due to the backward pawn on c6. (The backward pawn will have a hard time safely advancing after White plays 10.Nf3.) And Black's kingside is weaker because the pawn on f7 is missing. On the other hand, Black has also made some gains, in addition to equalizing space. Once Black castles kingside, the king's rook will be actively placed along the open f-file, and the bad bishop on c8 has a chance to escape into the outside world, either by playing …Bd7-e8 followed by …Bg6 or …Bh5; or, if Black does eventually manage to advance the e6 pawn safely, to f5 or g4. All in all, a tough fight is in store for both players, which is why there are grandmasters willing to play each side of this position.

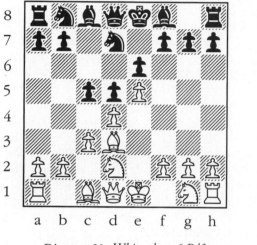

*Diagram 30: White plays 6.Bd3.*

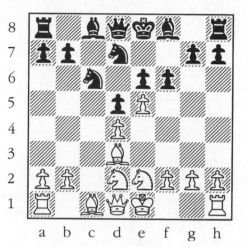

*Diagram 31: Position after 6…Nc6 7.Ne2 cxd4 8.cxd4 f6.*

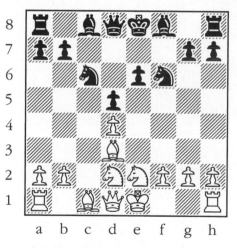

*Diagram 32: Position after 9.exf6 Nxf6.*

# Exercises

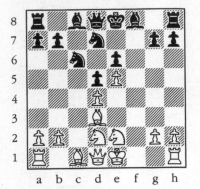

**Exercise 1:** *Black to move. This exercise is a review of your tactical skills. (Tactics are still important, you know!) The position comes from Diagram 31 if White plays 9.f4? fxe5 10.fxe5?? Can you see how Black wins a pawn? (Hint: Black uses a fork.)*

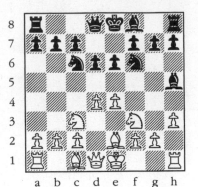

**Exercise 2:** *White to move (Wolff–Minasian, Los Angeles, 1994). White has two pawn moves to take more territory in the center. What are they? Which move is better, and why?*

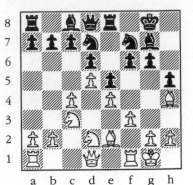

**Exercise 3:** *White to move (Reshevsky–Kavalek, Netanya, 1971). Who has more space? Assess the position, and suggest what White's next move might be and why.*

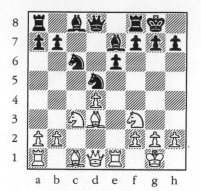

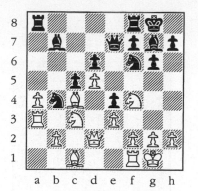

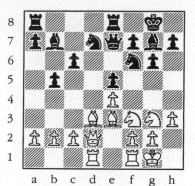

**Exercise 4:** *An example of the isolated pawn. Who has more space? Review the rules of thumb in Chapter 11 for playing with or against the isolated pawn. How do those rules relate to the rules of thumb for playing with more or less space?*

**Exercise 5:** *Black to move (Davies–Wolff, Preston, 1989). White has more space on the queenside, and Black has more space on the kingside. At the moment both players control about the same amount of space. Where should Black attack, and why? Suggest how Black should play.*

**Exercise 6:** *White to move (Wolff–M. Gurevich, Holland, 1993). Who has more space? I played 14.c4. Is this a good move or a bad move? Explain why.*

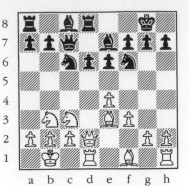

**Exercise 7:** *White to move (Fischer–Rossolimo, US Championship, 1965–66). Fischer, in his classic book* My 60 Memorable Games, *wrote that he should have played 13.Qf6 Rg8 14.h4 to attack on the kingside (where he has more space). Instead Fischer played 13.h4 right away. Do you see what Rossolimo played to gain more space on the kingside? (Hint: he used a pin to his advantage.)*

**Exercise 8:** *Black to move (Letelier–Fischer, Germany, 1960). Another of Fischer's memorable games shows the danger of rushing your pawns forward too quickly at the cost of development. White's center looks imposing, but Fischer smashed through it by playing 7...c5! 8.dxc5 Nc6! Analyze this position to see why Black has a good position. Compare your analysis with the answer to this exercise when you're ready. (This is a tough one! Do the best you can.)*

**Exercise 9:** *Black to move. What move can Black play to gain more space and to challenge White's spatial control? (Notice the connection between controlling the center and controlling more space.)*

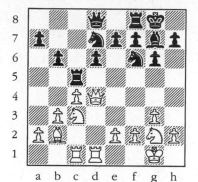

**Exercise 10:** *Black to move (Andersson–Portisch, Iceland, 1991). Who has more space? Do you think 14...Nd5 is a good move for Black? Why or why not?*

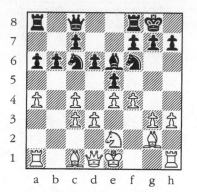

**Exercise 11:** *White to move (vanWely–Fritz Computer, Dutch Championship, 2000). Who has more space? How can White gain more space, and what is the right plan afterward?*

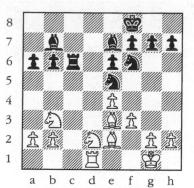

**Exercise 12:** *White to move (Kramnik–Kasparov, London World Championship match, 2000). How can White gain more space? How might play continue?*

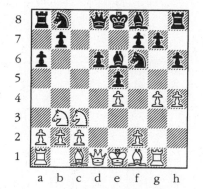

**Exercise 13:** *Black to move. White's plan is to play g4-g5 to push the knight away from the center and gain space. How should Black meet this plan?*

**Exercise 14:** *Black to move. White's d-pawn gives White more space in the center. Plus, White has the idea of playing e4-e5, gaining even more space in the center. How can Black fight for more space and stop White from taking more?*

**Exercise 15:** *Black to move. Black is considering two moves to neutralize White's space advantage: 1...Ne4 and 1...c5. Which is better, and why?*

**Exercise 16:** *Black to move. This position arises from the following opening: 1.e4 e6 2.d4 d5 3.e5 c5 4.c3 Nc6 5.Nf3 Qb6 6.a3. Identify the space-gaining move that is the idea behind White's last move, 6.a3. What moves might Black consider in this position?*

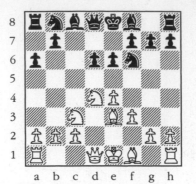

**Exercise 17:** *Black to move. This position arises from the following opening: 1.e4 c5 2.Nf3 d6 3.d4 cxd4 4.Nxd4 Nf6 5.Nc3 a6 6.Be3 e6 7.f3. Identify the space-gaining move that is the idea behind White's last move, 7.f3. What moves might Black consider in this position?*

**Exercise 18:** *Black to move (Stockfish 8–AlphaZero, London, 2018). Here, the AlphaZero computer sacrificed the a-pawn with 31…c5! 32.Nc2 g5! What was the idea behind these moves? Analyze and assess the position after 33.Nxa3.*

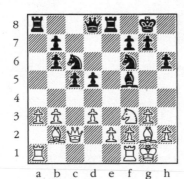

**Exercise 19:** *Black to move (Oparin–Carlsen, Saint Petersburg, 2018). Analyze and assess this position. What move do you think World Champion Carlsen played to gain space?*

**Exercise 20:** *White to move (Nakamura–Aronian, Belgium, 2018). What move can White play to gain space? Analyze and assess the position.*

# Chapter 13

# Weak Squares

In Chapter 12, we talked about the importance of controlling more squares than your opponent. But not all squares are equally important. Over time, some squares become difficult or impossible for one player to control with pawns. Such a square has the potential to become what chess players call a *weak square*, especially if the other player can still control it with pawns.

# Recognizing Weak Squares

A weak square is a square that one player can control but the other player can't. To recognize which squares are weak, just see which squares you or your opponent can't easily (or ever) control with pawns.

For example, let's look at Diagram 1. Does White have any weak squares? Obviously, we can ignore the first two ranks, because White's pawns can never control those squares anyway. The only square that could potentially be weak is d3 because White can no longer control that square with a pawn. But that's probably not something to worry about in this position because White retains full control of the d3 square with the major pieces, while Black is in no position to contest it.

Now what about Black? Even if we ignore the eighth and seventh ranks, we see that Black has no fewer than four weak squares: d6, d5, f6, and h6. (Did you remember to count d6? Don't forget that no piece or pawn controls its own square!) Should Black worry about these squares? Well, White certainly has full control of the d5 square and has both rooks hitting d6, so White might be able to take advantage of those squares. White doesn't control f6 at the moment, but if the knight goes to d5, it will attack the f6 square; plus, it's not hard to imagine White's queen controlling f6 by going to f3. White might be able to take advantage of the weak f6 square. The hardest square for White to control is h6, so that's probably the least weak of the bunch. On the other hand, h6 (like f6) is very near the black king, and Black should be especially careful about these two squares. If any white pieces land on those squares, they could be a serious menace to Black's king!

In Diagram 1, White controls the weak square d5 more than Black does. In addition, White attacks the d6 pawn several times, which forces Black to defend it several times. For these reasons, Black's weak squares are a serious liability. (Another thing that makes the weak squares a serious liability for Black is that two of them are so near the king. We'll come back to this theme later in the chapter.) Now compare Diagram 1 to Diagram 2.

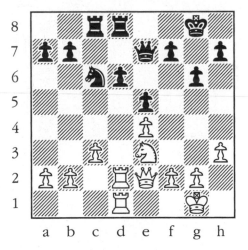

*Diagram 1: White has no weak squares, but Black has four: d6, d5, f6, and h6.*

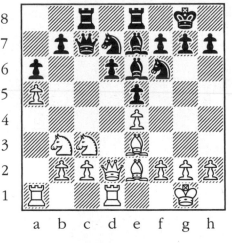

*Diagram 2: Black has three weak squares: b6, d5, and d6.*

Once again, Black has some weak squares: b6, d5, and d6. But these weak squares are much less of a problem than in Diagram 1 because Black controls these squares much better. The b6 square is controlled by the knight on d7 and the queen on c7. The d6 square (and the pawn sitting on it) is defended by the bishop on e7 and the queen on c7. And the d5 square is controlled by the knight on f6 and the bishop on e6. In addition, because it's impossible to see right now how White could attack the d6 pawn with a minor piece, the pawn is very well defended by the bishop on e7. All in all, even though Black has weak squares, they are not much of a liability because they are well controlled by the pieces.

When a square is weak, both players have an interest in controlling it. One way to exploit a weak square in your opponent's position is to put a piece on it (especially a knight). Often, the side with a weak square will want to control it with pieces to prevent the weak square from being easily occupied.

One of the important contrasts between Diagrams 1 and 2 is that in Diagram 1, White can play the knight to d5 without allowing it to be captured; whereas in Diagram 2, if White plays the knight to d5, Black can capture it and force White to recapture with a pawn, which would eliminate the weak square on d5. (Notice that the exchange would also change the status of the d6 pawn; it would no longer be a backward pawn because the square in front of it would be occupied by a white pawn.) It so happens that White can't safely play the knight to d5 because Black would win the pawn on c2. But in Diagrams 3 and 4, I've changed the position to illustrate what happens when White plays the knight to d5; Black captures it, and White recaptures with a pawn.

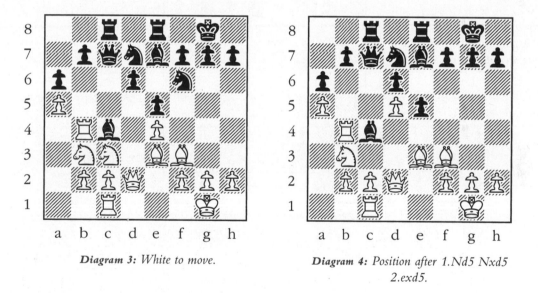

**Diagram 3:** *White to move.*

**Diagram 4:** *Position after 1.Nd5 Nxd5 2.exd5.*

Diagrams 3 and 4 show that after 1.Nd5 Nxd5 2.exd5, the d5 square is no longer weak because it's been occupied by a white pawn. There may be other reasons for White to carry out this exchange, such as to gain space in the center and the queenside. But the key idea here is how Black's pieces effectively defend the weak d5 square. When White tries to use the square for the knight, the exchange of pieces results in White occupying the square with a pawn, and the square is no longer a weakness for Black.

# Weak Squares and Pawn Structure

Perhaps you've noticed that weak squares and backward pawns seem to go together. That's not an accident. Since pawns capture diagonally, rather than forward, the square in front of a pawn is always a potentially weak square. It may be useful for you to review Chapter 11 and look for all the weak squares that go with each pawn structure. Keep in mind that when pawns are lined up side by side, there are no weak squares in front of them! That's one big reason the pawn duo is such a strong pawn formation.

In addition to backward pawns, one pawn structure that most naturally gives rise to weak squares is the isolated pawn. Since there are no pawns on the files adjacent to the isolated pawn, the square in front of the isolated pawn is weak. For example, in Diagram 5, the d4 square is weak and may be a useful square for White's knight or bishop to use.

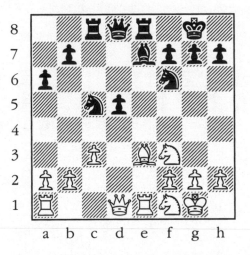

**Diagram 5:** *White can easily occupy the weak d4 square with the knight or bishop.*

# The Hole

Sometimes a weak square is called a *hole*. Think of it this way: when pawns are side by side, they control all the squares in front of them; but when one advances ahead of another, it may create a hole in the pawn structure because that square can no longer be controlled by a pawn. Diagram 6 gives an example of such a hole. White's knights occupy two of Black's weak squares: c5 and e5. The c5 square is not a hole because Black could eventually play the pawn to b6 and control c5. But the e5 square can never again be controlled by a black pawn, so it is a hole in Black's pawn structure. The white knight has a splendid post on this weak square, where it controls squares deep in Black's position.

A hole is often a particularly weak square, especially when your opponent can occupy it with a piece, as White has done in Diagram 6.

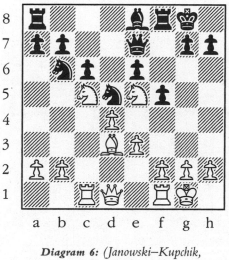

*Diagram 6: (Janowski–Kupchik, Havana, 1913).*

Although Black could, in theory, control this square by advancing the pawn to b6, the pawn on c6 makes it especially hard to do this because if the b-pawn advances to b6, it will leave the c6 pawn undefended. Therefore, the c6 pawn actually makes the c5 square weaker by making it harder to control that square without losing the pawn. This idea—a square made weaker because pushing a pawn to control the square leaves another pawn (or square) undefended—is a useful one to remember and comes up many times. (Two examples of this are Diagram 4 and Diagram 6 in Chapter 10.)

## The Weak Color Complex

Another advantage of White's position in Diagram 6 is Black's weak color complex on the dark squares, which goes together with the weak squares on e5 and c5. A *weak color complex* is a fancy way of saying that one side has many weak squares of the same color. In the case of Diagram 6, Black has a lot of weak black squares, such as e5, c5, d6, and maybe also f4 and g5. When a player has put a lot of pawns on squares of one color, it's usually important to keep the bishop that moves on squares of the other color. The bishop is a key piece for either exploiting or defending the weak color complex! (Notice that in Diagram 6, Black no longer has the black-squared bishop, which makes those squares especially weak.)

Since it's important for the player with a weak color complex to keep the bishop, it makes sense for the opponent trying to exploit the weak color complex to exchange that bishop. That was the strategy I used in a game at the North Bay Open in Canada (see Diagrams 7-11).

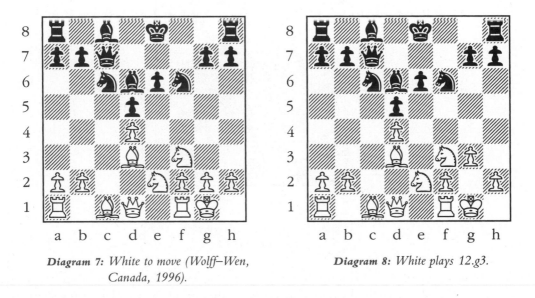

Diagram 7: White to move (Wolff–Wen, Canada, 1996).

Diagram 8: White plays 12.g3.

In Diagram 7, Black has just played the queen to c7 to prevent White from moving the bishop to f4 and exchanging it for Black's bishop. I decided to play 12.g3 (see Diagram 8) to increase my control of the f4 square so I could carry out the idea of exchanging bishops. There is some risk to making this pawn move because it weakens f3 and h3, two squares close to my king. But I had analyzed this position at home before playing this game, and I had decided it was more important to exploit Black's weak black squares than to worry about the white squares near my king.

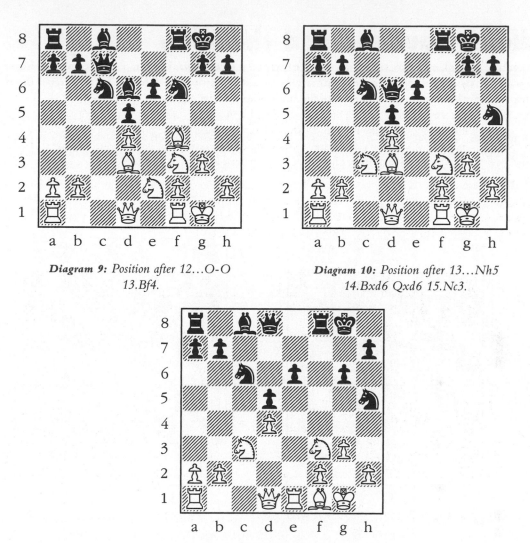

*Diagram 9:* Position after 12...O-O
13.Bf4.

*Diagram 10:* Position after 13...Nh5
14.Bxd6 Qxd6 15.Nc3.

*Diagram 11:* Position after 15...g6
16.Re1 Qd8 17.Bf1.

Diagrams 9, 10, and 11 show how I carried this idea out. Notice that in Diagram 11, White has several advantages, such as more space and more pieces developed. But one of the most important advantages is that White has almost all the pawns on black squares with a white-squared bishop, while Black has almost all the pawns on white squares with a white-squared bishop. White's pawns and bishop work harmoniously together, whereas Black's don't. As a result, Black's dark squares are much weaker than White's light squares, and White's bishop is good, while Black's is bad. (If you did Exercise 1 in Chapter 10, you saw a later position in this same game. Can you see how the color-complex advantage I gained here helped set up the strategy I was able to carry out in that exercise?)

# Weak Squares and the King

Having weak squares near your king is practically an invitation for your opponent to attack. Your opponent's pieces can use those weak squares to attack the king, and without pawns to repel them, it becomes much harder to defend. Let's look at an example.

There are a lot of good things about White's position in Diagram 12. White has an extra pawn, the two bishops, and a very strong pawn center. (Even the doubled pawn is a strength because it helps control the center, and it gives White the open a-file for her rook.) But White has a hole on g3, and this invites Black to line up the queen and bishop to set up a checkmate threat on h2. If White's h-pawn were on h2, White would have a large advantage. But with the pawn on h3, White is lost after 1...Qg3! (see Diagram 13).

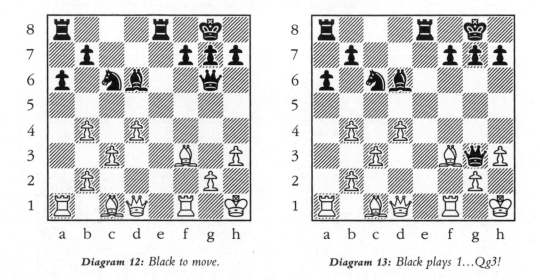

*Diagram 12: Black to move.*          *Diagram 13: Black plays 1...Qg3!*

Black threatens checkmate by 2...Qh2#. White's only defense is to run away with 2.Kg1, but then Black forces checkmate by playing 2...Qh2+ 3.Kf2 Bg3# (see Diagram 14). Every move of Black's attack was on one of those two weak dark squares: g3 or h2!

When you're attacking the king, find ways to create weak squares near the king and then move your pieces so they can control or occupy those squares. (Sometimes it's even worth sacrificing material to create weak squares near the king!)

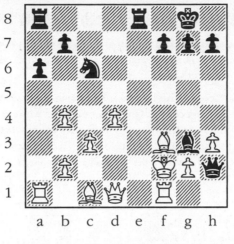

*Diagram 14: Position after 2.Kg1 Qh2+*
*3.Kf2 Bg3#.*

Even if there is no immediate checkmate, it's often wise to maneuver your pieces to any weak squares around the king. The pieces will then be well placed once the attack gets going in full. An example of this is my game against former World Championship challenger David Bronstein (see Diagram 15).

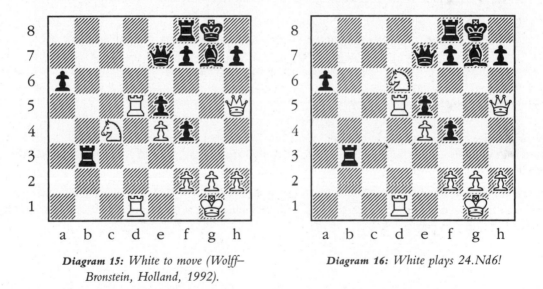

*Diagram 15: White to move (Wolff–*      *Diagram 16: White plays 24.Nd6!*
*Bronstein, Holland, 1992).*

Black is ahead one pawn. I could regain the pawn by playing 24.Nxe5, but this would open up the diagonal of Black's bad bishop on g7. Besides, Black's king is exposed, and with White's queen on h5 and the rooks doubled, most of my pieces are in good position to attack. I need to maneuver the knight to Black's weakest square near his king: f5. To this end, I played 24.Nd6!, as shown in Diagram 16.

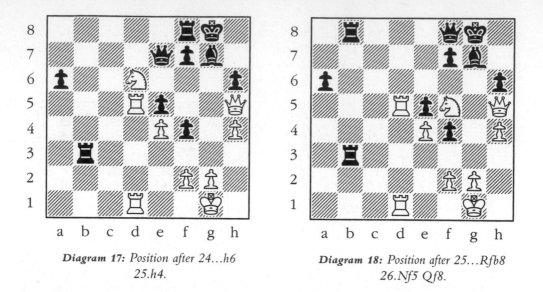

**Diagram 17:** *Position after 24...h6*
*25.h4.*

**Diagram 18:** *Position after 25...Rfb8*
*26.Nf5 Qf8.*

Black plays 24...h6? in an effort to offer the exchange of queens with 25...Qg5. White plays 25.h4 (see Diagram 17) to squelch that idea, after which Black's king position is even further weakened. Black then tries to activate the king's rook by playing 25...Rfb8, but after 26.Nf5 Qf8 (see in Diagram 18), the knight is on an ideal square to press the attack. In fact, White's attack is probably already winning. (Exercise 6, at the end of the chapter, asks you to find the best next move for White.)

Because it's so dangerous to have weak squares near the king, it's very much in your interest to create weak squares near your opponent's king if you're attacking it. One way to do this is to push your pawns up to the king's pawn cover. Even if the pawn is not protected, pushing it can put the defending side in a no-win situation. If your opponent lets you capture a pawn in front of the king, then the king's position is compromised. If your opponent moves the pawn or captures your pawn in response, the king's position may be compromised once again.

Diagrams 19 and 20 show an example of this. White has slightly more space and Black has a bad bishop, so we'd expect White to have an advantage. But White's advantage is larger than it might seem because 1.h6! is a powerful strike at Black's castled position.

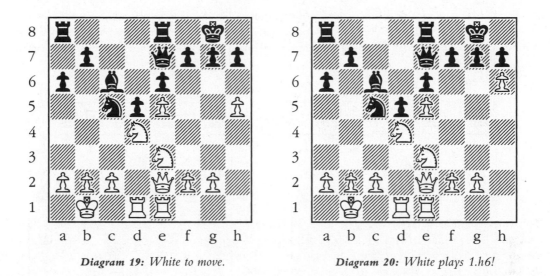

*Diagram 19: White to move.*        *Diagram 20: White plays 1.h6!*

White threatens to capture the pawn on g7. If Black plays 1...gxh6?, then 2.Ng4! is very strong because White will win back the h-pawn and gain the open h-file for his attack. (Notice that White also threatens to win material by playing Nf6+.) An attempt to counterattack the pawn on e5 doesn't work either; for example, after 1...Qg5 2.Ng4!, White's attack only intensifies. Black's best move is probably 1...g6, to keep the king as sheltered as possible. But after 2.Ng4 Nd7 (2...Ne4? is an inferior way to try to defend the f6 square: after 3.f3 Ng3 4.Qf2 Nh5 5.Rh1, Black's knight is off to the side of the board, and White will rip through Black's kingside defense with the sacrifice Rxh5 at the right time), the move 3.Qe3 increases White's space advantage and tightens White's control of the dark squares. Notice how Black's knight has been forced to a more passive square in order to defend the weak square f6.

# Repairing a Weak Square

Once you've pushed a pawn, you can't pull it back, but there are other ways to cope with having a weak square. One way to do this is to defend the weak square with a piece.

Diagram 21 shows a position that arises from a gambit called the *Marshall Attack*, invented by the great American player Frank Marshall a hundred years ago. White has an extra pawn, but Black has more pieces developed, and White's kingside is weakened. How can White cope with the weak white squares around his king?

Diagram 21: White to move (Tal–Witkowski, Riga, 1959).

Diagram 22: White plays 16.Bd5!

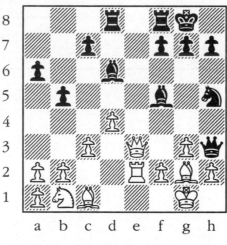

Diagram 23: Position after 16...Bf5
17.Qe3! Rad8 18.Bg2.

Diagram 22 shows the answer: White plays 16.Bd5!, which simultaneously serves both defensive and offensive purposes. Its offensive purpose is to attack the rook on a8. Its defensive purpose is to stop Black from taking the long white-square diagonal by putting the bishop on b7.

After 16...Bf5 17.Qe3! Black must move the rook on a8. Black can't move it to e8 because White would win material (two rooks for a queen) by capturing it. So Black plays 17...Rad8, and after 18.Bg2 (see Diagram 23), White succeeds in largely repairing the weak white squares around his king. Tal was then able to develop the rest of his pieces, and he quickly gained a large advantage because of his extra pawn.

Another way to cope with a weak square is to exchange whichever of your opponent's pieces is best able to attack it.

Suppose you are playing the black side of Diagram 24. Without question, Black is worse: Black's bishop is inferior to White's knight; Black has a glaring weak square on d5 and another weak square on f5. (White's knight would be very strong if it got to f5!)

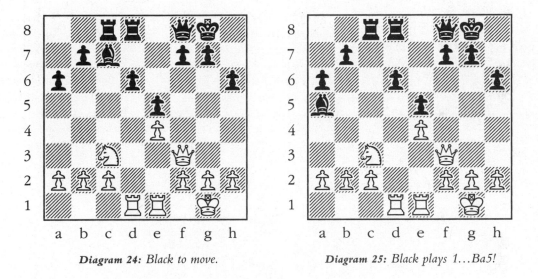

Diagram 24: Black to move.     Diagram 25: Black plays 1...Ba5!

But 1...Ba5! solves most of Black's problems. Because of the pin to the rook on e1, White can't avoid the exchange of bishop for knight. Black still has a worse pawn structure, but after exchanges, Black will be only a little worse and should probably draw. (For example, 2.Re3 Bxc3 3.Rxc3 Rxc3 4.Qxc3 Qe7.) The weak squares at d5 and f5 are much less of a problem once White's knight is off the board.

# Exercises

**Exercise 1:** *White to move. How can White weaken Black's control of the d5 square? (Hint: find a way to use White's black-squared bishop.)*

**Exercise 2:** *White to move. Each side is attacking the other's king. How can White use a weak square near Black's king to press through first? If Black's g6 pawn were on h7, what difference would this make?*

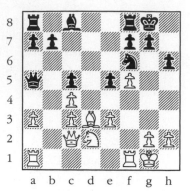

**Exercise 3:** *White to move (Botvinnik–Kan, USSR Championship, 1939). Botvinnik plays 16.Ne4! and after 16… Qd8, the game continues 17.Nxf6+ Qxf6. What is Botvinnik's idea? What weak square does Botvinnik want to exploit and with which piece?*

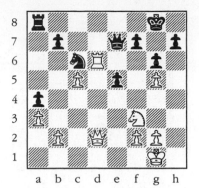

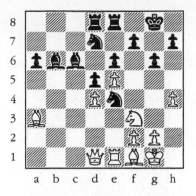

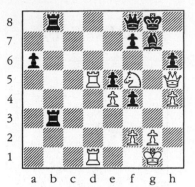

**Exercise 4:** *White to move (A. Ivanov–Gulko, US Championship, 1995). Black has just played 24...e5. Which squares near Black's king are weak? How can White maneuver a piece to control those squares?*

**Exercise 5:** *White to move (Adams–Wolff, New York, 1996). My last move (25...Bc6?) was a mistake because it allows White to maneuver the queen to a very weak square near my king by attacking my bishop. How?*

**Exercise 6:** *White to move (Wolff–Bronstein, Holland, 1992). Here is Diagram 18 again, after 26...Qf8, where we see White reap the benefit of maneuvering the knight to the weak f5 square. How can I win a pawn and also expose Black's king even more? (Hint: White makes a move that creates two threats at once.)*

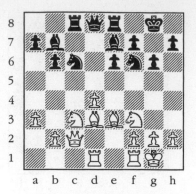

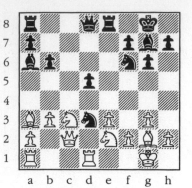

**Exercise 7:** *Black to move (Bernstein–Lasker, St. Petersburg, 1914). White has many weak squares near the king, which Black should try to exploit. The best move is either 35...Qg3 or 35...Qh2. Which is the right move, and why? (This is hard. Lasker himself, who was world champion at the time, played the wrong move! Here's a hint: figure out which move works out better for Black if White plays 36.Nxe6.)*

**Exercise 8:** *Black to move (Illescas–Wolff, Switzerland, 1993). It's my turn to play my seventeenth move. How can Black repair the weaknesses caused near the king by playing the g-pawn to g6?*

**Exercise 9:** *Black to move (R. Byrne–Fischer, US Championship, 1963–1964). This is a hard exercise! I've included it because it's both very instructive and very beautiful. Fischer finds an incredible way to exploit the potentially weak white squares around White's king. He played 15...Nxf2!! 16.Kxf2 Ng4+ 17.Kg1 Nxe3 18.Qd2 Nxg2!! (Fischer writes, "Removing this bishop leaves White defenseless on his white squares.") 19.Kxg2 d4! 20.Nxd4 Bb7+. Here Fischer writes, "The king is at Black's mercy." Analyze this position to see why Black has a winning attack against all of White's replies. Then compare your analysis with the analysis given in the answer.*

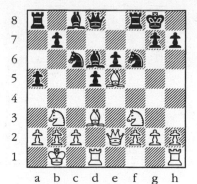

**Exercise 10:** *Black to move (Shirov–Kramnik, Holland, 2001). How can Black induce a weakness in White's castled position?*

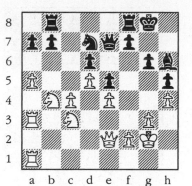

**Exercise 11:** *White or Black to move. If it is White's turn, what move should White play to create a very weak square that she can exploit? If it is Black's move, how should he defend against White's threat?*

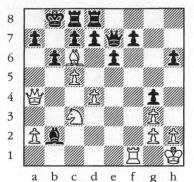

**Exercise 12:** *White to move. White has an attack, but White is behind in material and several pieces are attacked. How does White press home the attack by exploiting the weak squares around Black's king?*

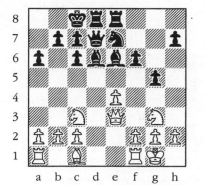

**Exercise 13:** *White to move. What squares are weak around the king? How can White exploit them?*

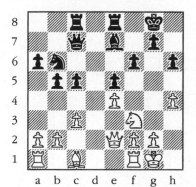

**Exercise 14:** *White to move. How can White exploit Black's weak squares?*

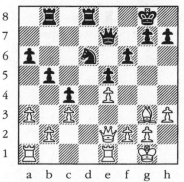

**Exercise 15:** *Black to move. How can Black exploit White's weak squares?*

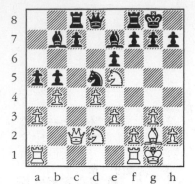

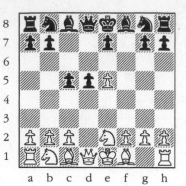

**Exercise 16:** *White to move (Kramnik–Carlsen, Dortmund, 2007). The obvious move is 17.bxa5, but White has a much better move, which brilliantly exploits the weak c6 square. What did White play, and why?*

**Exercise 17:** *White to move. This position arises after 1.e4 c5 2.Nf3 d6 3.d4 cxd4 4.Nxd4 Nf6 5.Nc3 e5. The idea of playing 5…e5 is fine, but Black should prepare this move by first playing 5…a6. How can White now use the b5 square to exploit Black's weakened light squares?*

**Exercise 18:** *White to move (Wolff–Shabalov, PRO Chess League, 2017). This position came from 1.e4 c6 2.Ne2 d5 3.e5 f6 4.d4 fxe5 5.dxe5 c5. Black's last move was a mistake. How can White exploit Black's weak light squares?*

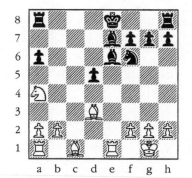

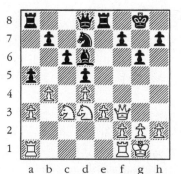

**Exercise 19:** *White to move (Fischer–Petrosian, Buenos Aires, 1971). Identify the weak squares in Black's position and formulate a plan to exploit them. What is White's best move and how might the game proceed?*

**Exercise 20:** *Black to move (Vaganian–Wolff, New York, 1990). Identify White's weakest squares and formulate a plan to exploit them. What is Black's best move and how might the game proceed?*

# Chapter 14

# All Good Things Must Come to an End

As the middlegame progresses, opposing forces come into contact. If neither side manages to mount a decisive attack, more pieces will be exchanged. When material for each side is reduced enough, the middlegame has ended, and the third phase of a chess game—the endgame—has begun.

"How reduced does material have to be? How much is enough?" you might ask. Unfortunately, there are no easy answers. I can't give you a simple way to tell when enough material has been exchanged so that the middlegame has become the endgame. But I can explain the two general principles that apply to the endgame. What you should do when some material has been exchanged is ask whether those principles seem to apply to the position you're playing. If they do, the endgame has begun.

# Don't Forget What You've Learned up to Now!

Before I explain these two general principles, I must make one thing very clear: *all the principles and strategies you've learned for playing the middlegame still apply to the endgame!*

Middlegame principles are principles for playing good chess, and the fact that there's less material on the chessboard in the endgame doesn't mean that those principles no longer hold true. Controlling the center, king safety, the advantage of active over passive pieces, pawn structure, space, weak squares—and more!—all still apply. However, the reduced material does have an effect on how to use these principles. The most important changes are listed here:

+ **Controlling the center.** It's still important to control the center. In fact, in many endgames it's absolutely essential to occupy the center before your opponent. But when material is drastically reduced, the center may become less important. For example, if all the pawns are on one side of the board, then all of the action will probably be on that side of the board, so the center will lose most of its importance. Diagram 1 shows an example of such a position.

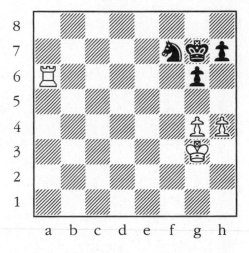

*Diagram 1: Example of a position where control of the center is not important.*

+ **Active vs. passive pieces.** In the endgame, it's more important than ever to keep your pieces active. The reason is simple: in the middlegame, when each side has lots of pieces, the rest of the army can compensate for one passive piece. In the endgame, that one piece may be your whole army or close to it! For example, in Diagram 2, White's rook and king are active, whereas Black's rook and king are passive. But other than pawns, king and rook are all that is left of each side's army! White is about to win Black's a-pawn, which should be enough to win the game.

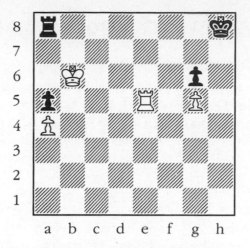

*Diagram 2: Example of a position where having the more active pieces is even more important than in the middlegame.*

+ **Good bishop vs. knight.** For similar reasons as above, whether the bishop or the knight is the better piece becomes more important as fewer pieces remain. The bishop is the better piece when it can roam freely and there are pawns on both sides of the board. In such cases, the bishop's greater mobility is an advantage over the knight. Diagram 3 shows such a position, taken from a world championship game between Kasparov and Karpov. Karpov drew, but Kasparov had good winning chances throughout. (Notice that Kasparov also has more space and better control of the center!)

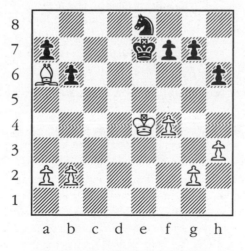

*Diagram 3: Example of a position where the bishop is better than the knight (Kasparov-Karpov, World Championship match, 1986).*

+ **Bad bishop vs. knight.** Sometimes the knight is the better piece. This happens most often when the bishop is bad (recall Chapter 10). Some endgames are lost just because of the bad bishop. Diagram 4 shows an example of this, taken from another World Championship match game between Karpov and Kasparov. Black's bishop can only attack one white pawn, whereas all of Black's pawns are targets for White's knight. Furthermore, the mobility of the bishop is reduced by having so many pawns on white squares. Karpov was able to exploit Black's ineffectual bishop using his active king and knight and winning this endgame. (This example illustrates why you should avoid putting too many pawns on the same color squares as your bishop without a *very* good reason. Even if it doesn't look like a problem in the middlegame, you may end up paying for it in the endgame!)

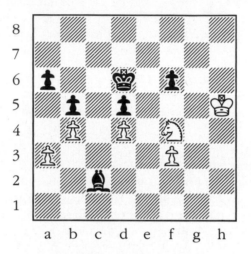

*Diagram 4: Example of a position where the knight is better than the bishop (Karpov–Kasparov, World Championship match, 1984).*

These are the most important ways that middlegame principles must be adjusted to fit the endgame. Experience will teach you others.

Now let's talk about the two general principles that apply explicitly to the endgame.

# Principle #1: The King Is a Strong Piece— Use It!

The first principle is also a quote from one of the strongest American grandmasters of all time: Reuben Fine. It was one of the pieces of advice he offered in his classic 1941 book, *Basic Chess Endings*, "In the middlegame, with so much material on the board, the king should be kept out of harm's way. But when material is reduced, the danger to the king decreases accordingly, and then the king should be used like any other piece."

Two examples will help me make this point. First, look at Diagram 5. White has an extra pawn, but White's rook is passive, while Black's is active. How can White activate the rook? Bring the king over to help! White should play 1.Kf1, 2.Ke1, 3.Kd1, 4.Kc2 to protect the pawn and drive away Black's rook. By using the king, White can get more out of her rook.

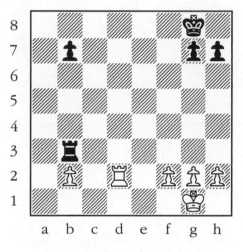

*Diagram 5: White needs to activate the king to exploit his extra pawn.*

Diagrams 6 through 9 show the second example. Diagram 6 shows the position of one of my games just at the moment that queens have been exchanged. (My last move was 25...bxc5, capturing White's queen.) While the queens were still on the board, it was much too dangerous for either side to bring the king to the center. But Diagram 7 shows that as soon as queens were exchanged, each of us rushed the king to the middle of the board as fast as possible. The king is a strong piece, and we each wanted to use it!

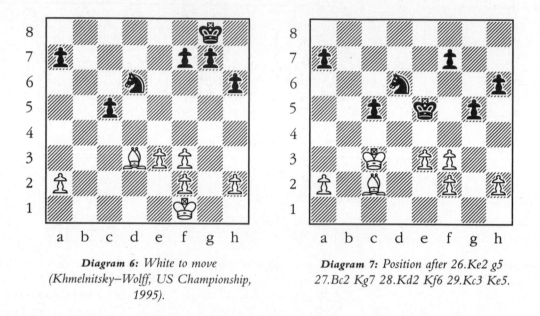

*Diagram 6: White to move*
*(Khmelnitsky–Wolff, US Championship,*
*1995).*

*Diagram 7: Position after 26.Ke2 g5*
*27.Bc2 Kg7 28.Kd2 Kf6 29.Kc3 Ke5.*

Diagram 8 shows the game at a much later stage. Although I have won a pawn, it's difficult to see how to win. The solution was to activate the king by playing 62...c4+! 63.Bxc4 Kc5 as shown in Diagram 9. Because the bishop was attacked, White had to allow the black king to reach d4 and then Black's active king and knight were able to force a win by attacking and winning White's pawns.

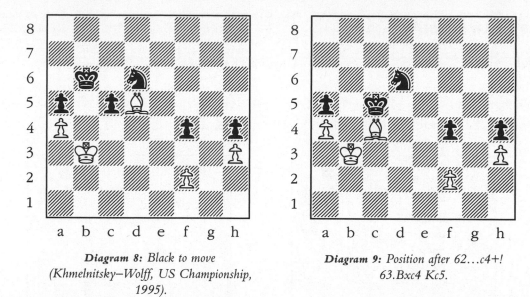

*Diagram 8: Black to move (Khmelnitsky–Wolff, US Championship, 1995).*

*Diagram 9: Position after 62...c4+! 63.Bxc4 Kc5.*

# Principle #2: The Passed Pawn Rules the Endgame

When there are no longer any opposing pawns that can block a pawn or control any of the squares between the pawn and the edge of the board, we say that the pawn is *passed*. (The name comes from the idea that the pawn has "passed" all of the opposing pawns.) In the middlegame, with lots of material on the board, it's hard to promote a passed pawn. (That doesn't mean that passed pawns are unimportant in the middlegame, just that the threat of pushing a passed pawn down the board doesn't usually feature prominently in the middlegame.) But in the endgame, with much less material on the board, the passed pawn becomes much more important. Ultimately, most endgame strategy comes down to creating and promoting a passed pawn. This is precisely why the advantage of even one pawn is often enough to win a game. Usually, one extra pawn makes only a small difference in the balance of forces of a complicated middlegame. But one extra pawn makes all the difference in the endgame when it promotes to a queen! Let's look at some of the most important aspects of passed pawns.

# The Pawn Majority

When a larger number of pawns faces off against a smaller number of pawns, it's called having a *pawn majority*. Where you have a pawn majority, you have the potential to make a passed pawn.

In Diagram 10, White has a pawn majority on the queenside, while Black has a pawn majority on the kingside. But White's pawns are much farther advanced than Black's, so White is much better positioned to make a passed pawn with 1.b6!

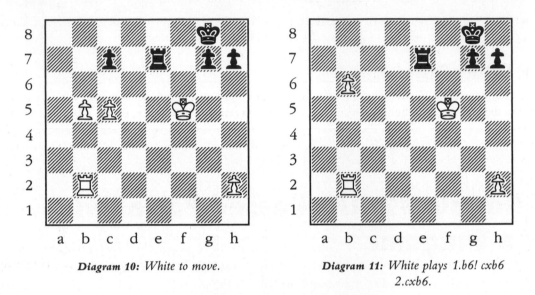

*Diagram 10: White to move.*

*Diagram 11: White plays 1.b6! cxb6 2.cxb6.*

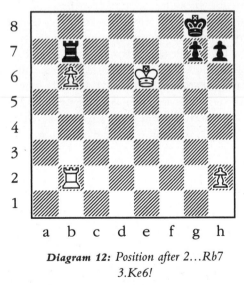

*Diagram 12: Position after 2...Rb7 3.Ke6!*

After 1...cxb6 2.cxb6 (see Diagram 11), White already threatens to play 3.b7 and 4.b8=Q. (Notice how well White's rook supports the passed pawn from behind it.) The only way Black can try to stop the pawn from promoting without giving up the rook is to play 2...Rb7, but then in Diagram 12, White uses the king with 3.Ke6! to drive the black rook away. White plays 4.Kd6 and 5.Kc6; after using the king to drive the rook away, White will push the pawn to b7 and b8. It will cost Black the rook to stop the pawn from making a queen, so Black has no way to defend.

Did you see how well placed White's rook was behind the passed pawn? Rooks belong behind passed pawns, regardless of whether that passed pawn is yours or your opponent's!

There are many, many ways to use a pawn majority. You should always look out for new ways to use the pawn majority in your own games and in any other games you study.

## The Outside Passed Pawn

In earlier chapters, I've stressed that center pawns are more powerful than noncenter pawns. That's true in the opening and the middlegame, and it's still sometimes true in the endgame when control of the center is important. But in the endgame, the outside passed pawn can be a definite advantage. (The outside passed pawn is a passed pawn that is very far over to either the kingside or queenside; it gets its name from the idea that it's "outside" the main theater of action.)

There are two reasons the outside passed pawn can be an advantage:

+ Since the outside passed pawn is far away from other pieces, it's harder for the defending side to get over to it and stop it from advancing. (Diagrams 10 through 12 give an example of this.)

+ Even if the defending side can get over to stop the pawn, the pieces may have been led away from many other important squares. In other words, the outside passed pawn sometimes acts as a decoy.

Diagrams 13 through 15 show how, by acting as a decoy, the outside passed pawn can be deadly. White plays 1.a6. To stop this pawn, Black must play either 1…Kc6 or 1…Kc7. But then White's king can infiltrate Black's pawns on the kingside by playing 2.Ke5. Because Black had to move the king over to catch the outside passed pawn, the kingside pawns are left defenseless to the white king.

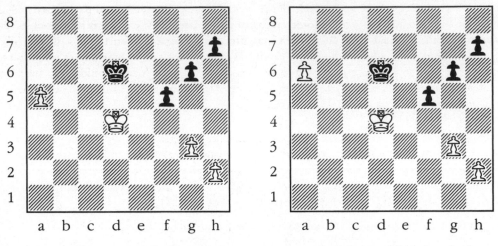

*Diagram 13: White to move.*     *Diagram 14: White plays 1.a6.*

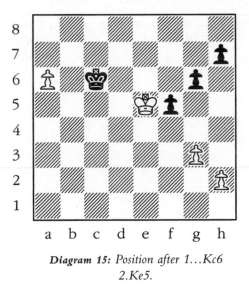

*Diagram 15: Position after 1…Kc6 2.Ke5.*

# The Protected Passed Pawn

A protected passed pawn is simply a passed pawn that is protected by another pawn. In the endgame, the protected passed pawn can be very powerful indeed. The point is that because the passed pawn is so powerful, you want it to be securely defended. And how better to defend it than with another pawn?

Diagrams 16 through 19 show an example of the power of the protected passed pawn. Each side has a pawn majority, but only Black has a protected passed pawn. Because the pawn is protected, White has no way to attack it with the king. (If White's king ever goes beyond the fourth rank, Black will play 1...b3 and make a queen, so the white king can never attack Black's queenside pawns.) Because the pawn is passed, White must keep the king close enough to catch it if Black should start advancing it. So the protected passed pawn severely limits the mobility of the white king. This turns out to be a large enough advantage for Black to win this position.

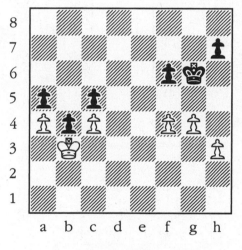

*Diagram 16: Black to move.*

Black starts by playing 1...f5! to break up White's pawns. Black's plan is to loosen the pawns in order to attack them with the king. If White plays 2.g5, then after 2...Kh5 (as shown in Diagram 18), Black will play 3...Kh4 and capture White's h-pawn, after which the other pawns will fall. (I haven't shown 2.gxf5+ Kxf5 in a diagram, but can you see that Black could then immediately capture White's f-pawn?) So White plays 2.Kc2, and after 2...fxg4 3.hxg4 h5!, Black exposes the pawns to attack by the king. Exercise 12 at the end of this chapter will challenge you to figure out how Black wins the position in Diagram 19.

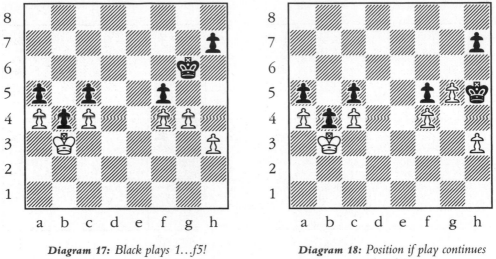

*Diagram 17: Black plays 1...f5!*

*Diagram 18: Position if play continues
2.g5 Kh5.*

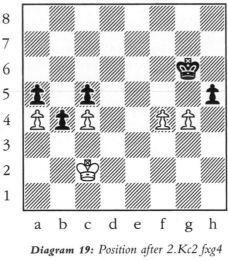

*Diagram 19: Position after 2.Kc2 fxg4
3.hxg4 h5!*

## Blockading the Passed Pawn

When your opponent has a passed pawn, you should stop it from advancing. The best way to do that is to stick a piece in front of it. When you do this, it's called *blockading the passed pawn*.

Diagram 20 shows an example of the blockade. White's e-pawn is passed, but because Black's knight is in front of it, it's not going anywhere. White can attack the knight with the king, but then Black will defend it with the king. Because White's bishop moves on black squares, it can't attack the square in front of the pawn, so Black can maintain the blockade indefinitely.

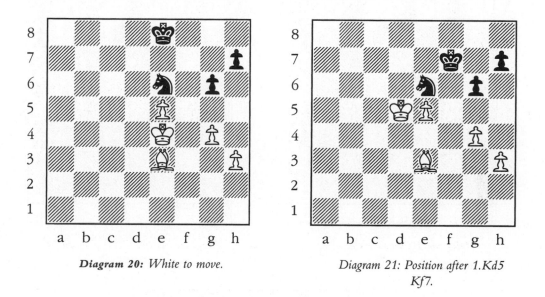

**Diagram 20:** *White to move.*  *Diagram 21: Position after 1.Kd5 Kf7.*

The only other way for White to try to break through is to use the king to attack Black's pawns, but so long as Black keeps the knight on e6 and the pawn on g6, all the fifth-ranked squares on the kingside are guarded and White's king can't get at the black pawns. If White plays 1.Kd5 as in Diagram 21, Black plays 1…Kf7, defending the knight with the king. Then Black moves the knight back and forth from e6 to any other square where the knight can't be captured and then back to e6 again. By following this plan, Black can only lose by running out of a safe square to move the knight to; but this should never happen, so the position is a draw. (Try playing this position out with a friend or a computer to see for yourself!)

When employing the blockade, make sure you leave yourself enough space so you don't run out of moves. This danger is shown in Diagrams 22 and 23. Black has blockaded the passed pawn just one square before promoting. Because White has a black-squared bishop, you might think that Black is safe. But Black's knight is on the edge of the board, which means it has very few squares to move to. Now White plays 1.Be5! and Black discovers that there is no good move. If Black could "pass" and not move, then Black would be safe because White still has no threat. But there's no such thing as passing in chess, so Black will lose: if Black moves the king, White's king will capture the knight; if Black moves the knight, White's bishop will capture it and then White will safely promote the pawn next move.

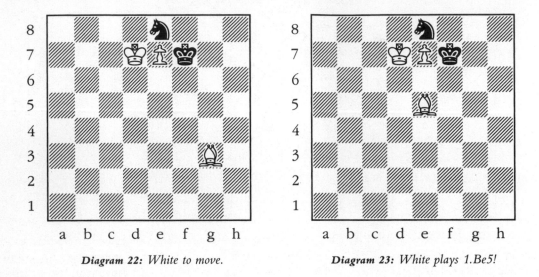

*Diagram 22: White to move.*    *Diagram 23: White plays 1.Be5!*

# Connected Passed Pawns

Recall from Chapter 11 that the pawn duo is very strong. Well, imagine the strength of a duo of passed pawns! When two pawns on adjacent files are passed, they are called *connected passed pawns*. Connected passed pawns are very, very powerful. Sometimes they are worth a lot of material.

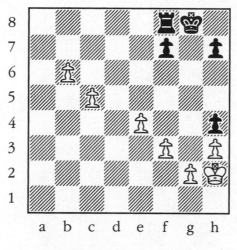

***Diagram 24:*** *Whoever moves wins.*

Diagram 24 shows a special case that illustrates the power of connected passed pawns. White to move wins by playing 1.c6! because Black can't stop White from making a queen. For example, play could continue 1...Rc8 2.b7 Rxc6 (or 2...Rb8 3.c7) 3.b8=Q+ and so on. Black to move wins by playing 1...Rb8!, which stops White from advancing the queenside pawns. Then Black moves the king over to the queenside and captures the queenside pawns, but Black has to be careful stopping the pawns: notice that 1...Rc8?? loses to 2.b7! Rb8 (2...Rxc5 3.b8=Q+) 3.c6 and 4.c7.

Connected passed pawns are so strong because they're so hard to blockade. Diagram 24 shows that sometimes they can overcome a rook all by themselves. With additional support from other pieces, they can be fearsome.

In Diagram 25, Black has two passed pawns that sit passively on their original squares, doing nothing, while White's connected passed pawns are far advanced. With White's king and knight nearby, Black has no chance of stopping them even though Black's king and knight are right in front of White's pawns. White wins by playing 1.e6+ followed by 2.d6 and then by advancing the pawns with the support of the knight and king. One sample line goes: 1.e6+ Kd8 2.d6 Ne8 3.Kc6 (White threatens 4.e7+ and 5.d7+) 3...Nf6 4.Kb7 a5 5.Nc6+ Ke8 6.Kc8! (Not 6.d7+?? Nxd7 7.exd7+ Kxd7, and White has no pawns left!) followed by 7.d7+ and wins.

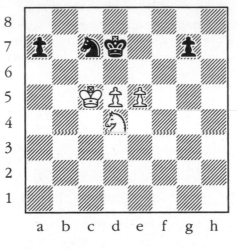

**Diagram 25:** *White to move.*

If you don't support your connected passed pawns well enough with your pieces, your opponent may be able to blockade them by getting one of them to advance and then blockading the backward pawn. An example of this is found in the exercises at the end of this chapter.

# Three Specific Endgames

Remember in Chapter 9, we had to distinguish between *the* opening and *an* opening. *The* opening is the opening phase of a game; whereas *an* opening is a specific sequence of moves at the start of the game that a player plans in advance. In a similar way, we have to distinguish between *the* endgame and *an* endgame. *The* endgame is the phase of the game for which you've been learning general principles. *An* endgame refers to a specific kind of endgame one learns how to play ahead of time. It is very valuable to learn how to play certain specific, typical endgame positions. Because endgames have a small number of pawns and pieces, the positions can be classified into certain types in which the plans and even specific tactics associated with those types of positions come up again and again.

There are many endgames to learn. A grandmaster knows thousands of them. I'm going to show you three. Each one helps to illustrate certain principles, and each is also useful in its own right.

# King and Pawn vs. King and the Opposition

Our first specific endgame is shown in Diagram 26. Notice the position of the two kings. When there is one square between the kings (horizontally or vertically), they're said to be *opposed*. Whichever side does not have to move has the *opposition*. So in Diagram 26, if it's White's turn, then Black has the opposition; while if it's Black's turn, then White has the opposition. The opposition is an advantage because when you have the opposition you can force the other king to give ground. In Diagram 26, if Black has the opposition, it's a draw; if White has the opposition, White wins. Diagrams 27 and 28 illustrate how the game could continue depending on whose move it is in Diagram 26.

(By the way, Diagram 26 shows us again that sometimes one side loses only because there is no such thing as saying "pass" in chess. Whenever this happens, we say that the player who would like to say "pass" is in *zugzwang,* which is derived from German and loosely translates to "a compulsive move." Chess has some odd words, doesn't it?)

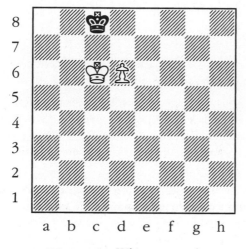

*Diagram 26: White to move draws; Black to move loses.*

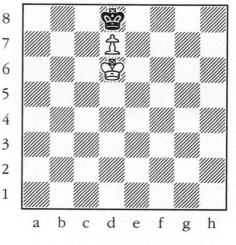

*Diagram 27: Position after 1.d7+ Kd8 2.Kd6.*

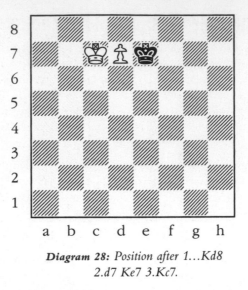

***Diagram 28:*** *Position after 1...Kd8*
*2.d7 Ke7 3.Kc7.*

If it's White's turn to move, White has no better move than 1.d7+. Black plays 1...Kd8, and now White must play 2.Kd6 to defend the pawn, but then it's a draw because Black is stalemated.

If it's Black's turn to move, Black has to move the king to either d8 or b8. If Black plays 1...Kb8, then after 2.d7 Black can't control d8 on the next move, so White will promote the pawn and win. Black plays 1...Kd8, and White plays 2.d7. Now the only legal move is 2...Ke7, after which White plays 3.Kc7, as shown in Diagram 28. White controls the d8 square, so White will again promote the pawn safely and win.

Suppose in Diagram 26, instead of pushing the pawn, White played the king back with 1.Kc5. Black might play 1...Kd7 and then after 2.Kd5, we arrive at the position in Diagram 29. Where should Black move the king now? Wherever Black moves it, Black wants to take the opposition when White brings the king to either e6 or c6.

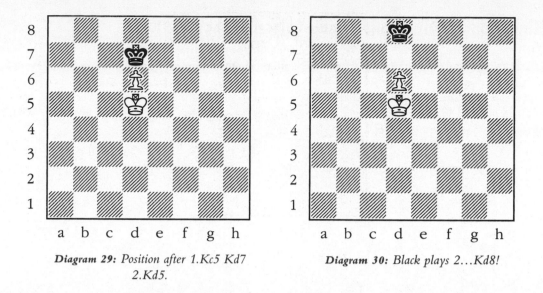

*Diagram 29: Position after 1.Kc5 Kd7 2.Kd5.*

*Diagram 30: Black plays 2...Kd8!*

Black should play 2...Kd8! as shown in Diagram 30. This is the only move to draw because otherwise White will take the opposition. Now if White moves the king to either c6 or e6, Black can take the opposition and draw. And if White moves the king to some other square—say e5—then Black just moves the king back to d7, and White is making no progress.

These king and pawn versus king endgames can get pretty tricky, and in the exercises, I give you a couple more to cut your teeth on. As you work on them, remember the importance of having the opposition!

## King, Rook's Pawn, and Wrong-Colored Bishop vs. King

This next endgame is either tragic or comic, depending on your point of view. In Diagram 31, White has an extra pawn and an extra bishop. Surely, Black should resign. But no: White can't win even with all that extra material! The problem is White can't force the king out of the corner with just the king and a pawn because, even if White takes the opposition, Black will be stalemated. The bishop is of no help because White has the wrong-colored bishop (i.e. it doesn't control the corner square where White wants to promote the pawn).

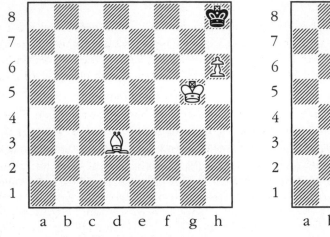

*Diagram 31: Even with an extra bishop and an extra pawn, White can't win.*

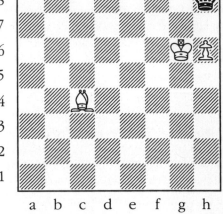

*Diagram 32: The best White can do is stalemate Black; there's no way to force the king out of the corner.*

Diagram 32 shows a typical position that might arise if White tries to win. White can advance the pawn to h7, but can't force the king out of the corner. The best White can do is give stalemate. Notice that the bishop is useless because all it can do is control g8, which just helps stalemate Black.

But don't think that having a bishop and a pawn always leads to a draw! Bishop and pawn against king is only a draw when all of these (very) special circumstances hold true:

+ The pawn is a rook's pawn, i.e. the pawn is on a file where a rook starts the game (which is to say either the h-file or the a-file).

+ The bishop travels on the wrong color to control the corner square where the pawn promotes.

+ The defending king can occupy the corner square where the pawn promotes.

## Opposite-Colored Bishops

In Chapter 10, we saw that having opposite-colored bishops favors the attacker, because what one side's bishop attacks, the other side's bishop can't defend (so it's like having an extra piece in the attack). But in the endgame, having opposite-colored bishops favors the defender, because the attacker's bishop often can't attack the defender's pawns, whereas the defender's bishop often can blockade the attacker's passed pawns.

Diagram 33 shows an example of an endgame with opposite-colored bishops that is drawn. Even though White has two extra connected passed pawns, White cannot make progress. White can't advance either of the passed pawns because they're blockaded by the black king and bishop, and White can't break the blockade because White's black-squared bishop is useless for controlling c6 or d5. If White could make another passed pawn, then White could advance that pawn, which Black couldn't blockade because the king and bishop would be too far away. But as the pawns stand, there's no way to make another passed pawn. And there's no way to attack Black's pawns, because Black's g6 pawn is protected by the f7 pawn, the f7 pawn is protected by the bishop, and White's bishop is useless for attacking Black's pawns. White's black-squared bishop is practically a spectator!

Here is an example of how the position from Diagram 33 might go: 1.Bf2 Ba2 2.Kf6 (or 2.d5+ Bxd5) 2…Bd5 3.Be3 Ba2 4.f5 gxf5 5.Kxf5 Bd5 6.Kf6 Ba2, etc. Black will just move the bishop back and forth between a2 and d5, and White can't break through. Black draws because even with two extra pawns, White can neither destroy Black's blockade nor capture Black's pawns.

Opposite-colored bishop endgames can get pretty complicated. The important thing to realize is that Black draws in Diagram 33 only because Black has a perfect blockade. A slight change can give White a winning position. For example, in Diagram 34, White wins by diverting Black's king with 1.d7! Kxd7 2.Kxd5. In Diagram 35, White wins by diverting Black's bishop with 1.h5! gxh5 2.gxh5 Bb3 3.h6 Bc2 (the diversion: Black's bishop must shift diagonals to stop the h-pawn from queening) 4.d5+ Kd7 5.Kf6, and Black's defense collapses.

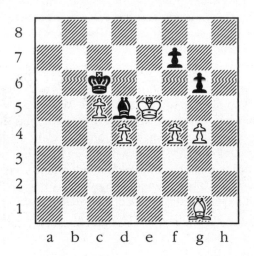

Diagram 33: Even with two extra pawns, White can't win.

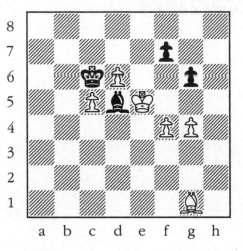

Diagram 34: White wins with 1.d7!

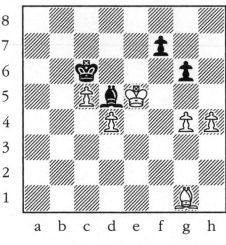

Diagram 35: White wins with 1.h5!

If you're trying to win an endgame, don't exchange down to opposite colored bishops unless you have a very good reason. And if you're trying to draw, grab any chance to exchange down to opposite-colored bishops. It might even be worth one or two pawns to do it!

Opposite-colored bishop endgames aren't always drawn; however, they give much better drawing chances than almost any other kind of endgame because the defending side can more easily defend the pawns and blockade the opponent's pawns. If you're trying to win an endgame, don't exchange down to opposite-colored bishops without a very good reason. And if you're trying to draw, consider carefully any opportunity to exchange down to opposite-colored bishops. It might even be worth a pawn or two to do it!

# Exercises

Exercise 1: *Black to move. This is Diagram 15 again, and your task is to show how White wins, even against Black's best defense. (Hint: Black is going to play 2...Kb6 to capture the a-pawn. While the king is distracted, have White capture Black's kingside pawns, but be careful not to let any of Black's pawns slip by!)*

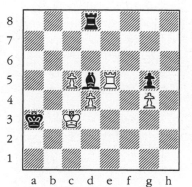

Exercise 2: *White to move. It looks like Black has White's pawns blockaded. Can White break Black's blockade and push her connected passed pawns? How?*

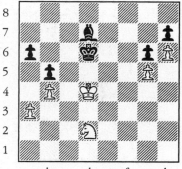

Exercise 3: *White to move. Who is better and why? How should White play?*

*Exercise 4:* White to move
(Capablanca–Germann,
Miller, and Skillcorn, London
Exhibition, 1920). In the old
days, grandmasters used to play
matches against teams of wealthy
amateurs. Capablanca played
this game against a team of three
players. It's Capablanca's turn
to make his twenty-third move.
Which move is better: 23.Ke2 or
23.O-O? Why?

*Exercise 5:* White wants to
win, Black wants to draw. If
it's White's turn, does White
win? If it's Black's turn, does
Black draw? Justify your answer
by showing how the game should
continue if it's White's turn and
if it's Black's turn.

*Exercise 6:* White wants to
win; Black wants to draw. If
it's White's turn, how does
White win? If it's Black's turn,
how does Black draw? (Hint:
remember the importance of
having the opposition!)

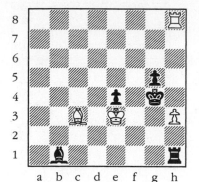

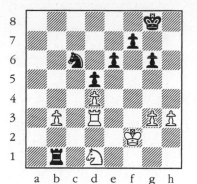

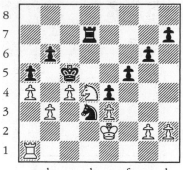

**Exercise 7:** *Black to move (Wolff–Browne, US Championship, 1995). This is one of the strangest games I ever won. Clearly Black can't lose after 55...Rxh3 56.Rxh3 Kxh3 57.Kf2, but Black can't win either. (Why?) So, Browne decided to play 55...Kf5?? to avoid exchanges. This move is a terrible blunder. How did I take advantage of Browne's mistake?*

**Exercise 8:** *White to move (Lasker–Capablanca, World Championship, 1921). Evaluate this position. Who do you think is more likely to win, and why?*

**Exercise 9:** *Black to move (Merenyi–Capablanca, Budapest, 1928). Capablanca played 30... Rxd4! 31.exd4+ Kxd4. Explain why this is a good sacrifice for Black to play.*

**Exercise 10:** *(Gutman–Wolff, Paris, 1987). It's White's turn, but rather than make a move, my opponent resigned. Does the fact that I had a rook's pawn and the wrong-colored bishop mean that White should have been able to draw? If White had played 57.Kd2, how should Black play?*

**Exercise 11:** *Black to move (Chow–Wolff, Sioux Falls, 1996). This is a tricky exercise! How does Black win this position despite being down a pawn? (Hint: find a way—any way at all—for Black to turn the h-pawn into a passed pawn.)*

**Exercise 12:** *White to move. This is Diagram 19 again (which came from Diagram 16 after 1… f5 2.Kc2 fxg4 3.hxg4 h5), and your job is to show how Black wins no matter how White plays. This is a difficult exercise. Analyze the position the best you can and then compare your analysis with the answer in the appendix.*

**Exercise 13:** *Black to move. This endgame is a draw. Analyze this position. After 1…Kc4, what is White's drawing strategy?*

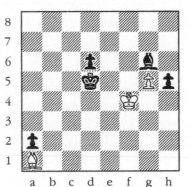

**Exercise 14:** *Black to move. Can White draw this position, also?*

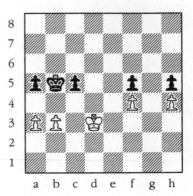

**Exercise 15:** *Black to move (Kasparov–Bareev, Holland, 2001). Black resigned in this position, but Kasparov later demonstrated that the position is drawn! Can you demonstrate how? (Warning: this is hard!)*

**Exercise 16:** Black to move (Turner–Pert, British Championship, 2000). It looks like White has stopped Black's king and pawns and can use the king to take Black's pawns. But Black found an extraordinary idea: 1...g4! What was Black's idea? Can Black draw?

**Exercise 17:** White to move. Black will try to draw by advancing the pawn and forcing White to give up the rook for it. Can White win? (Hint: This is hard until you find the right idea, but if you find the right idea then the win is easy. Look for a way to stop the black king from helping the pawn advance.)

**Exercise 18:** White to move. Can White win? (If you solved Exercise 17, can you see why the same idea won't work here?) Analyze the position to figure out what the result should be with best play by both sides and then compare your analysis to the answer.

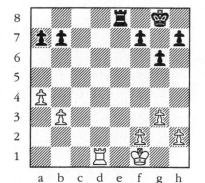

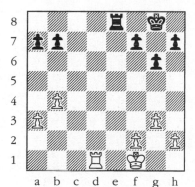

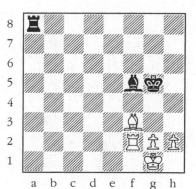

**Exercise 19:** White to move. What is White's strongest move, and why?

**Exercise 20:** White to move. Even after White plays the strongest move, Black has a key idea that does not exist in Exercise 19. What is it, and how does it change the evaluation of the position?

**Exercise 21:** Black to move. This position was first published four hundred years ago! Black is clearly trying to draw. What is the best defense?

**Exercise 22:** *White to move. The obvious move here is 1.h4, but this turns out only to draw. Why? What is the way for White to win this position?*

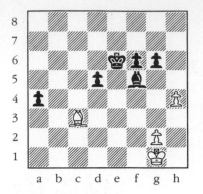

**Exercise 23:** *Black to move (Topalov–Shirov, Linares, 1998). Two top grandmasters played this game, and here Black played the absolutely extraordinary move 1…Bh3!! to win. Analyze this position. Can you see why Black wins after 1…Bh3, and why this incredible sacrifice is such a good idea?*

**Exercise 24:** *White to move. Can White force a win in this position? Justify your answer with analysis. (Hint: be sure to assess carefully what happens if White manages to capture the pawn on c2.)*

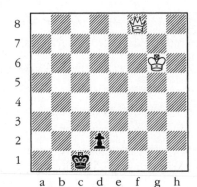

**Exercise 25:** *White to move. Can White force a win in this position? Justify your answer with analysis. (Hint: think carefully about what makes this position different from Exercise 24.)*

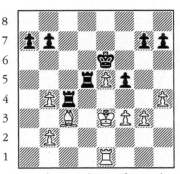

**Exercise 26:** *Black to move (Lombardy–Fischer, USA Championship, 1960–61). How did Fischer find a way to break down White's defense and exchange pieces to reach a clearly winning endgame?*

# Part 4

# BEYOND THE BASICS

If you've studied the first three parts, you've learned how to play chess well. But you've only scratched the surface of the possibilities chess has to offer. This part is your platform for diving into the world of chess.

Now that you've learned the basics, you're ready for more. Chapter 15 gives guidance in how to teach yourself far beyond this book—and how to find opponents so you can use your awesome chess skills. Then Chapter 16 explains how computers have played chess from the Stone Age (well, since the 1950s) up to the breakthroughs of artificial intelligence. Get ready to play chess like a boss!

# Playing Like a Boss and Beyond!

At this point, you've learned all the basic tactics and strategies for chess. You might be able to beat most or all of your friends, and you can certainly play better than most people who haven't studied the strategies and tactics you have learned so far. Maybe you've accomplished everything you want at chess.

But then again, maybe not. Maybe even after studying this book there's somebody you know who still beats you, and you'd like to turn the tables. Or maybe you've really gotten hooked on chess, and you'd like to start competing online, at a club, or in tournaments. I think you should! (But then I would, wouldn't I?) After all, chess is a great game, and there's a whole world of chess out there!

This chapter shows you how to take your game to the next level and beyond. I help you develop a training program to play chess competitively, and I guide you toward online resources for playing, learning, and watching chess. You learn how to play chess in clubs or tournaments. Finally, there is a section at the end of the chapter devoted to chess resources for kids.

# Design Your Own Training Program

Remember that there are three phases in chess: the opening, the middlegame, and the endgame. It turns out that the opening and the endgame are best studied independently. The middlegame is much harder to study on its own; the main way to improve your middlegame is through careful study of your own games and other people's games. Throughout all of this, it can be very helpful to use computers and, if you want, to work with a teacher or a coach.

Let's break this down step by step.

## Study the Opening

The opening comes first in chess, so we'll start there. From previous chapters, you'll remember there are lots of specific openings to learn. If you search chess books online, you'll quickly discover there's a huge amount of literature about openings. It may look daunting! Keep in mind that your goal is not to learn all chess openings for their own sake, but rather to take this knowledge and let it help you play better.

To play chess competitively, you need to develop an opening repertoire. Your repertoire is a set of specific opening sequences that allow you to reach a playable middlegame no matter how your opponent plays in the opening. If you don't want to play competitively, you may want to spend your time studying other aspects of chess. But if you want to compete for prizes in club competitions or amateur tournaments, it's essential to have an opening repertoire.

Developing an opening repertoire is a lot of work, and it is a personal thing. There's no right or wrong set of openings, just whatever lets you reach middlegame positions you like and play well. For that reason, I can't tell you what openings to play. But I can tell you how to go about selecting and studying your openings.

A good way to start the process is to play through some grandmaster games. Pay attention to the various openings they play and decide whether you like the kinds of middlegames and endgames that come out of those openings.

For example, do an internet search of "top-rated chess grandmasters" or go to the World Chess Federation's (FIDE) list of the top 100 players (ratings.fide.com/toplist.phtml). Each of these 100 grandmasters plays the opening differently and, as a result, gets different kinds of middlegame positions. Play through some games of these grandmasters and see whether you feel more comfortable with the positions of one versus another. (One useful website is chessgames.com, where you can search and select from almost a million games sorted in various useful ways.) Don't worry about the specific details of the openings; at this point, you are developing a sense for what kinds of positions you want to play.

Another way to develop an opening repertoire is to emulate a single grandmaster. When I started playing chess as a kid, I copied the opening repertoire of Bobby Fischer from his book *My Sixty Memorable Games*. It is more limiting to emulate a single grandmaster, but it is easier and will save you some time.

Once you have a general sense of the openings that grandmasters play and the kinds of middlegames they lead to, you need to start learning specific openings. The next step in developing your repertoire is to get an opening encyclopedia that covers all the different openings. I can recommend a few opening encyclopedias to consider:

+ *Chess Opening Essentials: The Ideas & Plans Behind ALL Chess Openings,* volumes 1-4 (2007). Written by Stefan Djuric and Dimitri Komarov, this encyclopedia is actually four books and is the most comprehensive of the choices listed.

+ *FCO: Fundamental Chess Openings* (2009) by Paul van der Sterren. This book explains the opening ideas, without being completely comprehensive.

+ *Modern Chess Openings,* 15th edition (2008) by Nick deFirmian. This is a very useful reference manual.

Using an opening encyclopedia will give you a holistic perspective. For example, suppose you decide that with White you want to start your games by playing 1.e4. Black then has a number of reasonable responses, including 1...e5, 1...c5, 1...d5, 1...c6, 1...d6, 1...e6, 1...Nf6 or 1...Nc6. You need to develop enough of an understanding about each of Black's moves to know what specific moves you want to play for the next 8 to 10 moves. Turning the board around, as Black you need to know how you plan to respond to each of White's most common first moves: 1.e4, 1.d4, 1.c4, 1.Nf3 and 1.g3. A good encyclopedia is a valuable resource for studying all of these moves and more.

Once you have outlined what you need to learn, it is time to study a few specific openings more deeply. For many, the encyclopedia may be enough, but you may also want to get some books written on specific openings. Be careful in your purchases, however. There's an enormous number of opening books, and you can quickly end up spending a lot of money here.

If you decide to go even deeper into learning chess openings, you will discover a nearly limitless world out there! For example, there are books devoted to opening traps, which are opening ideas that try to trick your opponent (or you!) into variations that look tempting but turn out badly. If you start using chess software databases, you will discover lots of opening analyses written directly for your chess database and supplemented by thousands of games to study. If you were to try to play openings at the same level as a grandmaster, which I do *not* recommend for you, you would have to study all the time to stay on top of all the latest ideas. A professional chess player spends more than half of his or her time just studying openings!

Don't get lost in studying the opening, however. Remember the point is simply to reach a middlegame position that you can play well. Study only what you need to achieve that goal so you can spend the rest of your chess time more effectively elsewhere.

## Study the Endgame

The reason we study the opening in depth is that a chess game always begins from the same position. The reason we study the endgame in depth is that once most of the pieces and pawns are off the board, there is a limited number of patterns to learn.

Fortunately, you only need to study a few books to learn everything you need to know to play the endgame well.

Here are some excellent endgame books:

+ *Chess Endings: Essential Knowledge* (1993) by Yuri Averbakh. Yuri is considered one of the finest endgame players of his generation and wrote many classic endgame books that grandmasters still study.

+ *Silman's Complete Endgame Course: From Beginning to Master* (2007) by Jeremy Silman. Jeremy has a real knack for explaining chess and has put that skill to good use in this endgame book.

+ *Understanding Chess Endgames* (2009) by John Nunn. John had a terrific career as a grandmaster, wrote dozens of very popular books, and was a math prodigy!

+ *Dvoretsky's Endgame Manual*, 4th edition (2014) by Mark Dvoretsky. Mark is perhaps the most revered chess trainer of his generation, and he is especially good at teaching endgames.

+ *Practical Chess Endings,* 2nd revised edition (2018) by Paul Keres. Originally written in 1972 by a grandmaster many chess historians consider one of the greatest players who never became world champion, this is a classic.

At this point in your training, you probably only need to study one or two of these books to get everything you need. Browse through the ones listed above, and pick those you like the most. If you read one or two of these diligently, cover to cover (especially if you use a chess set!), you can learn to play endgames well, and your results should noticeably improve.

## Study Games of Top Grandmasters

So far, we have outlined a training program for studying the opening and the endgame, so it would make sense for this section to be about studying the middlegame, right? But it doesn't really work that way because there is such an infinite variety of middlegame positions.

Once you have learned the basic tactics and strategies that we have covered in this book, the best way to improve your middlegame is to study the games of the top grandmasters, analyzed and explained by them. Let me repeat this for emphasis: *the best way to get better at the middlegame is to study the games of the top grandmasters, analyzed and explained directly by them!*

There is nobody better than the world champions, so I recommend you read the books that they have written about their own games. Here is a list of books written by most of the world champions since the 1950s:

+ **Viswanathan Anand (World Champion, 2007–2013):** *Vishy Anand: World Chess Champion* (2012) by Viswanathan Anand and John Nunn.

+ **Vladimir Kramnik (World Champion, 2000–2007):** *My Life and Games* (2000) by Vladimir Kramnik and Iakov Damsky.

+ **Garry Kasparov (World Champion, 1985–2000):**

  + *Garry Kasparov on Garry Kasparov, Part 1, Part 2,* and *Part 3.*

  + *Garry Kasparov on My Great Predecessors, Part 1, Part 2, Part 3, Part 4,* and *Part 5.*

  + *Garry Kasparov on Modern Chess, Part 1, Part 2, Part 3,* and *Part 4.*

  + Plus, any of Kasparov's books about his several World Championship matches.

+ **Anatoly Karpov (World Champion, 1975–1985):** Karpov wrote three chess books: *My Best Games, Anatoly Karpov's Best Games,* and *Chess is My Life.* Unfortunately, they are all out of print as of 2019. If you find them, they are worth reading!

+ **Bobby Fischer (World Champion, 1972–1975):** *My Sixty Memorable Games.*

+ **Boris Spassky (World Champion, 1969–1972):** There are no books written by Spassky that are translated into English, but Amazon does have a staple-bound book offered by the US Chess Federation for $15: *Boris Spassky: Fifty-One Annotated Games of the New World Champion* by Boris Spassky and Andy Soltis (1969). Get one if you can!

+ **Tigran Petrosian (World Champion, 1963–1969):** *Petrosian's Legacy* (2012). This is a compilation of his notes and some of his lectures, rather than a collection of games he annotated; but it is still very worth reading and studying.

+ **Mikhail Botvinnik (World Champion, 1948–1957, 1958–1960, and 1961–1963):** *Botvinnik: One Hundred Selected Games* (1960) by Mikhail Botvinnik and Stephen Garry.

+ **Mikhail Tal (World Champion, 1960–1961):**

    + *Life & Games of Mikhail Tal* (1997).

    + *Tal-Botvinnik 1960: Match for the World Chess Championship,* 7th edition (2016).

+ **Vassily Smyslov (World Champion, 1957–1958):** *Smyslov's 125 Selected Games.*

There are many other terrific books by some of the top grandmasters who were never world champion. But why start with anything other than the best? Once you have read a few (or more than a few) of the above books, then branch out and read some game compilations written by other top grandmasters. (Three grandmasters I can recommend you start with are Alexei Shirov, Paul Keres and Victor Korchnoi.) Whatever book or author you select, the key is to focus on reading only the best of the best!

## Study Your Own Games

In addition to studying the games of the greats, you also need to study your own games. Write down the moves of each game you play so you can analyze them afterwards. Look for all the ideas and hidden resources you and your opponent missed!

You should always analyze each game with your opponent right afterward—especially if you lost! This is called the *post mortem* and it is vital. You learn a lot by comparing how you and your opponent were thinking, while your impressions are still fresh.

If you are really serious about training, then you should also analyze your games at home with a chess computer or an engine, as chess players refer to it. (See Online Chess Resources for some recommendations.)

## Work with a Coach or a Teacher

My final recommendation, if you are really dedicated and want to get better, is to find a good teacher or coach. Back when I was a kid, there was no internet and instruction had to be done in person. (We also wrote things down on stone tablets!) But today, not only can you find a coach online, you can also interact online as well. At the time of publication (2019), these are two good online resources for finding a coach: lichess.org/coach and chess.com/coaches.

# Online Chess Resources

Keep in mind that the online world changes all the time, and this section might be out of date by the time you read it! Still, this list of resources gives you a good idea of the best of what is available online in all facets of chess as of 2019—and if anything is out of date when you read this, I'm sure something even better has taken its place.

The following resources are accessible as both websites and apps and are good general chess hubs:

+ **Chess.com:** Both a website and a mobile app. Through either one you can play games with online opponents, watch others play chess, solve chess exercises (like the ones in Chapters 5 through 14), find coaches (as noted above), download a chess-playing app, and more. This is a good place to start your online chess adventure! (They also have a popular chess app for young kids called Chess for Kids–Play & Learn.)

+ **Lichess.org:** A newer and fast-growing chess resource (website and app), it is kind of like chess.com but less commercial. You can play opponents, solve puzzles, find coaches, download a chess-playing app, and lots more.

These two resources are good for watching live chess tournaments:

+ **Chess24.com:** This is a popular website and app that offers online coverage of chess tournaments all over the world, as well as videos and other instructional tools.

+ **Chessbomb.com:** Similar to Chess24, it provides a way to follow chess tournaments online live with realtime computer analysis.

The following are some chess playing and training apps that I find helpful or interesting:

+ **Stockfish/Droidfish:** As you will read in Chapter 16, Stockfish is the strongest non–AI chess program in the world (as of early 2019) and far surpasses all human grandmasters. Would you believe you can download it for free? Go to stockfishchess.org and click "Download" in the menu section, or go to the App Store to download it onto an iOS device. (I use the official Stockfish app on my iPhone.) For Android users, there is a third-party app called DroidFish that can be accessed on the Download page or at Google Play.

+ **Chess–Analyze This:** This app makes it really easy to load a game and analyze it using multiple chess engines (using a ubiquitous online standard called *PGN)*.

+ **Chess Book Study:** Developed by the same chess-loving programmer as Analyze This, this app lets you import any chess book or article in PDF or e-pub format and integrates it on screen with a chess board. Instead of having a chess book in one hand and a chess set by your side—how quaintly twentieth century!—this program allows you to split the screen on your tablet or computer to read the book on one side and use a chessboard for analysis on the other. Neat!

+ **Chess Tactics Pro:** This app offers lots and lots of chess puzzles at different levels of difficulty. It's easy to use and allows you to track your progress.

These last two are resources for chess entertainment:

+ **Twitch and YouTube:** Obviously these online video sites have a lot more than chess! But if chess is what you want, you will find plenty here. Most top grandmasters provide lectures online, for example, and some stream their online games live and take questions while they are playing.

+ **PROChessLeague.com:** The PRO (Professional Rapid Online) Chess League is a growing online chess-team competition. The league has 32 teams and the season lasts from January to May, with qualifying matches in the fall months. Games are broadcast online with live commentary—and the time control is fast to keep the action going.

These online resources will get you started, but there are lots more. Have fun!

# Get Competitive

Are you ready to start playing in chess clubs or tournaments? That's great! While the online world is amazing, sitting down face to face with someone is still the best way to experience chess, in my opinion.

## Find a Club

Chess clubs are a wonderful way to meet people who share your love of chess. All large cities and most medium-sized cities have at least one chess club; you can find these easily online. Another way to find a club is to go to the United States Chess Federation (USCF) website: new.uschess.org. (You should get to know this website anyway if you are going to start playing chess tournaments.)

To find a club in your area, go to the USCF website, click the tab labeled "Play," and select "Upcoming Tournaments" from the pull-down menu. This will open a separate page, and you will see "chess clubs" located in the left-hand menu. Clicking that takes you to a link that coordinates with each of the 50 state affiliate chess organizations and generates a list of chess clubs in each state.

The USCF is the official governing body for chess in the United States. Here are some of the things the USCF does:

+ **Chess Ratings:** The way chess ratings work is explained in more detail in Chapter 16. The key point to know here is that chess ratings allow all players to rank themselves, track their progress, and be sorted into appropriate sections in any given tournament so the competition is fair and exciting. If you start playing chess tournaments, your rating will become a big part of your life, and the USCF manages and maintains all the national chess ratings.

+ **Magazine and Website:** The USCF publishes two magazines (one for adults and another for kids under 12) and maintains a website with lots of chess news and information from the United States and around the world. Most critically, it provides a comprehensive listing of all rated chess tournaments around the country so you can find a tournament near you and sign up to play.

+ **Championships, Youth Events, and more:** Most chess tournaments are independently organized, even if sanctioned by the USCF. But the USCF also organizes a number of events and championships for kids and adults.

## Tournament Rules

Before you play in your first tournament, there are five special competition rules you should know.

**Rule 1: Touch move**   In tournament chess, once you touch a piece (or pawn) you must move it (as long as it is legal to do so). This rule is strictly enforced! If you want to adjust a piece or pawn so that it is better centered on the square or if you want to touch it for any other reason than to move it, then you must clearly say "adjust" (or the French equivalent *j'adoube*) before touching it.

**Rule 2: Time controls**   Chess games played in a tournament are governed by a set of time controls, which regulate how long each player has for the game. Events can have a wide range of time controls. Standard time limits tend to fall between as little as 30 minutes for each side for the entire game to as long as 2 hours to play the first 40 moves (with an additional amount of time granted after the first 40 moves are played). You can use this time however you want. For example, if the time control is 1 hour to play the entire game, then you can bash out your first 20 moves in under a minute, or you can take 59 minutes to ponder your first 3 moves. Just don't go over the allotted time! If you use up all your time, then you lose.

Sometimes a tournament will use either a time delay or a time increment to supplement the allotted time. When a time delay is used, the chess clock is programmed to wait a certain number of seconds before debiting any time from you or your opponent during the move. When a time increment is used, the chess clock is programmed to add a certain amount of time to each player after the move is played. Back in the old days before electronic chess clocks, time delays and time increments were not technologically possible. But now with electronic clocks, delays and increments have become popular.

**Rule 3: Other ways to draw the game**   In tournaments, there are two additional ways that the game can end in a draw besides those mentioned in Chapter 3 (stalemate, perpetual check, insufficient material to checkmate, and friendly agreement).

The first is called *threefold repetition*. If the same position occurs three (or more) times during the same game, a draw may be claimed. The position must be the same in every way: The pieces must be in the same locations, the same moves must be legal (remember the castling and en passant rules), and the same side must be on move for a true repetition to occur. To claim a draw by triple repetition, you should not actually make the move that brings about the position for the third time. Instead, stop the clock and tell your opponent, "By playing [insert move here] I will repeat the position for the third time, so I am claiming a draw," or words to that effect. If you play the move and press your clock button, it's not your move anymore so it's too late to claim the draw; you must hope the position repeats yet again and that you remember the procedure the next time!

The second additional way a tournament game can be drawn is called the *50-move rule*. If 50 consecutive moves for each side have passed during which neither side has captured a piece or moved a pawn, either player may claim a draw. The point of this rule is to prevent someone from playing forever with no realistic chance of winning. However, another practical effect is to highlight the importance of mastering basic endgame technique. For instance, in Chapter 4 I explained how to give checkmate with just a rook plus your king versus a lone king. You learned that this ending should always be won by the side with the rook; wouldn't it be a shame to miss out on a deserved victory because you couldn't finish your opponent off in under 50 moves?

The procedure for claiming the draw under this rule is the same as for the triple repetition: stop the clock and point out that by making a certain move, 50 moves (or more) have passed with all the criteria met, and you claim a draw.

**Rule 4: Keeping score**   In tournaments, both players are generally required to keep an accurate score of the game. (Of course, you should want to do this anyway, so you can study and learn from your games later on!) You can also see how having a complete score sheet could be required to verify a triple repetition, 50-move rule claim, or a time-forfeit victory if there is any dispute.

**Rule 5: No talking, no computers, proper etiquette**   You are not allowed to have any outside help during the game. This means that you should not talk with other players about your game or their game. In fact, you really shouldn't talk to anyone at all; although in practice, people do sometimes chat quietly while it is their opponent's turn to move. Just don't talk about either of your games!

In the old days, the big worry was that people might sneak a look at a book or try to work something out on a chessboard during the game. Now that smartphones have gotten so good at chess, it has become necessary to crack down on their use. Many tournaments require all phones to be turned off during the game, and sometimes you can be forfeited just for having your phone on, even if you haven't been using it! Follow the rules at the tournament in question regarding smartphones, and please take them very seriously.

Finally, you should not disturb your opponent in any way. Think of chess as more like golf than basketball. No trash talking! And for that matter, no talking or making any noise at all. You will appreciate the same courtesy when you are deep in thought, trying to figure out the best move without using up all of your allotted time.

# Chess Resources and Activities for Kids

One of the great things about chess is that kids can use all the same chess resources as adults, compete against them on equal terms—and often win! Still, many times kids can benefit from resources that are aimed at a younger audience, so here are a few recommendations.

The best online resource for kids that I know of is ChessKid.com, which is affiliated with Chess.com. It has a kid-friendly user interface for playing other kids from around the world. Some other nice features of Chesskid.com are the following:

+ **Kid-Friendly Environment:** Lots of security measures to ensure privacy and safety; no personal information is ever displayed and the chat functions are monitored.

+ **Lots of Puzzles and Instruction:** There is an extensive database of puzzles designed for different skill levels, and there are lessons and tutorials that can be viewed online.

+ **Coach Portal:** If your child works with a coach online, the coach can use this feature to track your child's progress.

+ **School Resources:** Numerous tools for teachers to integrate chess into the Common Core curriculum for both elementary and middle school programs, as well as tools for organizing tournaments, managing clubs, and more.

Keeping in mind that any chess book that is good enough for a grownup is good enough for a kid, below are some books I like that are designed specifically for kids:

+ *Coach Jay's Chess Academy* **series:** These workbooks, designed specifically for scholastic players, were developed by Jay Stallings, who has taught scholastic players for over 20 years. They are ideal for young children who know the basic moves and understand the concept of checkmate.

+ *Learn Chess the Right Way* **series:** Written by former women's World Chess Champion Susan Polgar, this five-book series takes kids who have just learned the movement of the pieces and the concept of checkmate and teaches them basic tactics and strategies. Using puzzles grouped by category to learn techniques, there is a lot of material and it is accessible for young kids.

+ *The Standard Chess Workbook* **series:** This series is great for providing a solid foundation to supplement learning either in a class or at home. Written by Dylan Quercia, Director of Scholastic Programs for the Metropolitan Chess Club in Los Angeles, the series consists of three books, one for each playing level: beginner, intermediate, and advanced. The first book is designed for very new players and provides guidance for those who are learning the moves, while the other two books guide the developing scholastic player through tactics, checkmates, and endgames.

+ *Winning Chess Puzzles for Kids*: Written by Jeff Coakley, this book is a classic for scholastic chess. It supplies a wealth of chess puzzles that covers many topics, and it also incorporates some fun chess-related trivia puzzles. It is an enjoyable way for beginning scholastic players to learn chess.

There are many junior and scholastic chess events and tournaments around the country. Check the United States Chess Federation (USCF) website for events near you or contact your local chess club.

Finally, let me offer a few words of advice about the right competitive attitude for kids and parents.

**Kids:** Chess is the fairest game I know. It doesn't matter whether you are big or small, and it doesn't matter whether you are young or old. All that matters is how you play the game. That means you have just as good a chance to win as someone bigger or older than you! But it also means you have no excuses. If you want to win, you have to play good moves. If you lose, it means you made a mistake somewhere. Even if you won, you made some mistakes, because nobody ever plays a perfect game. Every mistake is a golden opportunity to learn! If you pay attention, work hard, and keep an open mind, you will be amazed at the progress you make over time. That is true for chess, and it is true for anything else to which you apply yourself in life.

**Parents:** Let your kids know that, while winning is definitely much better than losing (what is the point of playing if not to win?), it's okay to lose. Each loss is another opportunity to learn and to apply those lessons to improve. There is always another game to play. That is true for chess, and it is true for anything else to which you apply yourself in life.

Above all, remember that chess is a game, and the whole point of a game is to have fun and enjoy the challenge while constantly trying to improve!

Chapter 16

# How Computers Play Chess

Computer scientists first began building chess-playing programs in the 1950s. At the start of the 1990s, the best computers were still no match for the best humans, even after 40 years of trying. But in 1997, World Chess Champion Garry Kasparov lost a six-game match against the IBM supercomputer Deep Blue. In the following ten years, ordinary PCs decisively surpassed the best grandmasters. By the start of the 2010s, chess-playing programs were so far advanced that humans stopped playing against them in competition. Then in December 2017, a new artificial intelligence technology arrived on the scene and crushed the best existing chess-playing computer program in a match! Computers have made incredible progress playing chess. This chapter explores the fascinating topic of computers and chess.

# Chess: The Ideal Computer Challenge

Modern computers were first developed in the 1930s and 1940s. While early machines were primitive, the pioneers of computer science saw their nearly unlimited potential. A key question for computer scientists was what problem should they focus on trying to solve in order to best develop this new technology?

Claude Shannon, one of the most distinguished computer scientists of the era, argued that the answer to this question was chess. His highly influential 1949 paper "Programming a Computer for Playing Chess" begins:

> This paper is concerned with the problem of constructing a computing routine or "program" for a modern general purpose computer which will enable it to play chess. Although perhaps of no practical importance, the question is of theoretical interest, and it is hoped that a satisfactory solution of this problem will act as a wedge in attacking other programs of a similar nature and of greater significance.

Shannon argued chess was an "ideal" problem for developing the knowledge that would form the basis for lots of other computer programs. Why chess? (Other than because it's such a great game, of course!) Here is how he articulated the four reasons to focus on chess:

1. The problem is sharply defined both in allowed operations (the moves) and in the ultimate goal (checkmate).

2. It is neither so simple as to be trivial nor too difficult for satisfactory solution.

3. Chess is generally considered to require "thinking" for skillful play; a solution of this problem will force us either to admit the possibility of mechanized thinking or to further restrict our concept of "thinking."

4. The discrete nature of chess fits well into the digital nature of modern computers.

Shannon's insight was brilliant. He saw that chess was a well-defined problem where computers could eventually be successful while being sufficiently challenging to absorb generations of computer scientists. And as we will see toward the end of this chapter, he was also correct that developing chess-playing computers would enlarge our conception of what "thinking" really is.

# The Thinking Machine?

At first, when computer scientists went to work on the challenge of developing a chess-playing program, there was a robust debate about whether or not so-called artificial intelligence (AI) techniques should be used. Eventually, the AI approach was largely abandoned for chess programs until the mid-2010s. We will cover AI in much more detail later in the chapter. For now, let's focus on the way traditional computers played chess for decades.

It's important to remember that the way a human being experiences chess is completely different than how a computer experiences it. If you're a human being (and I assume that you are!), you have all kinds of thoughts and feelings during a chess game, and you think about things like pawn structure, weak squares, forks, pins, and the opposition.

But computers don't see chess that way. For humans, chess is something to be figured out and understood. For computers (and their programmers), chess is a mathematical problem that can be solved, at least approximately, with a massive number of rapid calculations. (As we will see later, this is every bit as true for AI as for traditional computer programs. AI is just a different computer programming technology for determining what calculations to make, and how to make them.)

Let's look at an example of how a traditional computer would find the best move and compare its thinking process with our own. Examine Diagram 1 and figure out how White can win. If you studied Chapter 8, you may recognize this problem, since it's taken directly from Diagram 23 in the section on the smothered mate tactic. Here is the winning sequence of moves: 1.Nf7+ Kg8 (if 1...Rxf7 2.Qxc8+ Rf8 3.Qxf8#) 2.Nh6+ Kh8 3.Qg8+ Rxg8 4.Nf7#.

If you solved this problem, you relied on recognizing a pattern of the pieces on the board and associating that pattern with an idea. The ability to rapidly recognize such patterns is invaluable, and as you get better at chess, you'll recognize more and more repeating patterns that will suggest moves and plans to investigate.

How would a computer deal with Diagram 1? Would it recognize the pattern and look up a solution plan (say, in the smothered mate file) in its memory? Nothing of the sort. Instead, the computer will simply list out every legal move White has in the position. For Diagram 1 they are Qa2, Qb3, Qb4, Qa4, Qb5, Qa6, Qc5, Qc6, Qc7, Qxc8, Qd5, Qe6, Qf7, Qg8+, Qd4, Qe4, Qf4, Qg4, Qh4, Qd3, Qe2, Qf1, Qc3, Qc2, Qc1, Nf3, Ne4, Ne6, Nf7+, Nxh7, Nh3, f3, f4, g4, Kf1, Kg2, Kh2, and Kh1.

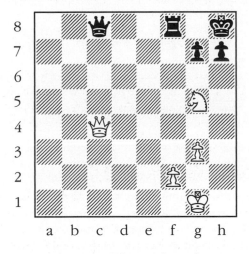

*Diagram 1: White to play and win.*

Did you know that there are actually 38 legal moves for White? When you looked at the position, you probably only thought about a couple: Qxc8 to capture the queen; Qh4, Qe4, or Qd3 to threaten checkmate on h7; and (hopefully) Nf7+. Most of the others just lose the queen right away or, at best, leave White still down the exchange (rook for knight) so you were wise not to waste time thinking about them. There's no reason to think of any other move, and considering them all would slow you down. (Just reading through them takes a few seconds!) Computers, on the other hand, can list out all the legal moves in a tiny fraction of a second.

What happens next? Well, when you consider a move, you assess how your opponent might reply. The computer does the same, but again unlike a human, it looks at every legal response to every legal move. Continuing with our example: the first move we listed for White was Qa2, which brings us to the position in Diagram 2.

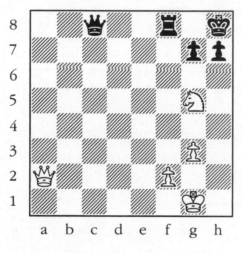

*Diagram 2: White plays 1.Qa2.*

To that, Black has the replies …Qc7, …Qc6, …Qc5, … well let's not list them all out again—the total number is 30, and the best one is 1…Qc1+ followed by 2…Qxg5, winning White's knight (and stopping the smothered mate threat). For most of White's 38 first moves, Black has about 30 replies to consider. So after one move by each player, there are 38 first moves multiplied by 30 replies equaling 1,140 possible positions. For each of those positions, the computer must repeat the process again, considering each of White's legal moves and all of Black's replies to each, and so on. In order for a computer to "see" the position after White's fourth move (Nf7# in the solution to the problem), a computer would calculate every single move by each side. If we estimate that there are 30 possibilities on average per turn, then the computer would analyze $30^7$ equaling 21,870,000,000 future positions that could potentially occur! (That is 30 moves for White times 30 moves for Black times 30 moves for White, seven times, up to 4.Nf7#.)

When it finally reaches the position that ends in checkmate, the program makes a note that 4.Nf7# was the best move in the position right beforehand, which is shown in Diagram 3. Now a backtracking process happens. Because 3…Rxg8 was Black's only legal move, the program knows that 3.Qg8+ was the best move in Diagram 4. Likewise, because Black had no alternative to 2…Kh8 a move earlier, 2.Nh6+ must have been the best move in Diagram 5, again because it leads by force to checkmate.

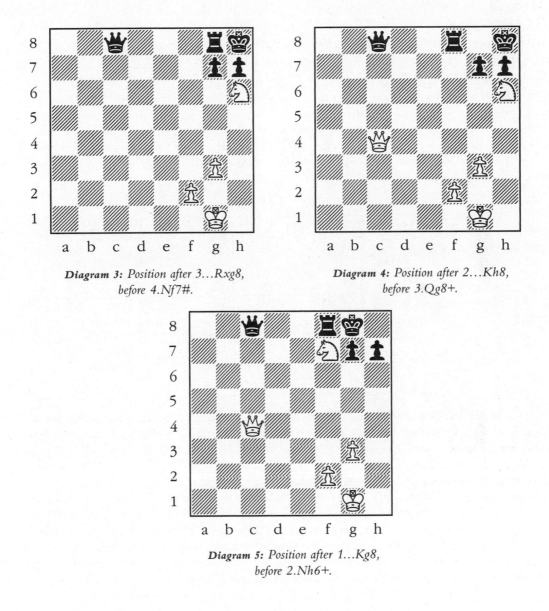

**Diagram 3:** *Position after 3…Rxg8, before 4.Nf7#.*

**Diagram 4:** *Position after 2…Kh8, before 3.Qg8+.*

**Diagram 5:** *Position after 1…Kg8, before 2.Nh6+.*

Finally, by comparing the backtracked consequences of the alternatives at move 1 (including the side variation starting with 1...Rxf7), the program can conclude with certainty that 1.Nf7+ is the best move in the starting position. If you were unfortunate enough to have Black in this position against your favorite chess program, it would waste no time in playing 1.Nf7+ (and it would probably helpfully inform you that checkmate was inevitable).

Note how different this was from the human approach. If you noticed the smothered mate theme you saw 1.Nf7+ and then only needed to investigate two variations, totaling perhaps 12 to 15 possible future positions, a minuscule fraction of all the legal possibilities.

Now try the position in Diagram 6. A computer would find the answer before you could blink because the winning combination is actually two moves shorter than that in Diagram 1. Here's a clue: look for a smothered mate. The position doesn't appear much like Diagram 1 at all, does it? But it uses the same tactic, and in a broad sense, the pattern is similar. Note how Black's king is surrounded by its own pieces. Although they are defending the king, they also hem it in (together with White's e6 pawn). If White could safely give check with a knight, it would be mate. Where can White give check with the knight? Not on d6, because the bishop controls that square. What about g7? No, the queen is on that square. But what if the queen could move off that square ...?

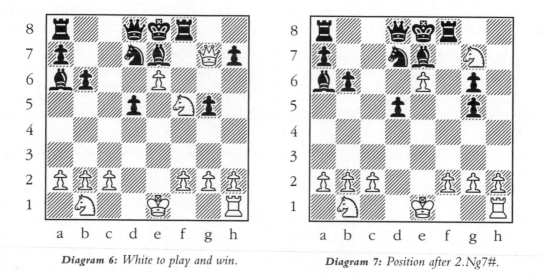

*Diagram 6: White to play and win.*          *Diagram 7: Position after 2.Ng7#.*

The solution is 1.Qg6+! hxg6 (1...Rf7 2 Qxf7#) 2.Ng7# (see Diagram 7), combining a clearance sacrifice with the smothered mate. Even though it was a shorter solution than Diagram 1, and therefore easier for the computer (because the search requires far fewer positions to find the right move), it was probably harder for you to find because it didn't quite look like any smothered mate you've seen. Plus, you had to combine two different tactics. As long as the computer has time to churn through all the possibilities, it will find the solution. But you can't use that method, so your solving ability depends on your ability to recognize patterns and form the appropriate plans in response.

In our first smothered mate example, finding a simple four-move combination required a computer to analyze billions of possible outcomes. That's a lot! As it turns out, computer programmers have developed tools to streamline the computer's analysis process to make it much more efficient. The programmers use a mathematical technique called *alpha-beta pruning* to eliminate redundant alternatives from the computer's analysis, and they use rules of thumb called *heuristics* that tell computers what kinds of moves to try first. (Without getting too thick in the weeds of computer science, the basic idea of alpha-beta pruning is that if the computer finds one way to refute a possible move, it can eliminate that move from its search rather than continuing to find more ways to refute it.)

Computers are often programmed to use the heuristic of looking first at checks and captures on the theory that these moves might be part of a forcing combination to win material or checkmate. (By the way, you should use the same heuristic!) And thanks to alpha-beta pruning, once one refutation for a move (that is, one line of play showing why a move is worse than its alternatives) is found, the computer doesn't waste time finding more refutations.

Of course, even with these time-saving measures, in most positions a computer can't possibly calculate out to checkmate. How does the computer decide what move to play? The search operates the same way as described previously. But instead of marking each position as a win, a loss, or a draw, the computer evaluates the position by assigning it a numeric score that represents how favorable (or unfavorable) that position is according to the computer's algorithm. Then the backtracking procedure finds the variation likely to lead to the best position a few moves down the road, as measured by the evaluation formula, even if it is not actually a checkmate.

In a way, we humans do something similar. We analyze the moves and assess the outcomes by trying to win material, gain space, increase the mobility of our pieces, develop an advantage in force near the king, create passed pawns, give our opponent weak squares, and so on. However, a big difference in how we evaluate each outcome is that where we make a judgment, the computer performs a mathematical calculation.

How can a mathematical calculation take the place of a judgment? The key is that all these strategic elements, to some extent, can be quantified. The computer adds up the point values of each side's pieces—remember the chart in Chapter 5?—measures how much space (by counting squares) each side controls, calculates how many squares each piece can move to, and so on. Some factors are harder to measure. For example, king safety—a critical factor—depends on the complex relationships between pawn structure, piece placement, the particular pieces on the board, and so forth, which makes it difficult to reduce to a single number. Other factors can be accounted for more easily by adjusting the values of the pieces; for example, a white rook might be worth 5 points normally, but 5.5 when it's on the seventh rank.

A numerical weight must be assigned to each factor to reflect its importance relative to each other factor. Generally, all else being equal, material is the most important factor (it takes a lot to compensate for, say, an extra knight), so material usually gets the highest number and the weights assigned to other factors are correspondingly lower. In the end, the weighted sum of all factors yields a single number, and this number is the computer's evaluation of the position.

In the very early days of computer chess, programmers decided to normalize their evaluations so that the material value of one pawn is the standard unit of measure. Doing so makes computer evaluations line up nicely with the traditional material point chart from Chapter 5. Thus, a computer evaluation might rate a particular position as +1.78, which means that the program thinks White has an advantage worth about 1.78 pawns.

"But chess is so complicated," you might object, "so how can all these different factors be precisely quantified and assigned accurate weights?" This is definitely a problem since all these weights have to be coded by human programmers. (AI operates differently, however, as we will see later in the chapter.) However, human programmers have had many decades to work on the problem, so the evaluation weights have now been well worked out. Although a human grandmaster still has much better judgment, the evaluation function of a traditional, modern chess-playing computer program has gotten very good. Combine this with the computer's ability to calculate millions of moves per second, and you can see why computers have gotten so good at chess!

You may have noticed another issue with this rigid numerical approach to evaluating chess positions. Suppose that a computer playing White reached the position of Diagram 6 in its analysis but didn't have time to search further. It would have to apply an evaluation function like the one just discussed to rate its (White's) prospects. With an extra rook and a minor piece, the score would be heavily in Black's favor since material considerations will outweigh the fact that White's pawn, knight, and queen are temporarily well-placed near Black's king. After all, if White couldn't give mate in two moves, Black would probably win.

An experienced human would probably "smell a rat" in this position and make the extra effort to make sure there isn't a checkmate somewhere. But the computer lacks these kinds of intuitive hunches. If it stopped its search here and applied its evaluation function to rate Black on top, it would be making a big mistake, since searching just one move further would reveal that White is winning. This mistake of cutting off the search too early is called the *horizon effect*.

The horizon effect used to be a big problem for traditional chess computers playing against humans, but today it rarely matters. One way this has been dealt with is simply by improving the evaluation function to the point where computer programs are not so easily lulled into stopping their search process at a position like Diagram 6. A second way traditional chess programs have coped with this issue is by developing a selective search technique. The basic idea here is that if the computer identifies a variation where each side's responses seem forced for a certain number of moves, it follows that variation out to the end. A third reason traditional computers rarely run into the horizon effect against humans is that the hardware has become so fast that they can search deeply enough to avoid it.

For these three reasons, even the very best human grandmasters are usually making analytic oversights and errors long before today's traditional computers are in danger of reaching a horizon. (But keep the horizon effect in mind when you see how the AI program AlphaZero defeats its non-AI computer opponent!)

All traditional chess programs use the basic process outlined so far to select moves, though some implement it better than others, and each has its own special evaluation function. Before we discuss how AI tackles chess, let's review the incredible progress traditional chess programs have made over the years.

# The Rise of Computers in Chess

Throughout most of the second half of the twentieth century, computer programmers were overly optimistic about how quickly computers would overtake humans. For example, in 1957, the renowned computer scientist Herbert Simon said a computer would be the world chess champion within 10 years.

He was off by 30 years.

David Levy, an international master (this is the title one level below grandmaster) made a $3,000 bet at the 1968 Machine Intelligence Workshop at Edinburgh University that no chess computer would beat him in 10 years. (By way of context, beating David Levy would have been impressive, but still far below becoming world champion.) In 1978, David Levy won his bet. Computers were still very far away from challenging top human players.

Ten years later, in 1988, the computer Deep Thought, the precursor to the IBM computer Deep Blue, shared first place in the US Open championship with International Grandmaster Tony Miles. At this point, it was clear that computers would eventually surpass humans. The only question was how long it would take.

Nine years later, the IBM computer Deep Blue defeated then—World Champion Garry Kasparov in a six-game match. Kasparov was probably somewhat off-form in that match: the match was tied after five games, and Kasparov played the final game very badly. Still, this was a milestone and there was no question computers would continue to get better and better.

By the middle of the 2000s, commercial PC chess-playing programs were consistently defeating top grandmasters. It's hard to pinpoint the exact moment when computers definitively surpassed humans, but it clearly happened during the first decade of the twenty-first century.

In the early 2010s, computers reached a level where top grandmasters totally gave up trying to defeat them. Top engines (as chess players call the computers) are universally used for analysis, but there is no longer any point competing against them.

Exactly how good have computers gotten? As it turns out, this question can be answered mathematically. There is a widely used method for quantifying chess skill called the *Elo rating system*, named after its inventor, physics professor Arpad Elo. The Elo system produces a four-digit number for each participant in any win/draw/loss (or win/loss) multiplayer competitive system. The system was originally developed for chess but has since been adopted in areas as diverse as video games, professional sports, and Scrabble. We won't get into the details (put "Elo rating system" into your search engine if you want to learn the math), but here are the key points:

+ The Elo ratings of chess grandmasters are generally above 2,500, while the ratings of world champions like Kasparov, Anand, and Carlsen tend to range between 2,800 and 2,850.

+ If you know the Elo ratings of two players, you can compute each player's expected score if they were to play a set of games against each other, with each player alternating between playing white and black.

+ Here are the expected scores of the higher rated player for a given point difference with a win = 1 point, a draw = ½ point, and a loss = 0 point. (Note that 100 percent is the highest possible score and means a player wins every game with no draws or losses.)

   + 100 points: 64%

   + 200 points: 76%

   + 300 points: 85%

   + 400 points: 92%

   + 500 points: 96%

   + 600 points: 98%

Keeping in mind that the world chess champion has an Elo rating between 2,800 and 2,850, take a look at the chart below showing the Elo rating progress that computers made from 1960 to 2018. (Please note that the "estimated rating of top computer" is only an estimate and should not be interpreted as a precise value. But it is accurate enough for our purposes.)

| Year | Estimated Rating of Top Computer | Expected Score: Top Computer vs. Human Champion (rated 2,800) |
|------|----------------------------------|--------------------------------------------------------------|
| 1960 | 1200 | 0% |
| 1965 | 1400 | 0% |
| 1970 | 1600 | 0% |
| 1975 | 1800 | 0% |
| 1980 | 2000 | 0% |
| 1985 | 2200 | 2% |
| 1990 | 2400 | 8% |
| 1995 | 2600 | 24% |
| 2000 | 2800 | 50% |
| 2005 | 3000 | 76% |
| 2010 | 3200 | 92% |
| 2015 | 3400 | 98% |
| 2018 | 3450 | >99% |

In 2000, the best chess computer was about as good as the world chess champion. By 2015, computers were in another league.

By 2010, the project proposed by Claude Shannon had clearly succeeded, yet nothing about the computer's success challenged our notion of "thinking." It just turned out that human-created weightings of known chess factors, mixed with superfast hardware and clever programming tricks (such as alpha-beta pruning and search heuristics) could surpass human judgment in the game of chess.

This was very impressive, but it seemed to say more about the nature of chess than about the nature of thinking.

And then came AlphaZero.

# The AI Revolution

Names sometimes create misleading associations. The name *artificial intelligence* (AI), leads some people to assume that computers using this technology must somehow be similar to human beings. Not so. While there are differences in the hardware configurations that AI computers use (which we won't get bogged down in), the only real difference between traditional computers and AI computers is how the machines are programmed.

In fact, AI is a catchall term that refers to many different approaches. The term originated in the 1950s when computer scientists pondered whether computers manipulating symbols could somehow give rise to "thinking." (Remember Claude Shannon's third point in his introduction!) To grossly oversimplify a complex topic, this kind of symbolic AI largely petered out in the 1980s.

These days, all the exciting developments in AI—and what gave rise to AlphaZero—come from a subfield of AI called *machine learning*. Machine learning really started going in the 1990s and then absolutely exploded in the early 2010s with the success of a particular technique called *deep-learning neural networks*.

Don't let the jargon scare you off. It's not that complicated. Let's take it one step at a time. (However, if you get lost at any point in the following explanation, you can skip ahead to the next section. I think this AI stuff is fascinating, but you can learn all about AlphaZero without knowing it.)

The term *machine learning* describes the general approach of programming a computer to develop its own rules for solving a problem. The following schematic diagram (adapted from the textbook, *Deep Learning with R,* by Francois Chollet with J.J. Allaire) illustrates the distinction:

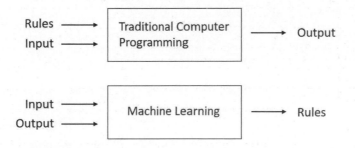

*Traditional computer programming versus machine learning.*

When using traditional programming to create a computer that does something, the programmer creates all the rules and defines the allowable input. The computer then follows the rules to run calculations on the input and generates output.

By contrast, when using machine learning to create a computer that does something, the programmer feeds in lots of sample input and output; the computer finds the statistical relationships between the input and the output that allows it to generate rules. Then the computer follows these self-created rules to run calculations on future input and generates output.

How does the computer run this statistical analysis to generate rules? The specific technique that has become by far the most successful in this decade—and the technique AlphaZero uses—is called a *neural network*. Although the phrase "neural network" is a reference to the biology of the human brain, that does not mean AI computers are anything like human brains! It's just an analogy. A neural network refers to the way the inputs, the manipulation of the inputs, and the final outputs are organized similarly to neurons in the brain. But I must emphasize that there is no physical similarity whatsoever between a human's and a computer's neural networks, and even the analogy to how human brain neurons are organized is tenuous. The bottom line? When you see the term *neural network*, just know that it means how the input data are organized so they can be manipulated using linear algebra to produce estimated values for the output.

The following schematic diagram shows how a simple (or shallow) neural network is typically represented.

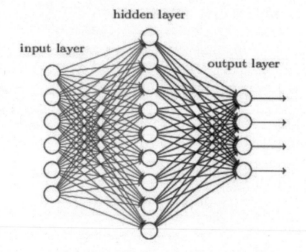

*Schematic diagram of a shallow neural network.*

Each circle represents a data point that is a number. The "input layer" is all the input data. (Don't get hung up on the number of circles: there could be thousands, millions, or more. This is just a schematic diagram.) The arrow from each circle in the input layer to each next circle in the hidden layer represents a mathematical manipulation by the computer. (I will explain soon why this layer is said to be "hidden.") Then there is one more manipulation from the hidden layer to the output.

Because there is only one set of manipulation operations in between the input layer and the output layer we would *not* say that this neural network is "deep." But what if we had more manipulations?

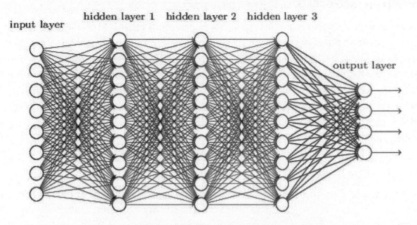

*Schematic diagram of a deep neural network.*

Each layer (each column of circles) represents another set of data manipulation. As more layers are added (more sets of intermediary manipulations of input data), the neural network becomes deep. Using the term *deep learning* to describe a neural network is just a way of saying that the neural network has lots of layers, i.e. it performs multiple sets of mathematical manipulations on the input data to map it onto the output data. The deep neural network in the diagram has three layers. As it turns out, the big breakthroughs in AI started happening in 2012 when the neural networks got to about six layers deep.

So, what have we learned so far?

+ Machine learning is the general approach by which computers develop their own rules for mapping input data to output data.

+ A *neural network* is the name given to the way all input data, manipulations on that data, and the output data are organized.

+ When there are more sets of manipulations on the data (i.e. more layers), a neural network becomes deep.

+ Once neural networks became deep enough, they started to do amazing things.

There is one last basic element of AI to learn: How the heck does the computer take raw data, manipulate it all somehow *without any human guidance,* and map it onto the output data? (A "map" corresponds to a set of input data going into the system, being manipulated at each layer, and then reaching the output layer.)

At the start, the computer has no idea how to manipulate the input data and map it onto the output data, so the first mapping is random. But the process doesn't end with the first mapping! After the first set of inputs is mapped onto the output, the computer uses a scoring system to see how close or far the mapping got to the desired output.

The computer then uses more math to adjust the weights of manipulations. This adjustment process is called *backpropagation* because it goes back to adjust the values assigned to the weights of the manipulations of the data through the layers. Then the next set of inputs that passes through the process is adjusted by the scoring system to produce a different output, which is then backpropagated to adjust the scoring system again, and again, and so on. As more and more data are fed through the system and the output keeps getting closer and closer to the desired end state, the computer develops a highly complex set of mathematical rules and weights for mapping any future input to output. The computer has used AI to write its own rules; it has learned how to map input data to output data!

But here's an important point: the final set of mathematical rules for mapping all the input data to the output data is not something that any human can interpret. It's not as if the computer has reached some understanding that can be translated into words. The machine developed these equations by performing enormous amounts of calculations on huge amounts of data, and those equations tell the computer how to map input data onto output data, but there is no written explanation for what the computer is doing. It is the proverbial black box. This is why we say those intermediary layers are "hidden."

The best chess computers before AlphaZero had sophisticated evaluation and search functions that were developed by human programmers after many years of tinkering and adjusting. AlphaZero, on the other hand, has far more sophisticated, complex evaluation functions that it developed on its own. *No human can observe those functions and explain why they are the way they are.* All we can do is observe what output AlphaZero produces for each input—in other words, what moves AlphaZero plays in any given chess position. In certain situations, AlphaZero might evaluate a chess position in a very different way than any other computer and play some very surprising moves.

And that is exactly what happened.

# Machine vs. Machine

On December 5, 2017 the DeepMind team at Alphabet (parent company of Google) released a paper titled, "Mastering Chess and Shogi by Self-Play with a General Reinforcement Learning Algorithm." (The term *reinforcement learning* refers to a particular kind of AI machine-learning technique.) The same team had used AI to develop a program that defeated the world's best Go player in March 2016. This paper announced that, by using similar technology, an AI program called AlphaZero had successfully mastered three different games and then convincingly defeated the best computer program in each one: shogi, Go, and chess. (The chess program that AlphaZero defeated was Stockfish, which had consistently won an annual competition of the top chess-playing engines.)

Because AlphaZero and Stockfish operate so differently, it is hard to figure out the best way to design a competition between the two programs that maximizes each one's ability. The DeepMind team focused on questions other than trying to quantify the exact Elo rating difference between AlphaZero and Stockfish. Chess grandmaster and computer scientist Larry Kaufman wrote a detailed article in early 2018 in which he estimated that AlphaZero might have an Elo rating of 3500, making it perhaps 50-100 Elo points stronger than Stockfish. Ultimately, the question of exactly how much better is AlphaZero than everyone else is unanswerable unless the DeepMind team decides to allow AlphaZero to play against multiple computer programs under standardized tournament conditions. Unfortunately, as of this writing, they have shown no interest in doing so.

Fortunately, however, we have many amazing chess games by AlphaZero to play through! In this chapter, we only have space to take a close look at one of those games. If you like this game, go online and find a website that lets you play through all the other games AlphaZero has played. Also, I highly recommend the book *Game Changer* by Grandmaster Matthew Sadler and Women's International Master and mathematics PhD Natasha Regan, which is devoted to analyzing AlphaZero and its approach to chess.

The game below was among the ten games released in the original 2017 paper, and it was universally thought the most beautiful. (Hundreds of additional games have subsequently been released.) Some of the commentary on this game is based on the commentary by Sadler and Regan from their book *Game Changer* (2019).

## AlphaZero—Stockfish, London, 2017

*1.Nf3 Nf6 2.d4 e6 3.c4 b6 4.g3 Bb7 5.Bg2 Be7 6.O-O O-O 7.d5*  This opening is called a *Queen's Indian Defense,* and it is one of the most commonly played openings among top grandmasters. Keep in mind that AlphaZero, unlike traditional chess computers, has not been programmed with any existing opening theory. It is making up its own opening theory! White's first six moves are standard, but the seventh move, 7.d5, is an unusual and sharp gambit. Although it is not the normal move for this opening (the normal move is 7.Nc3, developing the knight toward the center), it has been played at the highest level and is considered perfectly sound. By playing this gambit, White chooses to sacrifice a pawn to weaken Black's king position and to activate White's pieces. This is the sort of decision that turns out to be very typical for AlphaZero: sacrificing material in return for long-term compensation.

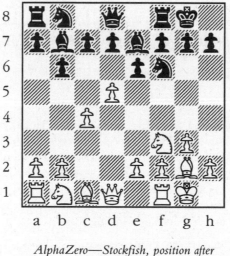

*AlphaZero—Stockfish, position after*
*7.d5.*

**7...exd5 8.Nh4 c6**   This move is the only way for Black to keep the extra pawn, but it comes at the cost of making the bishop on b7 passive and preventing the knight on b8 from developing easily to c6.

**9.cxd5 Nxd5 10.Nf5 Nc7 11.e4 d5 12.exd5 Nxd5 13.Nc3 Nxc3 14.Qg4! g6**   Black has no time to rescue the knight on c3 because White threatens 15.Qxg7#.

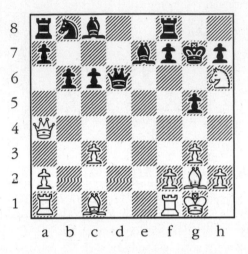

*AlphaZero—Stockfish position after 18...g5.*

**15.Nh6+ Kg7 16.bxc3 Bc8 17.Qf4 Qd6 18.Qa4 g5**   We are at the critical moment of the game. Each computer has anticipated this position. Stockfish's analysis indicates that White must withdraw the knight on h6 to safety by playing 19.Ng4, when White would have enough compensation for the pawn, but no more. AlphaZero has played for this position in order to make a very different move.

**19.Re1!!**   White allows the knight on h6 to be captured. When Stockfish analyzes this position as far as its horizon will allow, its evaluation function indicates Black gets a large advantage by capturing the knight. But AlphaZero is "thinking" very differently: it evaluates its chances after the knight sacrifice are somewhat (but not yet substantially) better than Black's. Subsequent analysis showed AlphaZero was right! We don't know what factors AlphaZero is weighing and in what proportions to reach its conclusion, but we can infer that AlphaZero highly values mobility, activity, and an attack against the king.

This is a good moment to highlight a difference between how AlphaZero expresses its evaluations versus traditional chess programs. Recall that a traditional chess program adds up all the factors into a single number. (For example, Stockfish might indicate that after capturing the knight, it has an advantage of 2.1 pawns.) AlphaZero doesn't express its evaluation by adding together a set of factors into a single number; instead, it expresses its evaluation as a percentage probability of winning or losing. (For example: AlphaZero might indicate that White has an expected score of 55 percent, meaning it has a very slightly better chance of winning than losing.)

This difference—summing all factors into a single score versus estimating a win probability—is due to the different structure of each approach. Stockfish's evaluation function was built up from hand-coded weights assigned to each factor; whereas AlphaZero's evaluation function was developed by repeatedly assigning and then adjusting (using backpropagation) an expected probability of winning to enormous numbers of positions that passed through its neural networks.

Now let's get back to the game. It's just starting to get really exciting!

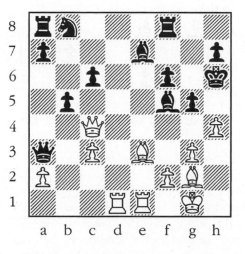

*AlphaZero—Stockfish, position after 23...b5.*

**19...Kxh6 20.h4 f6 21.Be3 Bf5 22.Rad1 Qa3 23.Qc4 b5**  At this point, AlphaZero plays a truly extraordinary set of moves. I have never yet met a chess player who anticipated White's next few moves when playing through this game for the first time.

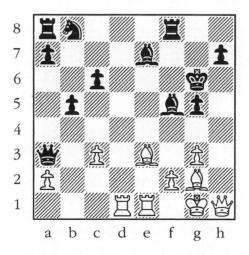

*AlphaZero—Stockfish, position after 26.Qh1!!*

**24.hxg5+ fxg5 25.Qh4+ Kg6 26.Qh1!!**  It is so unusual for the queen to be actively placed on the h1 square when White is castled kingside! Yet, upon deeper reflection, it makes perfect sense in this position. The queen supports the bishop on g2 along the long diagonal (which has the pawn on c6 and the rook on a8 as targets), while at the same time the queen can engage in the attack against the king along the h-file.

**26...Kg7**  AlphaZero believes this is the only good defense for Black. A key point is that 26...Nd7 is met strongly by 27.g4! Bxg4 28.Be4+ Bf5 29.Rxd7.

**27.Be4 Bg6?**  According to AlphaZero, the best move is 27...Bxe4, after which it believes White has a 61.9 percent expected score, a solid advantage, but one that is well within the range where accurate defense usually holds the draw. Therefore, we can identify 27...Bg6 as Stockfish's losing mistake.

Stockfish has fallen into a deep horizon-effect error in its calculations here. Recall that when Stockfish calculates, it is searching *nearly* every single legal move in each position, one at a time. The reason it is not looking at *every* single move is because of alpha-beta pruning and search heuristics. (On the high-end hardware Stockfish ran in this game, it was looking at 70 million positions per second!)

AlphaZero was also using very powerful hardware, but more of its computing resources were allocated for executing its more-complicated search prioritization and evaluation algorithms. This means AlphaZero was looking at fewer positions than Stockfish; in fact, AlphaZero was only looking at 80,000 positions per second or about one tenth of 1 percent the number of positions as Stockfish! The key to AlphaZero's success is that it successfully allocated its computer power to figure out which moves to focus on. This means AlphaZero was not following the kind of rigid search algorithms that would make it vulnerable to a horizon effect. When AlphaZero thinks something is worth looking into more deeply, it can do that. This helps explain why AlphaZero was able to see so much more deeply than Stockfish even though AlphaZero was looking at fewer positions.

**28.Bxg6 hxg6 29.Qh3! Bf6 30.Kg2!**  White's twenty-ninth move not only activates the queen along the h3-c8 diagonal, it also prepares the possibility of setting up the rook and queen battery along the h-file. White's thirtieth move gets the king out of the way to allow the rook to come to h1 and complete the setup of the rook-and-queen battery.

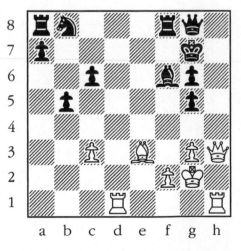

*AlphaZero—Stockfish, position after 31...Qg8*

**30...Qxa2 31.Rh1 Qg8** Black appears to have everything defended here. And indeed, there is no forcing move that breaks Black's defenses. Yet White has a very powerful move that tightens the noose further around Black's neck. This is the horizon effect moment for Stockfish, but the horizon is so far off that only a computer as strong as AlphaZero can see beyond it!

**32.c4!!** Believe it or not, this little pawn move is the key to breaking down Black's defense! The underlying idea is to restrict the mobility of the black queen.

**32...Re8** If 32...bxc4 then 33.f4! turns out to decisively open up more lines of attack against the black king—and the fact that Black's queen can no longer give check on a2 is the deciding factor in some of the variations. AlphaZero thought that 32...a5 was the best try for Black, but after 33.Rd6, White obtains a decisive advantage.

**33.Bd4** Once again the black queen is hemmed in by the pawn on c4, this time because check on d5 is no longer possible.

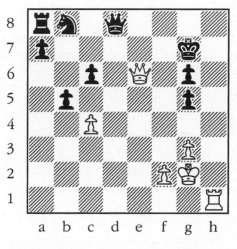

*AlphaZero—Stockfish, position after 36.Qe6!*

**33...Bxd4 34.Rxd4 Rd8 35.Rxd8 Qxd8 36.Qe6!** Incredibly, even though White only has the queen and rook left to press the attack, Black's king is defenseless! The threat is 37.Qe5+ Qf6 (37...Kf7 38.Rh7+ Kf8 39.Qg7+ Ke8 40.Qf7#; 37...Kg8 38.Rh8+ Kf7 39.Rh7+ transposes to 37...Kf7 38.Rh7+) 38.Rh7+ Kxh7 39.Qxf6 and, because Black's rook and knight are so passive and uncoordinated, White wins easily. Black would like to play 36...Qd5+ to exchange queens, but that darn c4 pawn is covering the d5 square!

**36...Nd7** Stockfish played the only move left to keep the game going. There is nothing better, but now AlphaZero's winning reply is so simple that even a human could see it!

**37.Rd1**   The pin along the d-file wins material, and the resulting endgame is lost for Black.

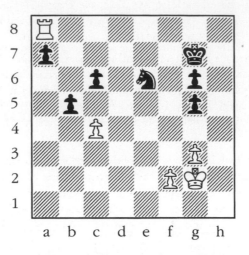

*AlphaZero—Stockfish, position after 39.Rxa8*

**37...Nc5 38.Rxd8 Nxe6 39.Rxa8**   Two humans might still have a tough fight here, but the computers can work out how White wins in all variations. Stockfish's programming dictates that it continue playing until the position reaches a point where the win is without doubt, which takes 17 more moves.

**39...Kf6 40.cxb5 cxb5 41.Kf3 Nd4+ 42.Ke4 Nc6 43.Rc8 Ne7 44.Rb8 Nf5 45.g4 Nh6 46.f3 Nf7 47.Ra8 Nd6+ 48.Kd5 Nc4 49.Rxa7 Ne3+ 50.Ke4 Nc4 51.Ra6+ Kg7 52.Rc6 Kf7 53.Rc5 Ke6 54.Rxg5 Kf6 55.Rc5 g5 56.Kd4 1–0**

## What Does the Rise of Computers Mean for Us?

In *The Idiot's Guide to Chess*, third edition (2005), I wrote the following about Garry Kasparov's defeat to Deep Blue:

> The ability of computers to play chess with the best grandmasters is extremely impressive. But it doesn't give us any reason to think about computers differently. Computers are still machines. They don't feel, they don't have any conscious awareness, and they don't even "think" in the way humans do. They do the same things they have always done. One of the things they do is play chess. Deep Blue played better than any machine ever had before, but it still played basically the same way that machines have always played. Kasparov lost because Deep Blue played a little bit faster and a little bit smarter than any machine had done before. (Plus, Kasparov did not play very well compared to some of his previous matches.) The IBM team deserves tremendous credit for their accomplishment; but in the final analysis, they built a better machine, not a different one.

With AlphaZero, it is clear that the DeepMind team did more than just build a *better* machine. They truly built a *different* machine, and we are only at the beginning stages of seeing what these new machines can do. To take just one example, in late 2018, the DeepMind team applied the AlphaZero technology in a scientific competition that predicts protein structures and it significantly outperformed all the other scientific teams from around the world.

We should not lose sight of the fact that these are still machines, however. AlphaZero does not and never will have conscious awareness any more than your smartphone, your PC, or your toaster does. What it does have is very sophisticated algorithms with tremendous capabilities. AI is technology with amazing potential that is still in its infancy. In a way, even though computers have now penetrated nearly every facet of our lives, we are still at a similar moment as when Claude Shannon wrote his 1949 paper!

Will chess continue to "act as a wedge in attacking other problems of a similar nature and of greater significance," as Shannon wrote? Maybe. But it is also possible that 70 years after Shannon wrote those words, chess may have outlived its special role in computer science. What we do know for sure is that computers have already developed to the point where they can greatly enrich our enjoyment and appreciation of the ancient game of chess. And computers will almost surely continue to develop by leaps and bounds.

What does the rise of computers mean for us? Computers are tools, so their rise means whatever we decide it means. Among the nearly limitless ways we can put computers to work for us, I hope we use them to enjoy chess even more!

# Glossary

**alpha-beta pruning**   A mathematical technique that allows the computer to cut down on the number of moves it must consider when it calculates the possibilities in a chess position.

**artificial intelligence (AI)**   A catchall phrase that refers to many different computer programming techniques other than the traditional approach of writing exactly what output the computer should generate for any given input.

**backward pawn**   Loosely speaking, a pawn in a pawn chain (in the strict sense of *pawn chain*) that protects another pawn in the chain. Strictly speaking, such a pawn that cannot be protected by another pawn, and that has no chance of safely advancing in the near future.

**bad bishop**   A bishop whose mobility is restricted by its own pawns.

**black-squared bishop**   The bishop that moves along the black squares. Each player starts the game with one black-squared bishop.

**capture**   The act of moving one of your pieces to a square occupied by one of your opponent's pieces, thereby removing your opponent's piece from the board. Once a piece is captured, it is gone for the rest of the game.

**castling**   A special move of the king. Under certain circumstances, the king can move two squares to the left or right toward one of the rooks and then place that rook on the square immediately next to it on the opposite side. See Chapter 3 for details on this move.

**check**   Refers to when the king is attacked. When the opponent threatens to capture the king on his next move, the king is "in check."

**checkmate**   Refers to when the king is attacked, and there is no way to prevent it from being captured in the next turn. Checkmate ends the game; the player whose king is checkmated loses, and the player who checkmates the other king wins.

**clearance sacrifice**   To sacrifice a piece in order to vacate the square it was standing on.

**closed**   Refers to when the center is filled with pawns that block one another. When the game is closed, there are few open files in the center.

**deep learning**   Refers to a neural network that performs multiple sets of mathematical manipulations on the input data to map it onto the output data.

**deflection**   Refers to when one piece is forced to move away from a square where it is needed for some reason. When this happens, the piece is deflected from the square.

**develop**   To move a piece (except for a pawn or the king) off its original square onto another square in the opening.

**discovered check**   A check that results because one piece moves, and the piece that was behind it gives check.

**double check**   When the king is put in check by two pieces at once.

**draw**   The chess term for a tie. When the game is a draw, neither player wins.

**Elo rating system**   A mathematical rating system named after its inventor, Arpad Elo, that produces a four-digit number for each participant in any win/draw/loss (or any win/loss) multiplayer competitive system, and is widely used in chess. If you know the Elo ratings of two players, you can compute each player's expected score against one another.

**en passant**   A French phrase that means "in passing." It refers to a special pawn capture, where one pawn captures another that has advanced two squares to land on the square immediately to its left or right. On the very next turn, and only on the very next turn, the pawn may capture the enemy pawn as though it had advanced only one square.

**exchange**   As a verb, a synonym for *trade*. As a noun, it refers to the material advantage of a rook versus a minor pieces. To be "up the exchange," for example, is to have a rook in return for the opponent having a bishop or knight.

**file**   A vertical row of squares. The chessboard has eight files.

**fork**   When one piece attacks two or more of the opponent's pieces at the same time, it is called a fork.

**forward pawn**   The most advanced pawn in a pawn chain (in the strict sense of *pawn chain*).

**friend or foe**   A convenient way to distinguish between one of your pieces and one of your opponent's pieces. Naturally, a friend is one of your pieces, and a foe is one of your opponent's pieces.

**good bishop**   A bishop whose mobility is not restricted by its own pawns.

**grandmaster**   The highest title one can earn as a chess player. It is awarded by FIDE, the World Chess Federation.

**horizon effect**   An issue that can arise from the rigid, numerical approach traditional computers use to evaluate chess positions, in which the search function is cut off too early during analysis, even though a similarly skilled human chess player would recognize that the position merits the extra effort to look more deeply.

**in-between move**   One that can be played between two moves you thought had to be played consecutively; it is often a check or a threat to capture some piece.

**insufficient material**   Refers to when neither side can possibly put the other king into checkmate. When there is insufficient material, the game is automatically a draw.

**machine learning**   The AI approach of programming a computer to develop its own rules for solving a problem.

**neural network**   An analogy to the biology of the human brain that refers to how the inputs for machine learning are organized so they can be manipulated using linear algebra to produce estimated values for the output.

**open**   Refers to when the center has no pawns that block one another. When the game is open, there are lots of open files in the center.

**open file**   A file that is either completely or relatively cleared of pawns and pieces, so that if a rook were posted on the file, it would control all or most of the squares along it.

**opening repertoire**   The set of opening sequences one has prepared in advance in order to reach a middlegame one is comfortable playing.

**opposite-colored bishops**   Refers to when you have one bishop and your opponent has one bishop, and each bishop moves on different colored squares. (For example, your bishop moves on the white squares and your opponent's bishop moves on the black squares.)

**outside passed pawn**   A passed pawn that is away from most of the other pawns and that is not a center pawn.

**passed pawn**   A pawn that can no longer be captured or blocked by another pawn so long as no pawn changes files by capturing.

**pawn chain**   Loosely speaking, any group of pawns of the same color on squares that touch each other; strictly speaking, a group of pawns of the same color on squares that touch each other diagonally. In the strict sense, the pawn is a chain because each pawn protects another and is protected, except for the base (which is not protected by a pawn) and the forward pawn (which doesn't protect any pawn).

**pawn duo**   Two pawns of the same color on the same rank and on adjacent files.

**pawn structure**   Any configuration of pawns of the same color.

**perpetual check**   Refers to when one side can put the other king into check forever. If one player announces he or she will give perpetual check, and there is no way for the other player to escape from the checks, the game is a draw.

**pin**   When a piece is on a square between a friend and a foe, and moving the piece would open a line that exposes the friend to capture by the foe, that piece is pinned to its friend; a pin refers to such a situation.

**protected passed pawn**   A passed pawn that is protected by another pawn.

**rank**   A horizontal row of squares. The chessboard has eight ranks.

**reinforcement learning**   A type of AI machine-learning technique that is generally applied to games and is specifically applied to chess.

**resign**   To concede defeat.

**sacrifice**   To voluntarily give up material for some reason.

**skewer**   An attack where a long-range piece (rook, bishop, or queen) threatens two or more opposing pieces along a single line.

**smothered mate**   Refers to when the knight gives check, and it's checkmate because the king is surrounded by its own pieces and so has nowhere to move.

**stalemate**   Refers to when the player whose turn it is to move has no legal move, and his king is not in check. When the position is stalemate for either player, the game is a draw.

**tactic**   A move or sequence of moves played to achieve some goal, such as the win of material or checkmate.

**trade**    To capture one of the opponent's pieces and allow the opponent to recapture some material in return. For example, to trade knights is to capture one of the opponent's knights and allow the opponent to capture a knight in return.

**weak back rank**    When your king is on the rank that is closest to you, and a check by the opponent's rook or queen along that rank would be checkmate, you have a weak back rank.

**weak square**    A square that one player can control but the other can't. It's not really correct to call a square "weak" unless it's also important, so whether a square is weak is a judgment call.

**white-squared bishop**    The bishop that moves along the white squares. Each player starts the game with one white-squared bishop.

**X-ray**    Refers to when a piece exerts control by following a foe along a diagonal, rank, or file.

**zugzwang**    Name for the situation when it would be a disadvantage for either player to move; it is derived from German and loosely translates to "a compulsive move."

**zwischenzug**    A German word that is sometimes used in chess parlance to mean *in-between move*.

# Answers to Exercises

# Answers to Exercises from Chapter 2

**Exercise 1:** The pawn on f5 may capture the bishop on e6, which is written "1.fxe6". The pawn on e2 may move to e3 or e4, which are written "1.e3" and "1.e4" respectively. The pawn on a4 may capture the pawn on b5, which is written "1.axb5". What about the pawn on c3? I played a little trick on you! This pawn may not move, because if it moved, the bishop on a5 would put the white king into check. You can *never* play a move that would put yourself into check.

**Exercise 2:** The knight on b7 has no moves. The knight on f6 can move to d7, e8, g8, h7, or h5, which are written "1...Nd7", "1...Ne8", "1...Ng8", "1...Nh7", and "1...Nh5" respectively. Or the knight may capture either of the pawns on d5 or g4, which are written "1...Nxd5" and "1...Nxg4" respectively. But the knight cannot move to e4, because the black pawn occupies this square.

**Exercise 3:** The bishop on f8 cannot move. The bishop on e6 can move to g8, f7, f5, d7, c8, d5, or c4, which are written "1...Bg8", "1...Bf7", "1...Bf5", "1...Bd7", "1...Bc8", "1...Bd5", and "1...Bc4" respectively. The bishop can also capture the pawn on g4 or the queen on b3, and these are written "1...Bxg4" and "1...Bxb3" respectively.

**Exercise 4:** This was another tricky question! White's king is in check from the black rook, so White must remove the check. The only way to do that by moving the rook is to capture the rook on e6, so this is the only move White can make with the rook. This move is written "1.Rxe6+". The + sign indicates that the move is check, as is explained in Chapter 3.

**Exercise 5:** The black queen can move to a2, b3, c4, e6, c6, e4, e5, f5, c5, b5, d4, d3, d6, d7, or d8. These moves are written "1...Qa2", "1...Qb3", "1...Qc4", "1...Qe6", "1...Qc6", "1...Qe4", "1...Qe5", "1...Qf5", "1...Qc5", "1...Qb5", "1...Qd4", "1...Qd3", "1...Qd6", "1...Qd7", and "1...Qd8" respectively. Black can also capture the pawn on f3, the rook on a5, or the queen on d2. These moves are written "1...Qxf3", "1...Qxa5", and "1...Qxd2+" respectively. Again, as explained in Chapter 3, the + indicates check.

**Exercise 6:** The white king can capture the queen on d5, but it can't capture the pawn on e5 because this pawn is protected by the queen, and if White made this move it would put the white king into check. The white king can move to e3 or f5, which are written "1.Ke3" and "1.Kf5" respectively, or it can capture the queen on d5, which is written "1.Kxd5".

**Exercise 7:** It must be Black's turn, because Black's king is in check. Black's legal moves are to move the king to e8 or g8 or to capture the bishop with the knight. These moves are written, "1...Ke8, 1...Kg8, 1...Nxc5" respectively.

**Exercise 8:** Black has exactly twenty legal moves. Black can move either pawn one or two squares forward, move the queen's knight (the knight on b8) to a6 or c6, or move the king's knight (the knight on g8) to f6 or h6. These moves are written respectively, " 1...a6, 1...a5, 1...b6, 1...b5, 1...c6, 1...c5, 1...d6, 1...d5, 1...e6, 1...e5, 1...f6, 1...f5, 1...g6, 1...g5, 1...h6, 1...h5, 1...Na6, 1...Nc6, 1...Nf6, 1...Nh6."

**Exercise 9:** White has eight legal moves with a pawn. These moves are written respectively, "1.a3, 1.a4, 1.c4, 1.d5, 1.dxe5, 1.g3, 1.g4, 1.h4." White has six legal moves with the king's bishop (the bishop on b3). These are 1. "Ba4, 1.Bc2, 1.Bc4, 1.Bd5, 1.Be6, 1.Bxf7+." White has no legal moves with the queen's bishop (the bishop on c1) because it is blocked by the pawn on b2 and the knight on d2.

**Exercise 10:** Black can make three legal moves with the king's knight: 1...Nf6, 1...Ne7, or 1...Nh6; notice that the second move is not written "1...Nge7" because there is no need to distinguish the knight on g8 from the knight on c6. Black cannot move the queen's knight because if this knight moves, the king will be in check. (The knight is *pinned* to the king; you learn more about the pin in Chapter 6.) Black can make two legal moves with the queen's rook (the rook on a8): 1...Rb8 or 1...Ra7. Black cannot move the king's rook (the rook on h8) because it is blocked by the knight on g8 and the pawn on h7.

**Exercise 11:** Black is in check; therefore, Black must eliminate the check. There are only two moves that do this: 1...Qc8 or 1...Qxg8. The best move is 1...Qxg8. After 1...Qc8, 2.Rxc8 is checkmate. However, after 1...Qxg8 the game will be a draw because even though White can capture the queen with 2.Nxg8, there is no way to checkmate the king with only a knight and king. (See Chapter 3 for more about when the game is a draw.)

**Exercise 12:** White has one legal move with the king: 1.Ka5. (All other king moves put White into check.) White has six legal moves with the knight: 1.Nc6+, 1.Nd5, 1.Nf5, 1.Ng6, 1.Ng8, 1.Nc8. White has nine legal moves with the rook: 1.Rg8+, 1.Rg6, 1.Rg5, 1.Rg4, 1.Rg3, 1.Rg2, 1.Rg1, 1.Rf7, 1.Rh7. After 1.Rg8+, we have the position in Exercise 11. However, the best move is 1.Nc6+ Qxc6+ (1...Ka8 allows 2.Ra7 checkmate, and 1...Kc8 allows 2.Rc7 checkmate) 2.Kxc6, and White can force checkmate with a rook and king. (See Chapter 4 for more about how White can win this position.)

# Answers to Exercises from Chapter 3

**Exercise 1:** Yes, White can capture this pawn. Black has just moved the pawn two squares, so White can respond by capturing *en passant* on the very next move. Were you thrown off by the fact that White is in check? But capturing the pawn en passant removes the check, so it is okay.

**Exercise 2:** The only way for White to promote the pawn to a queen on this move is to capture the rook giving check to her king, and the move is written, "1.cxd8=Q#". Notice the # is there because when White plays this move, Black is in checkmate! White can't play 1.c8=Q, because the king is in check and that must be dealt with.

**Exercise 3:** White castling queenside is written, "1.O-O-O". Black cannot castle queenside on the next move because the black king must pass through the d8 square to do so, and this square is controlled by the white rook on d1. By the way, notice that White could castle queenside even though the black bishop on g7 was attacking the rook on a1. There is no rule against castling if your rook is attacked! (If you got confused on this exercise, go back and review the castling rules in this chapter.)

**Exercise 4:** Black can play 1...Qg4+!, when White's only possible response is 2.Kh1. Black then plays 2...Qf3!+ but not 2...Qe4+? because after 3.f3 Qxf3+ 4.Rxf3, the checks stop. The game could continue: 3.Kg1 Qg4+ 4.Kh1 Qf3+ 5.Kg1 Qg4+ and so on, forever, until the game is declared a draw.

**Exercise 5:** White can play 1.Rg3+! Kh7 (or 1...Kh8) 2.Rh4#.

**Exercise 6:** Black is not in stalemate because Black has one possible move: 1...h3. And if White is alert enough to see that 2.Nc7# is checkmate, then White will win the game!

**Exercise 7:** White can't castle queenside, because then the king would pass through check on d1. But White can castle kingside, which is written: 1.O-O. Notice that White can castle kingside even though the rook on h1 is attacked.

**Exercise 8:** This position should not be declared a draw! Without the black pawn on h3, there is no legal way to construct a checkmate. But with the pawn, there is a way. In fact, this position is actually winning for White: 1.Ng4! h2 (the only legal move) 2.Nf2 checkmate. White forces the pawn to take the h2 square from Black and then White delivers checkmate with the knight. This is a good pattern to remember.

**Exercise 9:** Black should play 1...h2! when White must allow Black to be stalemated (e.g., 2.Ne4) or else Black will move the king to g1 and then promote the pawn safely (e.g., 2.Kg3?? Kg1 and 3... h1=Q). If Black plays 1...Kh2, then he loses after 2.Ng4+! Kh1 3.Kf1! h2 4.Nf2#.

**Exercise 10:** Yes, if White plays 1.g4, Black can play 1...hxg3+ en passant. Kasparov did not push the pawn, precisely because he did not want Black to capture en passant in this position. But as you will see in a later exercise, he made the wrong decision in this case.

**Exercise 11:** Black should play 1...c1=R!, when Black can easily win White's last pawn and force checkmate. (See Chapter 4 to see how to force checkmate with the rook.) Black should not play 1... c1=Q?? because then White will be in stalemate and the game will be drawn. Black also should not promote to a knight or a bishop, because then Black will not be able to force checkmate. Even though Exercises 8 and 9 illustrate positions where the knight and king can give checkmate against a pawn and king, that is a very rare case. Here, if Black made a knight or bishop, White would draw very easily.

**Exercise 12:** Black can't castle on either side because Black is in check. If Black blocks the check with either the knight or the bishop, Black will be in big trouble. (Do you see why? If not, you might want to ask yourself the same question after you read Chapters 5 and 6.) So Black will have to move the king either to f8 or d8, which will make it difficult for Black to get the king to a good square. Black should have castled earlier!

# Answers to Exercises from Chapter 4

**Exercise 1:** White plays 1.Qf7! Black has no other move than 1...Kc8, and then White has several ways to give checkmate: 2.Qc7#, 2.Qe8#, 2.Qf8#, and 2.Qg8#. But White should *not* play 1.Qe6? because then Black is in stalemate. (Give yourself credit also for 1.Qe2! which forces checkmate after 1...Kc8 2.Qe8#.)

**Exercise 2:** White plays 1.Ra1! Black has to play 1...Kc8 and then White plays 2.Ra8#.

**Exercise 3:** b4 and a6.

**Exercise 4:** White should push the pawn in order to promote it to either a rook or (better) a queen. Then White will be able to deliver checkmate. There are two ways to carry the plan out. The simplest is 1.b6 Kd8 (Black brings the king over to try to stop the pawn from reaching the edge of the board ...) 2.b7 (... but Black doesn't get there in time!) and White will promote the pawn on the next move. Another way is to play 1.Kc7, which prevents the black king from going to d8 or d7. The way is then clear for White to push the pawn to b8, make it a queen, and win the game.

**Exercise 5:** Black wins with 1...Kg6!, threatening checkmate with 2...Qf7, 2...Qe8, or 2...Qd8. White has no good defense. But see Exercise 6 for White's best try!

**Exercise 6:** Black should play 1...Kxf6 2.Kh8 Qg7#. Black should *not* play 1...Qxf6?? as then White would be stalemated.

**Exercise 7:** White plays 1.Re7! Kh5 2.Rh7#.

**Exercise 8:** After 1...c1=R 2.Kb2, here's how I did it: 2...Rc5 3.Ka2 Rb5 (there's nothing wrong with 3...Rc3 and 4...Rxa3 except that it requires move moves) 4.Ka1 Kb3 (*not* 4...Kxa3?? and it's stalemate!) 5.Kb1 (5.a4 Rd5 and 6...Rd1#) 5...Rc5! (quickest) 6.a4 (6.Ka1 Rc1#) 6...Kxa4 7.Kb2 Kb4 8.Ka2 Rc2+ 9.Kb1 Kb3 10.Ka1 Rc1#.

# Answers to Exercises from Chapter 5

**Exercise 1:** The knight on d4 attacks the pawns on b5 and e6 and the knight on c6. The pawns are each protected: the pawn on b5 is protected by the pawn on a6, and the pawn on e6 is protected by the pawn on f7. So White should not capture either of the pawns. But the knight on c6 is only defended once, by the bishop on b7, while it is attacked twice: by the bishop on f3 as well as the knight on d4. White can win a knight by playing 1.Nxc6+ Bxc6 2.Bxc6. Just as good is 1.Bxc6 Bxc6 2.Nxc6+, which wins a knight for a bishop. In either case, White gains a large material advantage.

**Exercise 2:** No. If White plays 1.Rxb7??, Black will play 1...Bxb7 and win a whole rook for a measly pawn! And if White plays 1.dxc5, Black wins the pawn back right away with 1...Bxc3+.

**Exercise 3:** White attacks the pawn on e6 with the queen and the pawn on h6 with the bishop on d2. White should not capture either of them because they are both protected. The pawn on e6 is protected by the pawn on f7, and the pawn on h6 is protected by the pawn on g7 and the rook on h8.

**Exercise 4:** Yes. Both moves win a pawn. White attacks the pawn on d4 three times, and Black defends it only twice, so he can capture it. The game might continue: 1.Nfxd4 Nxd4 2.Qxd4 Qxd4 3.Nxd4, and White has won a pawn. 1.Qxd4??, however, is a very bad move because it loses the queen after 1...Nxd4.

**Exercise 5:** Black should play 1...Qxg5!, which wins a bishop for nothing.

**Exercise 6:** Black should capture the knight on c4 and not the one on e6. The white rook protects each of the knights once, but Black attacks the white knight on c4 with two rooks (notice the power of doubled rooks), so he wins a knight by 1...Rxc4 2.Rxc4 Rxc4.

**Exercise 7:** No: 1...Nxc3 2.Rxc3 Rxc3 3.Kxc3 is a series of equal trades, as is 1...Rxc3 2.Rxc3 Nxc3 3.Kxc3.

**Exercise 8:** After 1.dxc6 Rxc6 material will be equal. But that does not mean White should not play 1.dxc6! because it is still the best move. In the diagrammed position, White has a material disadvantage: Black has a knight for White's pawn. White must grab the chance to even the situation with 1.dxc6.

**Exercise 9:** White can play three captures: 1.Bxf6, 1.Nxc6, and 1.Nxe6. None of them gives White a material advantage:

+ After 1.Bxf6 Bxf6, White has made an even trade. (Maybe Black has gained a tiny material advantage, because he now has a bishop for a knight.)

+ After 1.Nxc6 bxc6, White has made an even trade.

+ After 1.Nxe6? Bxe6, White has lost a knight for a pawn.

**Exercise 10:** White can play three captures: 1.axb5, 1.dxe5, and 1.Bxf7+. None of them gives White a material advantage:

+ After 1.axb5 axb5, White has made an even trade.

+ After 1.dxe5 dxe5, White has made an even trade.

+ After 1.Bxf7+? Kxf7, White has lost a bishop for a pawn.

**Exercise 11:** White should capture the rook on b6. After 1.Bxb6 Bxb6, White has won a rook for a bishop. (Capturing the knight on f6 is at best only an even trade.)

**Exercise 12:** No. The white queen is more valuable than either the black knight or the black rook. Because both of these pieces are protected, White should capture neither of them.

**Exercise 13:** Yes. After 1.Rxd7 Bxd7 2.Rxd7, White wins a knight and a bishop for a rook. According to the relative value of pieces chart, a knight and a bishop together are worth a little more than 6, while a rook is only worth 5.

**Exercise 14:** No. After 1.Rxd7 Bxd7 2.Rxd7, now that the king is on c8, Black can play 2…Kxd7, when White has lost two rooks for only a knight and a bishop. (Make sure you understand the difference between this exercise and Exercise 13.)

**Exercise 15:** No. In particular, notice that 1…Be5?? 2.Bxe5 is a disaster because Black loses a bishop for nothing, and also 1…Kg7? 2.Bxf6+ Kxf6 loses a rook for a bishop.

**Exercise 16:** No. Black still should not defend the rook, for the same reason as in Exercise 15. Black still cannot block the attack by moving a piece to e5 because even though he has one more piece which attacks this square (the knight on g6), White also has one more piece that attacks this square (the knight on f3), so they even out. (For example: 1…Be5?? 2.Nxe5 Nxe5 3.Bxe5.) Nor should Black capture the knight on f3 because it is defended by the pawn on g2: 1…Rxf3? 2.gxf3, and White wins a rook for a knight.

**Exercise 17:** Yes. Black can attack White's queen with 1…Nf4 then White should meet the threat to the queen rather than capture the rook; that is, 2.Bxf6?? Nxe2+ and Black wins a queen for a rook.

**Exercise 18:** The white knight attacks both the queen and the rook at the same time. This is called a *fork*, which you learn about in Chapter 6. Because both pieces are attacked at the same time, Black cannot move both of them to safety in the next turn. The best move is for Black to play 1…Bxe4, capturing the piece that attacks both the queen and the rook, removing the threat to them both. After 2.Qxe4, material is even.

**Exercise 19:** The white bishop attacks the rook, but the rook cannot move because if it did, that would expose the king to check, which is not allowed. This is called a *pin*, which you learn about in Chapter 6. The best move is 1...Nxe4, and after 2.Rxe4, material is even.

**Exercise 20:** No. The rook cannot move because that would expose the king to check, and there is no other way for Black to defend against the threat.

**Exercise 21:** Black can play 1...Ne4, which only loses a pawn after 2.Bxe4 dxe4 3.Rxe4. But losing a pawn is better than losing a rook for a bishop, so 1...Ne4 is the best move.

**Exercise 22:** After 1...Ne4, White has a better move than to capture the knight: White can play 2.f3! This move attacks the knight with a pawn, so Black should move the knight. But then White will capture the rook for the bishop. (Here's an extra question for you to solve on your own. Did you consider that after 1...Ne4 2.f3, Black could play 2...Rg3 to pin the pawn to the bishop? After 3.fxe4 Rxd3, Black saves the knight, by capturing the bishop on d3. But White can win the knight in several ways, two of which are 3.Bb1 and 3.Kh2. Can you see why?)

**Exercise 23:** White should play 1.fxe3 to keep material even because the knight on e3 attacked the rook. If White played 1.cxd5? or 1.Bxd5?, Black would play 1...Nxd1+ 2.Rxd1; if White played 1.Rxd5?, Black would play 1...Nxd5 2.Bxd5 (or 2.cxd5), in either case with the advantage of the exchange.

**Exercise 24:** No. After 1.Rxe8+ Rxe8 (or 1...Nxe8), if 2.Qxe8+? Nxe8 3.Rxe8+ Kg7, Black has a queen for a rook and knight, a material advantage for Black.

**Exercise 25:** Yes. After 1.Rxe8+ Rxe8 (or 1...Nxe8) 2.Rxe8+ Nxe8 3.Qxe8+, White has won a knight for nothing. Because the rooks are in front of the queen, White captures with less valuable material first and is left with the more valuable piece (the queen) in the end.

**Exercise 26:** No. Now that Black's queen is on c6 instead of c7, the rook is protected one more time. After 1.Rxe8+ Rxe8 2.Rxe8+ Qxe8 3.Qxe8+ Nxe8 material is still even.

**Exercise 27:** Black should play either 1...Qc5 or 1...Qd8 to move the queen out of the attack and defend the bishop at the same time. (Not 1...Qxd5, because after 2.Bxd5 Bxd5, White would have a queen for two minor pieces; not 1...Bb4, because after 2.Bxb4, White would win material; and not 1...Bc5, because after 2.Bxa5 Bxd4 3.Ne7+! Kh8 4.Rxd4, White is ahead a minor piece.) Then after 2.Nxe7+ Qxe7, material is still even.

**Exercise 28:** Black should play 1...Bxc1 2.Rxc1 b6 (to protect the knight), after which Black will be ahead a rook for a bishop.

**Exercise 29:** Black should still play 1...Bxc1 2.Rxc1 b6. However, after 3.b4! White will win the knight, as Black cannot move it without putting his own king in check. After White plays 4.bxc5, White will be ahead in material—two pieces for a rook.

**Exercise 30:** White cannot move the queen, as it will be captured on any square it moves to. White could block the attack with 1.Ne5, but then Black wins the exchange with 1...Nxe1 2.Rxe1, and on top of that can attack two pieces at the same time with 2...f6. And it does no good to block the attack with 1.Nf6+ or 1.Bf6 because Black can capture either piece with a pawn, winning material. But White can save the queen by counterattacking: 1.Nh6+! Now if 1...Kh8, 2.Nxf7+ Kg8 3.Nh6+ Kh8 4.Nf7+ is perpetual check. But if (after 1.Nh6+) 1...Bxh6, then 2.Bxh6! threatens checkmate on g7, gaining time to move the rook on e1 out of the attack by the knight.

# Answers to Exercises from Chapter 6

**Exercise 1:** White plays 1.f5!, which threatens to capture Black's pawn on e6. If Black plays 1…exf5 or 1…exd5, White plays 2.e6.

**Exercise 2:** White should be worried, because White's knight is pinned to the king, and if White defends the knight, Black will attack it again by playing 1…e6. Therefore, White will lose the knight.

**Exercise 3:** White should play 1.Rf1!, which pins the queen to the king. But notice that 1.O-O is illegal, because the queen controls the f1 square, which the white king would have to pass through.

**Exercise 4:** White cannot win the queen! White cannot play 1.Rf1+ because White's own king is in check, and White cannot play 1.O-O+ because it is not allowed to castle when it is in check. White's best move is to play 1.g3, which attacks the bishop on h4 and also threatens 1.Rf1+ or 1.O-O+. Therefore, 1.g3 wins the bishop because Black must respond to the threat to the queen instead of to the threat to the bishop.

**Exercise 5:** White should win. If Black plays 1…h1=Q, White skewers the king and queen by playing 2.a8=Q+ and then wins the endgame with an extra queen. Otherwise, White can stop Black from queening after he makes a queen, and should win.

**Exercise 6:** White should play 1.d4+!, which attacks both the rook and the king by discovered check, and so wins the rook.

**Exercise 7:** White's threat is to play 2.Qf3, attacking the knight again, and winning it. There is no defense, because Black cannot move the queen out of the pin without losing the knight.

**Exercise 8:** No, for two reasons. First, Black can move the queen out of the pin because the knight is protected by the pawn on g7. Second, Black can play 1…h6 to attack the bishop. If White plays 2.Bxf6, Black plays 2…Qxf6; if White plays 2.Bh4, Black can block the pin by playing 2…g5.

**Exercise 9:** If Black plays 28…Rxe6, White plays 29.Rc8! which pins the queen to the king and wins material. In fact, Black resigned after 28.Nxe6!, and I won the tournament.

**Exercise 10:** White should play 1.Nc5+!! Kb8 2.Na6#!

**Exercise 11:** Black should play 1…Nxe4!, which uncovers an attack against the queen. If White captures the knight with 2.Qxe4, Black pins the queen with 2…Re8.

**Exercise 12:** White plays 1.Qxa7+!! Kxa7 (if 1…Kc7, then 2.bxc8=Q+ gives double check, and White skewers the king and queen so that after 2…Kxc8 3.Qxe7 White is up a whole queen) 2.bxc8=N+!! and after 3.Nxe7 White should win.

**Exercise 13:** White's threat is to play 2.Nd6, checkmate! Because the e-pawn is pinned, Black cannot capture the knight. Clearly 1…Ngf6?? would be a terrible blunder, as White then plays 2.Nd6#. (But not 2.Nxf6+ Nxf6, which is just an even exchange of knights.)

**Exercise 14:** After 1…Qg1+!! 2.Kxg1 Nxe2+ captures the bishop and forks the king and queen. After 3…Nxc3, Black is a piece ahead and has a winning position.

**Exercise 15:** White combines the pin with the discovered attack, plus a mating pattern: 1.Be7!! Nxe7 (1…Qxg4 2.Rxd8#; notice that both 1…Qxe7 and 1…Qxd1 are illegal because of the pin!) 2.Rxd7 Rxd7 3.Nc3 and White has a winning material advantage.

**Exercise 16:** White won by combining the pin with the skewer with 1.Rd8!! Qxd8 2.Qh8+ Kf7 3.Qxd8. Note that 1.Qh8+ Kf7 doesn't work, because the king protects the queen on e8.

**Exercise 17:** White wins with 1.Rxf8+!! Kxf8 2.Ng6#. Remember always to look at a double check when you see it! (And notice that 1.Rd7+ does not win because 1...Nxc4 attacks the White queen so that 2.Rxd8 Nxd2 3.Rxd2 maintains material equality. Also, 1.Rxb7+ Nxc4 accomplishes nothing for White.)

**Exercise 18:** White combined the pin and the double attack with 1.Rd8!! Rxd8 (White threatened both 2.Rxh8 and 2.Rb7#, and 1...Ra7 is met by 2.Rxa7 Rxd8 [or 2...Kxa7 3.Rxh8] 3.c7+) 2.c7+ and 3.cxd8=Q+ with a winning material advantage and a mating attack to boot.

**Exercise 19:** Black continues 2...Ng3+!! 3.Kxg3 (3.Kg1 Rh1#) 3...f4#. A beautiful use of discovered check!

**Exercise 20:** White played 1.Bf3!! exf3 (the queen has no safe square to move to, and there is no effective counterattack) 2.exf3+ and the pawn captured the queen on the next move. A nice use of discovered check!

**Exercise 21:** Black won with 1...Nh4!, threatening 2...Qg2#. White has nothing better than either 2.Qf3 Nxf3+ 3.Nxf3, or 2.gxh4 Qxc3, in either case losing the queen for a knight.

**Exercise 22:** White cannot safely capture the knight. After 1.Nxd5?? Nxd5 2.Bxd8 Bb4+! 3.Qd2 (White's only legal move!) 3...Bxd2+ 4.Kxd2 Kxd8, Black has an extra piece. It's not enough just to see a pin: you must also calculate out all the consequences.

**Exercise 23:** Yes, 1...e5! does win a piece because after 2.Bxe5, 2...Qa5+! forks White's king and bishop.

**Exercise 24:** After 1...Rd3+! 2.Kc2 Nd4+, Black wins the rook thanks to the fork. The win is harder to see if White moves the king to b4, but the winning idea is similar: 2.Kb4 Nd4! 3.Re1 (moving the rook to any other square allows Black to safely capture the knight on e3) 3...Rxe3! 4.Rxe3 Nc2+ followed by 5...Nxe3, with a winning endgame for Black.

**Exercise 25:** The winning idea is to smash through the defending knight on c5: 1.Nxb6 Rxb6 2.Rxc5! dxc5 3.Qxc5. And after White wins the rook on b6, White will have a winning material advantage.

**Exercise 26:** 1...Re1+ 2.Rd1 (2.Nd1 Be4 pins the rook on d and after 3.Rxe4 fxe4, Black will have a winning advantage) 2...Be4+! 3.Ka1 (3.Rxe4 Rxd1+ 4.Nxd1 fxe4 is an easy win for Black, as is 3.Kc2 Rc2+ 4.Kb1 Rxc3+) 3...Rxd1+ 4.Nxd1 Rg1 and the pin wins the knight and the game.

# Answers to Exercises from Chapter 7

**Exercise 1:** White wins material by playing 1.Nxe5!, and if 1...dxe5 then 2.Nxc5. But White should not play 1.Nxc5, with the idea that if 1...dxc5 then 2.Nxe5, because after 1.Nxc5 Black has the "in between" move 1...Nxf3+! and after 2.gxf3 dxc5, material is still even.

**Exercise 2:** Fischer played 27...Bxa4! and Spassky resigned. Fischer's point was that after 28.Qxa4 Qxe4, he has the double attack of ...Qxe1+ and ...Qxg2#, to which Spassky would have had no defense (and 29.Qe8+ Kh7 does not solve White's problem).

**Exercise 3:** No, it would be a very *bad* idea! After 1.Rd1?? Re1+! Black wins material by combining deflection with the x-ray. If 2.Rxe1 Qxd6, Black wins a queen for a rook, and if 2.Kh2 Rxd1, Black wins a whole rook.

**Exercise 4:** If White could get the queen on g3 to g7, it would be checkmate. And there is a way to do it: 1.Rxh7+! and then 2.Qg7#. But notice that the clearance sacrifice does not work with 1.Rg8+?? because after 1...Rxg8, Black defends the g7 square!

**Exercise 5:** No, 1.Bxe7 is just an even trade after 1...R8xe7. But it would be a terrible blunder for Black to reply 1...R5xe7?? because then 2.Rxe7 would win a whole rook. Notice also that the in-between move 1...Rxe2?? would also be a disaster: after 2.Rxe2, White defends the bishop!

**Exercise 6:** The killer move is 1.d5!, deflecting the rook from the defense of the queen. If the rook moves, White captures the queen, and if 1...Qxa3, then White does not immediately recapture the queen, but plays the killer in-between move 2.dxe6+ Kxe6 3.Rxa3, winning a whole rook for only a pawn.

**Exercise 7:** The fact that Black's king and queen are lined up along the open diagonal should be a red flag that White would like to get his bishop to f3. The best way to do that is to play 1.Nxd4!, capturing a pawn, attacking the queen, and threatening to play 2.Bf3, pinning and winning the queen.

**Exercise 8:** I played 43...Rxb2! and after 44.Rxb2, I won the rook back with 44...Qc1+ and 45...Qxb2. The one extra pawn was enough to win the game.

**Exercise 9:** I played 59...Rxh3! to divert the queen away from the pin. If 60.Qxh3 fxg5, Black comes out a knight ahead. And neither of White's checks hurt Black: after 60.Qd7+ Kf8 or 60.Qg6+ Ke7, White has no follow up. (Always make sure the checks aren't dangerous when you calculate how to win material.)

**Exercise 10:** White plays 1.Qe2! Qxe2 (if Black plays 1...cxd3??, White plays 2.Qxe7; if Black moves the queen, White plays 2.Bxc4) 2.Bxe2, recapturing the queen and moving the bishop out of harm's way.

**Exercise 11:** White could play 3.Rxd4!! Rxd4 (3...Rxg3 4.Rxd8 Kxd8 5.Kxg3) 4.Nf5+ and 5.Nxd4, which is a nice way to combine attacking the defender (the rook defending the f5 square) with the fork. Kasparov drew the game but had he found this tactic, he would have played 1.g4, which would have given him tremendous chances of winning.

**Exercise 12:** 1.Ne6+!! fxe6 (if the king moves, White captures the queen on f6; the queen can't capture the knight because it is pinned) 2.Rc7+! followed by Qxf6. White wins the queen and has a mating attack.

**Exercise 13:** 1.Rb8!! threatens 2.Qg7# and leaves Black with no good defense: if 1...Qxb8 then 2.Nxf7#, and if 1...Rxb8 then 2.Qg7#.

**Exercise 14:** 1...Bc3+! wins the queen no matter what piece White puts on d2 (2.Bd2 or 2.Rd2 Qxd5; 2.Qd2 Bxd2+ and then 3...Qxh1+ just for good measure).

**Exercise 15:** 1.Qxe5! picked off the knight because 1...Qxe5 is met by 2.Rd8+ Ke7 3.Re8#.

**Exercise 16:** 1.Rg8+!! Kxg8 (1...Rxg8 2.Qxc1 is a winning material advantage for White) 2.Qg3+ Kf8 (2...Kh8 3.Qg7#) 3.Qg7+ Ke8 4.Qg8#.

**Exercise 17:** 1...Rh1+!! 2.Kxh1 (2.Kg2 Rxh5) 2...Nxg3+ and 3...Nxh5.

**Exercise 18:** Black wins material with 1...Rxd2! 2.Qxd2 (2.Rxe7 Rxd1+ and 3...Bxe7; 2.Bxd2 Qxa7) 2...Rxd2 (2...Qxa7? 3.Qxd8+! Bxd8 4.Bxd2) 3.Rxe7 Rd1+! (3...Bxe7 4.Bxd2) 4.Kh2 Bxe7 and Black is up a rook. Note that 1...Rxa7 does not win material: 2.Rxd8+! Qxd8 3.Qxd8+ Bxd8 4.Bxa7.

**Exercise 19:** White won with 1.Re7!! (not 1.Rd6?? Bxd6 2.Qxd5+ Kf8) 1...Qxe7 (if 1...Bxe7 or 1...Nxe7, then 2.Qf7#) 2.Qxd5+ and checkmate next move.

**Exercise 20:** 1.Rh8! Qxh8 (1...Qc8+ 2.Rxc8; 1...h6 2. Rxh6#; otherwise White plays Rxh7#) 2.g4#.

**Exercise 21:** Carlsen played 50.Qh6+!! and Karjakin resigned. It is checkmate after either 50...Kxh6 51.Rh8# or 50...gxh6 51.Rxf7#. A lovely way to defend the World Championship title!

**Exercise 22:** White plays 1.d5! Nb8 (as good as any other square) 2.Qa4+! followed by 3.Qxe4.

**Exercise 23:** Black played 18...Qxa2+ 19.Ka1 Qa1+ 20.Kd2 Qxd1+!! (but not 20...Bf3+? 21.Bd3 and White defends) and White resigned rather than allow 21.Kxd1 Bf3+! (double check!) followed by 22... Rd1# whichever way White moves the king.

**Exercise 24:** The threat is checkmate with either Nxc6 or Nd7. No, 1...Bh6 does not defend because 2.Nxc6 or 2.Nd7 is still checkmate due to the double-check. Black has no satisfactory defense.

**Exercise 25:** Black won material with 27...Rxc3! (but not 27...Qxd1+ because White plays 28.Rxd1 and defends, rather than 28.Nxd1?? Rxc1) 28.Qxb3 (28.Rxc3 Qxd1+; 28.bxc3 Qxa2) 28...Rxc1+ (28...Rcxb3 would also win) and White resigned since after White moves out of check and Black captures the queen on b3, White will be hopelessly behind in material.

**Exercise 26:** Anand missed 26...Nxe5!! 27.Rxg8 (not 27.Rxe5? Rxg4!) 27...Nxc4+ 28.Kd3 (or else just 28...Rxg8 next move) 28...Nb2+! (not 28...Rxg8 29.Kxc4) 29.Kd2 Rxg8. After missing this chance, Carlsen won the game, went ahead by a point in the match, and successfully defended the World Championship title. Had Anand played 26...Nxe5, he probably would have won the game, taken the lead in the match, and possibly chess history would have been very different. Always be alert for tactics!

# Answers to Exercises from Chapter 8

**Exercise 1:** I played 44.Bb7! and Black resigned. Moving the bishop off the d5 square threatens 45.Rd8#, and moving the bishop to b7 prevents both rooks from defending against the threat, because the rook on b6 is now blocked from moving to b8, and 44...Ra8 is met by 45.Bxa8.

**Exercise 2:** After 22.Bxe6+!, Black resigned. There is nothing better than 22...dxe6, after which 23.Rf8# is checkmate.

**Exercise 3:** If White plays 26.Nxd1, then 26...e1=Q# is checkmate. If White plays 26.Rxd1, Black wins with the beautiful move 26...Qxc3!! The point of this move is to threaten 27...e1=Q and also to deflect the white queen away from the defense of the rook on d1, so that if 27.Qxc3, then 27... exd1=Q+ mates next move. In fact, White has nothing better than either 27.Qb1 or 27.Rf1, both of which allow Black to capture the rook with check, gaining a decisive material advantage.

**Exercise 4:** If 1.Qxh5, then 1...Nf2# is checkmate. If 1.Qg3, then Black wins with 1...Qxh2+! 2.Qxh2 Nf2#. In fact, White is lost in the position in the diagram, even though White has an extra bishop!

**Exercise 5:** If it's Black's turn to move, then 1...Qh3! wins because Black threatens 2...Qg2# and White has no defense. If it's White's turn to move, White should play 1.Nd2!, which threatens to capture the bishop (so that 1...Qh3?? 2.Nxf3 would be a disaster for Black). Black must move the bishop away and then if Black brings the queen to h3 later to threaten checkmate again, White will have two defenses: either moving a pawn to block the diagonal (the pawn on f2 to f3 or the pawn on e3 to e4) and so cut off the bishop's control of the g2 square, or playing Qf1 to defend the g2 square directly. By the way, 1.e4? with the idea of meeting 1...Qh3 with 2.Ne3 does not work because then 2...Ng4! forces checkmate.

**Exercise 6:** White's idea was to march the king to h6 and play Qg7#. Incredibly, Black has no good defense. In the game, Black played (after 33.Kf4) 33...Bc8, and after 34.Kg5 he resigned. Black cannot stop the king from going to h6 by playing 34...Kh7, because after 35.Rxf7+ Rxf7 36.Qxf7+ Kh8 37.Kh6, Black will be checkmated. Please note that it's very rare to be able to use the king so aggressively when there are so many pieces on the board! This is an exceptional position.

**Exercise 7:** I played 14.Bxh6!, which wins a pawn because if Black plays 14...gxh6, then after 15.Qd3! White threatens both 16.Qxc4 and 16.Qg3+ followed by 17.Qg7#. Playing 14.Qd3 right away doesn't work because after 14...Nd6, 15.Qg3 is not check, and Black can just capture the knight on f5; playing 14.Bxh6 first exposes the black king to an important check.

**Exercise 8:** 1.Ng5!! Qxg6 2.Qxh7+!! Qxh7 3.Nf7#.

**Exercise 9:** 1...Ne5! attacks the bishop on d3 and also threatens 2...Qf3+ 3.Kg1 Bh3. White cannot defend against both threats.

**Exercise 10:** 1...Qxg3+!! (tamer moves don't work, for example, 1...Rd5 2.cxd5 Qxg3+ [or 2...Bxg3+ 3.Kg1] 3.Kh1 Qh3+ 4.Rh2!) 2.Kxg3 Rg5+!! 3.Kh3 (the only legal move) 3...Rf3#.

**Exercise 11:** White wins with 1.Ne6!! fxe6 (or else Black loses the queen) 2.Qh5+ g6 3.Qxg6#. This is a kind of smothered mate with the queen. Note that 1.Qh5 makes no headway against 1...g6!

**Exercise 12:** White plays 2.Rxe8!! Rxe8 3.Qg4+ Bg7 (or 3...Kh8 4.Bxf6+ Bg7 5.Qxg7#) 4.Bxf6 followed by 5.Qg7#. Notice how the attack worked: First, White exposed the black king (1.Nh6+ gxh6), then White eliminated a crucial defender of the f6 and g7 squares (2.Rxe8 Rxe8). Then White forced checkmate with the queen and bishop using the f6 and g7 squares (3.Qg4+ and 4.Bxf6).

**Exercise 13:** 1.Qc7+!! Nxc7 2.Nb6+! axb6 (or 2...Kb8 3.Rd8#) 3.Rd8#.

**Exercise 14:** 1.Qxf8+!! Kxf8 2.Bh6+ Kg8 3.Re8#.

**Exercise 15:** 1.Qa4+!! (not 1.b4 Qa3+! and Black gains time with the check to defend) 1...Qxa4 2.Nc7+ Kf8 3.Rxd8+ Qe8 4.Rxe8#.

**Exercise 16:** White played 18.Nxg6!! hxg6 (18...fxg6 also loses to 19.Bxg6) 19.Bxg6! fxg6 (Black has no good defense. For example: (a) 19...Bd6 20.Bxf7+! Kxf7 21.Rg7+ Kf8 22.Qf3 and White will soon crash through, or (b) 19...Bf8 20.Bc2+ Kh8 21.Bxf8 Rxf8 22.Qd2 Ng8 [White threatened 23.Qh6+] 23.Rh3+ Kg7 24.Rh7+ Kf6 25.d5 and Black will have to give up too much material to stave off checkmate), and now White played the very accurate 20.Qb1! (but not 20.Qd3? Ne5 or 20.Qc2 Ne5!).

21.dxe5 Ne4, in both cases using a pin against the queen to defend), and Black was helpless. The game concluded with 20...Ne5 21.dxe5 Ne4 22.Nxe4 Kh7 23.Nf6+ Bxf6 24.Qxg6+ Kh8 25.Bg7+ Bxg7 26.Qxg7#.

**Exercise 17:** White plays 1.Bxh7+! Kxh7 2.Ng5+ and there is no good defense, as the following analysis shows:

(a) 2...Kh6 3.Nxf7+ wins the queen, and 3.Nxe6+ is even stronger, eventually forcing checkmate.

(b) 2...Kg6 3.h5+ (White could also play 3.Qd3+ f5 4.exf6+ Kxf6 5.Qf3+ Kg6 6.h5+ etc.) 3...Kh6 (3...Kf5 4.Qf3#) 4.Nxf7+ etc.

(c) 2...Kg8 3.Qh5 Bxg5 (White threatens checkmate on h7; if 3...Nf6 then 4.exf6 wins, and if 3...Re8 4.Qh7+ Kf8 then 5.Qh8#) 4.hxg5 f5 5.g6 and White will soon checkmate Black with Qh8#.

(d) 2...Bxg5 3.hxg5+ Kg6 (3...Kg8 4.Qh5 transposes to variation "c") 4.Qh5+ Kf5 5.Qh3+ and it's checkmate after either 5...Kg6 6.Qh7# or 5...Ke4 6.Qd3#.

**Exercise 18:** The best move is 17.Bxh7+! and was played in the game. The game continued 17...Kxh7 18.Ng5+ and Black has the following choices:

(a) 18...Kg6 19.Rc3! and White has a very strong attack, but there is still plenty for both sides to play for. The best move may have been 19...f5, but in the actual game Black played the lesser move 19...Nxe5 and after 20.Rg3 (20.Qxe5 f6 is less clear) 20...f6 (better than 20...Kf6 21.Nh7+ Ke7 22.Qxe5) 21.Nxe6+ Kf7 22.Rxg7+ Kxe6 23.Rxa7 Rxa7 24.f4, White had a material advantage and eventually won.

(b) 18...Kg8? 19.Qh5 quickly forces checkmate after either 19...Nf6 20.exf6 or 19...Rfd8 20.Qxf7+ Kh8 21.Rc3.

(c) 18...Kh6? 19.Rc3! g6 (19...Kxg5 loses to 20.Rg3+ Kh6 [or 20...Kf5 21.Re1] 21.Rh3+ Kg5 22.Qh5+ Kf4 23.Re1 with checkmate to follow soon) 20.Rh3+ Kg7 21.Rh7+ Kg8 22.Qg4! is a winning attack, for example, 22...Nxe5 23.Qh4 Qe7 24.Rh8+ Kg7 25.Qh6+ Kf6 26.Nh7+ Kf5 27.Rxf8 Rxf8 28.Qh3+ Ng4 29.f3 and White wins the knight without slowing down the attack one bit.

The Bxh7+ sacrifice shows up all the time: it doesn't always work, but it is always worth a hard look!

**Exercise 19:** Black probably expected White to play 40.Nh6+ Kh8, when there is no good discovered check (except for 41.Nf7+, which gets back to the same position after 41...Kh8). But White found a much stronger move: 40.Qh8+!! and Black resigned since it is checkmate after 41...Nxh8 41.Nh6#.

**Exercise 20:** Black played the brilliant 36...Nxh3+!, and White resigned because there is no defense: 37.gxh3 (37.Kh1 Qxf1#) 37...Bh2+! 38.Kxh2 (38.Kh1 Qxf1+ 39.Kxh2 Qg2#) 38...Qxf2+ 39.Kh1 (39.Bg2 Qxg2#) 39...Qxf1+ 40.Kh2 Qg2#. This game shows how finely balanced attack and defense is in chess. A few moves earlier, White had a winning position, but because the player playing White (a very strong grandmaster, by the way) missed 36...Nxh3+, the player playing Black (another very strong grandmaster!) won the game.

# Answers to Exercises from Chapter 9

**Exercise 1:** Black has played better. White's first move does little to control the center and weakens the kingside. (If White wants to fianchetto the king's bishop, 1.g3 is a much better move.) Black's move, on the other hand, is superb. It fights for control of the center, and it helps develop his pieces. If White plays 2.f3??, it does nothing to develop the pieces and little to fight for the center. But its worst feature is that because it weakens the diagonal e1–h4, which leads to the king, Black can give checkmate with 2...Qh4#. This is called the *Fool's Mate*, and it is the fastest possible checkmate.

**Exercise 2:** It would be an excellent move; 1...d5 not only fights for control of the center and helps to develop the queenside pieces, it does all that with gain of time, because it attacks the bishop on c4. Notice that the pawn on d5 is adequately protected, because the queen on d8 protects d5. One of the advantages of pushing the d-pawn is that doing so increases the scope of the queen along the d-file.

**Exercise 3:** Black's second move allows White to exchange the less valuable c-pawn for the more valuable d-pawn. White's extra center pawn will give White better control of the center than Black. Black's third move exposes the queen to attack and allows White to develop a piece with gain of time by playing 4.Nc3.

**Exercise 4:** This is a good position for Black to fianchetto the king's bishop. Because White's d-pawn has pushed forward to d5, and because Black has pawns on d6 and c5, the bishop will have very good control of the diagonal, and it will be strongly placed there. Notice how the bishop's control of the diagonal will go right through the center and reach White's queenside!

**Exercise 5:** White should castle queenside. Castling kingside would be a very bad idea, because White's king would be exposed there. Not only does it lack some protection by its pawns, it would be especially susceptible to attack because Black already has the open h-file which leads right to the king's position.

**Exercise 6:** It is a bad move. Although White makes two attacks at the same time (4.Qxc5 and 4.Qxf7#), Black defends both easily with 3...e6 (the pawn blocks the bishop's control of the f7 square, and the bishop on f8 defends the pawn on c5). Black defends both threats by making a very useful developing move that he would want to make anyway. Meanwhile, White's queen is exposed and out of play. Black will soon play ...Nf6 and gain time to develop his knight to the center while attacking the queen. Always be very suspicious of double-attacks that bring the queen out too early in the opening!

**Exercise 7:** Black threatens to capture the pawn on e4, and White must respond to that threat. White's best moves are 3.exd5 (meeting the threat with gain of time), 3.e5 (gaining space), 3.Nc3 (defending the pawn with a knight, while keeping the diagonal open for the bishop on c1), and 3.Nd2 (defending the pawn with a knight, while ensuring that if Black tries to pin the knight with 3...Bb4, White can break the pin with 4.c3). It is less good to defend the pawn with the bishop or with the queen, because Black will capture the pawn and then play ...Nf6, gaining time to develop. (This is an example of the principle, "Develop knights before bishops.") Also not good is 3.Bb5+, as after 3...c6 White must retreat the bishop and so must defend the e4 pawn with the bishop. Finally, while 3.f3 has a worthy idea behind it (recapture a center pawn with a wing pawn), it fails tactically: 3...dxe4 4.fxe4 Qh4+ and 5...Qxe4. This is an example of how dangerous it is to move your f-pawn too early in the opening!

**Exercise 8:** The bad move is 3...Be7?, which allows White to gain a huge advantage in the center with 4.e4. Both 3...Bb4 and 3...d5 are good moves, as they not only develop in the center, but they also hinder White from playing 4.e4. Notice that after 3...d5, if White plays 4.cxd5, then Black can recapture with 4...exd5, keeping a strong pawn in the center. This is a huge improvement over Exercise 3, where Black was not able to keep the strong pawn in the center, and where Black lost time by moving pieces several times in the opening.

**Exercise 9:** The problem with each move is that it is too passive. Moving first gives White the initiative, but this will evaporate if White does not develop the pieces as aggressively as is reasonably possible. Moving the bishop to b5 or c4 places the bishop on an active square; on b5 it harasses Black's knight, while on c4 it controls a central diagonal. On e2 the bishop does not contribute to the fight for the center, so this move does not put any pressure on Black's game. Moving the bishop to d3 is even worse. At least on e2, White can continue developing normally. But on d3, the bishop blocks the d-pawn from moving forward, hindering White's future development.

**Exercise 10:** The big drawback of 5...exd4? is that it opens the e-file. White continues 6.Re1! and Black's knight is in trouble. If 6...d5 then 7.Nxd4! threatens both 8.Nxc6 bxc6 9.Bxc6+ and 10.Bxa8, and 8.f3, attacking the pinned knight. If 6...f5 then 7.Nxd4 threatens both 8.f3 and 8.Nxf5. Black might try (after 6...f5 7.Nxd4) 7...Nxd4 8.Qxd4 Be7, but after 9.Qxg7, White has restored material equality and has a raging attack against Black's king. The moral is to be very careful about opening files against your king in the opening, especially when playing Black!

**Exercise 11:** Both 1...e5 and 1...c5 are fine moves, but they lead to very different positions. After 1...e5, the position is dynamically imbalanced: Black stakes out a position in the center and the kingside, while White will play more on the queenside. After 1...c5, the position is symmetrical, with both sides fighting for the queenside. Other common moves for Black in response to 1.c4 are 1...Nf6 (developing the knight), 1...g6 (preparing to fianchetto the king's bishop), 1...e6 (opening the diagonal of the king's bishop and preparing the pawn move ...d7-d5), and 1...c6 (also preparing the pawn move ...d7-d5). But 1...d5? is not a good move, because after 2.cxd5 Qxd5 3.Nc3, Black has lost ground in two respects: First, Black has exchanged a center pawn for a noncenter pawn. Second, Black is losing time with the queen as White is able to develop the knight with gain of time.

**Exercise 12:** There are three main moves for White: 3.Nc3, 3.e5, and 3.exd5. The developing move 3.Nc3 is the main line; it develops a piece and keeps the center intact. Black continues 3...dxe4 4.Nxe4 and then Black tries to develop the minor pieces and prepare the move ...c6-c5 to chip away at White's center. Another popular move is 3.e5 to gain space. The third major response is 3.exd5 cxd5 4.c4, when White accepts the weakness of an isolated d-pawn in return for more space and pressure on Black's center. (See Chapter 11 for more about isolated pawns!) The move 3.f3 is not commonly played, although it is not quite as bad as it is in the French Defense. (See Exercise 7.) Black can try to exploit the weakness near White's king by playing 3...dxe4 4.fxe4 e5, but then 5.Nf3 (5.dxe5? Qh4+!) 5...exd4 6.Bc4 is a dangerous pawn sacrifice. More commonly, Black responds to 3.f3 with 3...e6, when the move f2-f3 is not very useful for White, and so Black has a good version of a French Defense.

# Answers to Exercises from Chapter 10

**Exercise 1:** White should aim for a position with a knight against Black's bad bishop. That is why I played 22.Bxf5! Qxf5 23.Nxc6! Bxc6. Black's bishop is terribly restricted by its own pawns; not only the pawns on d5 and e6, but even the pawn on g6 restricts it, because the bishop has no hope of becoming more active by playing …Be8 and …Bg6 or …Bh5. White has a very large advantage in the position, and I won by maneuvering the knight to the kingside and attacking Black's king.

**Exercise 2:** The knight goes to h1 in order to go to g3 and then to either f5 or h5. But moving the knight has another advantage: it enables the queen to shift to h2, where together with the rook (and the knight once it completes its journey), it will put great pressure on Black's kingside. The game continued: 17…f6 18.Qh2 h6 19.Ng3 Kh7 20.Be2 Rg8 21.Kf2! (the king is perfectly safe on this square in this position, and moving it off the first rank allows the rook on a1 to move over to the kingside to join the attack), and White won by virtue of an attack against the black king.

**Exercise 3:** The correct move is 15…f6, which blunts the diagonal b2-g7 leading straight to the king. Notice that this move follows the rule of putting pawns on the opposite color of the one bishop Black has. (Black puts the pawns on black squares because Black has the white-squared bishop.) Doing so would accentuate the power of Black's bishop, and lessen the power of White's extra bishop. The move played was 15…f5?, which makes it impossible to block this diagonal with a pawn. After 16.f4 Nc6 17.Bc4+ Kh8 18.Bb2 Qe7 19.Rae1 Rf6 20.exf5 Qf8, White had already won back one pawn, and the attack was stronger than ever. In fact, Morphy won this game very nicely with 21.Re8!! Qxe8 22.Qxf6! Qe7 (22…gxf6 23.Bxf6#) 23.Qxg7+!! Qxg7 24.f6. I urge you to study this position and understand why Black must lose material here.

**Exercise 4:** Black has good play after 17…Rdc8! which attacks the knight on c3 and, in general, puts great pressure on White's queenside. Notice how the two bishops put pressure on the b2 and a2 pawns. It is very common for the two bishops to give enough compensation for a pawn in such a position. White decided not to defend the pawn by playing 18.Rfc1 (18.Rac1 loses the a-pawn after 18…Bxc3 19.bxc3 Qxa2) because he did not like his position after 18…Rc7 followed by doubling rooks on the c-file. But even after giving back the pawn, White's a-pawn remained weak, and Black won the game by attacking on the queenside.

**Exercise 5:** White should exploit Black's weakest point: the f7 pawn. One way to do this is to play 1.h5 and 2.g6. Also possible is to play 1.Qf3 before pushing the kingside pawns, and still another idea is to play 1.Rh3 with the intention of playing 2.Rf3 and then push the kingside pawns. A final idea is to play 1.g6 hxg6 2.Rxg6 to open lines to attack Black's king. Notice how much more active White's bishop is than Black's bishop!

**Exercise 6:** White should play 1.Bh6! to exchange off the fianchettoed bishop. In fact, whenever you want to attack a king that stands behind a fianchettoed bishop, it is usually a good idea to exchange off that bishop—it is a valuable defensive piece, and once it is removed the king is much more exposed. In this position, the move has the additional virtue of enabling the queen to move closer to Black's king with decisive effect; for example, 1…Bxh6 2.Qxh6 and the threat of checkmate is devastating. If Black allows White to capture the bishop and then give check with the queen on h6, once again the queen's power will overwhelm Black.

**Exercise 7:** Black should play 1...Red8! to seize control of the open d-file and then after taking control of the d-file, Black should put one (or both) rooks on the second rank by playing ...Rd2. Black has an enormous advantage in the endgame.

**Exercise 8:** White has a large advantage because of White's greater control of the center and because White's knight and queen are so much better than their black counterparts. There are many ways to exploit these advantages, but the best way is 1.e5! fxe5 2.fxe5 dxe5 (Black must not allow this pawn to get to e6, or it will become much too powerful) 3.Qxe5, and the threats of 4.Nxc7 and (much more important) 4.Ne7+ are very difficult for Black to meet. The following variation is especially instructive: 4...Qg7 5.Ne7+! Kf8? (5...Kh8 6.Qxc7 is better, but still winning for White) 6.Qd5! (threatening not only 7.Qxa8+ but also 7.Qd8+! which mates on the back rank) 6...Re8 (the only rook move to defend both threats) 7.Nxg6+!! Qxg6 8.Rxe8+, and White wins material because Black cannot recapture the rook: 8...Kxe8 9.Qd8#.

**Exercise 9:** The idea is to continue 3.Nf3! and 4.Ne5! because the knight is a powerhouse on e5. If Black captures the knight, then Black gives up the bishop pair and trades off the stronger bishop to do so. (The dark-squared bishop is more powerful because most of Black's pawns are on light squares.) After 1.e5 Be7 as played in the game, White's pieces (particularly his knight) are very passive, and this eventually led to White's defeat.

**Exercise 10:** White has the advantage because White has the two bishops well placed in an open position. One possible plan to neutralize this advantage is to exchange a pair of bishops by playing 1...Nd7 and 2...Bf6. For example: 1...Nd7 2.Qc2 h6 (White threatened 3.Bxh7+ and 4.Bxh7+) 3.Rad1 Qc7 (not 3...Bf6? 4.Bxf6!; and if 4...Qxf6 or 4...Nxf6, then 5.Bh7+!) followed by 4...Bf6. White still has the advantage, but after the exchange of Black's more passive bishop for White's powerhouse bishop, Black will be closer to an equal game.

**Exercise 11:** In contrast to Exercise 10, here White's bishops are passive, while Black's pieces (including the queen and bishop) are active. In addition, although White has an extra pawn, it is doubled and isolated. (See Chapter 11 for more about doubled and isolated pawns.) So Black has a very good game. The obvious move is 16...Qxc5, and this is enough to give Black an advantage. But Anand found an even stronger way to play: 16...Qe5!, threatening 17...Nd4. After 17.Qa4 (attacking the knight on c6) 17...Rad8! 18.Be1 Nd4!, Black had a fantastic initiative, and soon won.

**Exercise 12:** Black played 1...Rd8!, with the tactical justification that 2.Rxb5?? Rd1+ 3.Bf1 Bh3 forces 4.Nd2 Rxa1 when Black is winning. White has no way to prevent the rook from penetrating with the rook to d1, and this allowed Black to develop a dominating position and win the game.

**Exercise 13:** White has a winning advantage. Black's queen is so passive that Black is practically playing without it. Meanwhile, Black has no active play elsewhere; notice how the bishop on e3 and the pawn on d4 restrict Black's bishop and his rooks. White's light-squared bishop is a monster. So long as White is careful not to allow Black's queen to get out, the winning plan is to attack the king. The game continued 22...h6 23.a6! f5 24.Bh3! Rf8 25.a7+ Kc8 26.Qb1! (forcing the g-pawn to advance, giving White the f4 square for the bishop) 26...g4 27.Bf1 Kd7 28.Bd3 Ke6 29.Bf4 Rf7 30.Qc2 Bf8 31.Qe2+ and Black resigned because it will be mate shortly. See how horrible the queen was on a8. You can't play without your most powerful piece like that!

**Exercise 14:** White should play 1.Nh4! and maneuver this knight to f5. White should follow this up with moving the rook on a3 to the kingside (either Rg3 or Rh3) and then bringing the queen into play via g4 or h5. The passive Black bishop will be more of a target than a defensive piece, and the knight on f5 will be a powerhouse. The attack should be decisive. For example: 1.Nh4! Qf7 2.Nf5 Kh8 3.Rh3 Rg8 4.R1e3! (this threatens 5.Rxh7+! and 6.Rh3+) 4...Bf8 5.Rh5! followed by 6.Reh3, with a devastating attack. This is a good example of how an advantage in having more active pieces (the white knight versus the black bishop, and also the white rooks versus the black rooks) can lead to an opportunity to attack the opponent's weakest point. (In this case the king, because the knight on f5 looks straight at the kingside.)

**Exercise 15:** Black can play 1...Bd8! followed by 2...Ba5 or 2...Bb6, activating the bishop by getting it outside the e5 and d6 pawns. Black would be no worse in the resulting position.

**Exercise 16:** The idea behind 19.h6 is to force Black's bishop to a permanently passive position on h8 after 19...Bh8. Black will now try to free the bishop by playing ...f7-f6, so AlphaZero formulates an amazing plan to prevent this, even at the cost of one or more pawns. The game continued 20.Ng5! Bxg2 21.Rhc1 Bd5 22.Rc7 Nf5 23.Ne4! Rfc8 (23...f6 may have been a better try) 24.Rbc1 Rxc7 25.Rxc7 Bxa2 26.Nc5 Bd5 27.Nd7, and even though Black has two extra pawns (which are connected and passed pawns, no less!), White's far more active pieces versus Black's very passive bishop on h8 and king on g8 give White a winning advantage.

**Exercise 17:** White sacrifices the exchange for a pawn in order to accomplish the following goals: (1) eliminate Black's most active piece, the knight on c5; (2) make the remaining white rook on b7 superactive; (3) shut down the activity of Black's queenside rook, bishop, and king; and (4) establish a superstrong pawn on c6. After 28.Rxb7+! Nxb7 29.Rxb7+, the game continued 29...Kd8 30.c5! Ra8? (30...dxc5 was better, but after 31.Bxa6 Rxa6 32.Rxh7, White has won a pawn and should win the resulting endgame) 31.c6. Although Black has a nominal material advantage, the contrast between White's active pieces and Black's passive pieces is stark and gives White a winning position. In particular, Black has no good defense to the plan of White playing Nb5-d4. In desperation, Black sacrificed the bishop with 31...Rc8 32.Nb5 Bxc6 33.dxc6 Rxc6, but this barely slowed White down and Black soon lost.

**Exercise 18:** After 26...Qe6! 27.Rxh5 f5! the rook on h5 is cut off from the rest of the board, and even though it looks menacingly close to Black's king, it turns out to be ineffective and trapped. Meanwhile, Black's very strong knight on e4 dominates the center, and Black's a6-b5-c4 and f5-g4 pawn chains hem in White's bishop. The game continued 28.Kh2 Rac8 29.Bb4 Rfe8 30.axb5 axb5 31.Re1 Qf7, and White had to sacrifice the exchange with 32.Rg5 Nxg5 33.fxg5. But after 33...Rxc6, Black had complete control of the board and easily won. Winning this game helped Viswanathan Anand capture the World Championship title in 2007, which he held for six years, until losing to rising star Magnus Carlsen in 2013.

# Answers to Exercises from Chapter 11

**Exercise 1:** If it's Black's turn, he should play 1...h4! to attack the g3 pawn. In fact, White must lose a pawn after this move; she can't protect g3 enough times—don't overlook that the black queen on c7 also attacks it!—and after 2.gxh4 (2.g4 fxg4 3.hxg4 Rxg4) 2...Rxh4 3.Rh1 Rgh8, Black wins the h-pawn. If it's White's turn, she should play 1.h4! to stop this move.

**Exercise 2:** White can create a pawn duo and increase his control of the center with 10.f4.

**Exercise 3:** After 27...Nxd5 28.exd5, White can create an extremely strong pawn duo next move with 29.c5. White should attack Black's weakened queenside and advance the pawns. The strong pawns and pair of bishops will completely dominate Black's position. (In particular, Black's bishop on f8 will remain very passive.) By advancing the pawns and threatening to promote one of them, Black will be forced to lose material. Black will try to attack White's king, but he will not have enough material in that part of the board for his attack to succeed. This is a *very* complicated position, so don't worry if this explanation leaves you unconvinced. Study the continuation of the game at your leisure, and see if you can understand why White won. Notice in particular the strength of the pawn duo (after 27...Nxd5 28.exd5) 28...Qg6 29.c5 e4 30.Be2 Re5 31.Qd7 Rg5 32.Rg1 e3 33.d6 Rg3 34.Qxb7 Qe6 (Black threatens 35...Rxh3+!) 35.Kh2!. (But now Black must lose material because amazingly after 35...Qe5 36.Qxa8, Black doesn't have a good discovered check!) Black resigned.

**Exercise 4:** The doubled pawns are nothing to be concerned about. Although moving the pawn from f2 to e3 does create another pawn island, all of White's pawns are well protected so it is not too much of a drawback. On the plus side, the pawn controls the center better on e3 than on f2, and most importantly, White gains the useful f-file for her rook. In fact, Black decided to play 20...Qe6 21.Qxe6 fxe6, doubling his own pawns to neutralize the open f-file by putting his own rook there.

**Exercise 5:** Here the doubled pawns are a serious weakness. Not only does the pawn on f6 block the fianchettoed bishop's diagonal, even more seriously the d6 pawn is isolated and very weak. Kasparov drew this position, but only after suffering for many moves.

**Exercise 6:** Black should play 1...c3!, after which White is much worse. For example, after 2.bxc3 Qxc3 3.Rfc1 (to protect the c-pawn) 3...Nf4! 4.gxf4 Rxd2, White's pawns are a shambles, and Black's pieces are much more active than White's.

**Exercise 7:** White played the very strong move 21.Rd1! when the game continued 21...Bxc5 22.Bxc5 Qe5 23.Bxf8 Kxf8 24.Rd4!, and White has a large advantage. Black's d-pawn is isolated and weak, and Black has no threats against White's position. (Notice how useful it is for White to exchange several pairs of pieces when playing against the isolated pawn: the exchange of pieces has neutralized any hope Black would have of causing trouble to White's king, but White has kept enough pieces to put pressure on Black's d-pawn.) White won a long game.

**Exercise 8:** White wins with 1.a5!. This move stops Black from making a passed pawn on the queenside, because if the b-pawn moves White can capture it (en passant, if necessary) and White's passed pawn will be further advanced than Black's. Black cannot use the king to capture the pawn, because then White will make a passed pawn on the kingside and win; for example, 1...Kc5 2.f4 Kb5 3.g5 Kxa5 4.h6 and White queens before Black. So Black must keep his king near the kingside, but then White will distract the king by making a passed pawn on the kingside and then win on the queenside. Here is one sample line to illustrate how this might happen: 1...Ke5 2.Ke3 Ke6 3.f4 Kd5 4.g5 fxg5 5.fxg5 Ke5 6.h6 gxh6 7.gxh6 Kf6 8.Kd4 Kg6 9.Kc5 Kxh6 10.Kb6 Kg6 11.Kxb7 Kf6 12.Kxa6 Ke6 13.Kb7 followed by a6-a7-a8=Q and wins.

**Exercise 9:** White should play 1.fxe5. Remember, as a general rule, you should capture toward the center. Here there are three specific reasons why this capture is correct: (1) It opens the f-file, activating the rook on f1. (2) It opens the c1–h6 diagonal, activating the bishop on c1. (3) It maintains the pawn on d4, which keeps the knight on c5 passive. Kasparov, in fact, played 1.fxe5! and won without trouble. Had White captured 1.dxe5, Black could have gotten counterplay with 1...Nc5!

**Exercise 10:** White has a pawn structure advantage because he has four pawns to Black's three on the kingside, while Black's extra pawn on the queenside is doubled. But this advantage is currently limited because Black's h-pawn restrains White's g-pawns and h-pawns. (See "When One Pawn Holds Two" in Chapter 11.) If White plays g2-g4 and allows ...hxg3, White will have split pawns on the kingside, and the h-pawn will be isolated and weak. But if White can play g2-g4 without allowing ...hxg3+, White will have a powerful pawn duo on f4 and g4 and will be able to establish an even more powerful pawn duo via f4-f5 on e5 and f5.

**Exercise 11:** White to move should play 1.c5!, threatening both 2.cxd6 and 2.c6, in both cases undermining Black's pawns. Black to move should play 1...b6, stopping c4-c5.

**Exercise 12:** Black should play 1...f4!. This move undoubles Black's pawns and it attacks White's pawn on e3. In addition, it activates Black's bishop on c8. White is faced with a difficult choice. If 2.exf4 Nxf4, Black suddenly has very active pieces close to White's king (the knight on f4, the bishops on c7 and c8, and the rook on e8). If White defends the e3 pawn, e.g. with 2.Qd3, then after 2...fxe3 3.fxe3 Qe7 4.Nd1, Black has the better pawn structure and more active pieces, plus the two bishops to boot.

**Exercise 13:** It may appear at first to be a bad move because it allows Black to exchange off the weak, doubled pawn on c5. But in fact, it is a very good move because it accomplishes three things: (1) It takes control of the weak c5 square (see Chapter 13 for more about weak squares), which allows White to post a knight strongly on c5. (2) It exposes the a-pawn as a weakness on the open a-file. (3) It weakens the d-pawn, by undermining the c5 pawn that defends it. The game continued 1.b4 Nf5 2.Ne5 Bxe5 3.fxe5 cxb4 4.axb4 Qxe4 5.Rxe4, and White quickly had an overwhelming position. It is not always a good idea to exchange a doubled pawn, but in the right situation it can be a powerful idea if executed well.

**Exercise 14:** White should play 1.h5! followed by 2.hxg6. This opens the h-file against the king, which will enable White to bring her queen and rook into the attack, with deadly force. Play might continue 1.h5! b5 2.hxg6 hxg6 3.Bh6! with a winning attack. By the way, this position is taken from the Dragon Variation of the Sicilian Defense (see Chapter 9). Black can avoid this fate if he plays the opening better than this, but still this is a good illustration of the dangers he faces when White employs this strategy.

**Exercise 15:** White should play 1.cxd4. This capture is correct because (1) it captures toward the center, and (2) other captures leave White with three pawn islands, instead of two. (Remember, all things being equal, you want to have fewer pawn islands!) The game continued 1.Nxd4?! Bd7! 2.Nb3?! (correct was 2.Nxc6 Bxc6 3.Bxc6 bxc6, but Black is better here as his pieces are more active) 2...Qc7 3.Nc5 Be8 and Black was better because of his superior pawn structure.

**Exercise 16:** White should play 2.Nf5! gxf5 (there is nothing better because the pawn on d6 is attacked) 3.exf5, and the very strong pawn on e6 shuts down Black's position and gives White a large advantage.

**Exercise 17:** This game was played at the 1948 World Chess Championship tournament, between Mikhail Botvinnik (White) and Paul Keres (Black). White played 25.Rxb6! cxb6 26.Nc6 Qc7 27.Nxd8 Qxd8 28.Qc2 and soon won, thanks to Black's ruined pawn structure. Botvinnik went on to win the tournament and to become the world champion in 1948, a title he would hold (with only two brief interruptions) until 1963.

**Exercise 18:** Black played 22...f5! to eliminate the e4 pawn's defense of the d5 pawn and quickly got the advantage after 23.exf5 gxf5 24.Be3 (no better is 24.Ne3 Bxe3 followed by 25...Nxd5) 24...Nxd5 25.Bxd4 cxd4 26.Rd2 e5. Black's central pawns dominate the board, while White's two queenside pawns are merely targets.

**Exercise 19:** The AlphaZero computer played 25...g5! with the plan of playing ...g5-g4. This plan turns out to be very strong, as White's pieces are too far away to defend in time. The game continued 26.Qc1 g4 27.hxg4 Qxg4 28.Qf1 Qg5! and Black had a winning attack, which the AlphaZero computer converted beautifully.

# Answers to Exercises from Chapter 12

**Exercise 1:** Always be on the alert for a tactic. Black wins a pawn by 10...Nxd4! 11.Nxd4 Qh4+.

**Exercise 2:** The two moves are 7.e5 and 7.d5, but 7.e5 is less effective, because after 7...dxe5 8.dxe5 Qxd1+ 9.Bxd1 Nd7 (9...Bxf3 10.Bxf3 Nxe5 doesn't win a pawn because of 11.Bxb7) 10.Bf4 Bb4, all of Black's pieces are active, and White's e5-pawn is weak. I played 7.d5! exd5 8.exd5. Now Black didn't want to retreat the knight to e7 or b8 (notice that after 8...Ne7, Black wouldn't be threatening to capture the d5-pawn; notice also that 8...Ne5? is a mistake because 9.Nxe5 wins a pawn), so he played 8...Bxf3 9.Bxf3 Ne5 10.Be2 Be7 11.O-O O-O, but I had the advantage because of my two bishops and more space. By pushing my d-pawn instead of my e-pawn, I kept Black's dark-squared bishop constrained and avoided the exchange of queens. Also, the pawn on d5 is supported by the queen, which makes it harder for Black to attack than the e5-pawn would have been after 7.e5.

**Exercise 3:** Count squares and it's clear that White has more space. In particular, the strong pawn on d5 gives White more space on the queenside, so that's where White should attack. A very good move here is 14.b4!, as Reshevsky played. This move gains more space on the queenside, and it also prepares the pawn push c4-c5 (after White controls the c5 square enough times so that this move doesn't lose a pawn, of course), which will put even more pressure on Black's queenside and center.

**Exercise 4:** White has more space. One of the advantages of the isolated center pawn is that it usually gives the side who has it more space than the opponent. With more space, you can attack. One of the most important reasons you should not trade too many pieces when you have the isolated center pawn is the same reason you should not trade too many pieces when you have an advantage in space: the more pieces you keep, the more effective your attack will be.

**Exercise 5:** Black's space advantage is on the kingside, so Black should find a way to attack there if possible. I found a way to press my attack and also gain more space: 17...g5! 18.Nge2 Ng4! Because White's knight has been driven back, White has less space; because Black's pawn and knight have advanced on the kingside, Black has more space. Now Black's attack in the center and the kingside more than compensates for the sacrificed pawn. (Part of Black's compensation comes from the fact that the d3 square is weak, and Black has the possibility of maneuvering the king's knight to that square with ...Ne5-d3.) In fact, White quickly lost after 19.b3 Qe5! 20.g3? (20.Ng3 was forced) 20...Qf5, and the threat of 21...Ne5-f3 with a winning attack forced White to play 21.Nxe4 Qxe4 22.f3. But after 22...Qxe3+! 23.Qxe3 Nxe3 24.Bxe3 Nc2, I won easily with the material advantage I gained from the knight fork.

**Exercise 6:** The space count is roughly equal, although Black is threatening to gain more space on the queenside by playing ...a6 and ...c5. My move 14.c4? was terrible because after 14...b4!, my bishop on d3 had become a very bad piece, and Black threatened to gain a huge amount of space on the queenside by playing ...c5. I couldn't play 15.c5 because after 15...Nxc5 16.Qxb4 Nxd3 17.Qxe7 Rxe7 18.Rxd3 Ba6! Black wins material. I tried to get tricky with 15.a3, hoping for 15...a5, when I planned to play 16.axb4 axb4 17.c5 Nxc5 18.Qxb4 Nxd3 19.Qxe7 Rxe7 20.Rxd3, and if 20...Ba6, then 21.Ra3! pins the bishop to the rook on a8. But Gurevich was too smart for that, and he played 15...c5! Now if 16.axb4 cxb4 17.c5 Nxc5 18.Qxb4 Nxd3 19.Qxe7 Rxe7 20.Rxd3 Ba6, there is no pin along the a-file, so Black wins material again. I had to let Black gain lots of space on the queenside, and he won a nice game.

**Exercise 7:** Fischer overlooked that Black could play 13...f5!, gaining space on the kingside. (not 14.exf6?? because of 14...Qxf4+). Fischer won the game, but in Fischer's opinion, the space that Black gained on the kingside gave Black about equal chances in this position.

**Exercise 8:** The game continued: 9.cxd6 (Fischer says that White should give back the pawn in order to complete his development and castle, and he suggests that the best way to do this is 9.Nf3 Bg4 10.Be2; although I think that after 10...dxe5, Black is better.) 9...exd6 10.Ne4 (Fischer quotes Grandmaster William Lombardy as saying that 10.Nf3 would have been "more realistic," although after 10...Bg4, Fischer still likes his position. Notice that after 10.exd6 Nxd6, Black will play ...Re8 next move, pinning the bishop on e3 to the king. White will not be able to castle, and Black will have a huge attack against the king for only one pawn.) 10...Bf5! (Black continues to develop with gain of time. Notice that 10...dxe5? 11.Qxd8 Nxd8 12.Bc5 loses the rook for bishop.) 11.Ng3 (Fischer thinks that 11.Nxd6 Nxd6 12.Qxd6 Qxd6 13.exd6 is a better chance for White, but he concedes that after 13...Nb4! Black will get back the pawns and maintain an attack.) 11...Be6 12.Nf3 Qc7, and because White could still not afford to open the e-file and the fianchettoed bishop's diagonal with 13.exd6, Black regained the pawn next move with 13...dxe5 and also kept his attack.

This is a complicated and difficult position, and I don't expect you to be able to see everything, even if you study it for some time. The most important thing for you to understand from this exercise is when the center opened up, and White was far behind Black in development, Black's active pieces were able to exploit White's weaknesses and the exposed king. Those advantages were worth more for Black than the one or two extra pawns were worth to White. If you want to push your pawns to gain space, you must be certain that your opponent can't open the center and use developed pieces to attack your undeveloped position!

**Exercise 9:** Black gains space and strikes at White's strong e4 pawn by playing 1...d5! White must either allow Black to capture on e4, which will weaken both White's pawn structure and White's dark squares, or White must capture on d5, which will allow Black to take more control of the center. Two sample lines:

(a) 2.Qe1 dxe4 3.Rxd8+ Qxd8 4.fxe4 e5 and Black has equal space and better pawns.

(b) 2.exd5 Nxd5 3.Nxd5 Rxd5 4.Qe1 Rxd1+ 5.Qxd1 e5 and Black has at least as good a pawn structure as White and controls more space. Notice how Black's game improves once he exchanges off White's strong center pawn on e4.

**Exercise 10:** White has more space, as a space count shows, so 14...Nd5! is an excellent move to trade pieces. Because White's queen is attacked, the knight can't be captured. The game continued 15.Qd2 Nxc3 16.Bxc3 Bxc3 17.Rxc3 Nf6 18.f3 Qc7 19.e4 b5 20.Rdc1 Rc8 21.Ne3 Qa5 and chances were equal because Black had solved his problem of a space disadvantage.

**Exercise 11:** White played 1.f5! Bd7 2.g4!, taking a terrific amount of space on the kingside. Notice that although White's light-squared bishop is very bad, Black's light-squared bishop is even worse! Meanwhile, White's grip in the center prevents Black from getting counterplay there, so White can focus on attacking on the kingside, where the extra space gives White a large advantage. After 2...Ne8 3.Ng3 Qd8 4.g5! Bc8 6.h4 f6 7.Qh5! White's attack was in full swing, and White soon won.

**Exercise 12:** Kramnik played 1.g4! h6 2.h4! Bc8 3.g5 hxg5 4.hxg5 Nfd7 5.f4! Ng6 6.Nf3, and White had a large advantage because of his space advantage and more active pieces. A very important thing to note is that the plan beginning with 1.g4! was only possible because Black's pieces did not have active squares to go to when they were attacked, and so they had to retreat. For example, when White played 3.g5, Black had to retreat the knight to d7 and couldn't go to e4 or d5, and when White played 5.f4, Black had to retreat the knight to g6, and couldn't go to c4, d3, f3, or g4. If you are going to push your pawns forward to take more space, be sure that your opponent can't move the attacked pieces forward to more active squares!

**Exercise 13:** Black should play 1...d5! so that 2.g5 can be met by 2...hxg5 3.hxg5 Nxe4, and 2.exd5 can be met by 2...Nxd5. Always look to meet an attempt to gain space by a counterthrust in the center!

**Exercise 14:** Black should play 1...c5! so that 2.e4 can be met by 2...cxd4! 3.Nxd4 Bb7. By exchanging the c-pawn for the d-pawn, Black has neutralized White's space advantage.

**Exercise 15:** 1...c5 is less effective because after 2.d5! White's space advantage has increased, not decreased. Striking with ...c7-c5 against this pawn formation can be effective in positions where the dark-squared bishop is fianchettoed on g7 because it increases the power of the bishop along that diagonal. (For example, see Exercise 4 in Chapter 9.) But here, Black's bishop is in no position to operate along that diagonal, and so Black simply loses space for nothing. Much better is 1...Ne4! to exchange knights. After 2.Qc2 Nxc3 3.Qxc3, Black can now play 3...c5 much more effectively because White's queen no longer supports d4-d5 in response. Grandmaster practice has shown this position to be roughly equal.

**Exercise 16:** White's idea is to play 7.b4. For example: 7...Nh6 8.b4 cxd4 9.cxd4 Nf5 10.Bb2, and practice suggests that White has an edge here, although the position is perfectly playable for Black. Two common responses here for Black are 7...c4 and 7...a5, both of which seek to stop the b2-b4 thrust.

**Exercise 17:** White's idea is to play 8.g4. For example, 7...Be7 8.g4 O-O 9.Qd2 Nc6 10.O-O-O, and practice suggests that White has an edge here, although the position is perfectly playable for Black. Black has several ideas in this very sharp and complex position. One is to take space on the queenside with 7...b5, which is sometimes followed by development with 8...Bb7, and sometimes followed by pushing the pawn right away to b4 with 8...b4. Another idea is to play 7...d5, although practice suggests that 8.exd5 Nxd5 9.Nxd5 Qxd5 10.Qd2 is slightly better for White. In recent years, the move 7...h5!? has become popular for Black. Grandmasters used to think this move would weaken the kingside (especially the g5 square) too much at this early stage to be good for Black, but the benefits of taking space on the kingside and stopping g2-g4 now seem to outweigh these drawbacks.

**Exercise 18:** Black's idea was to gain space on the kingside with ...g5-g4-g3. The pawn on g3 will severely crimp the white king, and together with the pawns on c5 and b6 also severely crimp the white bishop. The game went 31...c5! 32.Nc2 (32.e6 Bc8 33.Nb5 Rxd2 34.Rxd2 Bxe6) 32...g5! 33.Nxa3 (33.fxg5 Bxg5 is good for Black as the rook on d2 is attacked and the bishop is poised to play ...Bf4+) 33...g4! 34.Kg1 g3, and Black had more than full compensation for the pawn thanks to the very strong h4-g3 pawns and Black's far more active pieces. Black eventually won.

**Exercise 19:** Black has more space in the center and could pressure White along the e-file. White has a strong dark-squared bishop and wants to organize counterplay in the center to open up the position for the two bishops. Carlsen played 15...d4! to gain more space, increase the pressure along the e-file, and shut down White's dark-squared bishop. The game continued 16.b4 Qd6! 17.Rfc1 Nd7! (it is far more important to maintain the strong pawn on d4 than to try to win the relatively unimportant b-pawn with 17...cxb4), and Black had the advantage. Notice that this is a case where the doubled pawns are actually helpful to Black because if White ever plays bxc5, then after Black recaptures with ...bxc5, the resulting pawn structure is favorable for Black. The game continued 18.Qd2 Re7 19.Re1 Rae8, and the significance of Black's space advantage was clear. Note, in particular, how the powerful pawn on d4 both neutralizes White's bishop pair and also accentuates the power of Black's rooks along the e-file.

**Exercise 20:** White played 13.b4! threatening 14.bxc5 since 14...bxc5?? would lose the bishop to 15.Rxb7. If Black plays 13...c4 in response, then after 14.Bc2, Black's light-squared bishop would be very passive. Black decided to play 13...cxb4 14.cxb4 Rac8, but after 15.Qa4 Rc3 16.Rb3 Rxb3 17.Qxb3, White had the advantage due to White's greater activity. Although White's d-pawn is isolated and f-pawns are doubled, here these factors are not much of a drawback as White's pieces more than adequately control the weakened d4 and e4 squares; meanwhile, the open e-file makes White's pieces even more active. White had the advantage throughout the game and eventually won a hard struggle.

# Answers to Exercises from Chapter 13

**Exercise 1:** White can play 1.Bg5! and then 2.Bxf6. The bishop can't control d5 directly, but it can contribute by exchanging itself for Black's knight, which does control d5.

**Exercise 2:** White can play 1.Ng5! which exploits the weakened g5 square. White threatens 2.Bxf6 and 3.Qh7+ followed by 4.Qh8#, and Black has no defense. For example, 2...bxa4 3.Bxf6 axb3 (3...gxf6 4.Qh7+ Kf8 5.Qxf7# or 5.Qh8#; 3...Bxf6 4.Qh7+ Kf8 5.Qh8#) 4.Qh7+ Kf8 5.Qxg7# or 5.Qh8#. If Black's g6 pawn were on h7, however, then Black's attack on the queenside would win because White would have no way to get to Black's king in time. For example, 1.Ng5 would be easily met by 1...h6!

**Exercise 3:** Botvinnik's idea was to exploit the weak d5 square by putting his bishop on it. The game continued 18.Be4! Rb8 19.Rad1 b6 20.h3 Ba6 21.Bd5, and White had a large advantage thanks to the space advantage and the superstrong bishop on d5.

**Exercise 4:** Black has very weak squares on f6 and h6, which White exploited by playing 25.Nh2! Nd4 26.Ng4. The game continued 26...Rd8 27.Nf6+ Kg7 28.Qe3!, and Black couldn't play 28...Rxd6 29.cxd6 Qxd6?? because of 30.Ne8+ forking the king and queen. White soon won this game thanks to the grip on the dark squares.

**Exercise 5:** I overlooked the very strong move 26.Qc1! Bb5 (there's nothing better) 27.Bxb5 axb5 28.Qh6!, and White had a winning attack because of the threat of 29.Rxe4! and 30.Ng5. I soon lost.

**Exercise 6:** I played 27.Qg4!, which threatens 28.Nxh6+, but more importantly threatens 28.Rd8!, which deflects the queen away from the bishop, allowing Qxg7#. Bronstein defended against the second threat by playing 27...Rb1 (27...Kh7? 28.Rd8! Rxd8 29.Rxd8 still wins; the pin is not as important as the deflection), but after 28.Nxh6+ Kh7 29.Nf5, I quickly won because Black's king was so exposed.

**Exercise 7:** The correct move is 35...Qg3! because after 36.Nxe6 Ra2! 37.Re2 (What else?) 37...Ra1+, Black wins. White would have to play something like 36.Ne2, but then 36...Qh2 is very strong. Instead, Lasker played 35...Qh2?, and after 36.Nxe6 Ra2 37.Re2 Ra1+ 38.Kf2, there was no checkmate because 38...Qg1+ 39.Kg3 is okay for White. Lasker played 38...fxe6, but after 39.Qg6! he lost a pawn, and eventually the game.

**Exercise 8:** I played 17...Bf8!, and after 18.Qe2 Bg7, not only were the squares around my king well defended, my bishop also had a strong post where it could attack White's isolated d-pawn.

**Exercise 9:** White must move the king because any attempt to block the check loses material (for example, 21.Nf3 Qxd2 22.Rxd2 Bxc3). Let's look at each king move:

(a) 21.Kh3 Qd7+ 22.g4 h5 23.Qf4 hxg4+ gives Black a fearsome attack, because 24.Qxg4? loses material to 24...Re3+ 25.Kh4 Bf6+.

(b) 21.Kg1 Bxd4+! 22.Qxd4 Re1+! 23.Kf2 (23.Rxe1 Qxd4) 23...Qxd4 24.Rxd4 Rxa1 wins material, as Fischer points out.

(c) 21.Kf2 is a tough nut to crack, but Fischer gives the following beautiful variation: 21...Qd7! 22.Rac1 Qh3 (threatens 23...Qg2#, as well as 23...Qxh2+) 23.Nf3 Bh6 24.Qd3 Be3+ 25.Qxe3 (25.Ke2 Qg2+ 26.Ke1 Qf2#) 25...Rxe3 26.Kxe3 (White still has a material advantage, but because of the weakness of the white squares, it won't last.) 26...Re8+ 27.Kf2 Qf5!, and Black pins and wins the knight on f3. Notice that White can't defend it by playing 28.Rd3 because the queen would capture the rook.

(d) 21.Kf1 is what Byrne played, but after 21...Qd7! he resigned. Fischer gives two variations to explain why:

(d1)　　22.Qf2 Qh3+ 23.Kg1 Re1+!! 24.Rxe1 Bxd4, and Black will soon play ...Qg2#.

(d2)　　22.N4b5 Qh3+ 23.Kg1 Bh6, and the check on e3 will be deadly.

This is a very difficult exercise, so don't worry if you had trouble finding all these moves. In fact after the game, Robert Byrne said that until he resigned, two grandmasters who were explaining the game to spectators thought that White (Byrne) was winning!

**Exercise 10:** Black can (and did) play 1...a4! 2.Nc1 (2.Nxc6 bxc6 3.Nd4 is strongly met by 3...Qb6!, as 4.Nxe6?? Re8 5.Bf5 Ne4! loses material for White.) 2...a3! 3.b3 Qa5. Black quickly got a strong attack thanks to the weakness of the b2 square. Indeed, Black already threatens 4...Qc3 with checkmate to follow!

**Exercise 11:** White to play should play 1.a6! to get the knight to c6, e.g. 1...Nc5 2.axb7 Rxb7 3.Nc6! with a large advantage. Black to play should play 1...a6 to prevent this move and maintain the c6 square. Although this weakens the b6 square, the knight already covers this square, so that weakness is less important.

**Exercise 12:** 1.Qa6!! (not 1.Nb5? a5 and there is no easy way in) 1...dxc6 2.Nb5! cxb5 3.c6! and checkmate.

**Exercise 13:** The a7 and a8 squares are weak. In addition, Black's king is blocked in by the queen and rook. White can exploit this with 1.Qa7! when Black has no way to prevent 2.Qa8# next move.

**Exercise 14:** 1.h5! followed by 2.Nh4 is very strong. The knight will come to f5 or g6, and the queen can come to g4.

**Exercise 15:** 1...Nb7! Followed by 2...Nc5 is very strong. The knight will come to d3, and Black can press his advantage on the queenside by playing ...a5 and ...b4.

**Exercise 16:** White played 17.Nb3! axb4 18.Na5 Ba8 19.Nac6 Bxc6 (or 19...Qd6 20.Bxd5! exd5 21.axb4) 20.Nxc6 Qd7 21.Bxd5! exd5 (not 21...Qxd5?? 22.Nxe7+) 22.axb4 and White's iron grip on the c6 square, coupled with the very weak pawn on b5, allowed Kramnik to defeat future–World Champion Carlsen.

**Exercise 17:** White plays 6.Bb5+!, and Black has a set of bad choices now:

(a) 6...Nc6?? 7.Nxc6 is lost.

(b) 6...Bd7 7.Bxd7+ Qxd7 (7...Nbxd7 8.Nf5 is even worse for Black) 8.Nde2 (8.Nf5?! Nxe4! 9.Nxg7+ Bxg7 10.Nxe4 d5 is good for Black) 8...Qc6 9.Ng3, and White has a solid advantage thanks to Black's weak light squares.

(c) 6...Nbd7 7.Nf5 a6 8.Bxd7+ (8.Ba4 b5 9.Bb3 is also good for White) 8...Qxd7 (8...Bxd7 loses a pawn to 9.Nxd6+) 9.Bg5! Nxe4 (or 9...Qc6 10.Bxf6 Bxf5 11.exf5 gxf6 [11...Qxg2 12.Qd5!] 12.Nd5, with a clear advantage for White) 10.Nxg7+! Bxg7 11.Nxe4, and White is much better because 11...d5 11.Nf6+ Bxf6 12.Bxf6 is quite bad for Black.

While the details of this analysis are complicated, the core idea is that the check on b5 either exchanges Black's light-squared bishop or causes Black's pieces to interfere with the defense of key squares like f5, which allows White to play aggressively for advantage.

**Exercise 18:** I played 6.Nf4! to threaten both 7.Qxd5 and 7.Qh5+. If Black plays 7...e6, then after 8.Qh5+ Kd7 (both 8...g6 9.Nxg6 and 8...Ke7 9.Ng6+ give White a decisive material advantage), White has a crushing attack after, e.g. 9.Be2 or 9.Bd3 (but 9.Ng6? Qe8! is less clear). My opponent played 7...Nh6 to defend against Qh5+, but after 8.Qxd5 Nc6 9.Bb5, White had a huge advantage, and I won easily. It's dangerous to weaken the squares around your king early in the opening, especially when playing Black!

**Exercise 19:** Black's weakest squares are the c5 and b6 squares, as well as the pawn on a6. Fischer played 15.Be3! O–O 16.Bc5! to exchange Petrosian's dark-squared bishop. After 16...Rfe8 (16...Bxc5 17.Nxc5 is even worse since the bishop on e6 and pawn on a6 are both attacked and Black must play the very passive 18...Bc8) 17.Bxe7! Rxe7 18.b4!, White had a strong grip on Black's weak queenside. Fischer proceeded to win elegantly.

**Exercise 20:** White's weakest squares are the c4 square and the pawn on a3. In particular, a knight would be very well placed on c4 and would attack the weak pawn on a3. I played 18...Nb6! 19.Nc5 (19.b5 Nc4 would be awkward for White since Black threatens both 20...Nd2 and 20...Bxa3) 19...Qc7 (defending the b7 pawn while also attacking the h2 pawn) 20.h3 Nc4 (threatening 21...Nd2) 21.Rfd1 Qe7! (intensifying the pressure against the a3 and b4 pawns and also preventing 22.b5 because of 22...Bxc5) 22.Ra2 b6 23.Nd3 axb4 24.axb4 Rxa2 (24...Bxb4? 25.Rxa8! Rxa8 26.Nxd5! cxd5 27.Qxd5 forks the knight and rook, and after 27...Rc8 28.Rc1, White wins material) 25.Nxa2 b5 26.Nc5 Ra8, and Black's very active pieces gives Black a clear advantage; I eventually won the game. Notice how the exploitation of weak squares leads naturally to the activation of the pieces. Also notice that you must be constantly vigilant for tactics!

# Answers to Exercises from Chapter 14

**Exercise 1:** After 2...Kb6, White wins by playing 3.Kf6 Kxa6 4.h4! (But be careful. Don't play 4.Kg7?? g5! because suddenly Black wins by making a queen with the f-pawn!) 4...Kb6 5.Kg7 Kc6 6.Kxh7 Kd6 7.Kxg6 Ke6 (to protect the f-pawn) 8.h5, and White advances and promotes the h-pawn. For example: 8...Ke7 9.Kg7! followed by h6-h7-h8=Q.

**Exercise 2:** Black's bishop prevents White's king from supporting the advance of the pawns. The solution is for White to remove the bishop: 1.Rxd5! Rxd5 2.Kc4 wins. For example: 2...Rd8 3.d5 Ka4 4.c6 Ka5 5.Kc5 Ka6 6.c7 Rc8 7.Kc6!, and White wins by pushing the d-pawn. Notice that 1.Rxg5? Ka4 is not nearly as effective, as this allows Black to bring the king back into play to draw.

**Exercise 3:** White has a large advantage, because Black's bishop is bad, and because White's king is better centralized. In particular, Black's a-pawn and h-pawn are both weak. White wins by playing 1.Ne4+ Ke6 2.Nf6 (2.Nc5+ Ke7 3.Nxd7 Kxd7 4.Kd5! also wins because by taking the opposition, White is able to capture Black's pawns no matter how Black moves the king, for example 4...Ke7 5.Kc6-b6xa6, or 4...Kc7 5.Ke6-f6-g7xh7. But notice that 4.Ke5? Ke7! or 4.Kc5? Kc7! are drawn.) 2...Kf5 3.Nxh7, and White will play 4.Nf6 5.h7, and 6.h8=Q to win.

**Exercise 4:** Capablanca played the correct move: 23.Ke2! The king is in no danger because of the reduced material, and so it should be centralized. Capablanca won a very nice endgame, thanks largely to his powerful king position.

**Exercise 5:** White to move wins by 1.c6! (Not 1.b6? Nd4 2.b7 Nc6, blockading the pawns and allowing Black to capture them with his king) 1...Nd4 (or 1...Ne5 2.c7) 2.c7 and promotes to a queen. Black to move draws by 1...Nd4! (or 1...Ne5! 2.c6 Nc4! 3.c7 Nb6) 2.b6 (2.c6 Nxb5 captures the b-pawn and stops the c-pawn) 2...Nc6!, and now that the pawns are blockaded, Black can bring the king over to capture the pawns.

**Exercise 6:** White to move wins most easily with 1.Kd6! Ke8 (or 1...Kc8 2.Ke7) 2.Kc7 Ke7 3.d5 and pushes the pawn to make a queen. White can also win with either 1.Ke6 or 1.Kc6. For example: 1.Kc6 Kc8 (1...Ke8 2.Kc7 Ke7 3.d5; 1...Ke7 2.d5 Kd8 3.Kd6! takes the opposition and wins) 2.d5 Kd8 3.Kd6! Kc8 (or 3...Ke8 4.Kc7) 4.Ke7 followed by pushing the d-pawn to make a queen. Notice that 1.Ke5? Ke7! and 1.Kc5? Kc7! both draw. Black to move only draws by taking the opposition with 1...Kd7!; one sample variation goes 2.Ke5 Ke7! 3.d5 Kd7 4.d6 Kd8! 5.Ke6 Ke8! and draws.

**Exercise 7:** After 55...Rxh3 56.Rxh3 Kxh3 57.Kf2 followed by 58.Be5, White blockades both pawns. The best Black can hope to do is to win the bishop for both pawns, but then with only a bishop left Black can't win. (You should analyze the position to convince yourself that there is no way for Black to break White's blockade.) Browne saw this and realized it would be a draw, so he tried to avoid exchanging rooks by playing 55...Kf5??, but then after 56.Rh6!, he was threatened with 57.Rf6#. Black can only avoid checkmate by giving up the rook, for example 56...Re1+ 57.Bxe1 or 56...Rxh3+ 57.Rxh3. Browne played 56...g4, but after 57.hxg4+ he resigned, because 58.Rxh1 would be next, leaving him with a lost position.

**Exercise 8:** Black has a large advantage for two reasons: Black's pawn structure is much better than White's (one pawn island against three), and White's pieces are passive, whereas Black's pieces are active. White's passed pawn is useless because it can't be advanced. In fact, Black is about to win the pawn by playing the knight to a5, when White won't be able to defend it again. Capablanca won the b-pawn, and then won the game.

**Exercise 9:** By making this sacrifice, Black gains several things: (1) Black's king becomes very powerful. (2) Black gets rid of White's only active piece. (3) Black gets a powerful protected passed pawn on e4, and the potential for connected passed pawns by advancing the kingside pawn majority. (4) White's queenside pawn majority is useless, because Black's two pawns hold White's three, and because Black's knight and king attack the pawns. (5) White's rook is terribly passive. Black won by advancing the kingside pawns. White had no hope of blockading the pawns because Black's king and knight supported them so powerfully.

**Exercise 10:** White can't draw because it's impossible to move the king into the corner. After 57.Kd2 Kb3! 58.Kc1, Black wins by simply advancing the a-pawn. Notice that Black's bishop serves double duty along its diagonal: it stops White's king from crossing b1 to get to a1, and it controls the h7 square, thereby stopping the pawn from promoting.

**Exercise 11:** The trick that my opponent missed is 41...Bh4! Normally it would be insane to put the bishop on a square where it can be captured, but here the idea is that if 42.gxh4, then 42...g3! 43.hxg3 (or else 43...gxh2) 43...h2 makes a queen. Meanwhile the threat after 41...Bh4! is 42...Bxg3! 43.hxg3 h2 and Black wins. White had to play 42.e4 Bxg3 43.Bg1, but after 43...Bxf4, I won the bishop by playing 44...g3 45.hxg3 Bxg3 and 46...h2 and then I soon won the game.

**Exercise 12:** Black's plan is to capture White's kingside pawns and then win on the queenside. It turns out that by using the protected passed pawn as a decoy, Black can win both of White's remaining queenside pawns and then the game. The game might go as follows: 4.gxh5+ (4.g5 h4 wins because Black can blockade White's connected passed pawns, but White can't stop both of Black's passed pawns) 4...Kxh5 5.Kd3 Kg4 6.Ke4 b3! 7.Kd3 Kxf4 8.Kc3 Ke3 9.Kxb3 Kd3 10.Kb2 Kxc4 11.Kc2 (11.Ka3 Kc3 12.Ka2 Kb4 wins one a-pawn anyway) 11...Kb4 12.Kd3 Kb3 13.Kd2 Kxa4 14.Kc3 Kb5, and Black wins with the two pawns. The winning plan is to push the c-pawn and then when White tries to make Black stalemate the king, Black forces White's king to move by pushing his a-pawn. For example: 15.Kb3 c4+ 16.Kc3 Kc5 17.Kc2 Kb4 18.Kb2 c3+ 19.Kc2 Kc4 20.Kc1 Kb3 21.Kb1 c2+ 22.Kc1 a4! (This is the difference of having the extra pawn!) 23.Kd2 Kb2, and Black makes a queen and wins. (Notice again the key role played by the opposition!)

**Exercise 13:** White holds the draw by blockading all of Black's pawns. With 1...Kc4, Black is trying to penetrate with the king to b1 to win White's bishop. White must stop the king from penetrating, so White plays 2.Ke3! Kb3 3.Kd2!, (White must stop the king from getting to the d3 square and then stop the king from getting to the c2 square.) If Black tries to advance the d-pawn, White makes sure the king covers the key d4 square when the Black king covers it: 1...Kc4 2.Ke3 d5 3.Bh8. If Black brings the king back to e6, White stops the king from penetrating to f5 and g4 (where it might threaten the g3 pawn) as follows: 1...Kc4 2.Ke3 Kd5 3.Bh8 Ke6 4.Kf4. Black has no way to break the blockade, so White draws.

**Exercise 14:** No, Black wins this position. The difference is that Black has another passed pawn, while White's passed pawn is securely blockaded. Black begins the same way as in the last position: 1...Kc4 2.Ke3 Kb3 3.Kd2, but now Black plays 3...h4! and White's king is overloaded. White must use the king to stop the h-pawn, but this lets Black's king penetrate. The game could continue 4.Ke3 Kc2 5.Kf4 Kb1 6.Bh8 a1=Q 7.Bxa1 Kxa1 8.Kg4 d5 9.Kxh4 d4 10.Kg4 d3 11.Kf3 Kb1 followed by 12...Kc2, 13...d2, and 14...d1=Q.

**Exercise 15:** Black draws by 1...Kc6! (not 1...a4?? 2.bxa4+ Kxa4 3.Kc4 Kxa3 4.Kxc5, and White wins with Kd5-e5-xf5, or 1...Kb6?? 2.Kc4 Kc6 3.a4! Kd6 4.Kb5, and White wins a crucial tempo over the main line; for 1...Ka6 2.Kc4 Kb6, see variation "a") 2.Kc4 and now there are two moves:

(a) 2...Kb6 3.Kd5! (3.a4 Kc6 gains the opposition and White cannot break through; 3.b4?? cxb4 4.axb4 a4! 5.b5 a3! 6.Kb3 Kxb5 7.Kxa3 Kc4 and Black wins!) 3...Kb5 4.Kd6! (4.Ke5 a4! 5.bxa4+ Kxa4, and because Black's c-pawn is so fast, White must play 6.Kd5 Kb5 7.a4+ Kb4 8.a5 c4 9.a6 c3 10.a7 c2 11.a8=Q c1=Q, and White has winning chances, but the queen endgame is not clear) 4...c4 (not 4...a4?? 5.bxa4+, or 4...Kb6?? 5.a4) 5.bxc4+ Kxc4 6.Ke5 Kb3 7.Kxf5 Kxa3 8.Kg5 Kb3 9.f5 a4 10.f6 a3 11.f7 a2 12.f8=Q a1=Q, and because White wins Black's h-pawn, this endgame is known to be winning for White. White's plan is to try to exchange queens while advancing and promoting the pawn. Black's plan is to try to give perpetual check. In this position, it turns out that White's plan should win. These endgames have been analyzed extensively by computers, and probably only computers can play them without making tons of mistakes!

(b) 2...Kd6! 3.Kb5 (again, 3.a4 Kc6 is drawn after 4.Kc3 Kd5 5.Kd3 Kd6! 6.Kc4 Kc6) 3...Kd5 4.Kxa5 Ke4 5.a4 (not 5.b4?? c4! 6.b5 [6.Ka4 c3 7.Kb3 Kd3] 6...c3 7.b6 c2 8.b7 c1=Q 9.b8=Q Qxa3+ and 10...Qb3+, winning for Black) 5...Kxf4 6.Kb6 Kg3 7.a5 f4 8.a6 f3 9.a7 f2 10.a8=Q f1=Q, and Black is not worse.

It's amazing how complicated chess can be with just kings and pawns, isn't it?

**Exercise 16:** There are two key variations after 1...g4! as explained in the following list:

(a) The game continued 2.Nxg4 Kh3 3.Kb3 Kg2 4.Ne5 (4.Kxb4 Kxf3 5.Ne5+ Kg2 gives White no chances to win) 4...Kxh2 5.Kxb4 g5 6.Kc3 Kg3 7.Kd2 g4! 8.fxg4 (8.Nxg4 Kxf3) 8...f3 9.Nxf3 (9.g5?? f2; 9.Ke1 Kf4) 9...Kxg4, and the game was called a draw.

(b) 2.fxg4 g5!! 3.Kb3 f3, and White has two choices: White can capture on b4 and make a draw by stalemate. Or White can play 4.Ne4 Kxg4 5.Kxb4 when Black can force a draw with 5...Kh3.

**Exercise 17:** White wins with 1.Rb5! Black can make no headway without advancing the pawn, but if Black advances the pawn, the king will not be able to defend it: 1...g3 2.Rb3! g2 3.Rg3 followed by capturing the pawn. So Black must wait, while White brings the king down the board (making sure not to block the rook's control of the key rank!) to capture the pawn.

**Exercise 18:** This position is drawn. Black uses the king to shepherd the pawn forward, while keeping the White king away. The game could continue: 1.Kc6 g3 2.Kd5 (2.Ra4 g2 doesn't help White at all) 2...Kf4! (Not 2...g2?? 3.Rg8! or 2...Kg4? 3.Ke4! g2 4.Rg8+ Kh3 5.Kf3, and White catches the pawn) 3.Kd4 g2 4.Rg8 Kf3 5.Kd3 Kf2 6.Rf8+ Ke1 7.Rg8 Kf2, and White will have to give up the rook for the pawn.

**Exercise 19:** White should play 1.Rd7! taking the seventh rank. Black has a very difficult game after this move. If Black defends the pawn with 1...Rb8, then White keeps the rook on the seventh rank, and both Black's king and rook are very passive. But if Black keeps the rook active, for example, with 1...Re6 2.Rxb7 a6, then Black loses a pawn for nothing. White should probably win the endgame in either case.

**Exercise 20:** After 1.Rd7, Black should play 1...Re6! Now after 2.Rxb7 Ra6!, Black counterattacks White's a-pawn and restores material equality with active play. White can try to keep some pressure by playing 2.b5!? Rb6 3.a4 a6! 4.Rd5 axb5 5.axb5, when White's rook is more active than Black's, but here Black has relatively active pieces and is only slightly worse. Can you see why this idea of 1...Re6 and 2...Ra6 works in this position but not in the position in Exercise 19? These little details can make a big difference in chess! Always, always, *always* look for ways to keep your rook active in rook endgames, whether you're attacking or defending!

**Exercise 21:** Black has a neat resource here: 1...Ra1+ 2.Rf1 Rxf1+ 3.Kxf1 Bh3!! 4.gxh3 (on any other move Black will play 4...Bxg2 with the same result), and now it's a dead draw after Black heads to the corner with 4...Kh6 (followed by ...Kg7 and ...Kh8). The extra h-pawn doesn't help Black one bit.

**Exercise 22:** After 1.h4 c5 2.h5 (or 2.Kd2 Kb2 3.Kd3 Kb3 4.h5 c4+ 5.Kd2—5.Ke2 Ka2! 6.h6 c3 draws—5...Kb2 6.h6 c3+ draws) 2...c4 3.h6 c3 4.h7 c2 5.Kd2 (5.h8=Q c1=Q draws) 5...Kb1! lets Black queen in time (but not 5...Kb2?? when 6.h8=Q+ wins because the check stops Black from making a queen). The winning idea is as follows: 1.Kd2! Kb2 (1...Kb3 2.h4 Kc4 3.h5 Kd5 4.h6 Ke6 5.h7, and the pawn outraces the king) 2.Kd3! (2.h4 c5 transposes to the drawn 1.h4 lines above) 2...Kb3 3.Kd4! (3.h4 c5 transposes to the drawn 1.h4 lines above) 3...Kb4 4.h4 c5+ 5.Ke3 c4 6.h5 c3 7.h6, and now White wins after either 7...c2 8.Kd2 Kb3 9.Kc1 followed by pushing the h-pawn or 7...Kb3 8.h7 c2 9.Kd2 Kb2 10.h8=Q+. Pretty clever, huh? King and pawn endgames are tricky!

**Exercise 23:** I know this bishop move looks crazy, but it actually all makes perfect sense once you analyze the position logically. Black needs to break through the blockade that the white bishop has along the a1-h8 diagonal. Moving the king around to the queenside doesn't work: 1...Kd6 2.Kf2 (not 2.Bxf6?? Kc5 and 3...d4, winning for Black) 2...Kc5 3.Ke3, and White is in time with the king to hold the blockade. So Black wants to bring the king around to e4 via the f5 square, but the problem is that the bishop on f5 is in the way, and moving the bishop gives White time to bring the king up to e3 in time. For example, if 1...Bg4 2.Kf2 Kf5 3.Ke3 draws. Or if 1...Be4 2.Kf2 Kf5 3.g3 (to move the pawn off the g2 square), and now the bishop on e4 is in the way of the black king. Black can try 1...Bc2!? 2.Kf2 Kf5 3.Ke3 Kg4! 4.Bxf6 Kg3, followed by ...Kxg2, but this allows more pawns to be exchanged, and it is not clear that Black can win this endgame.

The idea of 1...Bh3!! is to clear the f5 square for the king with gain of time, attacking the g2 pawn, while keeping the e4 square open for the king. Yes, there is the little detail that the bishop can be captured! But once White takes the bishop, the doubled h-pawns are stopped by Black's g6 pawn, and what will matter is that Black's king gets to e4 in time. So the game went 1...Bh3!! 2.gxh3 (2.Kf2 Kf5 3.Ke3 Bxg2 wins for Black because now Black has a third passed pawn outside of the a1-h8 diagonal) 2...Kf5 3.Kf2 Ke4 4.Bxf6 d4 5.Be7 (5.Ke2 a3 wins by pushing the a-pawn to a1) 5...Kd3 6.Bc5 (6.Ke1 Kc2 7.Bc5 d3 8.Bb4 a3 9.Bxa3 [or else Black pushes the a-pawn to a1] 9...d2+ and 10...d1=Q) 6...Kc4! 7.Be7 Kb3, and White resigned because White cannot stop both of Black's pawns. If 8.Bc5 d3 9.Ke1 Kc2, then Black decoys the bishop away with the a-pawn and queens the d-pawn; if 8.Ke2 Kc2, then Black will push the d-pawn to d3, use the a-pawn as a decoy, and queen the d-pawn. Wow!

**Exercise 24:** The position is a draw. The key idea here is that when White uses the queen to separate the king and pawn, if White captures the pawn on c2, it will be stalemate. Here is a representative variation: 1.Qb4+ Ka1 2.Qa3+ Kb3 3.Qb3+ Ka1!, and there is nothing better than 4.Qxc2, stalemate.

**Exercise 25:** This position is a win for White because there is no stalemate trick for Black. Here is a representative variation: 1.Qc5+ Kb1 (if 1...Kd1 then 2.Kf5 lets White bring the king closer to the pawn) 2.Qd4 Kc2 3.Qc4+ Kb1 4.Qd3+ Kc1 5.Qc3+ Kd1 (5...Kb1 6.Qxd2) 6.Kf5 Ke2 (6.Qc2 Ke1) 7.Qe4+ Kf2 8.Qd3 Ke1 9.Qe3+ Kd1 10.Ke4 Kc2 11.Qd3+ Kc1 12.Qc3+ Kd1 13.Ke3 Ke1 14.Qxd2+ Kf1 15.Qf2#. In general, the queen versus pawn that is one square away from queening is a win for the queen against b-pawn, d-pawn, e-pawn, or g-pawn and is a draw against c-pawn, f-pawn, a-pawn, or h-pawn. You have seen why the endgame is a draw against c-pawn or f-pawn. Can you figure out for yourself why it is a draw against either a-pawn or h-pawn? (Here is a hint: it also uses a stalemate trick.)

**Exercise 26:** Fischer played 30...Rxc3+! 31.bxc3 Rxe5+ 32.Kd2 Rxe1 33.Kxe1 Kd5 34.Kd2 Kc4. This king-and-pawn endgame is an easy win for Black by playing ...b7–b6 and ...a7–a5 to make an outside passed pawn. White's king has to go over to the a-file to capture the pawn, allowing Black to capture the c-pawn with the king and then run over to the kingside to capture White's pawns. Fischer won without any trouble.

# Other Chess Notations

Throughout this book I've used a form of algebraic notation to describe chess moves. In this appendix, I explain the other major system for describing chess moves called *descriptive notation*. Descriptive notation is no longer commonly used, but many older books and magazines still in print use it, so if you want to be able to read them, then you should learn it.

First, you should be aware that there are also variants of algebraic notation in use. Each language has its own names for the chess pieces; for example, if you encounter a French chess publication, you will see the symbols R (*roi*, "king"), D (*dame*, "queen"), T (*tour*, "rook"), F (*fou*, "bishop"), and C (*cavalier*, "knight"). This may be confusing at first, but you'll be surprised how quickly you can figure out which letter stands for which piece. Fortunately, more and more publications use a language-independent figurine algebraic notation, in which the pieces are referred to with the same pictorial symbols used in chess diagrams.

You should also keep in mind that some versions of algebraic notation leave out the "x" for capture moves and the "+" for checking moves, and sometimes, when one pawn captures another, only the files are listed. (For example, instead of cxd4 you might see cd4 or even just cd.) No information is lost by compacting the notation in these ways, but because it does get a bit more confusing, you don't see these variants as frequently as the standard notation used in this book.

Finally, there are two minor variations to keep in mind. First, the initials *e.p.* are sometimes put after an en passant pawn capture. Second, sometimes a win for White, a draw, or a win for Black is indicated by "1-0", "½-½", and "0-1" respectively.

Now, about descriptive notation. Actually, "descriptive" is a misnomer; in my opinion, this old-fashioned system is less descriptive and more confusing than algebraic. Chess notation is a case in which the United States has caught up with the rest of the world since most countries have been using algebraic notation for decades. (It might take a bit longer for the United States to catch up with the metric system, though!)

In descriptive notation, the pieces are referred to just as in algebraic, except the pawns are "P," and in very old books, "Kt" is sometimes used instead of "N" for the knight. But the similarity between the two notations ends there. For one thing, each square on the board has two different names, not just one as in algebraic. Each square is named by putting its file in front of its rank (as in algebraic notation), but in descriptive notation each file and rank is named both from White's point of view and Black's point of view. Furthermore, the files are referred to according to the piece that stood on them at the beginning of the game: K for king, Q for queen, KB for king bishop (the bishop on the king's side of the board), QB for queen bishop, KN for king knight, QN for queen knight, KR for king rook, and QR for queen rook.

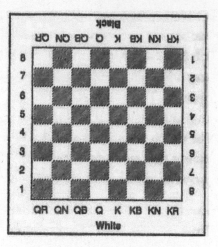

***Diagram 1:*** *The names of the ranks and files from each player's perspective in descriptive notation.*

Diagram 1 shows the names of the files and ranks from each player's perspective. (Note that if no ambiguity is introduced, the K or Q can be omitted from before the B, N, or R in the name of a square or a piece.) A move consists of a piece name, followed by a hyphen, followed by a square name; a capture consists of the capturing piece name, an x, and the captured piece name. (Castling is exactly the same in both descriptive and algebraic notations.) If this all seems cumbersome compared to algebraic, that's because it is. You don't even want to know how they did it in the nineteenth century before this "simplified" system was invented!

You'll probably understand descriptive notation better if you play through a brief game in it: 1.P-Q4 N-KB3 2.P-QB4 P-K4 3.PxP N-N5 4.B-B4 B-N5+ (+ for checks or "ch" sometimes) 5.N-Q2 N-QB3 6.N-B3 (not N-KB3, because the knight at Q2 is pinned and cannot move) Q-K2 7.P-QR3 KNxKP! (the punctuation marks are the same) 8.PxB?? N-Q6 mate (no # in descriptive). In algebraic that game went: 1.d4 Nf6 2.c4 e5 3.dxe5 Ng4 4.Bf4 Bb4+ 5.Nd2 Nc6 6.Nf3 Qe7 7.a3 Ngxe5! 8.axb4?? Nd3#.

If you've read Chapter 3 and this appendix, you know how to read and write chess moves in all the major chess notations. The whole world of chess is open to you now! Don't worry too much about descriptive notation; you're better off sticking to algebraic anyway! If you've got an old book or magazine in descriptive notation that you want to read, take another look at this appendix and go over the sample game above. With a little practice, you'll have no trouble understanding whatever you want to read.

# Index

first mapping of input data, 326
machine learning, 323–324
neural network, 324
origin of term, 323
traditional programming, 323
traditional programming, 323
attack success, 150
Averbakh, Yuri, 306

## B

backpropagation, 326
backward pawn, 213, 216, 217, 257
*Basic Chess Endings*, 277
battle lines, drawing of, 13–38
  aim of the game, 13
  chessboard, 14–15
    placement, 14
    squares, 14–15
  exercises, 36, 38
  movement of chess pieces
  bishop, 20–22
  king, 26–28
  knight, 18–19
  movement with capture (notation), 34
  movement without capture (notation), 32
  pawn, 16–18
  queen, 24–26
  rook, 22–24
  notation of chess moves, 28
  movement with capture, 34
  movement without capture, 32
  pawn, with capture, 30
  pawn, without capture, 29

pieces, 15–16, 28
  rules of movement, basic, 15–16
  sides, 15
Bergman, Ingmar, 9
best way to experience chess, 309
b-file, 14
Bisguier, Arthur, 141
bishop
  fianchetto, 182
  forks, 104
  knight vs., 275–276
  passivity, 226
  pins, 111, 114
  weak color complex, 260
bishop, effective use of, 192–199
  activity, 192
  bad, 193
  companion bishop, 196–199
  advantage, 196
  blocking by pawns, 198
  doubled pawns, 198
  example, 196, 198
  position, 196–197
  rules, 198–199
  coordination with pawns, 193
  example, 192
  good, 193
  opposite-colored bishops, 199
  pawn placement and, 194
  positions favoring knight or bishop, 194–196
  favoring bishop, 196
  favoring knight, 194–195
bishop, movement, 20–22
  diagonals, 21
  example, 21
  origins, 20
  placement, 20
  power, 22

black box (AI), 326
*Black Panther*, 10
Black side, 15
blockading the passed pawn, 285–286
  danger, 286
  example, 285
  trying out position, 285
books, 306
  *Anatoly Karpov's Best Games*, 307
  *Boris Spassky: Fifty-One Annotated Games of the New World Champion*, 307
  *Botvinnik: One Hundred Selected Games*, 307
  *Chess Endings: Essential Knowledge*, 306
  *Chess is My Life*, 307
  *Deep Learning with R*, 323
  *Dvoretsky's Endgame Manual*, 4th edition, 306
  *Game Changer*, 327
  *Garry Kasparov on Garry Kasparov, Part 1, Part 2, and Part 3*, 306
  *Garry Kasparov on Modern Chess, Part 1, Part 2, Part 3, and Part 4*, 306
  *Garry Kasparov on My Great Predecessors, Part 1, Part 2, Part 3, Part 4, and Part 5*, 306
  *Idiot's Guide to Chess, The* (third edition), 332
  *Life & Games of Mikhail Tal*, 307
  *My Best Games*, 307
  *My Life and Games*, 306

*My Sixty Memorable Games*, 307
*Petrosian's Legacy*, 307
*Practical Chess Endings*, 2nd revised edition, 306
*Silman's Complete Endgame Course: From Beginning to Master*, 306
*Smyslov's 125 Selected Games*, 307
*Tal-Botvinnik 1960: Match for the World Chess Championship*, 7th edition, 307
*Understanding Chess Endgames*, 306
books (kids)
  *Coach Jay's Chess Academy* series, 312
  *Learn Chess the Right Way* series, 312
  *Standard Chess Workbook, The*, series, 312
  *Winning Chess Puzzles for Kids*, 312
*Boris Spassky: Fifty-One Annotated Games of the New World Champion*, 307
Botvinnik, Mikhail, 136, 268, 307
*Botvinnik: One Hundred Selected Games*, 307
Broadway musical, 9
Byrne, Robert, 240

## C

Capablanca, José, 9
capturing a piece, 16
Carlsen, Magnus, 147, 210, 254
Caro-Kann Defense, 186
castling, 44, 46
  defense, 151
  example, 44, 46
  grabbing space, 238
  key consideration, 175